SCENT OF HERBS

'Look my boy, look!' he exclaimed in childish excitement, stretching his arm towards the hills. 'Look behind Yssandon! See how they're streaming towards Perpezac, see them! My God! What a mass! Can you see them? Oh my goodness! It's years since I've seen such a big flight of pigeons! And look, look at the one coming behind! Can you see? And the other one after it, you see?'

'Of course,' murmured Félix after a few seconds of watching, 'they're beautiful, and so many . . . Well it's the season, it'll soon be Saint Luke's day! Yes, they're very beautiful,' he repeated, suddenly grasping why Pierre-Edouard was worried by the approach of winter and questioning whether he would ever see May again.

For in the cold grey sky, amongst the low, heavy clouds which foretold further showers, there was not the shadow of a pigeon, not even a tiny flock of starlings, nothing. And already, Pierre-Edouard's eyes seemed to have forgotten what he believed he had seen.

Claude Michelet was born in Brive in Limousin in 1938. He still lives on his land at Marcillac, close to Brive, where one of his six children now farms with him. He is the author of a trilogy about the people of Saint-Libéral which begins with *Firelight and Woodsmoke* and many other works, including a biography of his father, Edmond Michelet, who was a minister in General de Gaulle's government.

ALSO BY CLAUDE MICHELET

Firelight and Woodsmoke
Applewood

Scent of Herbs

CLAUDE MICHELET
Translated by Sheila Dickie

PHŒNIX

A PHOENIX PAPERBACK

First published in Great Britain by Orion in 1994
This paperback edition published in 1997 by Phoenix
a division of Orion Books Ltd,
Orion House, 5 Upper St Martin's Lane,
London WC2H 9EA

A CIP catalogue record for this book
is available from the British Library.

ISBN: 1 85799 871 5

Printed and bound in Great Britain by
The Guernsey Press Co. Ltd, Guernsey,
Channel Islands

For my grandchildren

The Earth cannot end if one single man is still living. Have pity on the exhausted Earth, without love it would no longer have reason to exist . . .

Jules Michelet (1798–1874)

THE VIALHE FAMILY

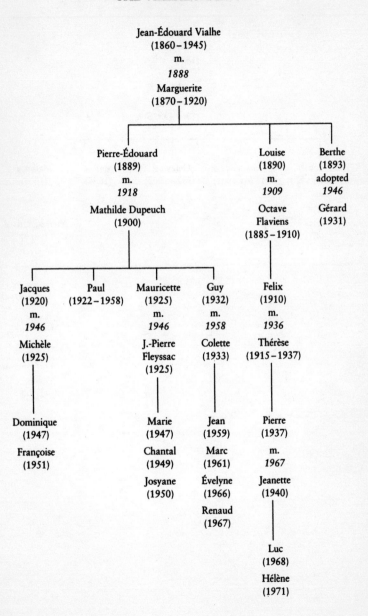

Jean-Édouard Vialhe
(1860–1945)
m.
1888
Marguerite
(1870–1920)

Pierre-Édouard
(1889)
m.
1918
Mathilde Dupeuch
(1900)

Louise
(1890)
m.
1909
Octave
Flaviens
(1885–1910)

Berthe
(1893)
adopted
1946
Gérard
(1931)

Jacques
(1920)
m.
1946
Michèle
(1925)

Paul
(1922–1958)

Mauricette
(1925)
m.
1946
J.-Pierre
Fleyssac
(1925)

Guy
(1932)
m.
1958
Colette
(1933)

Felix
(1910)
m.
1936
Thérèse
(1915–1937)

Dominique
(1947)

Françoise
(1951)

Marie
(1947)

Chantal
(1949)

Josyane
(1950)

Jean
(1959)

Marc
(1961)

Évelyne
(1966)

Renaud
(1967)

Pierre
(1937)
m.
1967
Jeanette
(1940)

Luc
(1968)

Hélène
(1971)

THE DUPEUCH FAMILY

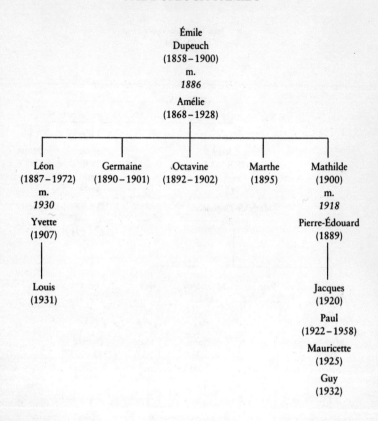

Émile
Dupeuch
(1858–1900)
m.
1886
Amélie
(1868–1928)

Léon
(1887–1972)
m.
1930
Yvette
(1907)

Louis
(1931)

Germaine
(1890–1901)

Octavine
(1892–1902)

Marthe
(1895)

Mathilde
(1900)
m.
1918
Pierre-Édouard
(1889)

Jacques
(1920)
Paul
(1922–1958)
Mauricette
(1925)
Guy
(1932)

A Reminder

Firelight and Woodsmoke

SAINT-LIBÉRAL is a village in the lower Corrèze, very close to the Dordogne, which subsists on its local produce – stock-rearing and mixed crops – and by the work of its one thousand inhabitants, farmers and craftsmen. At the beginning of the century, when *Firelight and Woodsmoke* begins, it is a real town, with a priest, a teacher, a doctor, a solicitor. Life is hard. The children run around in clogs; the family gathers round the fire by the light of oil-lamps; there is a strict moral code. In these days a man is respected if he owns more than ten hectares and ten cows. This is the case with Jean-Edouard Vialhe, also esteemed for his courage and his high standards; as is customary, he rules absolutely over his property and his people – his wife and their three children, Pierre-Edouard, Louise and Berthe. As in every community, Saint-Libéral does not include only good citizens; there is Emile Dupeuch and his son Léon; the sort of people, of irregular incomes and principles, whom the Vialhes keep at a distance.

This rural France has hardly changed throughout the nineteenth century, but now, with the new century, 'revolutionary' ideas and techniques are slowly emerging and taking over. And the old world is crumbling. Jean-Edouard, who has been one of the principal architects of this modernisation – by introducing the first machine into the village, by fighting for the building of a railway (1907–1909) – will be the first victim too, within his own family. His children rebel against his authoritarianism: Louise marries against his wishes a young man who is not from the land, Octave Flaviens; Pierre-Edouard, after his military service, leaves the farm; Berthe flees in search of adventure in Paris as soon as she is twenty-one. Meanwhile the village experiences happy years; Léon

Dupeuch profits by them, becoming a very able stock-dealer, and gaining in notoriety.

Then comes the war, the Great War, which will engrave forty-three names on the memorial to the dead of Saint-Libéral. A terrible time when the village, deprived of its men, turns in on itself. Pierre-Edouard and Léon are wounded, the latter losing his left hand. During his leave Pierre-Edouard has met Mathilde, Léon's sister; when, demobilised after the armistice, he announces to his parents that he is to marry this girl – a Dupeuch! – it leads to a parting of the ways. The newly married couple set up home outside the village on a wretched smallholding, Coste-Roche, which they courageously bring to life again. In 1920 their son Jacques is born, and three other children follow: Paul, Mauricette and Guy.

The immediate post-war years see Jean-Edouard widowed, alone on his farm, locked in gloom. His two daughters experience different fates: Louise, the shy one, is lady companion in a château in the Indre, at Cannepetière (she has one son, Félix); Berthe, the vivacious one, has created under the name of Claire Diamond, a fashion house which prospers in the Faubourg-Saint-Honoré.

Applewood

Time has passed; it passes . . .

1930: the countryside has not recovered from the blood-letting of the war, the great depression is looming, Saint-Libéral encompasses no more than five hundred and ninety-four inhabitants. Léon Dupeuch, now a notable citizen, succeeds Jean-Edouard Vialhe as mayor and marries Yvette, who gives birth to Louis. Jacques, Pierre-Edouard's eldest son, enters the Veterinary School at Maisons-Alfort following his baccalaureat, whilst Paul works with Léon.

1939: once more it is war, and once again the young men leave. June 1940 – defeat: Jacques is taken prisoner, Paul reaches London. Berthe passes through Saint-Libéral, entrusting to Pierre-Edouard young Gérard, the son of her fiancé, a German assassinated by the Nazis. She is already in the

Resistance; after being arrested she is deported to Ravensbrück.

Even wars come to an end. The indomitable Berthe has survived the horror; she resumes the management of her couture house. Jacques returns from captivity and marries Michèle – from their union is born a boy, Dominique, and a girl, Françoise (he is to become an agricultural engineer, she a veterinarian: they are the future of the family and the village). He tries to modernise and extend the Vialhe property. Of his two brothers, one, Paul, a professional army officer, falls in Algeria in 1958; the second, Guy, opens a law office in Paris – of his eldest son, Jean, we shall hear more. Likewise the daughters of his sister Mauricette, a teacher in Saint-Libéral . . .

Jacques is elected mayor in 1959, taking over from Léon Dupeuch – who, in 1946 became the owner of the château which stands above Saint-Libéral!

It is 21 December 1968, and Mathilde and Pierre-Edouard celebrate their golden wedding amid the assembled family. When they find themselves alone together:

> 'As for us,' said Pierre-Edouard, 'I think we've done all we had to do, and we didn't do it too badly. So we've every right to rest a while or go for a stroll. Come on, let's climb to the top of the peak; from up there you see better and further.'
>
> Hand in hand like two lovers who have an eternity before them and are careless of time, years or weather, they ascended the heights of the White Peak.

Six years later, in 1974, Mathilde and Pierre-Edouard await us on the first page of *Scent of Herbs*. Their children and grandchildren are not far away: three generations of the Vialhes.

PART ONE
The Sleeping Village

1

Saint–Libéral was sparkling, all the windows open in the September sun. With the new moon had come at last the stormy showers so longed for throughout two dry months. Too light and fleeting to soak the coarse red soil of the village thoroughly, they had nevertheless revived the green of the meadows and lucerne fields. In the woods the drab summer dust was at last washed off, and they resumed the dark, lustrous green of their summer foliage. However, here and there in the thickets of chestnuts and poplars, a few russet patches already presaged autumn.

In places, still scattered but all the more treasured and sought-after, the boletus mushrooms pushed up their brown or black domes beneath the bracken and heather.

Preceded by a dog still young and foolish enough to gallop and bound after butterflies and grasshoppers, Pierre-Edouard emerged from the chestnut grove which encircled the plateau. After two hours of painstaking search in familiar corners – the same ones over more than eighty years – he had found at least three pounds of beautiful cep mushrooms, healthy, young ones, and several dozen chanterelles. He made for the broad oak stump where he paused on each of his walks, and sat down with a sigh.

He was delighted with his collection, but weariness now dragged at his legs and the small of his back; a cruel ache gnawed at his shoulders too, where rheumatism had set in long ago. As for his heart, it was beating a little too fast, much too fast even . . . He had perspired so much that his shirt was wringing wet. He thought how Mathilde would, once again, scold him for his rashness. She might even force him to change his shirt and flannel binder, and make him promise not to venture out on such long walks any more.

I bet I'll have earned the right to a tirade about my

3

irresponsibility, as she calls it! he thought, smiling to himself. Irresponsible, me? Yes, maybe, but if you can't be at my age! It's the same with the tobacco – he took his pipe and packet of shag from his pocket – not supposed to touch it! And other things as well . . . A pipe, and a little plum brandy, from time to time is very pleasant!

He shrugged at the memory of the recommendations made by the doctor whom Mathilde had called during his last attack of bronchitis, just before the summer. It was a young stranger who was acting as locum at Ayen, a pompous lad whom he had instantly disliked.

'This time, Grandad, you'll have to leave off the tobacco!' he had summarily announced. 'I've seen your file at Doctor Martel's. Firstly you have severe bronchitis, and on top of that a very much weakened heart. So from today, no more tobacco! I forbid it! I hope Grandma will watch out for that! And of course, no alcohol either, just half a glass of wine with meals!'

'What a little squirt!' grumbled Pierre-Edouard to himself, filling his pipe. 'Ten years ago I'd have kicked him up the backside and out through the window! Oh yes – but then ten years ago I had a strong heart . . .' he murmured, flicking his lighter.

He sucked at the stem with little puffs; pressed the tobacco into the bowl with his thumb.

'Never mind,' he told the dog, who had come to lie down in front of him, 'that's no reason for that pimply young incompetent to come reading me sermons! I know very well that I have a weak heart! And so, what's that to him, the little worm? It's my heart, isn't it?' He bent towards the dog, stroked it absentmindedly between the ears. 'You don't care; you're right. And after all, to finish like that, it's still better than poor Léon . . .'

Pierre-Edouard had taken the death of his brother-in-law two and a half years earlier in February 1972, very badly. And although he had so often seen death at close quarters – the carnage of the Great War was ever-present in his memory – he had been deeply affected by the loss of his old friend. A slow and painful parting, interrupted by that useless operation

4

which Yvette, his sister-in-law, had not wanted to refuse, such was Léon's suffering from the stomach cancer which had finally carried him off. But after four extra months of hell!

'Bloody awful thing,' he murmured, shaking his head as if to banish those uncomfortable memories.

It was shortly after the funeral of his brother-in-law that he had experienced his first warning of heart trouble. Oh, nothing too bad! First this unaccustomed weakness and these twinges high up in the side of his chest. Sufficient symptoms for Mathilde to call Doctor Martel, their family physician, immediately: a real doctor, him, a good one, not some locum!

At least he didn't forbid me to smoke, he thought, sucking on his pipe. He knows that I've run most of my race already, and whatever I do, I'm in my eighty-sixth year! Since Léon's no longer here, I'm the patriarch of Saint-Libéral, a nice step up! Well, everyone makes a fuss of me, that's not unpleasant!

Not unpleasant, but occasionally annoying. He had quickly realised that Doctor Martel had recommended to all his household that he should be protected from strong emotions, and especially anything which caused anger. Since then it was a competition to see who would tell him the most lies, conceal the truth best, suppress everything which might shock him. Despite that, he knew everything, everything! He had an accomplice in the place.

Definitely not Mathilde! She depended on him too much, and did not want to risk causing a heart attack by revealing some bad news. Not Louise either; she also believed it was essential to cushion him from all surprises, and therefore to draw a veil over, among other things, the rash behaviour of certain members of his family. And God knows, some of them knew how to get into impossible situations!

However, despite these two mutes, there was nothing he did not know; every detail of all the matters concerning the family. He laughed about it to himself.

Yes, thankfully Berthe was there to keep him informed; to tell him day in, day out, everything which logically speaking he should know; was he not the eldest?

Since Berthe's return to Saint-Libéral some fifteen years earlier, a real bond had grown up between the two of them.

5

This alliance could not have developed earlier, for Berthe had spent part of her life far from the village. She had led a life which had nothing at all in common with Pierre-Edouard's; a life which he had criticised severely for a considerable time. It seemed to him to have little to recommend it and to be unworthy of a Vialhe daughter.

But the war had intervened, then her incarceration, and Berthe had amazed them all. Full first of admiration for his sister, he now felt great affection for her, and in particular was grateful that she did not treat him like an old man. It was she who occasionally slipped a packet of tobacco into his pocket, warning him not to overdo it. Advice which astounded him, for his sister smoked like a chimney. Above all it was she who, each day during their shared walk up the track to the peaks or their chats by the fireside, kept him in touch with family life, the neighbours, the village. Thanks to her he knew it all. And if some of the news had caused him much sorrow, not to mention anxiety, none of it struck the mortal blow Mathilde and Doctor Martel feared. With age he had acquired great detachment. Only death touched his heart, especially that of someone near and dear to him, especially Léon's.

But as for the rest! Bah, that was life! You had to go along with it and keep telling yourself that nothing was the same as before, that you were only an observer, one of the last representatives of a vanished time, a defunct era. Everything became outdated, and most of the values which he had defended were no longer current. If you accepted that, it was all normal, logical, and Berthe was right not to hide anything from him.

What good would it do to conceal from him, for example, that his granddaughter Marie, Mauricette and Jean-Pierre's eldest, a maths teacher in Lyon, was filing for divorce after five years of marriage? Fortunately she had no children; but still, what a mess!

And her twenty-five-year-old sister Chantal, she was a one too! She had been favoured by Berthe, who had introduced her into the fashion house revived and managed by Gérard, her adopted son. Chantal, it seemed, was a resounding success as representative of the Claire Diamond label, but was also a hit with all the men who pleased her. And according to Berthe, who laughed about it, there were plenty of them . . .

As for Josyane, the third and youngest, she had suddenly thrown up her law studies one day and left to go round the world arm in arm with a little fool who purported to be a photographer. It was scarcely credible, such an I-don't-give-a-damn attitude! But according to Berthe, there was nothing extraordinary in all this.

Of course that was not the opinion of their parents, unhappy Mauricette and poor Jean-Pierre, who already had enough to worry about as it was. Jean-Pierre was still teaching in Saint-Libéral but was forced to fight each year against the threatened closure of his school. Thanks to some Portuguese he still had twelve pupils, but did not foresee the intake rising in years to come. On the other hand he was not of an age to retire and could not imagine, at forty-nine, leaving for a school in Brive, or still further away. Really, the poor fellow did not need his daughters to add to the complications of his life!

Pierre-Edouard was not supposed to be au fait with all that, so he never talked about it, except to Berthe . . .

Similarly he was not supposed to know that during his last visit to Saint-Libéral, two years earlier, his grandson Dominique had exchanged harsh words with his father. The culmination was that he had the audacity to reproach him for working himself to death for nothing on the Vialhe land! And he continued to say it in his letters. Dammit, who the devil had paid for the wretched boy's education? And who was still paying for his sister Françoise? Jacques, every time! And he would not see the end of back-breaking work on his fifty hectares until the girl had her veterinary certificate! But the younger generation were ruthless. Not content with finding a job with Arabs – as if there were not better things to do in France – that scamp Dominique had considered his father to be working too hard and inefficiently, his mother wearing herself out to earn a few sous, and that everything could be easier with good advice, better management and a well-organised development plan.

What a nerve, the rascal, thought Pierre-Edouard with a

smile. He had a real soft spot for his eldest grandson, a true Vialhe.

Yes, cheeky as a Vialhe, that boy, but lost to the Vialhe land. An agricultural engineer and well on the way to success, if he decided to leave Algeria and return to his job in the company whose name Pierre-Edouard had forgotten. But Jacques assured him that it was a good firm and Dominique would have a very creditable situation in it.

Then he could help out his parents, which would be only fair. He felt slightly depressed at the thought. He knew that Jacques had recurring health problems. From working too long on his old tractor, a machine now ten years old, his back was ruined, his spine crumbling. Doctor Martel even said they might have to operate one day if he continued at that rate. But what else could he do? He was alone with Michèle to manage the farm, take care of thirty-five Limousin cows, ten sows and their litters for fattening. Added to that were the usual crops, especially grass and maize for forage. Also half a hectare of tobacco and double that of beets. So how could he stop when faced with such a burden of work! Not forgetting, besides, the time he devoted to his role as mayor. Saint-Libéral might well be in decline, but there were still three hundred and four inhabitants with expectations, and always plenty of forms to fill in.

Basically, Jacques had been right not to stand in the last regional elections. Firstly because he would have been beaten for certain. People don't want to be represented by someone from the land any more. They want town-dwellers who don't have calloused hands – doctors, lawyers, industrialists, but not farmers. Jacques had realised this. Better to go before you're kicked out, less upsetting. And then if by chance he had been returned, he wouldn't have been able to keep the farm going, and that . . .

To Pierre-Edouard, that was the essential point. Jacques was the last of a very long line of Vialhes. Of all those Edouard-Mathieus, Edouard-Benjamins or previous Jean-Edouards who had toiled over the Vialhe fields for more than two centuries. Like them all he was the eldest, the heir. But

8

unlike them, his son was not preparing to relieve him. And that – yes, that gave Pierre-Edouard heartache.

The sunset was magnificent. Leaning on the rough trunk of an old tamarisk tree, Dominique Vialhe awaited the most beautiful, supreme moment. That dazzling flash of the last ray thrown out by the sun before being sucked below the deep purple horizon of the stony desert. Afterwards darkness would fall very quickly; magnificent, luminous, blue-tinged night, alive with all its fiery stars.

But for the moment, gold and crimson suffused everything. They shimmered on the black stones of the rocky plateau which opened to the north, and on the huge dunes of the great western desert which curled away to the east, soft and voluptuous as the pale thighs of a sleeping woman. They sparkled in the occasional, stagnant pools of water scattered in the pebbly bed of the river Guir. And the sight was so dazzling that Dominique felt he was experiencing one of the most beautiful sunsets in the world. One of the most perfect, the most delightful; and that despite the suffocating heat, the myriad fierce, pursuing insects and that sand dust which irritates the eyes and throat. A close of day such as he had never seen elsewhere. Not even when two years earlier, having fulfilled his national service as a voluntary overseas worker, he had treated himself to a three-month tour of the world before settling down in a job. A sunset which eclipsed those of Greece, Egypt, Indonesia or Australia; outshone those of Peru, Mexico, California or Quebec. Such an awe-inspiring sunset that it would even make you forget those of the Corrèze and Saint-Libéral! And God knows, those were magical indeed! Regal even, but not to this degree. Not to the extent that they filled you with such serenity, such happiness. Not to the point of inspiring tears on your eyelashes which were maybe not entirely caused by the dazzling light.

'We'll definitely have a sandstorm tomorrow,' predicted Dominique's companion as he turned over the spicy sausages sizzling on a bed of embers. And since his friend was still absorbed and did not reply, he continued: 'How much do you bet? At least three days' sandstorm. Bet on it, okay?'

Dominique watched the last rays, a little disappointed not to see that turquoise flash which occasionally, very rarely, flares up for a fraction of a second, and turned round. Now darkness would come very quickly.

'I don't bet anything at all,' he said, moving closer to the fire. 'What a try-on! I'd like to remind you that it's almost four years I've been living in your damned country, two years I've been ruining my health in all four corners of your Sahara Desert! Have to be an idiot not to see that damn sandstorm coming to destroy all our work! As if your buddies and the goats weren't enough! As if there weren't enough locusts! I tell you, I've had a basinful of it, your rotten dump!'

'You're just a dirty immigrant worker who does nothing but eat poor people's couscous and merguez!' retorted the young Berber with a laugh. 'Oh yes, a dirty immigrant, an evil, reactionary capitalist and colonialist!' he affirmed with a broad smile. He sprinkled the merguez sausages with a cloud of grey pepper, stirred the embers and continued: 'You haven't the slightest respect for the country and people who feed you with such generosity, we ought to deport you, pronto!'

'Funny guy!' said Dominique, sitting down beside the fire. 'Well, is it cooked? I'm hungry!'

When he had got to know Ali four years earlier, he had immediately appreciated his professional abilities. The young Berber, also an agricultural engineer, had a mission to benefit his people through his knowledge and to assist in the improvement of his country. After several months of contact with an administration which appeared to enjoy juggling with plans, alternative ideas, projects and other abortive attempts at action, he had retreated behind an impudent sense of humour which he shamelessly exploited.

'Joking apart,' he said, tasting a sausage, 'what have you decided? I really need to know whether I'm going to have to ask for another team-worker. Watch out, they're burning hot!' he said with a grimace.

'What I'm going to do? I've no idea. First take my holiday; there'll be plenty of time to see after that.'

That was untrue, and really a way of postponing the decision. An excuse not to choose between the profession he had pursued for four years in Algeria, and that tempting position offered by the huge and all-powerful multinational Mondiagri. On the one hand a life of liberty and the unexpected in a country he loved; on the other the rigours of research. On one side, real work as an agronomist, a livestock specialist, spending his time on down-to-earth experiments; on the other, a much better paid job which would probably take him to the four corners of the world, but also oblige him to spend more time in front of a typewriter or calculator than in the middle of a flock or a field of lucerne.

At present he needed the open air, space, the smell of grass and livestock – all that he had found here in Algeria, where his overseas work had brought him four years earlier. As a young agricultural engineer, he had found himself appointed technical assistant in the Algerian agricultural service where Ali was already working.

For two years they had laboured together in the fertile areas around Oran and Algiers, trying to establish both some flocks worthy of the name, and high-yield forage crops.

When his overseas service was finished, and after several months spent on holiday in Saint-Libéral and especially in travelling, he had accepted the Algerian government's offer and resumed his work with Ali for a further two years.

But they had both had to bid farewell to the rich soil of the north, and devote themselves solely to the agricultural development of the oases and semi-desert zones in the south. Unrewarding and frequently demoralising toil, consisting of attempts at irrigation and cultivation and the establishment of herds. Exhausting work as well, for it was carried out under a terrible, scorching heat, beneath a deadly sun, with devastating sandstorms and occasionally clouds of locusts which ravaged all the crops within a few hours. Difficult work, ultimately, for it was effected with the help of a workforce more inclined to take a siesta than to set to hoeing.

Despite that, Dominique was neither disheartened nor discouraged, and it was with continuing interest that he moved from one oasis to the next, from an experimental farm to a trial dam in the hills.

Stationed in Bouhamama for a week, he still had before him several days of lab and desk work – soil and milk analyses, crop evaluation, animal weighing, insemination and treatment plans to establish. He would then fill his last month with a brief final tour of inspection. First to the palm groves of Beni-Abbès and Tarhit, then the few small trial fields in Abadla where the production cost of a quintal of wheat was among the highest in the world. On to Béchar, just to dip back into the atmosphere of town life. Then by aeroplane sorties to the test areas around El Goléa, Ghardaïa, Touggourt, Laghouat, all those isolated patches which needed to be protected and saved despite the wind, sand, sun and at times even the incompetence, negligence or stupidity of men. Finally to Algiers, the transfer of authority and instructions to his successor, and then France. And above all the decision to be reached on which his whole future depended, Mondiagri, with his sights set on the salary and promotion they offered, or a further tour, without much future but still very attractive, of the Saharan oases.

'Shall I tell you something, you shouldn't talk so much while you're eating, it's bad for the digestion!' teased Ali, intrigued by his companion's silence.

'He who speaks sows, he who listens gathers the harvest; it was you who taught me that proverb!'

'And is the harvest good?'

'No, not particularly. But I have to say you're talking nothing but rubbish this evening!' laughed Dominique. 'Come on, don't get angry, I'm only joking,' he added, nibbling a merguez. 'I understand, you'd like to know who you're going to be working with!'

'Just a little, I wouldn't mind! We've put in some hard graft together, produced some good results, and we get on. But what if they send me a pen-pusher to follow you, a good-for-nothing? That'll be hard. So I'd really like to know what you're reckoning on doing, to be prepared.'

'I told you, first my holiday, then we'll see . . . Well, I hope I'll know how to assess things and choose . . .'

Ali shook his head, stoked the fire with charcoal, and set to cooking a few more merguez.

'What's your problem?' he asked eventually.

'You know very well! We've talked about it a hundred times! I'm twenty-seven: it's now or never. If I sign on again here, God knows how many years it'll be for! I love it dearly, your country, I really do. But I've no illusions, it's like a goat! It finishes by devouring people who stay too long. Look, I can't see myself suggesting to a woman that she wait for me in Oran or Algiers while I tour the oases. To tell the truth, I can't even see myself suggesting she move to Algeria for several years. Not unless she's pretty well used to Africa.'

'Filthy racist!' joked Ali.

'Okay, but you know I'm right.'

'Yes.'

'And besides, you have to admit that the professional future here is rather restricted, at least for a Frenchman. It's true. You know fine that your government is not rolling in money, and salaries . . .'

'I know. And yet you've been four years here, you've enjoyed it. You still enjoy it!'

'Sure. But I'm twenty-seven,' repeated Dominique, 'time's passing; if I wait too long, I'll have nothing left in France. And if I let Mondiagri's offer go . . .'

'So basically, it's a pointless discussion,' said Ali. 'You've already chosen. It'll be Mondiagri. And frankly, even if I'm sorry to see you go, I can't say you're wrong.'

2

JACQUES turned round to examine the rotavator's work and his face contorted. Although he had pulled tight the broad belt which supported the small of his back, the pain was still there, low down in the region of his kidneys, fierce and throbbing, radiating through his buttocks and into his legs. But if all went well it would gradually fade as the muscles and nerves were warmed by the vibrations of the tractor. And especially when the liniment had penetrated the painful area.

The trouble with this green-coloured, stinging counter-irritant supplied by a veterinary friend, was that it stank horribly and was so caustic that it transformed a scratch into a crater. However, lightly spread on unbroken skin it had unparalleled efficacity. As proof, it cured cows of injury-induced arthritis! It was therefore quite logical that it should bring relief to a human de-sensitised to the normal creams suggested by Doctor Martel.

For several years now Jacques had had little faith in the virtues of medicine. He had seen so many specialists – physiotheraphists, chiropractors, acupuncturists, not to mention the healers, manipulators, hypnotists and other charlatans – that he no longer had confidence in any of them. So when the pain came he treated it in his own way. But he knew very well that a day would come when he would find it impossible to get up. Meanwhile, he worked.

Thanks to some recent stormy showers the soil on the plateau had become pliable, less resistant to the prongs attacking it. Providing he did not attempt to set it too deep, the rotavator did an excellent job on this old, artificially sown pasture which he had decided to turn over. In its place, after a good winter, he was going to set spring barley, which should be a success. In this soil, rich in humus and nitrogen, which had not been exposed to the sun for six years, it would be surprising if barley did not do remarkably well.

'And make sure you don't overdo the fertiliser, watch out how you tip it on!' his father had said to him the previous evening. Attracted by the rumble of the tractor the old man had come to cast an eye over his son's work, the condition of the Vialhe land, and especially over the plot called the Long Piece. It had quite a history, quite a past.

Fertile and deep, it was this field that had, in 1901, received the thirty-one walnut trees which Pierre-Edouard was proud to have planted with his father. There remained only eight of these veterans; luxuriant trees with magnificent trunks which produced exceptionally fine wood for carving. Eight trees out of thirty-one, it wasn't a lot: the penalty of time, frost, storms and disease. Amongst them now grew eighteen of the twenty specimens Pierre-Edouard had replanted after the great frosts of 1956. But these eighteen were nowhere near equalling the old stock, their yield was still minimal; promising, certainly, but in ten or fifteen years. To tell the truth, if it had been up to him Jacques would never have chosen specimens with tall trunks which required twenty years to become profitable. He would have put in low, fast-growing ones, and already be harvesting a fine crop today. But his father had prevailed; he wanted to leave some real trees for his grandchildren.

Oh yes! They don't give a damn about trees, the grandchildren! thought Jacques. If I listened to Dominique and his agronomist ideas, I'd have to cut down every single thing which pokes its head up on the plateau, plum trees, apples, walnuts, the lot! and then – intensive farming! It suits him fine to talk about farming, the lout, the advisers aren't the ones who pay for it! As for his sister, the only thing she's interested in is technical research in zoology; apart from that, nothing!

He reached the end of the field, lifted the rotavator, turned on the headland, and set off again across the pasture on the old Massey-Ferguson. He noticed that the small of his back was less painful, less sensitive to the jolting, and increased the acceleration.

He had been distressed to witness the paths chosen by his three nieces. Distressed for them, because he loved them dearly and was afraid of seeing them unhappy; distressed for Mauricette. Neither his sister nor Jean-Pierre deserved that. They had done their best to bring up their children, to instil what they thought best, to prepare them for the future, to give them good jobs. And then, hey presto, the young people chuck it all away, morals and all. Goodbye parents and their outmoded ideas! The world is our oyster!

Now us, we've been lucky, we can't complain. Dominique is pig-headed and impudent but he's good at heart and a worker. As for Françoise, she's almost too serious, especially if you compare her with her cousins . . . But I prefer her like that!

He thought his brother Guy and sister-in-law Colette had also been lucky with their children. Jean, the eldest, was only fifteen, Marc thirteen, Evelyne eight and little Renaud a year younger. They were polite and never caused trouble when they came in the summer with their parents. Not for long, just a few days before heading for the beaches with their mother, whilst Guy went back up to Paris and his work as a lawyer.

He'd steered his boat cleverly, that one! You had only to look at his cars, always Mercedes, and his apartment too, nine rooms in the Avenue Bosquet, on the top floor, with a terrace and a pretence at a little garden! That was not the home of a poor man!

But what was so pleasant about him was that he was not ashamed to admit that he made a very good living, had an exciting job and was happy in Paris, surrounded by a wife who adored him and delightful children. Added to that he was generous, and made sure that his parents lacked for nothing. Jacques knew that he sent a cheque to his mother every month, and was grateful for it. He would have liked to do the same, but it was impossible, fate had decreed otherwise.

Occasionally he started to speculate bitterly what his life could have been like if the war had not intervened and messed everything up, spoilt everything. That was what had prevented him from becoming a veterinarian, as he had dreamed. It had virtually forced him to take over the Vialhe land. He did not regret it, not too much ... And besides, today he was almost avenged, with his son an agronomist and his daughter soon to be a veterinarian; he had the right to be proud.

Mathilde could have managed without running down to the church square when the travelling grocer stopped his van on Wednesday afternoon beside the disused wash-house.

For the last three years Saint-Libéral had had no grocer; no baker any more, either. As for the butcher, he had closed his shop nearly twenty years ago.

So on Tuesday mornings Mathilde accompanied her daughter-in-law on her drive to the shops in Objat or Brive; Louise and Berthe frequently made the journey too. So nothing was forcing her to patronise a trader who, however pleasant he was, nonetheless marked up all his products by a fairly hefty sum; it was needed to pay for the petrol, the depreciation of the vehicle and for the service! Mathilde felt that she owed him this premium. To her, who had known the era when Saint-Libéral provided a livelihood for a baker, two grocers and a butcher, and even accommodated a market and livestock sales, this decent fellow represented the last meeting point. It was around him that almost all the women of the village gathered once a week. Because one might as well face facts: there was nothing else in the village to produce the slightest sign of life. It was a fair old time since the forge had rung out, since the wheelwright had died. As for the masons, carpenters and roofers, it was decades since they had disappeared.

Even the priest was seldom seen. He had an incredible number of parishes to serve, and could only come to say Mass once a fortnight. And more often on Saturday evening than on Sunday, which to Mathilde was not real Mass at all.

So where could they now meet their neighbours, get everyone's news, find out a bit about what was going on in the community, if it wasn't around the grocer's van? In addition, thanks to him, one heard the gossip from Perpezac-le-Blanc, Yssandon, Ayen or Saint-Robert. And as he visited the most isolated farms you could discover how your distant cousins

18

and acquaintances were getting on in Laval, Louignac or Berquedioude.

Mathilde would therefore have felt guilty if she had missed the grocer. For two packets of biscuits, half a pound of coffee and a litre of oil she could, if she wished, have an hour's conversation with her old friends in the village. In addition, her attendance was a sort of thank-offering to a shopkeeper who had the consideration to come at sensible times, which allowed for a chat, especially in fine weather. Unlike the butcher, who arrived in Saint-Libéral at the end of his round, that's to say, late in the evening. What's more, his meat was not top quality. And he was rather surly and talked little.

As on every Wednesday afternoon, Mathilde laid down her work when the van's hooter sounded in the church square.

'The grocer's there, do you need anything?' she asked quite loudly, for Louise was getting a little deaf. As for Berthe, she was so absorbed in her sketches that she did not seem to have heard.

Her eighty-one years and her retirement did not prevent her from having just as many ideas as ever about fashions. She therefore drafted sketches of blouses, skirts and gowns which she sent to Gérard. Her taste was still reliable, and a number of lines at Maison Claire Diamond had first seen the light of day on the corner of the Vialhe family's table. She treated herself to a stay in Paris during the shows, and thereby kept in touch with everything.

'No, I don't need anything,' she said closing her sketch-book, 'but I'll come with you anyway, it's nice out. Look at poor Louise, she's getting more and more hard of hearing!'

In truth, busy with her knitting, the old lady appeared to have heard nothing. After living for several years in the house which she had had built on Combes-Nègres, Louise had returned to her childhood home six years ago. For however comfortable, pleasant and well-situated the new house was, she felt lonely there, too isolated. And on some winter evenings, when darkness fell so quickly and so early, she was afraid.

But she was glad, all the same, to have had it built when

summer came. For, then her grandson Pierre and his wife Jeannette came to spend their holidays and with them – oh joy! – her two great-grandchildren: Luc, six years old, and Hélène, three.

And to see the children running and playing around the old chestnut tree which rose imposingly thirty paces from the house, filled her with a strange happiness. A joy suffused with nostalgia which had become very sweet over the years; poignant memories indeed, but mostly fond and tender ones. For it was there, under the chestnut which wore its three or four centuries well, its dense crown so luxuriant, so reassuring, its enormous trunk all bulging with callouses and burrs, streaked with folds and fissures, seemingly indestructible, that she and Octave had outlined their plans for the future some sixty-five years ago. A future which then seemed to belong to them, which appeared so beautiful and secure . . . It had not fulfilled its promise. Nevertheless, despite everything and against all odds, Octave Flaviens' great-grandchildren danced around it every summer; laughed and sang in the same spot where their forebear used to sit to watch the path along which Louise would appear.

The holidays over, quite rejuvenated by several weeks of children's laughter, Louise would close up her house again, already counting the months which separated her from next summer. For she no longer even opened it for her son. When Félix came, on average for about twelve days every three months – he had now retired, and could please himself – he also preferred to stay at the Vialhes. He knew that Pierre-Edouard greatly appreciated his company, his conversation, the walks they took together. The old man grew rather bored surrounded by three women, especially since the demise of Léon, with whom he had got on so well. He no longer had a friend, an ally, to comment on the news, criticise politicians and their politics, answer back to the TV journalists or simply evoke memories and count absent friends . . .

'The grocer's there, do you need anything?' asked Mathilde again, leaning down to her sister-in-law.

Louise stopped knitting, thought about it, shook her head but still got up.

'I'll come with you, I'll find some little thing to buy. And it'll give me some fresh air,' she said as an excuse.

Soon afterwards, taking short steps, the three old ladies set off in the direction of the church square where the housewives of Saint-Libéral were already assembling.

Berthe and Mathilde took Louise's arms and made sure that she avoided the cracked paving-stones; she was older than them. They walked without urgency, certain that the grocer would wait for them. He was accustomed to it, they always arrived last. Then there would be many more people, and a little more time to chat while waiting to be served.

'Instead of howling like a jackal, why not tell me about your *douar*!' insisted Ali as, with customary ceremony, he decanted the mint tea he was in the process of preparing, flavouring it with a sprig of mugwort.

As predicted, the sandstorm had been blowing for two days. Such a fierce wind that it rendered impossible Dominique and Ali's work: namely, to harvest in the normal way and then to weigh a crop of sorghum of which Dominique had had great hopes. Hopes which were evaporating hour by hour. For despite the protection of the oleander, prickly pear and palm hedges, and even wattle fences, he very much feared that the crop would already be burned by the sandstorm, lost.

Unable to fulfil their planned programme, Dominique and Ali had taken advantage of an apparent lull, that morning, to extract about fifteen soil samples, with a view to analysis. Subsequently the storm had resumed with greater violence.

Its fury was such that a suffocating reddish dusting of sand penetrated even inside the room where the two men were sheltering. For try as they might to plug the chinks in the doors and windows, the sand still got in. It drifted everywhere, insinuated itself, clung around their eyes in a stinging crust, crunched between their teeth, parched their throats. As for the noise, it was simply a long, deafening whistle which frayed the nerves like a stonemason's saw.

Although accustomed to phenomena of this sort, Dominique had difficulty in remaining good tempered and calm after several hours of wind. And here it had lasted two days. Ali, who knew his companion well, foresaw the moment when he would react in his own way.

Illogically, instead of trying to forget the storm by retreating into a soothing siesta, he would wind his turban cloth around his nose and mouth, tighten his sandgoggles to the maximum, strip to his underparts, and go out to face the elements. He would take a turn around the building for less than five minutes, but that was quite enough! He would walk until he could no longer feel his body, such was the force and sting of the millions of grains of sand launched at over a hundred miles an hour in a dry but suffocating shower. Afterwards, red as a pimento pepper, his skin almost raw, he would come back in, throw a bucket of water over his head and, his calm restored, would suggest that his friend try the experience. But Ali was in no way partial to that type of adventure. The wind hardly disturbed him. All you had to do was tell yourself that it would stop one day, and wait. Without getting irritated.

He poured himself a little tea, tasted it, and filled the glasses. 'Come on, tell me about your *douar*!' he repeated.

'Go and get stuffed!' muttered Dominique. 'My *douar*, I assure you has better weather than here! Over there you're not bored to death by sandstorms! Dead right! Oh dammit! I'll have to go out!' he shouted, getting up.

'Well go, then! I'll keep the tea warm for you! But take care,' warned Ali earnestly. 'Don't let the hut out of your sight: you can't see further than ten metres. If you get lost, you'll be cured for good! And covered in sand, too, for sure!'

'You must visit my village some day or other,' said Dominique later. His skin was on fire, but he had recovered his peace of mind.

However, not only had the wind not diminished; it had strengthened as darkness fell. By now, it was certain, apart from the root vegetables, tubers and melons, there would be nothing left in the experimental plots.

'Yes, you should come. Anyway, I've already told you that.'

'I know. I'll try to. One day, maybe.'

Ali did not know France except by reputation, and that was a mixed one. He retained detailed memories of his childhood close to Tizi-Ouzou. At that time France, and especially her army, was everywhere. It was often necessary for his parents – market gardeners and tree growers – to show their papers when they went to town to sell their produce, or to see friends.

And then, one summer's day, the three colours which waved above all the official buildings had been replaced by the Algerian flag – the real one, his father had told him.

Subsequently, according to those who spoke of her, France was completely evil, colonialist, murderous. Others, the more discerning, assured him that she was not so bad, rather fine even. No one remained indifferent to her. In any case, everybody agreed in saying that France was a rich country, very rich, and they lived well there.

As he grew older, Ali realised that it was all much less simple. By associating with Dominique and several volunteers, he had gained an insight into what the French might be like. But there again, he mistrusted generalisations, and vowed to go there one day to form his own opinion about the place. Meanwhile he stored away what Dominique told him about his country. And to listen to him, you were forced to believe that it really was a beautiful land.

'You'll see, I'll take you to the prettiest parts of the Limousin and the Corrèze,' insisted Dominique.

Saint-Libéral, for example?' joked Ali, who felt he knew each walk, each house, such was the stream of words flowing from his companion on the subject of his birthplace.

When he was in a bad mood, it was enough for Ali to touch upon his *douar*, as he called it, for him to launch immediately into a poetic description. What Ali found hard to understand, on the other hand, was that his companion could remain so long far from a land which he talked of with such fervour.

His attitude became even more blatantly contradictory since he envisaged, without any apparent problem, going away again when working for Mondiagri. And it was rather the same when it came to his relatives. If you were to believe him, he got on with them extremely well; spoke of his grandfather with great feeling and of his grandmother with touching affection. Ali was equally certain that he had a great deal of respect and regard for his father, but he did become less voluble when the conversation turned to him.

At the end of that afternoon it was perhaps out of devilment, or because he felt Dominique had relaxed after his sand shower, that Ali dared to go further.

'You're trying to tell me your village is the most beautiful, your family the best, and it's two years since you've been there. It doesn't seem to worry you very much!'

'There's a grain of truth in that,' admitted Dominique, after considering it for a few moments. 'I've taken a while to learn it, but I know now that there's no point in wanting to change a situation if you haven't the means to do so.'

'You've lost me.'

'Well it's simple. I'm in a rage every time I go there. I even manage to lose my temper in my letters. My father is killing himself, wearing himself out for nothing. The poor old thing really hasn't had any luck in his life. He found himself managing the farm by accident, and for thirty years it's sapped his spirit and health. First of all it was to enlarge the holding, then to pay for our education, my sister and myself, and to repay the loans too. And now he's struggling to reach retirement in ten years' time. But you may ask what state he'll be in when he gets there. And what annoys me is that I can't do a thing about it.'

'You mean to say that your father doesn't earn a good living? I thought you had a fine farm!'

'You know all these things are relative. Anyway, what's the use of a fine farm if it's badly managed? And it is. Well, my father looks after it as best he can, as well as he knows how, but his thought processes are twenty-five years out of date. That's the whole problem. And you see, when I go there, I notice how everything's deteriorating, that the equipment's worn out, that production's stagnant. And I don't need to be told that the income is diminishing, it's obvious. Like it's obvious straight away that my father's exhausting himself. And that makes me furious.'

'Why don't you tell him?'

'But I *have* told him! And do you know what he answered?

24

"You've only to take my place, it's open, we'll see if you do better"!'

'I see, and that's not your idea at all?'

'You must be joking! I've got better things to do elsewhere! And look here, be serious, I'm not a farmer. No, what it needs is for my father to change tack altogether, to look for something different. But it's not very likely; at fifty-five you don't change your habits . . . Well, I understand him and it drives me wild. Do you get it now, why I don't often go to Saint-Libéral? It's so that I don't have a shouting match with my father. I know my mother can't bear our arguments, so it's damage limitation, okay? And if you add to that my grandfather sticking his oar in . . .'

'I thought you worshipped him! You always told me he was fantastic.'

'So he is! Only he thinks nothing of my degree in agronomy, nothing! The only thing he's worried about is finding someone to follow my father in looking after the Vialhe land. And he knows it won't be me! Oh, not that he reproaches me about it, no, but still . . . Look, even if I were appointed Minister of Agriculture, I bet the first thing he'd ask me would be: "When are you going to resign from that useless job and work on something serious, on the Vialhe land?" He's like that, Grandpa, a great character. What's so funny?'

'Nothing, nothing! When you talk about your land, I don't know whether it'll stay in the family; on the other hand, when it comes to character, in your case the succession seems to me to be assured!'

3

DESPITE the admiration and affection Jean Vialhe felt for his father, his relationship with him had changed in the last few months. It quickly became strained when the conversation turned to a subject on which neither wished to give ground. For, however much they agreed with each other on questions of sport, cars, films, books, or even politics, the dialogue became bitter-sweet when it touched on the future.

Almost a year ago, Jean had baldly announced to his father that he did not want to be a lawyer or a civil servant and that all the other supposedly 'good jobs' were a load of rubbish. He was going to be a stock-breeder, there was no other route possible for him!

He had understood that it came as a terrible shock to his father. All the more so because Guy had every reason to hope that his eldest son would follow him, if not in his footsteps at the bar, then at least by achieving a position in society as comfortable as his own.

For Jean was one of those pupils who, from kindergarten to graduation, seem to absorb knowledge like delicious sweets, greedily and with enjoyment. Always at the top of the class, he was about to enter his second to last year at school at the age of fifteen, and could thereafter quite reasonably aim for the highest qualifications.

At first Guy had thought he was playing the rebel, it was his age. After all, he had always been inclined to kick over the traces. Less than Marc, however, his junior by two years who proclaimed the need to reorganise the world from A to Z, gun in hand if it came to it. And without letting feeling get in the way! But given his age he could be forgiven for sticking up a photo of Che Guevara in his bedroom. Guy remembered it well, knew that everything changed at a great rate and you had to allow for what was in fashion. Since 1968, it had been protests.

So in the first instance he had not taken his eldest son's pronouncements very seriously. But he had begun to worry when he had discovered, six months earlier during Agriculture Week, that Jean was using every spare moment to go and admire the animals on the showground at Porte de Versailles. Annoyed, for he felt at a loss, he had talked to Berthe about it during one of her trips to Paris. The old lady had laughed until she cried.

'The genes, my dear Guy, the genes! There they are and in some strength too! Think of your parents! A Vialhe plus a Dupeuch, that's not going to give you a mandarin in the civil service. All the better!'

'And why not? None of us were born peasants! It was an accident that Jacques stayed on the farm. When he worked with Léon, Paul champed at the bit behind those cows. Mauricette wouldn't rest until she became a teacher. As for me, I left Saint-Libéral as soon as I could, you know that, you gave me a home in Paris!'

'Well, it's skipped a generation, that's all! Oh, if your father hears this, he'll be over the moon!'

'I forbid you to tell him, he'll do everything to encourage the boy in this mad idea! Stock-breeder, I ask you! When he has everything he needs to make a success of himself! Come on, joking apart, tell me what I could do to get this nonsense out of his head?'

'He hasn't talked about leaving school? So what's the problem? Don't spoil his dream, let it run its course.'

He was not convinced by this advice and felt it useful to relaunch the debate with his son:

'If I understand you properly, all you want to do is to copy those young fools who set off to live up-country in Larzac with three goats and two sheep, and would starve to death without daddy's cheques?'

'No way! I told you, I'm going to be a stock-breeder! The sort you're talking about are just mucking around. In the first place they don't know a thing about it. If they really wanted to raise livestock they wouldn't go there, where nothing grows except stones! I know, I've been finding out. It's one of the regions hardest hit by the rural exodus. Think about it, if the land were that good, the farmers would stay there! No, that's not where you need to go.'

His son's seriousness had rather shaken him. And he, who knew how to be so composed and calm when defending clients in court, had raised his voice:

'Oh, I see your drift! You'll be setting up in Saint-Libéral maybe?'

'If I could, yes, but there's not enough space free, I mean enough ground. But if one day Louis were to sell Uncle Léon's land, and not for building on, well yes, then it would be worth it.'

The wretched boy thinks of everything! thought Guy, gritting his teeth.

'Right, enough dreaming,' he cut in. I don't know who put these notions in your head, but we'll discuss it again later. At the moment I don't want to hear any more of the sort of rubbish you might expect from romantics like Giono or Lanza del Vasto! All those utopian ideas have already caused enough damage as it is! If at least you wanted to copy your cousin Dominique!'

'But I *am* reckoning on on doing the same as him! Only I want to set up on my own account, to rear stock.'

'Well that . . .' Guy had sighed, realising that the discussion was turning against him.

Instead of unsettling his son, as he had hoped, it had allowed him to formulate out loud what had perhaps until then been only a rather vague plan, poorly researched, barely thought out. Thanks to the soapbox inadvertently provided by his father, Jean had been able to explain his ideas, clearly and seriously, and had thus taken an important step forward in his commitment. Since then, Guy had avoided reopening a debate which he was no longer certain of controlling.

When informed of it, Colette, his wife, had supported him. She, too, hoped that time would cure everything, that their son would one day realise for himself just how impractical his idea was. She herself had suffered too much when her own parents had ostractised her on learning that Guy was the son of small-time farmers in the Corrèze. The breach had lasted until the birth of Jean. And now this brilliant child, pupil at one of the best schools in Paris, who could honestly call himself a Parisian, son of a lawyer and grandson of an antique dealer – there was no need to remember the other grand-parents – was taking pride in referring to his country origins and wanting to go back to his roots? It was grotesque!

When Guy had sought to rent a shoot with a few friends three years earlier, he had considered that his cousin Félix would be well placed to advise him. He still lived a few kilometres from Mézières-en-Brenne in the forestry cottage, long ago bought for a token sum, where he had spent the greater part of his life. He therefore knew the area like the back of his hand, and had no difficulty in pointing Guy towards a very fine piece of land.

It had originally been part of the twelve hundred hectares belonging to the Château of Cannepetière, where Louise had worked for so long. The shoot now comprised six hundred hectares of woods, heath and thickets, all dotted with pools and marshes. A paradise for game, a delight for hunters who could shoot according to their tastes at roe deer, wild boar, pheasant, hare or partridge. But also, and most importantly, a selection of mallard, teal, shoveller and tufted duck; not forgetting the rail, woodcock and snipe.

During the hunting season, Guy went down once a fortnight for the weekend. He never omitted to go and say hello to his cousin – admittedly the shoot lay less than a kilometre from his house. Occasionally he even accepted the bed offered by Félix. Exhausted by a day's shooting in the fresh air, he slept soundly there, lulled by the song of the wind in the huge oak trees.

For the last two years Jean had nearly always accompanied him. Not to hunt – he was not old enough yet, and was not attracted by the sport – but to fish with Félix and especially to accompany him on long ornithological expeditions.

Félix had always felt a great affinity for birds; since his retirement they had become his obsession. He amazed Jean with his knowledge and the speed of his observation, which allowed him to differentiate in an instant a sedge warbler from a grasshopper warbler. So, whilst the shots and barking echoed in the distance, Félix and Jean, binoculars around their necks, practised a more peaceful form of hunting. During the last six months Jean had taken up photography and discovered how much patience, calmness and determination were needed to capture a simple coot with the lens.

What also interested Jean a great deal, and astonished him, was when Félix talked to him of the Vialhe family. He knew a lot about them and willingly related it. He seemed to know everything about the family circumstances, the important events, the character of each person, the tragedies, quarrels and reconciliations.

And when one day Jean had wanted to know how he had learned all that, he explained:

'It's true, the first time I set foot in the village I was already twenty-six! But thanks to your great-aunt – yes, your Aunt Louise – I was almost as familiar with it as I am with every little footpath in the woods around us. Your aunt told me all about the family, and the neighbours, the fields and meadows, the woods, the countryside of Saint-Libéral too. She was so unhappy here, poor woman. She told me, she pined for her village for forty years! So she used to re-read the letters which came from there. First the ones from your grandfather – she had a whole packet of them, which she knew off by heart. Then, after the war – the Great War I mean – it was your grandmother who wrote. And that went on until your aunt returned to live in Saint-Libéral in 1956, no, '55, October '55. Since then it's she who writes to me and tells me everything. That's how I know the history of the Vialhe family and the village, I should perhaps say the sagas . . .'

'So you know all about my cousin?'

'Which one?'

'Come on, you know very well: I mean Jo! Papa won't have her name mentioned at home!'

'Then I shan't talk about her either.'

'Is it true that she's gone off around the world with a boyfriend? Go on, you can say it, can't you? You can see I know!'

'Well you know as much as I do, don't expect any more. And the main thing is she'll be back one day. That's how the

31

Vialhes do it. When they've a mind to it, they give up everything and go away for years to the devil knows where! And then one day they reappear in Saint-Libéral. It's hereditary. Your grandfather and your two aunts did it. And if your Uncle Paul didn't have time to do the same, it was because the heavens decreed otherwise.'

'You're sure it'll be like that with Jo? I hope so. She's nice, Jo. She lived with us before she took off . . . I remember, she wasn't stuck-up, *sympa*, you know! It was she who looked after us when our parents went out in the evening. Do you think we'll see her again?'

'Of course. Look, you remember those nightjars we saw last summer? They're migratory, they leave at the end of the summer, but they always return the following spring. The urge is overwhelming, they always return to where they were born, like the Vialhes. And they're similar in other ways too!'

'Oh, right?'

'Yes, they're very imposing. As a result they're often mistaken for small falcons or sparrowhawks; they pretend to be raptors, really! But they're showing off, you know, they only eat insects. And they have big mouths too! Can't stop puffing, churring, getting worked up, right! Don't you remember?'

'Of course I do!'

Jean recalled the whole scene. It was at the end of July. His father had come to shoot duck, and he had stayed with Félix, as usual.

At dusk, when thousands of starlings were whirling in search of a roost above the pools and reedbeds in unpredictably twisting, noisy clouds, Félix and he had set off walking across the heath. They were hoping to catch a glimpse of one of the two short-eared owls which were nesting there. Everywhere in the pools and ditches, in the slightest speck of water, toads were croaking. And now timidly, almost self-consciously, for the season for love was over, a few warblers were trilling from their perches in the bulrushes.

It was then that the shadow of a bird, seeming to shoot out of the ground in front of them, spun skyward, twisted round and immediately disappeared in a flurry of wings.

32

'Did you see that? Like a cuckoo or a kestrel, but smaller,' Jean had murmured as he stopped.

'Not quite, wait for it. The family lives there. Here, listen! Listen to the nightjars calling to each other.'

And suddenly, emerging from the night and diving straight back in to it, three other birds had circled round the observers for a few seconds. Then, following the repeated chucking call from one of the parents, they had all disappeared, swallowed up by the darkness.

'What are they looking for?' Jean had whispered, still surprised.

'The grasshoppers and moths we've put up by walking in the long grass. Usually they follow the animals, they disturb the insects too. See, that gives them their old name of "goat-sucker". Not so long ago I used to know some quite sensible people who firmly believed that nightjars came to suck their goats in the dark! Yes, they did! You'll be telling me they're the same ones who were convinced that adders and grass-snakes suckle as well!'

'But where do they come from?'

'From Africa, they spend all the cold months there. They arrive here at the end of April when they can find something to feed on. They nest and leave again. Those ones, well that family, I've known them since I was old enough to watch birds, that takes us back to the twenties! They lay in that heath-land every year, over there to the right, beside that aspen grove. You know, since I've been observing them that makes several generations of nightjars! One year, more than fifteen years ago, I ringed the two young; yes, they only have two per nest. They were magnificent. I don't know whether it annoyed them to know they were discovered, but it was three years before they returned! I saw some in other places, but not here. And then one evening at the beginning of May, they shot up like just now, they were back. Since then they've been there every year.'

'And you say the Vialhe family is the same?' Jean was amused.

'Yes, a bit, on account of their weird characters! But you don't need to go and tell you father and grandfather in

33

Saint-Libéral that I'm calling them birds! You keep it to yourself, okay?'

Settling down at the far end of the Long Piece, Pierre-Edouard expertly evaluated the work accomplished by Jacques a few days earlier. His rotavator had worked miracles. Apart from a few green tongues which licked round the feet of the walnut trees, there was no sign of the old meadow. Cleanly scalped and turned under, it had given way to long smooth beds of rich, red earth. The clods were still too dry and brittle for ploughing, but a short day's rain would make it superb, ready to be opened by the share. And seeing it already so beautiful, Pierre-Edouard knew that the furrows would be smooth, regular. He was constantly amazed by the work modern machines were capable of producing.

In his time he would never have been able to obtain such results, make the soil so clean, so yielding. For even if his oxen had been equal to pulling the Canadian cultivator with its 'goose-foot' tines, the machine's prongs would have been broken by jamming between the interstices of the lucerne roots, which were broader than a man's thumb. Besides, in earlier times, even on pliable, damp ground, nothing would have pulverised the earth so well, mixed so thoroughly the humus, turf and that generous layer of limestone clay which made the Long Piece so productive.

And yet, despite this fantastic progress and all the care and manure lavished on it, the earth could give no more. What had nourished generations of Vialhes and, before them, over the centuries, other unknown generations, was year by year becoming less able to feed those who were maintaining it to an ever higher standard. From one harvest to the next, it grew weary of being forced to produce more each time, always give something extra. And what had been the yield of the century ten years earlier – and would have been inconceivable fifty years ago – now counted as a mediocre result, hardly sufficient to cover the costs of production. It was crazy, stupid. This was the outcome of the senseless dash forwards in which Jacques was involved in order to survive.

Over the years, like hundreds of thousands of his

colleagues, he had been obliged to bend to the demands of the time. Producing more, always more, to try to compensate by increasing the volume for the losses caused by totally stagnant, or even falling prices. But how could he reach a target which was rapidly disappearing into the distance without running out of breath or courage!

Even during the worst periods of crisis, before the war, Pierre-Edouard had never seen such a mess, such a gloomy future for those who were clinging to their land. They clung on, for it was their only means of survival, their final struggle. They knew of no other way than to turn to it with loving care. But it was no surprise that as a result Saint-Libéral, which had counted 1,100 inhabitants at the beginning of the century, now harboured only 304, whose average age was over fifty! The dozens of little farms which formed its wealth, gave it standards and pride, were reduced to just eleven concerns.

They were of course much larger, more productive, more modern. But what use was that since they seemed, despite this, less and less able to meet the needs of their owners? Moreover, the majority had no one to carry on the work. And everything seemed to indicate that they would not even attract purchasers when the last smallholder gave up. How would they find someone crazy enough to invest in such a marginal way of life?

And yet, *miladiou*, that's a bloody fine, rich earth we've got there, fulminated Pierre-Edouard, sweeping his eyes over all the Vialhe lands on the plateau.

He bent down with some difficulty, collected a fistful of earth, crumbled it, kneaded it. Then with a broad movement he cast in front of him, as sowers do.

Poor old Jacques, what with this and the fifteen hectares at the Heath, it gives him a fair old lot of work. And he's killing himself with it. Good God! he needs some help, a fellow like poor Nicolas . . . Or if that's hoping for too much, someone like that idiot my father employed in the years . . .? Huh! I've forgotten . . . And what was his name, that old cackler? Doesn't matter, I'll ask Mathilde, she has a good memory . . .

He reflected for a few moments, searched his memory to try to remember the christian name of the man whose inane and toothless smile he could still picture clearly, but whose name had faded away with time.

The devil with that ass! Never mind, even he would be of use to Jacques! But that's over! It's a long time since we've seen tramps passing with their bundles over their shoulders! Nobody wants to get their hands dirty any more. Besides, even if by some miracle Jacques discovered a rare pearl, he wouldn't have the means to pay him! Well, that's how it is, seems that's par for the course . . .

He pulled on his unlit pipe for a long time, knocked it against his palm, and continued his solitary walk. Above the Long Piece, not far away, a lone kestrel on the look-out for fieldmice hovered like the Holy Ghost.

Pierre-Edouard was at the edge of the plateau, at the foot of the White Peak, when he heard the Saint-Libéral bell strike eleven o'clock. He quickened his pace a little, for he knew Mathilde would worry if he were not home by a quarter to twelve. They had come to an understanding. Mathilde had long ago abandoned the idea of keeping him around the house, of confining him to the garden, main street or even church square, where everyone could have seen him and above all come to help him in case of need.

He had waved away the arguments she put forward to persuade him. Just as he had openly laughed when she had proposed, seeing he was bored at home, that he spend a little more time at the bistro – the last and only business in Saint-Libéral – still kept by Nicole, daughter of Noémie and granddaughter of Ma Eugène, whose reputation as an incorrigible hussy was well-established. Naturally, she had suggested, it wouldn't be to drink there, but to talk things over with the last of his old friends, Edmond Duverger and Louis Brousse, who liked to meet there to share a hand of rummy.

'So now you want to send me to Nicole's? Well what d'you know, how times change! Only fifteen years ago you'd have scratched out my eyes if I'd stepped into her place! I was barely allowed to buy my tobacco there! And still you almost resented that!'

'No I didn't! You always exaggerate! I've never stopped you enjoying a game of cards if you felt like it! So now that you should be taking things easy . . .'

'That's it! Go on, say it, I'm allowed to see Nicole now that she's fifteen years older! Now she's as ugly as anything and I'm past it! But I don't want to call trumps. I don't particularly want to hang around with poor old Brousse, who's getting more and more doddery. Nor Edmond, who cries like a child over the slightest thing. I don't want to be with those dotards who are younger than me. I like them all fine, well, almost all, but they irritate me.'

What he craved was to walk in the woods and the fields, whatever the weather; to tend the last five hives he had kept; to take out his gun occasionally and try, without a great deal of conviction, to track and shoot a woodcock. What he loved was to see the Vialhe lands over the seasons, to admire Jacques' herd of Limousin cows and his enormous sows. What he wanted was to be free to climb as far as the White Peak one day, to the Caput Peak the next and another time up to Coste-Roche, to greet his daughter-in-law there and be given a cup of real coffee; Mathilde had a tendency to make it weaker and weaker.

But as he hated to see the ugly lines which worry etched on his wife's forehead, as he knew the extent of her fear for him, how she watched for the slightest sign of tiredness and stood ready to call the doctor, he had established a sort of system, a tacit agreement. Before leaving, he always revealed his itinerary and the aim of his walk. As for his timetable, it was fixed. Thanks to this, neither of them needed to express their thoughts. They both knew that this information would direct the search if one day he were to be a little late . . .

All the same he had smiled on discovering at the bottom of a pocket of his hunting jacket, the one he slipped on for his walks, a big whistle, which Mathilde had put in without saying a word, knowing that he would understand. He had refrained from telling her that he would have little chance of whistling into that tiny spout if his heart was causing him trouble. He knew just how short your breath was when that happened . . .

Thus for two years he had regulated his outings. And such was his understanding of her after fifty-seven years, he was persuaded that Mathilde knew where he was to be found at such and such a time. It was reassuring, for him as well . . .

On this day he checked with his watch that the church clock was right – since the electric chimes were installed, for lack of a sacristan, it had a tendency to wander – and stepped down the path which plunged towards the village. He took it carefully, for the slope was steep. He had known the track for over eighty years, was familiar with each turn, each hump, each big rock. Now, instead of running down it thoughtlessly and happily in ten short minutes, it would take him almost three-quarters of an hour. The key was to recognise and accept it, without resentment.

4

SINCE his first election as town councillor, Jacques ⟨...⟩ no difficulty in getting re-elected at each ballot; he ⟨...⟩ won by a large margin in the first round. But that di⟨...⟩ not make his work as mayor any easier.

Firstly, Saint-Libéral was ageing at a catastrophic rate, the whole community was in a state of collapse and therefore lacked financial resources. Secondly, the representation within the council had changed since the last election, in March 1971.

It was not even politics which had set them at loggerheads. The relationship between the left and the right remained roughly the same, and as Jacques kept himself strictly aloof from all that, it was not the various opinions and their differences which gave him trouble.

Besides, it was a far cry from the battles of yesteryear. And it was really very amusing to see, seated side by side and promoting the same values, Jean Delpeyroux, Henri Brousse or Jacques Duverger. Thirty years earlier, the father of the first-named swore by Marshall Pétain alone, the father of the second took only Stalin as his model, while the latter's father never hid his sympathy for Léon Blum and his friends.

Today the sons were upset – and they were not the only ones – that they could not vote for Chirac, his constituency being too far from Saint-Libéral! So even if Peyrafaure or Delmas were susceptible to the smooth approach of a Communist like Duclos, political sparring did not present any problems for Jacques. On the other hand, a certain lack of understanding had crept into the council since the new arrivals in the village had been elected. It was not that they were unpleasant, far from it, but they were totally ignorant of the life of a rural community and its organisation.

Living for some years on the edge of the village, on the plots

..s, Léon's son, they worked outside the village. ..of them were employees at the hinge-factory in La Rivière-de-Mansac, Claude Delmas and Alain Martin; another, Michel Lacombe, kept a small shop in Terrasson; the fourth, Mathieu Castellac, was with the electricity company EDF in Brive, and the last, Roger Peyrafaure, lived on his pension from the SNCF railway company.

Certainly their numbers did not give them the majority on the council, but the ideas they expounded, and which sometimes found a favourable echo with other councillors, frequently left Jacques speechless, they were so unrealistic. In fact, although living in a rural parish, the five newcomers expected to have the benefit of the services they had enjoyed in town. And they were not the only ones making such demands. So Jacques had to fight every inch of the way not to waste his already slender budget on trifles.

For to him, everything which was not absolutely essential was unnecessary. Unnecessary, and how costly, this construction of pavements at the beginning of the track up to Coste-Roche. Of course there were four recently built houses there, but their owners should consider themselves lucky to have the use of a surfaced and maintained roadway. So why the devil were they asking for pavements? To make out they were posher, and to be the envy of those in the village who had none?

Jacques knew full well that if he gave in on this point the fashion for pavements would gain ground in Saint-Libéral: everyone would want one, would demand it even! so, no! since the beginning of the century only the main street had had a pavement, and that was quite sufficient. There was therefore no question of embarking on new works.

Equally pointless, and even grotesque, the extension of street lighting along the track which led up to the plateau, where several new houses had been built.

'But, good God!' swore Jacques, 'they knew there were no lamp posts when they bought! And no main's drainage either! That's why they didn't have to pay too much for their land! Street lights in the middle of the country! I ask you! And what for, eh? For their dogs to pee up against, maybe? There are still plenty of trees hereabouts!'

It was also unnecessary, and unaffordable, to renovate and refit the inside of the youth club. It would have to do, old as it was. But what was the good of investing in a building shunned by the few young people in Saint-Libéral?

And yet, if there were one parish property which Jacques would have liked to see revived, that was the one. It embodied his entire adolescence. It was enough to think of it to hear once more the laughter of Paul, all his friends, of Father Verlhac; to remind himself of the vibrant, happy village it had been. A community where there were so many young people they had once needed a games room and a library of their own.

Today, the remaining kids were so few and far between that they could not even make up a football team!

After considering ongoing business, the discussion on the subject of youth did, however, resume in the council meeting that evening in October.

Jacques, already worn-out by a day's ploughing, realised that it would be a long time before he got to bed when Roger Peyrafaure began to speak. Not only was he as long-winded as a lawyer, but he loved the sound of his own voice. He knew too that his position as a civil service pensioner gave him a certain authority in the eyes of some, and he never denied himself the pleasure of holding forth.

'Messieurs,' he commenced, 'I regret to say that we are behaving extremely badly with regard to our young people. Extremely badly, and I choose my words carefully . . .'

He's got a nerve, the old crab, thought Jacques, massaging the small of his back. Our young people, he says! He never wanted any, if I'm to believe what his wife told Michèle!

'Yes,' continued the orator, 'one day they will judge us severely, will call us to account. And they will be right! For I pose the question, messieurs, what are we doing to prevent them jumping on their motorbikes every Saturday evening, and sometimes even during the week, to go all the way to Ayen, or still further, to hang about the cafés playing at some pinball machine or table football? I ask you . . .'

'Well, and so what?' interrupted Delpeyroux suddenly.

'What d'you want us to bloody well do about it? You can't tie them down, can you?'

He was the first deputy, and a friend of Jacques. Like him, he was one of the last farmers in the village, had spent all day picking walnuts, and was also in a hurry to get to sleep.

'But how can you say that, Monsieur Delpeyroux!' broke in Peyrafaure. 'Precisely! We have to bloody well do something, as you put it! Yes, monsieur!'

This too was a departure. Previously – friends or enemies, political adversaries or not – all the men of Saint-Libéral had called each other by their Christian name, or their surname, and used the familiar 'tu'. Only the very old had a right to the formal 'vous' and to be addressed respectfully, as père such-and-such. Nowadays, with the newcomers, you were almost always required to stick on a 'monsieur' as long as your arm and to juggle with 'vous'. But as Delmond had one day said with regret:

'Say what you like, it was much easier when you could say: "My dear old Jacques, you're really bloody stupid!" Nothing was inferred, you knew there was no harm meant! But today, if I say that to one of these fellows, using the formal "vous", he might take it amiss! And I'd be lucky if he didn't complain to the gendarmes!'

Jacques smiled, thinking of the anecdote, and decided to take a turn at moving the discussion along.

'Right,' he interrupted, 'I think we've all understood that there's practically nothing for the young people. But I believe I have explained my views. We cannot invest crazy amounts solely to keep a few adolescents amused. It's a pity maybe, but that's how it is. We are not rich, you know, so what would you suggest, Monsieur Peyrafaure?'

'Oh! It's very simple,' said the latter, drawing a Gauloise from his cigarette-case. He lit it slowly, to create the maximum effect, took a long drag and leant back in his chair: 'It's quite simple,' he repeated. 'I suggest we build them a tennis court . . .'

'A what?' breathed Brousse in alarm.

'A tennis court,' said Jacques, who had understood very well.

42

'That's not so stupid, that would allow some grown-ups to keep fit too,' approved Martin, with the manifest encouragement and support of Castellac, Delmas and Lacombe.

Jacques looked at his old friends, those born and bred in the village, and pictured them, racquet in hand, galloping after a ball.

'Listen,' he said eventually, 'I've nothing against tennis, it's an extremely healthy sport – well, I presume it is – but do you really think that we can afford this . . . this luxury? Yes, it is a luxury!'

'It's not a luxury! Other villages have built them, and everyone's very pleased,' Martin assured him.

'Well, those villages are richer than ours!' cut in Jacques, with a flash of temper. 'Those are villages where there are children! Where the average age is not over fifty, like here! Those are not retirement colonies!'

'There's nothing wrong with being retired!' cried Peyrafaure angrily, for he felt under personal attack.

'I wasn't thinking of you,' Jacques reassured him. 'But bloody hell!' he exploded, 'do I need to spell out just how meagre our budget is? We should be redoing the roof of the mairie and of the church; there's not enough money, even with grants! To buy a big mower, a proper one, to clear the verges, not enough money! Repair a section of the water piping, no money! No money, my God! And you come rabbiting on about a tennis court? Why not a golf course and a swimming pool while you're at it? Or a racecourse? Eh?'

'When it comes to money, all you have to do is ask your friend Chirac, it seems he's handing it out to all his buddies!' growled Peyrafaure, getting more and more annoyed.

Jacques shrugged. He knew that Peyrafaure was not of his persuasion. So sometimes, when the discussion grew lively, a few barbed remarks were thrown around. It wasn't serious. But he promised himself the satisfaction of returning a ball to hit Peyrafaure in the face one of these days, like at tennis, right?

'No, let's be serious, messieurs. I'm not denying that we need to consider the young people, and the not-so-young. But have a heart, don't talk about a tennis court any more, it's beyond our means! That's the situation and that's all there is to it,' he said, rising and so indicating that the meeting was closed.

'All the same, we'll have to find some idea to pull this village out of the doldrums!' cried Martin.

'Right, there I'm in complete agreement with you,' Jacques assured him. 'And believe me, that idea, I've been looking for it ever since I came to the council as second deputy. I remember it well, it was twenty-seven years ago this month! You were only just born, Monsieur Martin, for if I'm not mistaken, you're hardly older than my eldest son! Yes, I've been looking for it since the year he was born. And I'll have you know, the electors are aware of that and trust me. Because it's twenty-seven years they've been voting for me!'

Even as he told himself repeatedly that he had made the right choice, that it wasn't sensible to base his whole future in Algeria, Dominique felt rather like a deserter. He didn't enjoy that. So now that everything was decided he was in a hurry to finish, to climb into the aeroplane and draw a line under it. But, as ill-luck would have it, his Super Caravelle had already been delayed for two hours, and no one in the airport had been able to tell him what time they could hope for take-off. No one even seemed to know why the aeroplane was not there.

Good thing nobody's waiting for me at the other end, he thought as he watched the indicator board on which flight 108, his, had still not been announced.

'Say what you like, things still aren't up to scratch here!' he called to Ali.

The Berber smiled and shrugged resignedly.

'So it took you four years to find that out!'

He had absolutely insisted on accompanying Dominique and watching with him for the promised Caravelle. But neither had anything further to say to each other; the wait was becoming uncomfortable.

'Honestly, you could go,' suggested Dominique once more. 'It might be a long wait yet.'

'I've got plenty of time. And it'll teach the new boy some patience!'

'He'll bloody well need it, dealing with you!' joked Dominique.

As soon as he met his successor, he understood that all would not be going smoothly between him and Ali. Young Sliman was still a little too full of his agronomy course and all the theory in his studies. Too sure of himself and tactless, he had cut short the explanations which Dominique was prepared to provide. To listen to him, he already knew everything about Saharan agriculture, and had no need of a Frenchman's experience. His attitude displeased Ali, who had vowed to lick him into shape without delay. Dominique had no doubt that the matter would be sorted out quickly. One or other of them would have to give in, and it would not be Ali. But knowing that this youth might perhaps try to ruin his work annoyed him. In the same way he was troubled by a sort of regret, almost a bad conscience, which had haunted him from the moment of decision was taken.

'Look, maybe it's good news this time!' he said suddenly, hearing the display board clicking over. He watched it and turned to Ali. 'The bloody plane's ready at last; I hope they've tightened all the nuts and bolts! Right, I'll be leaving you then, mate. But don't forget you promised to visit.'

'Don't worry, I'll keep it in mind. And you, if your Mondiagri sends you anywhere near ... Well, I mean, perhaps to Morocco; they've got a subsidiary over there, so ...'

'You bet, I'll pop over here. Go on then, look after yourself, and hey, man, you watch our experimental fields. Don't let that junior muck up our work. Because between us we've done a bloody good job! You know, what annoys me about going is that I may never find such an interesting and useful job again ...'

They shook hands, then Dominique turned on his heel and marched along the corridor to board.

Dominique adjusted his seat, stretched himself out more comfortably and glanced discreetly in the direction of his neighbour. He noticed immediately that she was young and good-looking, then that she was wrestling with her safety belt, which was much too long and all twisted up.

45

'Would you like some help?' he suggested.

'I'll manage, thank you,' she assured him as she got up.

She unravelled the strap, shortened it, sat down and fastened the buckle. Already the aeroplane was taxiing towards the runway.

When his eyes came to rest on his neighbour's hands, Dominique noticed that she was trembling. She was shaking so much that despite gripping the armrests with her fingers, her whole forearm was twitching. He observed her more closely, saw her closed eyes, mouth clamped shut, chin quivering. And despite her very deep suntan, two nasty pale blotches marked her cheeks.

He guessed that she was younger than him, and ventured in a joking tone: 'Is it malaria, fear, or both?'

She shrugged; gripped even tighter at her chair. Already the Caravelle was entering the final turn which would bring it to the beginning of the runway.

'If you're scared. I've got a trick to deal with it,' he reassured her, 'and if it's malaria, I've got what you need for that too.'

'Yes, I'm scared!' she blurted out. 'Now leave me in peace! Well, what's your trick?' she asked, biting her lips.

'Very easy. Look, as soon as the plane has switched to full thrust and begins to gather speed you start counting slowly. Or better still, you look at the second hand of your watch.'

'And what then?' she asked, smelling a rat.

'Well if we haven't taken off within forty seconds, at least we'll only be five seconds from heaven!'

'Oh, you think you're so clever!' she retorted and closed her eyes.

He saw that she was really very frightened. Already the sound of the jet engines was becoming deafening. He leaned over to her and offered a suggestion:

'It's not a joke! It works because it keeps you busy. But if you want to, you can hold on to my arm and squeeze as hard as you like, it seems that helps.'

He was surprised by the strength of the fingers which grasped his forearm and locked on. Pinned against the backrest by the acceleration and the Caravelle's amazing

46

angle of ascent, he did not move so long as he felt the fingers digging into his muscles. Then the machine gradually levelled off and the hand clutching him relaxed.

'Please excuse me,' said the young woman. 'It's better now.'

'My, that's a really strong grip you've got there!' he said, pushing up his sleeve to view the red marks left by her nails.

'I'm sorry,' she said again, with a smile. 'I've flown often enough, but I'm still just as frightened at take-off. Silly, isn't it?'

'No more than being frightened of other things; that's just the way it is. And does it affect you at landing?'

'No, no. You're safe, I won't scratch you any more.'

'Oh, it doesn't worry me. Although it's common know-ledge that landing's more risky than take-off,' he added wickedly.

'It's so kind of you to reassure me like that!' she replied, leaning towards him to look out of the porthole which he was partially blocking.

He noticed that she had very beautiful blue eyes, an exquisite, delicate profile, but her extremely short, dark brown hair showed evidence of a disastrously unprofessional cut.

She did that herself and made a complete mess of it! he thought. Or one of her friends, not a very talented one!

'Would you like my seat?' he suggested.

'No, no,' she said, curling up in her reclining chair, 'it's over, you can't see anything any more, there are too many clouds.'

'Yes, you can,' he said. 'Look back there, you can still pick out a bit of the coastline.'

She leaned over once more, saw it, smiled and resumed her place.

'Well, that's it, farewell Africa!' she said.

'At your age, it's a bit melodramatic to be saying goodbye! You've got all the time in the world to go back to Africa!'

'Yes, probably. It's just a figure of speech.'

'Are you a teacher?' he asked suddenly.

'No, why? Do I look like one?'

'Not particularly. No, I was asking because I've met several Frenchwomen like you during my years in Algeria. They were

47

almost all lecturers in something or other. The last one was a shrink and spent her time trying to understand the behaviour of countries recently released from the colonial yoke, her very words! A vast programme, don't you think?'

'And you, are you a teacher?'

'No, why? Do I look like one?'

'Not look, but sound – talk, talk, talk!'

'If that's all, there's nothing wrong with that. But come on then, instead of chattering away I'll nail my flag to the mast: Dominique Vialhe, agronomist, two years in Algeria, two in the Sahara.'

'Béatrice Laurignac, paediatric nurse, three years in Upper Volta.'

'Married?'

'Single.'

'Congratulations.'

'Because I'm still single?'

'Not at all, that's easy enough! But because of Upper Volta; that must be a tough job, down there!'

'You have to like it . . .'

'Of course. But tell me, your name comes from round our way.'

'Where's round your way?'

'The Corrèze.'

'That's in the north!' she said with a shrug. 'No, I'm from Agen.'

'That's not too bad,' he granted her. 'But tell me, why didn't you take the direct flight from Ouagadougou to Paris? What have you been doing in this dump? I may as well tell you that you were quite right to be frightened. You saw it, more than two hours delay we had! Seems they lost an engine . . . And just look at this cabin, it's rotten all through! If it were to rain, we'd be soaked!'

'Thank you for informing me so tactfully. I know very well that there's a more direct flight, but I had friends to visit in Algeria. There you have it. Any more questions?'

'No, that'll do. But please don't switch off. If I'm a bit too chatty it's because it's so nice to talk about something besides my job, especially with a fellow countryman.'

48

He looked at her, saw that she had closed her eyes, thought that maybe she wanted to sleep, and kept quiet. It was she who restarted the conversation after a few moments of silence.

'Are you leaving Africa too? For me, it's finished. And what about you?'

'Me too. But you said "It's finished", why?'

'Perhaps for the same reasons as you!'

'I bet you're going to get married,' he said, without really knowing why. 'Is that it?'

'What an idea!' she said with a laugh. 'But is that why you're going back then?'

'No way!' he retorted.

'Well why, then?'

'Oh, it's a long story!'

'Well tell me anyway, we'll see whether we've had the same experiences.'

'No, no, after you, ladies first.'

Dominique and Béatrice had not travelled the same road. Whereas one had worked in his younger days to reach the goal he had set himself – and it wasn't easy for the son of small farmers – the other had flitted happily from one thing to the next.

Daughter of a chemist, Béatrice had jogged along with classical studies up to her baccalaureat. Then, under the false pretext that the Universities of Toulouse or Bordeaux were less highly rated than Paris, she had persuaded her parents that her sudden enthusiasm for history deserved the best professors. That was in October 1967, and the only history which really interested her was her own!

She was then nineteen, and desperate to escape the smell, the tubes, creams, lotions and other patent products of the family chemist's shop. Anyway her elder brother was already preparing to succeed his father in the business, and she had no wish to compete with him for it.

From an attic shared with a girlfriend in the Rue Saint-André-des-Arts, she had gaily discovered all the pleasures of independence. And since it seemed quite natural that her parents should regularly send her a monthly allowance, she had no money worries.

She toyed lightly with the lectures in her course and developed a parallel education in theatre and cinema studies. As there was often a little time between two performances, she undertook to explore some museums.

It was not therefore to fill her spare time that she fell in with the protesting students; it was pure curiosity. She did not regret the experience, at least not at first.

She had discovered, in all those debates, meetings, shouting matches, controversies and good-natured chaos, a pleasant way of asserting herself and finding her own voice. And as she loved to take the floor, she had realised with delight that she could defend, with just as much determination, ardour and conviction, exactly the opposite of what she had advocated that same morning in front of a different audience! It was all very exciting. Much better than stupidly going out in search of a beating or a painful lungful of tear-gas, just for the childish pleasure of poking out your tongue at the riot police or calling them the SS.

However, since some of the listeners lacked the most basic sense of humour and the sneaks had told them that the little brunette with blue eyes had, two hours earlier, been proclaiming the opposite of what they had just applauded, she had been forced to abandon her career as an orator. Trapped at the end of a grimy corridor, she had understood that imagination and humour were not to the taste of the unyielding disciples and guardians of the new revolution; they were expressly forbidden.

'Right, you little bitch, you're busy sabotaging the movement! Is it that bastard Fouchet who's paying you?'

As she did not know the name of the Minister of the Interior, she had thought it was a joke and shouted back:

'No, it's Talleyrand!'

The clout she got brought tears to her eyes. But she had stood up to them, wrestled with them, striped her attacker's face with three sharp nails, lashed out with the toe of her shoe at the shin of another, and escaped under a shower of insults and threats:

'Stupid cow! If you come back we'll smash you up with crowbars!'

Considering the matter carefully, and not completely convinced it was absolutely necessary to sweep away a whole society and way of life which suited her very well, she had refrained from setting foot in the meetings or any of the other interminable discussions which proliferated everywhere. Since it was necessary to approach all this with the solemnity of a pope, it was not much fun. Likewise she had shunned all the demonstrations and marches which had followed throughout the whole month of May.

'That was it, shortly after all that fuss I changed tack,' she concluded.

'Funny, we might have met each other before during that period,' he said.

'Why? You were in Paris too?' she asked, switching to the familiar student form of address and using 'tu' without noticing.

'No, at Grignon. But I came and had a look.'

'Did you follow the events? Did you join in?'

'In the disturbances? No, I didn't have the time. And what's more I couldn't afford such luxuries! But you, after that, why paediatric nursing? Why Africa?'

'Because I like it, a great deal! As for Africa . . .' She fell silent, and shrugged. 'Why not Africa?'

'Well if you look at it like that . . .' he said. He watched her, saw that she seemed to be lost in memory, and continued, just as a joke: 'Africa wasn't to mend a broken heart, I hope? In Algeria I saw girls in that sort of situation. They were cured!'

'A broken heart?' she was amused. 'No, no, not especially. It was simply the first job I could find when I wanted a change of scenery, to make a break with my parents; give myself a bit of space, you know! But what about you, how did you get there?'

He looked at his watch and smiled.

'It would take too long to tell, we'll be landing in ten minutes. We'll have to meet again if you're interested in finding out. Shall we see each other again?'

'Who knows? . . . I believe in fate.'

51

'Why not! But we could still try to increase the odds a bit, couldn't we? Shall we exchange addresses? No obligation.'

'Okay, if you put it like that, no obligation. I mean we don't have to respond to a letter or call, right?'

'Well I certainly agree that gives fate more of a chance!'

5

SINCE Saint-Libéral no longer had a priest or a sacristan, Mathilde and Louise had committed themselves to looking after the church. They undertook to open it each morning, to close it after the evening angelus bell, to sweep it and set it to rights again after the few rare services. They made sure that there was always a good supply of candles, and holy water in the stoup.

Thanks to this, any old ladies who slipped into the church during the day did not have the feeling of entering an abandoned shrine. It was quite upsetting enough not to see the red lamp glowing above the tabernacle, empty of the blessed sacrament since Father Soliers had found the wafers all blue with mould after he had been away a fortnight. So, not being able to meditate in front of that, the female parishioners would kneel beneath the statue of Saint Eutrope, patron saint of the parish; Mathilde lit a small flame in front of it each morning.

For a long time now, a deep understanding had existed between these two. It was always at his feet that Mathilde came to draw courage when she had need of it. That habit dated from October 1917, after she had accompanied Pierre-Edouard to the train taking him back to the front line, when she had needed to feel she was not alone in the struggle against her overwhelming despair.

And then, over the course of the years, other events had brought her there, trustingly, to face the brightly painted statue. It was a very fine piece; thirteenth century, the experts maintained. Still well preserved, it had developed a sheen over the centuries and offered the faithful the rather tight-lipped but gentle smile of a man with a comforting expression and a beard of delicate ringlets. The hand raised in blessing had long ago lost the middle finger down to the second joint; in the other he held at his heart a thick missal embossed with a gold cross. Mathilde carefully dusted the statue each week, and used the opportunity to clean the niche where the spiders enjoyed weaving delicate haloes around the saint.

On this last Wednesday in October, two days before All Saints', Mathilde and Louise were happily chatting as they turned their steps towards the church. It was fresh but dry, and the day had begun pleasantly enough. But best of all was the news which delighted the whole family: Dominique had announced he would be arriving the next day. He had telephoned from Paris where he had been spending a short week sorting out some business with his new employers. According to Jacques, who was very proud of it all, he had secured an extremely interesting and very well paid job.

Unfortunately he would not be working in France, at least not at present. His first assignment would be to Guyana, which was not exactly a suburb of Saint-Libéral!

'Well, well, so that's it!' Pierre-Edouard had murmured on learning the news. 'That's his reward for wanting so many diplomas! Now they've sent him to a penal colony! Really, if you'd told my poor father that a Vialhe would one day go to Cayenne!'

But he too was very proud to know that his grandson had an important job. Anyway, Guyana was still better than Algeria. To Pierre-Edouard, that was the God-forsaken land where his son had died. He did not like it, and did not want his grandson to live and work there.

Well, the main thing is that he'll be here tomorrow, thought Mathilde, climbing the steps of the church. And as she was in a very good mood she decided to thank Saint Eutrope with a fat candle; a beauty, bearing that clever transfer of Notre Dame de Lourdes.

The empty niche was horrible, like an eyeless socket, obscene. Mathilde stood speechless, dazed, petrified to discover the cavity where there was nothing but a little heap of rubble and the pale outline of the statue printed on the grey stone, marking its presence there over the centuries. She jumped when she heard behind her the cry Louise emitted as she reached one of the two side chapels. It was the one where the altar housed the tiny casket containing the relics of Saint Eutrope, a fragment of jawbone. The reliquary had disappeared.

Then, all of a tremble, each transfixed by the same thought, the two women scurried to the other side of the apse, to the chapel of the Virgin Mary. And the same gasp of horror shook them when they saw that the magnificent door of Limoges enamel enclosing the tabernacle had been torn off.

'They've stolen everything, everything! How dare they!' Mathilde was incoherent, bitting her lips so as not to cry at such patent sacrilege. Then she saw, behind the great altar, a huge hole in the stained glass at the back of the church, giving on to the garden of the Vergnes' house.

'They've taken everything, everything!' she repeated, wandering to and fro.

Here, two big chandeliers were missing. There, the beautiful lectern of solid walnut, the eagle with outstretched wings on which the missal was placed. And in the vestry, horror of horrors. Everything had been pulled out of the cupboard through its broken door. Tossed into the middle of the room, there lay the capes and stoles, the old chasubles, the surplices. All those holy vestments which testified to the time when Saint-Libéral had its own resident priest, when the church was full each Sunday and Holy Day, and High Mass resounded with great pomp when His Lordship the Bishop honoured the church with his annual visit.

'Look,' whispered Louise, 'they've stolen it all . . .'

Stolen, the beautiful chalice donated in 1910 by Madame Duroux, the squire's wife, in honour of her elder daughter's marriage. Gone, the ciborium and the paten for the consecrated bread, the graceful crystal cruets for the wine, the ones they never dared to use because they were too fragile, and the monstrance. And even the old censer, which had not seen the smoke of incense for years, was no longer hanging from its nail.

'They got out that way . . .' said Mathilde, pointing to a little door, which had been unused for the last twenty years and led into the Vergnes' garden.

'Yes. We must call the gendarmes,' decided Louise.

'Of course, but first let me warn Pierre-Edouard quietly. It'll give him a shock, you understand.'

Carried by the postman from Perpezac – there had been no post office in Saint-Libéral for five years – the news had circulated around the village before it struck noon. Everyone, whether practising Christians or not, felt this theft like a violation. For by breaking into a holy place, it was rather as if the robbers had penetrated into the sanctum of every home. And everyone felt defiled by this incomprehensible act.

The oldest were the most shocked and scandalised. For even if some of them, especially the men, had not entered the church in years, it was still no less theirs. Within its walls all those born in the village had been baptised, taken their first Communion. It was there that many had been married. There, most importantly, had rested, for the duration of a service, the coffins of their parents, their friends, their partners, sometimes their children. There finally, before long, they too would be welcomed to begin their last journey. And those who had known an era when the church could remain open day and night without it occurring to anyone to desecrate it, were barely able to conceive of a person sufficiently immoral to plan and then carry out such a vile deed.

There was therefore a group gathered in the church square, reverberating with outraged and vengeful remarks, when the police car eventually arrived.

'They took their time!'commented Jacques.

'Yes, it must be more than three hours since they were called,' agreed his brother-in-law Jean-Pierre.

As teacher he naturally filled the post of secretary at the mairie, and was able to make an inventory of all the works of art the church contained.

'Come a bit quicker when it's a matter of confiscating a few demijohns of moonshine brandy!' said Pierre-Edouard sarcastically.

He had been in a bad mood ever since Matilde had told

him, and was cursing an era capable of producing individuals so foul that they would dare to sully consecrated ground.

Preceded by Jacques and Jean-Pierre, the two gendarmes entered the church, where Mathilde and Louise were waiting for them. Pierre-Edouard fell into step behind them.

'They must have come in through there!' said one of the gendarmes, after having examining the broken window.

Huh! No need to wear a kepi to work that one out!' grumbled Pierre-Edouard. He was growing angrier and angrier as he saw just how upset Mathilde was.

'Yes, they came in that way, the slobs!' he continued. 'And I can even tell you how! By climbing on to the lean-to by the Vergne house and jumping into the garden. It would never have happened when the house was inhabited! But that dump, with it's For Sale board to alert every passer-by, and it's been up more than a year, is almost an invitation to help yourself! It's like the empty presbytery – a signal for looters that's all!'

'Undoubtedly,' agreed the gendarme, turning to Jacques. 'And what have they taken?'

'Everything they could, but my brother-in-law will give you the details of the important pieces.'

'Here it is,' said Jean-Pierre, holding out a type-written sheet.

The officer read it and nodded his head:

'Very accurate description, but how did you know all that?'

'I helped with the inventory which the people from the Ministry of Cultural Affairs made five years ago.'

'Very good, we'll be able to circulate that,' said the gendarme, filing the document. 'But what I'd like to know is how they could do it without anyone hearing anything. And above all, how they got away so quietly.'

'By the vestry door which opens on to the garden,' explained Jacques.

'Look here, if you were a bit better at your job, you'd know that already!' interrupted Pierre-Edouard. He was aware of the two gendarmes' offended expressions, but took no notice. 'Exactly! If you came more often you'd know what was going on round here! Oh, I tell you, in the old days your colleagues weren't any cleverer, but they didn't need to ask questions like that! they would have known straight away!

'Listen,' Jacques intervened, 'let the gentlemen do their work! We've come on a bit since the mounted constabulary!'

'And more's the pity!' Pierre-Edouard was carried away. 'I'm going to tell you,' he shouted at the gendarmes who were more and more discomfited by the attack, 'instead of your pretty blue van driving through Saint-Libéral once a fortnight, only when the weather's good and without stopping of course, if you were to walk about a bit you'd know that the Vergnes' garden backs on to the lane which goes down to the Combettes. Yes, there's a lane, and that's where the robbers' car must have been waiting. They won't have needed to walk more than eighty metres, and cool as a cucumber! There's no one left around there, or only a few old people. And they're not of age to go out in the middle of the night when the dogs bark. The old people know it takes you three hours to arrive! So they're not in a hurry to get bashed up waiting for you outside! That's what you ought to know!'

'Listen, monsieur, we're not here to be lectured! We're here to investigate!' cried the officer.

'A lecture; I'll give you a lecture if I feel like it! That's just it: if you came more often we wouldn't be robbed by the first thieves who turn up!'

'Calm down,' Mathilde put in. 'These gentlemen are doing what they can.'

'All right! Can't do much, those old jackdaws! This proves it, can't even prevent a break-in in the middle of the village! I'll tell you something, you won't be seeing your Saint Eutrope in a hurry. He's a long way off by now, poor fellow! And nobody's after him! Right, I'm off out for some fresh air. I can see that I'm holding up the smooth running of the investigation!' he hurled, as he strode towards the far end of the church.

He went out, and the noise of the heavy door slamming behind him echoed all along the main street.

'Well I must say, Mayor, your father's still in good form!' said the officer as soon as Pierre-Edouard had left.

'Oh, you think so?' Jacques smiled. Then he saw his mother quite downcast and sad, and his black mood returned. 'Yes, that's as maybe, but he's right – I mean about the route taken by our visitors.'

'We'll go and have a look at that in a moment.'

'And apart from that, what will you actually do?'

'We'll take statements from the witnesses, I mean these two ladies. We'll try to find out what time the robbery happened, look for tracks behind the church . . . all that, the usual routine.'

'That means there's no chance of getting anything back?'

'Sadly, your father's right on that count too,' sighed the gendarme. 'The stolen objects are several hours away by now. They're probably already in Paris, Lyon or Bordeaux. Or somewhere else just as distant! Or even sold already . . .'

'But who would dare to buy such things?' Louise intervened.

'What's that?' The gendarme was amazed. 'Anybody, my dear lady! You know, maybe I shouldn't say it, but since some priests have taken to selling statues and pictures which they no longer wanted in their churches, everybody's got used to finding them in the dealers and antique shops. So . . .'

'But . . . even the chalice? Even the ciborium?' Mathilde asked indignantly.

'Of course, madame! There are people who even enjoy using one as an ordinary dish, or as a vase!'

'Mon Dieu . . .' she murmured.

She was from an era when the worshippers had no right to touch the sacred vessels without express permission; it would have been a grave sin. And she felt so sad she could have cried as she pictured the Saint-Libéral chalice in impious hands.

'Well yes, that's how it is,' said the gendarme. 'It's a funny old world we're living in.'

It was then, and only then, that Mathilde realised how much times had changed, the world had turned upside down, for ever probably. Further proof lay in the fact that no one had yet thought to inform the vicar who served the parish. It was staggering, for that demonstrated that nobody in Saint-Libéral recognised good Father Soliers as the village priest. He was not and would never be more than a caretaker. Not unknown, naturally, but still forever a stranger, the vicar of other parishes, the one who could only come once a fortnight and not even on Sundays.

'We should perhaps tell Father Soliers,' she said eventually.

'Oh yes, that's true,' said Louise, 'but where is he?'

'Um . . .' murmured Mathilde as she considered the matter.

'It's Wednesday morning? He must be taking Catechism in Yssandon or Perpezac, at least I think so . . .' reckoned Jacques. 'But you're right,' he said to his mother, 'I'll go and telephone right away.'

He came back a few moments later to announce that the priest was neither in Yssandon, nor in Perpezac; he was at a meeting in Tulle, at the bishop's palace.

'So did you leave a message?' asked Mathilde.

'No, I didn't dare,' he said thoughtfully. He shrugged his shoulders before replying: 'They explained to me that he and his colleagues were discussing Christian activities in the rural framework. I didn't think it would be in very good taste to tell them what's happening here in Saint-Libéral, in the way of activities . . .'

It was almost midday before the gendarmes left the village. Mathilde watched the police car disappear, and turned to Jacques.

'They won't find anything, will they?'

'I'm afraid not . . .'

'And you, what do you think?' she asked her son-in-law.

'The same, sadly!'

'So they were wasting our time with their stupid questions. Pierre was right,' she said.

'I wouldn't be surprised,' said Jacques.

'Great!' she sighed. 'Right, it's time I went back, your father will be waiting for his soup and he'll be getting impatient. Especially as he's already in a bad mood . . . By the way, as he's not here, have you any news of the girls?'

She had a longstanding agreement with her daughter and son-in-law that she would continue to hear news of her granddaughters, whatever their behaviour, or misbehaviour, might be. She considered she had the right to know. So she kept herself informed whenever she got the chance, which was to say when Pierre-Edouard was not around. For although Mauricette dropped in on her parents every day, that was of course when her father was at home; and as they were supposed to keep it all from him . . .

'Marie telephoned yesterday evening, she's okay,' Jean-Pierre assured her.

'She didn't say any more about the problem with . . . uh . . .'

The fact that one of her granddaughters was prepared to break her marriage vows was heartrending for her, so that she did not even wish to say the word divorce; she was shocked by it.

'Yes, of course, it seems it's all done already,' said Jean-Pierre resignedly.

'Aah . . .' she breathed out. 'I won't ask you for news of Chantal. Aunt Berthe speaks to her on the telephone every fourth morning. I know she's very well. That is, if you like that sort of thing . . .' she sighed.

There again, the life led by her granddaughter was far from pleasing to her. All the while she consoled herself by telling herself that Chantal at least, if she went on the way she was going, would never need to get a divorce . . .

'And the little one?' she continued.

She had always had a weakness for Josyane. Of Mauricette's three girls, it was she who most resembled Mathilde. Lively and graceful, as she had been in her youth. But stubborn too, and deceitful if need be. And with a will of iron when it came to completing a project she considered worthwhile. To that she added an independent streak which Mathilde had understood. At least until the day when Josyane had gone too far. To leave like that for the ends of the earth, on an impulse, that was really unforgiveable! Well, almost . . . She saw that her son-in-law was delaying his reply, and asked again:

'So what about Jo?'

'We received a postcard this morning,' he explained. He seemed so unhappy that she should not really have enquired further. But she needed to know.

'She's well at least?'

'Oh! That, yes, seems to be! Well, you know, she never complains and especially not when things are going badly . . .'

'And where did this card come from?'

By now she was used to it. On account of her grand-daughter, she had been forced to get down one of those old atlases out of the loft. A book dating from her days as a pupil with the nuns at Allassac, before the 1914 war. A completely obsolete work which showed the colonies, French and others, but which still allowed her to follow her granddaughter's movements a little better, when Jo thought to write.

After spending almost a year in the United States, she had headed straight for Mexico. Subsequently a postcard arrived from Colombia; then another from Peru. Three months later Josyane was in Rio. So it was hard to guess where the next message would come from!

'Come on, say it! Where is she now?' she repeated the question.

'In Tahiti!'

She needed several seconds to realise fully that it was a long way off, a long, long way . . .

'But what's she doing over there?'

'Who know's!' said Jean-Pierre with a shrug. 'I've given up trying to understand!'

'But doesn't she explain anything?'

'No,' he sighed. 'At least since she left she never has explained anything, why should she start now?'

The robbery from the church earned Saint-Libéral the attention of the local press. The afternoon had hardly started when a journalist from the Brive office stopped his car in the church square. Preceded by a dachshund which was nearly eaten by the first dog it met – a brute almost as big as a calf, which was always ravenous and belonged to Delmond – the man walked without hesitation to the door of the bistro and pushed it open. Here was a very fine professional who knew his area and his trade like the back of his hand. He reckoned on garnering a mass of information at Nicole's, all the details of the general atmosphere, which he was very keen to capture.

His disappointment was great when he found only two old men sipping coffee. As Edmond Duverger was as deaf as a post and Louis Brousse wary and disinclined to speak, the conversation did not even get off the ground. That left Nicole. But she had seen nothing and if she was, like everyone, aware of the crime, her information was second-hand, vague.

'Do you know whether Monsieur Vialhe is about?' asked the journalist.

'Which one?'

'Well, I only know of one, the former regional councillor, the mayor, you know! He's still the mayor, isn't he?'

'Yes. Maybe he's at the mairie.'

'Right, I'll go there,' said the man, carefully sniffing the beverage called coffee which he now regretted having ordered. 'But tell me,' he continued, 'it's astonishingly quiet here, what's going on? There used to be a few more people, didn't there?'

'At one time, yes, there were more people. But not now. It must be a long time since you've been here, eh?'

'Yes, I suppose it is if I think about it,' he said, fiddling with his Rolleiflex. 'Four or five years maybe. I was doing a report on a plan for redistributing the land.'

'Oh yes, that rubbish! But luckily the redistribution was never done! Just as well, it was only good for stirring up quarrels between neighbours,' explained Nicole. 'Yes,' she continued, 'redistribution, that costs money, even when it doesn't produce any!'

She observed him closely, searched her memory and then exclaimed happily:

'Now I remember you! One day you were taking pictures at Delpy's and his whole herd chased after you! We had a good laugh then, I'll say!'

'Yes, yes,' he tried to dismiss the subject.

'But tell me, you didn't have a beard then? Ah, I thought so! That made you look younger, yes, really! Although the beard's not bad either. Yes, I quite like it, it's soft, like being stroked . . .'

'So you're saying the village is always as empty as this?' he continued, indicating the completely deserted square.

63

'Huh, a few people turn up on days when there's a funeral, but otherwise . . . oh yes, and a few come for the grocer, but you're too early . . .'

He gave a little smile, for he was absolutely convinced that she was making fun of him, and returned to the reason for his visit.

'So you don't know anything of the theft?'

'Well, no, not much. Except it seems it's worth hundreds and thousands, what they took! All the church plate, you know! But what were they thinking of leaving all that stuff where it's never used? I must say, as far as I'm concerned, the church . . . I've got nothing against it. But I don't have anything to do with it either. Except for funerals . . .'

She regarded him eagerly; nodded her head:

'All things considered, it suits you, that beard. Yes, it does, it looks very attractive! And then, the best part is it hides the wrinkles, eh?'

She's well tanked up! Incredible, she must run on neat Pernod! he thought, contemplating the blotchy, swollen face of his hostess. He drank a mouthful of coffee and put down the cup.

'Well, I'll go and find out what the mayor can tell me,' he said, striding to the door.

'Aren't you going to take photos?

'How do you mean, photos? Who of?'

'Well, of me! Usually in the paper there's a photo of the people who have been doing the talking, with their names too!'

'Of course, you're right,' he said with a smile.

And since he was a kind man who would have been sorry to disappoint Nicole, he took two photos of her, posing jauntily behind her bar.

'I'll send them to you,' he promised as he went out.

Still pulled along by his dachshund, who yapped himself hoarse on the end of his lead each time he caught sight of a hen or duck, he headed for the mairie.

Luckily he found Jacques and Jean-Pierre there, who supplied all the information he wanted. He constructed from this a very fine and moving article, illustrated with a photo of the broken window and the empty niche, which appeared three days later. However, he had been so struck by the silence and emptiness of Saint-Libéral that he began his piece thus: *In a village which seems abandoned, so sleepy and deserted as it is, the criminals were able to empty a church of its exquisite treasures with complete impunity* . . .

'So, now I'm the mayor of an abandoned village . . .' muttered Jacques, putting down the daily paper. He was a little annoyed, and almost telephoned the reporter to communicate his resentment. But he refrained; the man was simply making an observation.

Whether you liked it or not, even if Saint-Libéral was not abandoned, it was well and truly deserted and silent, motionless as a village about to die . . .

PART TWO
The Migrants

6

FROM the moment he was old enough to think, Dominique had always done his best to look on the bright side of life. That did not preclude periods when he felt bad-tempered or discouraged; but at least he did all he could not to give in to these feelings.

He therefore reproached himself, after a week at Coste-Roche, with not being as happy as he should have been. Happy to see his parents again after an absence of two years, to plunge back into the world and the scenery of his childhood. Happy as a man taking a well-earned holiday. However, despite his pleasure at being with his family again, in a place he loved, he was not completely content.

He had expected to find that his parents had aged, but the reality was worse than he had imagined. His father in particular was worn out. What was more, he had the appearance of a man haunted by fatigue, whose worries had become his constant companions. Dominique might well remind himself that the break-in at the church had affected him deeply, but that was not enough to explain it all. Not enough to warrant his limping and obviously painful gait, his bent back and the deep lines etched in his face. Not enough to excuse the state of his land either . . .

Not that it was bad, but Dominique was too observant not to notice immediately that many of the pastures showed signs of depletion, and the majority needed to be resown. He had also too professional an eye not to register that the Limousin herd was ageing; many of them should have been culled and replaced. And he was not too blind to see that the plum trees on the Perrier field were no longer well tended. To cap it all, just about everywhere ugly fringes of brambles and thistles were springing up, all those weeds which take advantage of the slightest relaxation in the maintenance of the land.

But since he had decided before coming to say nothing which might upset his father, he was forced to keep his opinions to himself. Likewise he could not in all fairness blame his mother for having let herself go in her old age, and done nothing to alleviate its effects. She was only forty-nine but sometimes seemed nearer sixty. Lastly, he was saddened by the state of Coste-Roche.

For the house had an aura, if not exactly of poverty, at least of want. Here the shutters needed repainting; there a window with a broken catch no longer opened; here again a cracked downpipe poured all its water over a corner of the yard at the slightest shower.

And everywhere inside, yellowing wallpaper, sagging furniture, a collection of crockery which grew less well-matched and more chipped. There as elsewhere, as with the land and farm buildings, the gradual wear and tear caused by lack of maintenance and limited means. The thought that he was at last going to be able to help his parents a little – it looked as if his salary would be three times what he had received in Algeria – was not enough to improve his temper. He was not convinced that lack of resources was the only thing depressing his father.

'You're on the right track, my dear; what's eating your father is more serious than all the financial difficulties he's experiencing. And God knows he's got enough of those!' Berthe assured him.

She was taking advantage of a trip Dominique was making to Brive in his Ami 6 to accompany him and do a bit of shopping.

'They're very comfortable, these little cars,' she admitted, spreading herself out on the bench seat. 'You know, if I were still driving, this is what I'd have.'

'You should have gone on,' he suggested. 'You've never had any problem!'

'Exactly! It was to avoid any that I gave it up. I had always decided to stop driving on the day of my seventy-fifth birthday. That's what I did, and I don't regret it. Is it second-hand, this one? It doesn't look like it,' she noted.

'Yes, a bargain; it's a 1970 model but it only had thirty-five thousand on the clock. I took it right away.'

'You were right. At your age you need to lead your own life and be independent.'

'But I've decided to give it to Papa when I leave,' he continued. 'That'll allow him to get rid of the old Aronde; it's in a dreadful state, possibly even dangerous. This one will last him for a bit.'

'That's kind of you,' she said, patting him gently on the shoulder. 'Yes, very kind. Does he know?'

'No, it's to be a surprise when I leave.'

'And then it'll be a comfort to him after seeing you go, is that right?'

'I suppose so.'

'That's kind,' she reiterated. 'Slow down a bit, there are always loonies shooting out at these crossroads!'

He smiled, for he loved the rather slangy vocabulary his great-aunt liked to use, and took his foot off the pedal.

'So what's eating Papa, do you think?' he asked, resuming the conversational thread.

'Lots of things.'

'What in particular?'

'First of all, whatever he may have said and even if I think he was right, he's missing not being regional councillor any more. You see, there at least he felt he was achieving something.'

'You're sure he would have been beaten?'

'Yes. You know, it's all connected. He'd have been beaten because people nowadays don't want a small farmer to defend them. So that's one thing, that affected him deeply. He felt rejected. But that's not all. I hope you've been keeping in touch with what's been happening in France while you've been away. Well, you have to see things as they really are: nobody's interested in agriculture any more.'

'Well you have to admit that what's going on at our place . . .'

'That's not the point, it's your father's profession. He's already poorly paid, then people tell him he's useless as well! No, just look at that idiot, the speed he's overtaking us! What a wally!'

'And then what else is wrong with him?'

'Right, I could say his health. It's staring you in the face, his back's killing him, but that's almost by the by. No, what's eating him is not being able to jog Saint-Libéral out of its coma, not finding anything to revive the village. It's not for lack of looking or trying, but you get tired of it all . . .'

'I'm sure. But it's true, the village has got pretty gloomy. It's terminal, and I don't see any solution.'

'There it is, you can see the whole picture. All that stops him feeling happy. He's always taken everything to heart, and now he's frightened he'll end up without making a success of anything. Anyway, luckily there's your sister and you. That makes a difference. But you don't need him any more, Françoise only a bit, and not for much longer. Yes, your father needs to feel useful and to be successful. There's only the mairie to put his heart into, but as he has less and less hope . . .'

'And what could I do to help him?' asked Dominique as he slowed down to enter the industrial area of Brive. 'Just look, what a lot of development here! Bloody hell, not so long ago this was the middle of the country!'

'Yes, you see! It's developing here and dying thirty kilometres away, at home . . . The town is gaining ground and we're mouldering away. And everyone seems to think that's quite all right. So to come back to what you can do for your father? I don't know. Simply tell him he's right to fight on, even if it's apparently for nothing.'

'Better to find him something which would be worth fighting for, eh?'

'Of course, but have you got any ideas?'

'No.'

'So, you see . . .'

Never would Josyane have imagined that she could experience such a sense of relief as she did on seeing the Boeing transporting Gilles disappear.

And yet God knew how precarious her present situation was! Alone, more than twenty hours by plane from the mainland of France, with hardly enough to live on for a month, on an island where everything was arranged to fleece the tourist: not a very comfortable position. However, despite all that, she was happy, free.

Contrary to what her companion had perhaps hoped, it was not to try to persuade him to stay that she had accompanied him to Faaa airport, but to make sure he was actually leaving! He had tried that trick so often, saying, 'You're really too stupid, I'm going back to France!' that she had ended up wondering whether he would ever actually do it, and fearing he would not.

She had been fed up for a long time with the childish outbursts with which, like a spoilt brat, he greeted the slightest opposition. She had quickly realised that the impulse which had seized her when he had suggested she accompany him round the world was a monumental error; an idiotic whim which she was still paying for and regretting.

For although Gilles knew how to be pleasant and witty, although he was well educated and interested in everything, he was also often disagreeable, boorish, bad-tempered and spiteful. And always dramatically infantile. In fact when he had one day asked her to go away with him, it was not so much because she was a pretty, funny, jolly girl: it was to have someone permanently around to lean on. She had realised that as soon as they arrived in the United States, when, far from his own kind and already feeling lost, he considered jumping into the first available aeroplane to return to the calm of Parisian life!

She had also discovered that he was not much more of a photographer than she was, that his journalistic projects were pipedreams based on vague contacts with an equally nebulous agency. Although she had quickly appreciated that he was inspired and athletic when the time came for tenderness and more energetic activities, she had also immediately observed that he was very lazy when he needed to earn his living. Always ready to escape to pastures new, as well! For it was he who, after a few months or weeks of little bits of work picked up by chance during their journeys, made a reverse charge call to his father, to get something sent for air-tickets so that they could change countries!

He declared that his father could easily afford to indulge his whims. He was a Member of Parliament, of fluctuating persuasion, who had grown grey but never blushed under two Republics and several different portfolios, without actually renouncing his profits from industry. Swept out in 1968 by a young tiger who had had the wit to chant 'Vive de Gaulle!' a quarter of an hour earlier than him, he now slumbered in the Senate and was in clover.

'I promise you it won't worry him to send us a bit of cash, he's got enough! I'm not joking,' Gilles reassured her, when she reproached him with the dreadful way he called for help the moment he felt bored or a little at sea. She had never accepted that sort of hypocrisy which consisted of declaring yourself free and independent, all the while reaching shamelessly into the paternal pocket! She would not stoop to that. So to draw the line, she had always managed to provide her share of the budget through her own work. But their differences of opinion on this matter had soured their relationship very early on.

Despite this, and all his other shortcomings, Josyane had not immediately envisaged cutting the ties and leaving him to extricate himself alone from his fits of depression, bad temper and fury. Wisely, she did not yet feel sufficiently confident to venture alone on the exploration of all the countries she wanted to get to know. And as he for his part was incapable of making any progress without support and clung to her like a toddler to its mother, they had remained together for almost two years, somehow or other, a strange couple, rather ill-matched.

But she had very quickly realised that it would all fall apart one day, that he would end up hating her for being made of sterner stuff than him, and she herself would tire of his outbursts, his insults and his cocksure arrogance, thinking he was irresistible the moment he slid his hand into her blouse. She had no doubt that there existed at least one other man in the world capable of satisfying her just as well as him, without being quite so emotionally disturbed. She only had to find him, or to wait for him.

The rift between them had been accentuated during their

first week in Tahiti. The idea of visiting Polynesia was his. He wanted to make a photo-reportage for which the agency with whom he very sporadically collaborated would, this time, pay him a fortune! That was what he had given her to believe . . . But he delivered the same speech at each new foray, and she knew that he would be doing well if he even managed to get paid for the films! She had no more illusions about his abilities to earn his living as a photographer!

She was nevertheless happy to follow him to Tahiti, for her job as nanny to a rich family in Rio was beginning to weigh heavy. The three children she had charge of were really too badly brought up and in need of a cuff or two. Exactly what she was not allowed to give them! And after all, Tahiti – that was the ultimate destination, paradise on earth! She had quickly understood that it might be true for those who arrived with solid financial backing; lacking that vital ingredient, it was close to purgatory.

For despite the sun, the scent of mallow, the warm blue water and thousands of brightly coloured fish slipping through your legs, life was not simple for those who needed to earn their daily bread. Especially if they arrived totally unprepared, without any contacts, nor knowing who to turn to.

But Gilles and she had something to survive on for a while without too much trouble, and had therefore begun to snap away at a great rate. For she too had taken to the business, and often achieved better results than him. She had a superior sense of composition, of perspective, an eye for a fleeting image to be captured, for the light.

Their first serious row had arisen four days after their arrival. With all the pessimism of which he was capable, Gilles had decided that Tahiti was a real trap for suckers; it was tiny, you could get round it in an afternoon; two rolls of thirty-six were enough to photograph everything, and it was therefore imperative to leave such a miserable spot.

'Don't you think you're exaggerating a bit? We've only just arrived, and we've seen nothing of the interior!' she had said.

'The interior? You didn't think I was going to wade through that bloody jungle! There's not even a road! No thank you, to slog up fifteen hundred or two thousand metres for the sake of coming down the other side, not likely! No there's really nothing in this dump! Ah, except the girls! Their mugs could frighten the life out of you, but some lovely bums! And their boobs! Have you seen?'

'To me, you know, girls . . .'

'Right, it's not the article, I'm not staying here!'

'Where do you want to go?'

'To Bora Bora, seems it's worth a detour. And I'd like to pop over to Raiatea.'

'But you're crazy! You know our budget won't allow for that!'

'Yours may not, but mine will. You don't think I came here to sit around doing nothing!'

She had seen that he had made up his mind and knew already that he would make no allowances for her reservations. And as she was fed up with always having to make him see reason, she had given up the struggle.

'Fine, do as you like, I'm staying here.'

'You want to leave me?'

'Don't twist things; it's you who's leaving, not me!'

'Okay. Right, you muddle along by yourself then, old girl. Cheerio!'

'And to emphasize his displeasure, he had picked up his bag and camera and left the modest hut they had rented on the outskirts of Papeete.

She had then spent her first night alone since she had known him. To her great satisfaction, not only was she not frightened, she had actually slept better! As he had not reappeared the following morning she had set out at once to look for work in Papeete. Enquiring at every business, shop or enterprise run by Europeans, she had offered her services to each one either as a saleslady, or as an interpreter – she now had a very good command of English, could get by respectably in Spanish and Portuguese – or again as a secretary. And, as a last resort, as a nanny.

Demoralised by a week of futile searching, she was on the point of giving up hope when the manager of a travel agency almost flung her arms around her neck and at once adopted the familiar 'tu' commonly used in Tahiti.

'You speak American? This is really true?'

'Yes.'

'Well, you've come at the right moment, my dear! Oh yes! Our guide has been blackmailing us for a rise and I refuse to give in! I must say that's really not on here, because once you start . . .! Yes, she's Chinese, a beautiful girl, the sneak! And she speaks four languages! But that's no excuse! Is it really true, you can speak American with that authentic nasal accent?'

'Yes.'

'Great! Where are you actually from? I'm from Avignon. Well, we arrived one day, my husband and I, and we stayed. I really love this country, on account of the sun. Where did you say you were from?'

'From the Corrèze, but it's years since I left there. I've worked in Paris and in the United States too, a bit in Mexico, in Colombia and in Peru, and several months in Brazil. So if you need an interpreter, because, as for being a guide, I . . .'

'Sure I need you! We're expecting twenty-three Texans the day after tomorrow! You know all the atolls round about, I presume? Yes that's obvious, you're so nice and brown! Perfect, I'll give you a try. Come tomorrow, I'll explain everything to you.'

She had rushed in bewilderment to the nearest library and got hold of several works on Polynesia. By the early hours she knew Bora, Raiatea, Huahine and Moorea inside out, and was even familiar with Rangiroa!

All smiles, she presented herself to her employers. Only fantastic self control prevented her from bursting into tears on learning that she would not be getting the job.

'Well yes, my dear,' the lady from Avignon had explained to her, 'the Chinese girl's won, she's come back . . .'

'But I thought . . .'

'Yes, I know. But as I told you yesterday, she's pretty, that kid; my husband gave in, so . . .'

'So there's no work for me?'

'Well no, not at the moment. But come back in a few days. I haven't finished with this yet. When it comes to the locals, it doesn't worry me too much if my husband runs after them a bit. It's to be expected, eh? They're always wiggling their hips and rubbing up against anything in trousers! Fine. But if he starts with Chinese girls, then I shall have to say something, especially that one, she's the sort to take over my business and give me the heave ho! So if you haven't found anything in a few days' time, come back and see me, I'll deal with the Chinese girl myself . . .'

And now, as the Boeing heading for San Francisco was nothing but a silent, shining point in the distance, she was wondering rather anxiously how she was going to survive. But she was still very relieved to be alone at last and finally free of Gilles.

He had reappeared one evening after a fortnight's absence. He was not alone. At his side, a fat hibiscus flower in her ear, a Tahitian girl swayed languidly, her pareo accentuating her curves. She was magnificent, but Josyane had not experienced the slightest jealousy. On the contrary, she felt liberated: this girl proved that the break was final, that there was no point in discussing anything. They only needed to say goodbye to each other, without shouts, arguments or tears. It was much better like that.

'I'm going back to France the day after tomorrow, do you want to come?' he had suggested.

'No. I'll come back one day, but not with you.'

'You'll regret it. I tell you, you should stick with me.'

Then she had understood that he was actually hoping to resume their life together. The very idea of it revolted her.

'I'm staying here. But what about her, are you taking her to Paris?'

'You must be joking! No seriously, come with me. Come on, let's forget all the cock-ups and get going.'

'No way, and don't keep on about it, it's getting absolutely ridiculous, especially in front of this young lady. Come on, we'll part friends if you like, but it's over. And don't ever try to come after me again, I'd take a very dim view of that!'

He seemed genuinely upset, but she had often seen him like that and had no time for it.

'Right, will you at least come to the airport with me?' he had sighed. 'I'll be alone. I mean without her. She lives on Moorea and is going back tomorrow.'

'Okay, I'll come.'

And she had kept her word. But they had nothing left to say to each other and the wait had seemed long before his flight was called.

'So you're sure you won't come with me? It's not too late. I asked, there are still seats. I've got enough to pay for it.'

'Don't be ridiculous.'

'Have you got some money left? Do you want any?'

'No, I'll manage.'

'Look,' he had suddenly said, taking off the bag which held his Leica and lenses, 'at least take this; you could always sell it if you're really broke. And after all I owe you that much. I'm fed up with photography anyway, I don't ever want to hear about it again!'

He had passed the pouch-strap over her head, kissed her on both cheeks, and made off towards the boarding gate.

As she passed the shop selling souvenirs and postcards, she chose a sunset over Moorea. And having written her parents' address, she jotted down the first words which came into her head: *Love and kisses from Tahiti. It's all wonderful. Everything is fine!*

It was almost true.

Despite the doctor's advice, Pierre-Edouard could not resign himself to doing nothing all day long; his walks were not enough. He needed to make himself useful, or at least to pretend so to himself. He was still sufficiently aware to know that the tiny bits of work which he attended to were not essential, except to him.

Thus, for example, when the kitchen garden no longer needed careful weeding – he had cleaned between the carrots plant by plant as meticulously as a watchmaker – he busied himself raking the courtyard, trimming the old box hedge with the secateurs or, in season, shucking a few corncobs for Mathilde's geese and ducks. Sometimes too, when the late autumn sun permitted, he would sit on the steps by the door to shell walnuts or peel chestnuts which Mathilde would later blanch.

But what he also very much enjoyed was to set himself

down in the woodshed. There, resting on an old oak log which had served as a seat for three generations of Vialhes and whose clawlike roots were cut short to form firm legs, hatchet in hand, he split the kindling for the kitchen stove. Of course he cheated a little in his choice of billets, rejecting any that were not of chestnut, or were knotty or too thick; he knew he would not be able to split them. But the rest, what joy!

Firstly they smelt nicely of good dry wood, cut in the right season, after frost, then properly stacked and left for several hot summers. Wood which held no more sap and would burn without spitting, but whose heartwood emitted a tang of old wine cellars as it split open; slightly acrid and bitter but pleasant, still living.

Then they were good to touch, just rough enough to grip easily without slipping, but never becoming too harsh or prickly. And finally they split without difficulty, giving a cheerful crunch, in long, even sections falling one each side of the blade. Small logs which it was a pleasure to divide again, then split once more, before piling them up beside him.

That morning it was the dry crack of the axe landing in the middle of a log which attracted Dominique to the woodshed. He smiled to discover his grandfather there. The old man – muffled up to the ears, for the cold was biting – was so happy and absorbed in his work that he made a delightful picture, like a child enthralled by his favourite toy.

'You'll catch cold, Grandfather,' he scolded him nonetheless.

'Hey! It's you! No, no, quite the opposite, it's keeping me warm!'

'Would you like a hand?'

'Not on your life! You can see I'm enjoying myself!'

In that case . . .' said Dominique, sitting down on a wide log.

'So, just like that, you're going off to the devil knows where? There are no jobs in France?' asked Pierre-Edouard, turning over a log to find the direction of the grain and so discover which end he should deliver the blow.

'Yes, I'll be off again, but not for a fortnight.'

'I know. But it still seems a pity that you have to go so far away.'

'Oh, it's not so far, only a few hours by plane.'

'Of course, it's not as far as Tahiti . . .,' smiled Pierre-Edouard, lowering his voice as if Mathilde, whose silhouette could be seen occasionally through the kitchen window, thirty feet away, might hear. 'Hah! It surprises you to hear me tell you that,' he said, amused. 'I'm not supposed to know what's going on! I know they take me for a feeble old stick who shouldn't be told anything! Well you see, I find out anyway! But don't tell your grandmother whatever you do, she'd have a fit! Promise!'

'Okay,' said Dominique, laughing.

'What do you think she could be doing there, little Jo?'

'Impossible to tell . . . But you really shouldn't worry about her, she always gets by!'

'That's so! Eh, she's as stubborn as a mule; she's a real Vialhe too, isn't that right? Talking of Vialhes, did you hear about your cousin?'

'Which one?'

'Jean.'

'Is he ill?' asked Dominique. Then he looked at his grandfather and continued: 'What's so funny?'

'You lot! Since you suppress any bad news which might reach my ears, you don't know anything yourselves any more! And I'm well informed! But don't tell a soul, not even your mother!'

'Tell what?'

'That your cousin wants to do the same as you, and I'm very pleased!'

'The same as me? In what way?'

'The same college, the same profession, that's what! All right, it's not exactly farming, but it's better than ending up a pen-pusher, eh?'

'Absolutely. But he's still young, he's still got time to change his mind!'

'I'd be surprised, he's pigheaded as well. No, that's not why I'm mentioning it to you.'

'Oh? Why then?'

'The problem is that his father won't agree to it. You know your Uncle Guy: he must have got it into his head that his son should be an ambassador, or a minister, or some other useless rubbish like that! So you'll do me a favour, won't you?'

'If I can, I will.'

'You're passing through Paris before you leave? Right. The thing is to explain to your uncle that there's nothing to be ashamed of in liking farming and wanting to do something with the land, like you are. And then tell the boy from me that he's right, he must stick to it, we need people like him! Will you tell him?'

'Listen, it's not that easy! Especially when it comes to my uncle . . .'

'Bunkum! I'm not asking you to lecture him! Simply talk to him about your job, in a casual way, about everything you do, your future, your salary . . . You can do that, can't you?'

'Not so easy . . . You have to understand,' Dominique hummed and hawed.

'Do it for me. If I were twenty years younger I'd see to it myself,' Pierre-Edouard assured him with a smile, 'but now, I really can't do a thing. Besides, you know, I haven't even been told about it! So . . .'

7

PREOCCUPIED and irritated by the mongrel's boisterous search, for it was too young to control its speed and enthusiasm when it found a trail, Jacques did not notice the hare getting up. Actually, instead of staying in its form until the last moment, then springing out straight ahead, the leveret, terrified by the yapping and over-zealous zigzags of the dog, crept from the tuft of ling under which it had taken cover at first light and slipped away. It was therefore fifteen paces ahead of the dog and forty from Jacques. And when he did make out the tawny arrow heading straight for the White Peak, it was much too late to aim his twelve-bore between the fugitive's ears. Nevertheless he hoped that Dominique, who was positioned by the mine-cutting, would understand the signal and let off a couple of shots to trim the tops of a few brambles.

'This dog is really useless!' he grumbled, shouldering his gun again after having ejected the empty cartridges.

With a bit of luck, although this confounded mongrel did the exact opposite of what was required and was at present barking away three hundred metres in the opposite direction from the hare's trail, their quarry would cut across the slope of the White Peak, traverse the plateau, then run back down, straight towards the mine cutting, to plunge into the valley of the Diamond. Unless Dominique sent it head over heels on the way.

All the hares flushed at this end of the plateau had followed the same track since time immemorial. And Jacques knew from his father that in olden days even the wild boar and wolves took this path. It was immutable.

So logically speaking, if Dominique was in a good position he would be able to take aim at the hare in the pass and stop it there, in the tumbled mass of reddish, iron-bearing rocks of the mine workings.

A broad chestnut tree, crooked and worm-eaten but still solid, stood twenty-five metres from the cutting; settling down at its foot, Dominique knew that he was well placed.

Ever since reaching an age to accompany his father on hunting expeditions, he had been familiar with all the good spots for game in the area; all the routes and haunts of partridge, pheasant or woodcock, the oak groves for pigeons and the broom bushes on the Caput peak where the thrushes lingered. Unfortunately that was not much use any longer, for the game had become very scarce for lack of opportunity to browse.

In fact the decrease in cereals sown had gradually limited the numbers of partridges breeding without any parallel diminution in the number of hunters. And the plateau, which formerly provided cover for eight or ten coveys of red-legged partridge, now harboured only one or two, and that was in a good year! As for the migratory birds, their numbers shrank from one season to the next, frightened away by the advancing houses which were popping up here and there on the edge of the plateau.

Added to that, car drivers were not slow to crush the few pathetic young hares which the hunting clubs persisted in releasing against all better judgement. And as myxomatosis had decimated the rabbit population . . .

The amazing thing was that none of this prevented the foxes, wild cats, civets, martens and other predators from multiplying at a great rate, but it did explain why it was becoming normal to beat around the countryside all morning without flushing anything.

It therefore grew to be almost the exception to fire a gun, and it was really to please his father, who was convinced that a hare was lying low at the end of the plateau, that Dominique had agreed to accompany him. But he was sceptical as to the outcome of their hunting expedition. What was more, he had the honesty to admit that he had little interest in what he was doing. There only remained just under a week of leave for him, but since the previous day the time had lost some of its savour; a few words had changed everything.

After serious consideration, having weighed the pros and cons, finally telling himself that he was a fool to wait, that his silence might ruin everything, he had made a decision. So, on the back of an aerial view of Yssandon he had written: *Wasn't the journey from Algiers to Paris rather too short?* and had then posted it to the address which Béatrice had given him.

That was brief, frivolous and harmless enough to allow for no response if the answer proved to be negative. But it could also be construed as an appeal. Especially as an appeal which might be answered. And it had been, by return of post. The single sentence conveyed on an aerial view of Agen had filled him with happiness: *Of course! But I didn't dare try a hijacking!*

Now he was floating on air, filled with elation which he wanted to share with the world, to proclaim to anyone who would listen. But he had not yet said a word to a soul!

And what amazed him was the discovery that none of the women he had previously met, and liked more or less, had made such an impression on him. Above all, the parting from one of them had never seemed so unpleasant, so difficult to accept. For, since he was sure that the feeling was mutual, the separation from Béatrice was becoming unbearable. And just as he had seriously considered and reflected on the matter before deciding to write, he now allowed his ardour the same rein.

Only the fact that he could not exactly recall the young woman's face clouded his happiness a little. Certainly he remembered her lively blue eyes, the short, brown, badly-cut hair, the rounded, tanned cheeks, but that was all. And much as he felt capable of recognising her in a crowd of ten thousand, he could not picture her exactly in his memory. He could make out the silhouette he had seen at Orly, disappearing in the direction of the bus, but he was frustrated by the vagueness of the little face when he tried to recollect it precisely. The smallest picture of her would therefore have delighted him and calmed his nerves. For he had to wait a little longer, be patient for two more days before taking the road to Agen.

Having received the card, he had rushed to the telephone to

inform Béatrice that he was coming immediately, or almost. An anonymous and rather cold voice had brought him down to earth by informing him that she was away, would not be back for three days, and had not left a telephone number where she could be reached. Vexed, he could only grin and bear it and count the hours . . .

Although lost in tender thoughts, he still heard the two shots echoing from the plateau. Immediately on the look-out, he fixed his gaze on the path where the hare would shortly arrive if his father had missed it. But, treacherously, when he should have devoted all his attention to that particular corner of the mine cutting, the image of Béatrice, still cloudy but so comforting, floated before his eyes.

He raised his rifle briskly nevertheless, and aimed at the leveret as soon as he saw it. The animal, a fine beast weighing more than seven pounds, was trotting along unhurriedly since the dog had lost its trail, and was an easy mark.

With thumping heart he pressed the first trigger, the one for the right barrel. Nothing happened. Already the hare, having spotted him, was bounding away with lightning acceleration. He squeezed the second trigger and then remembered that, his thoughts being everywhere but on the hunt, he had forgotten to load his gun.

'The biggest fool on earth, that's me, I can't believe it!' he muttered in frustration.

Then he imagined the ironic comments which his father would surely aim at him on learning of his stupidity.

'That's bound to go all round the village!'

So, to cut matters short, preferring to be considered clumsy rather than a bashful lover, he slipped two cartridges into the chamber and let off a magnificent double in the direction of a fat cumulo-nimbus cloud which seemed to be mocking him as it hung motionless above the White Peak.

'I thought you were more skilful! Or you really have got out of practice in Algeria; isn't there any game there?' asked Jacques, crouching down to try to relieve the pains shooting through his loins.

'That wretched hare was too far away . . .'

'Get away with you! I hope at least you didn't wound it?'

'Oh, no danger of that!' Dominique assured him, trying not to smile. 'But where's the dog?'

'That idiot? God knows! I expect he's waiting for me by his feeding bowl. That's about the only thing he can do! I don't think I'll ever make anything of him,' said Jacques with a wry smile.

'Are you in pain?'

'Bah, no more than usual, no less; have to get on with it.'

'You should get some treatment.'

'Don't talk about that,' said Jacques curtly. 'Get some treatment, that means have an operation! So are you going to look after the farm while I'm in hospital? Are you going to take care of the animals?'

'No, of course not.'

'Well then, don't mention it again,' said Jacques, rising painfully to his feet. 'You see, if I seize up one day, I don't know what we'll do. Your mother wouldn't be able to hold out by herself. Okay, the neighbours would rally round a bit, the Brousses, the Delpeyroux', the Valades, but they couldn't do it all! So what would happen? Your grandfather wouldn't be able to help me either!'

Dominique nodded, and very nearly revealed the ideas which had been going round in his head about the farm. As his Aunt Berthe had realised, his spell away from France had not prevented him from following the development of the political situation in agriculture, in Europe or elsewhere; quite the opposite. And everything which he had been able to discover by reading the reports, articles, plans, theses and other projections had been painfully recalled since he had seen how his father was living and working. But his conclusions were so pessimistic that he now hesitated to relay them to him.

To tell him, for example, that he needed to look with fresh eyes at some modern ideas, to consider some projects which might perhaps seem crazy, but which were probably the only means of extricating the farm from this impasse.

To explain to him that everything was in a state of flux. That above all it was vital to understand that a farm like the Viahles', however good it might be, was viewed as a dead

87

weight which the admirers of a certain sort of Europe, under American influence, had no wish to support. That those people were merely anxious to see the disappearance of all the rank and file in the farming world, whose work was of no interest to anyone. And those who said the opposite were liars and charlatans, for they were the same ones who defended and propounded the Malthusian economic theory current in Brussels! The same ones who, incapable of managing supplies, preferred to destroy them, when only three hours' plane-ride away children were dying of hunger!

And that a farm like the Viahles' was irrevocably condemned, from the moment the discussion included the malign schemes of individuals perverse enough to advocate the set-aside and the slaughter of milking herds! All these observations, painful as they were, only gave a brief glimpse of what awaited all the Viahle farms in France. Those hundreds of thousands of small units whose only mistake was to want to continue in a world which considered it much simplier and more economical to snuff them out, in the face of universal indifference.

If he, an agricultural engineer, had been so happy in Algeria and especially in the Sahara, it was because there at least he had the feeling of doing something useful; of putting his intelligence and skills at the service of an agricultural system which it was vital to develop. And he was pleased to be setting off again for distant parts for the same reasons. Reasons which he was not at all sure of finding in France . . .

But he remained silent, for he was afraid of further demoralising his father. Besides, for all he knew, Jacques had probably analysed the situation in the same way himself. Only he had maybe not the health or strength to draw the necessary conclusions. So what was the good of turning the knife in the wound?

'Incidentally, how do you think he's doing?' asked Jacques to break his son's silence.

'Who?'

'Your grandfather.'

'Rather well. I mean he's aged, naturally, but he's still just as scathing.'

'Ah that, yes! But he's got a weak heart, and in my opinion he doesn't look after himself properly!'

'You're a fine one to say so! I'm sure he feels the same about you!'

'Maybe,' admitted Jacques with a smile. 'Same family! Shall we go back? Hopeless to try to hunt any longer, there's nothing left. And without a dog . . .'

'But why the devil are you lumbered with a mongrel like that?'

'Bah, it was Delpeyroux who gave him to me. Well you need a hunting dog, and as old Frisette died . . . Anyway Delpeyroux assures me that the beast will improve with age; I rather doubt it myself . . .'

'Is Delpeyroux still a town councillor?'

'Yes. And a good thing he's there, with our friends, the ones born in the village. With them we're still just in the majority, but it may not last long! Have you heard the latest idea from the others? They want to build a tennis court! Can you credit it?'

'If it can be done at low cost, it may not be as stupid as all that . . .' considered Dominique.

He had got wind of this plan from Berthe, knew his father's opinion, and was aware just how carefully he had to tread so as not to clash with him.

'That's wonderful! You too? Have you all gone off your rockers or what?' cried Jacques.

He was surprised and a little disappointed by his son's reaction. In his eyes, that put him with the group living in cloud-cuckoo-land, the ignoramuses who would never understand the rural mentality, still less the financial difficulties of a small-town mayor. But as he did not wish to break off the conversation, he persisted:

'No, joking apart, can you imagine Delpeyroux and Brousse in shorts hitting balls to each other? There are others I could mention . . .'

'No,' Dominique admitted. 'To tell you the truth, apart from a few kids, I can't see many people in Saint-Libéral getting enthusiastic about it, although . . .'

'What? No, believe me, much as I need to find something to

liven up the village, I must avoid making mistakes and spending money unnecessarily as well. So your tennis court – you jest! The people of Saint-Libéral aren't interested in that!'

They had reached the plateau, where the view reached in every direction, to each far horizon.

'I agree, that goes for the inhabitants of Saint-Libéral,' said Dominique, stopping to admire the countryside, 'but what about the rest? The ones who come for holidays over there, for instance!' He stretched his arm in the direction of a distant hill where lay the newly completed bungalows of a holiday village. 'Yes,' he insisted, 'think about the people who choose to come here in the summer! There's nothing in Saint-Libéral, so we must try to attract people who might come from elsewhere.'

'I've tried! Look at those new houses in the village. They're there because I did what was needed. Well, it wasn't a very good idea. I had people come who know nothing about our problems, our way of life as farmers. And yet there's a chance that they may take our places and decide how we should live! They're already asking for pavements, soon it'll be lamp-posts! Next thing they'll want a school bus! And if you listen to them, there's more than one who'd like to stop the cocks crowing because it wakes them up too early! Or who wants the church clock to break down, for the same reason! No, no, it was *not* a good idea!'

'I'm not talking about that sort of settlement,' said Dominique, walking on, 'and I grant you, it must be difficult to integrate them all! No, if I say a tennis court or something else of that sort isn't a bad idea, it's because that might encourage someone to spend an afternoon in Saint-Libéral without dying of boredom! Right now there's nothing! You can't even visit the church any more. Nothing left; no restaurant, no grocery store, not even a decent bistro!'

'And for a very good reason! Nothing begets nothing!'

'So we must think of something. And if you're allergic to tennis courts, imagine a pool, a ranch with horse-riding, a . . .'

'Stop!' Jacques interrupted. 'You'll end up suggesting a fair at harvest or threshing time, or some other pathetic tomfoolery, making us look like clowns! As long as I'm mayor I'll never ask one of my electors to make a spectacle of our work, and especially not the old ways of doing things! I'll never lower myself to pretend to feed sheaves into an old threshing machine when they've already come out of a combine-harvester! And all to amuse a few miserable idlers who are only too happy to look down on us! If you start that you'll end up like a theme park! Nothing doing! I don't want to see town children throwing me peanuts and chewing-gum one day!'

'I'm not talking about that sort of display,' said Dominique, 'and I'd be very disappointed too, if Saint-Libéral had to come to that!'

'Well you see the problem! Believe me, it's years now I've been thinking it over and I've found nothing acceptable, nothing!'

'That doesn't mean to say there isn't anything! If you don't want the village to wither away completely, there must at least be some people here in the summer.'

'That's easier said than done, without degenerating into quaint folklore! But believe me, I wasn't waiting for you to come along before I started considering all that!'

'I've no doubt. Well, all I can say is . . .'

'Yes, you come back every two years to give some advice!' Jacques laughed without the slightest bitterness, but not sorry to put things in their true perspective. 'By the way, I'm really surprised, this time you haven't made any comments about the farm!'

'What's the use!' said Dominique with a shrug, likewise keeping his remark casual. 'Anyway,' he added, 'I haven't said anything, but that doesn't mean I'm not thinking about it!'

'Right, then we're quits,' joked Jacques. 'By the way, are you really in such a hurry to go? Your mother told me you're leaving the day after tomorrow.'

'Yes, but I'll drop in again before I leave properly, at the end of the week probably.'

Dominique glanced at his father and was grateful to him for not persisting, for not trying to winkle out why he was going away or where he was going.

Then suddenly, without understanding quite why, he felt the urge to talk, to confide, to communicate all the happiness which filled his heart. And he was pleased that it was, rightly, his father who was at hand to be entrusted with his secrets.

'Must tell you, P'pa, I've found my wife!'

'What?' Jacques jumped. 'That's not what you're going away for, is it?'

Since his three nieces, who had been such good little girls, now rivalled each other in seeking independence and dissipation, he was ready to hear anything. And to tell the truth, he was sometimes amazed that he had so far escaped very lightly as far as his own offspring were concerned; but he knew that everything has to start somewhere!

'No joking,' he insisted, 'tell me that's not why you're leaving? You're not going to get married that quickly?'

'Get married? Of course not! I'm only going to ask Béatrice to go with me to Guyana.'

'Ah . . . Just like that, without any formalities! You don't bother about conventions, you young ones! Well, I must be getting too old to understand . . .'

He was disconcerted by his son's apparent irresponsibility in organising his emotional affairs. He felt like telling him that it was not very wise to plan your future in such a casual way, then thought better of it. Dominique was old enough to paddle his own canoe as he pleased, even if his technique seemed at first bizarre.

'You say she's called Béatrice?' he continued.

'Yes.'

'And you're absolutely sure in yourself? And of her?'

'Completely.'

'After all, it's your problem. Have you known her long?'

'It will be exactly a month the day after tomorrow. Yes, that'll be a month we've been apart, and it's damned long! You can't know how long!'

'Oh yes I can! I've got a good memory,' murmured Jacques. Twenty-eight years earlier, he too had realised that the young girl he had just got to know would be his wife. And from that moment the minutes separating him from her had seemed unbearable. Dominique was the proof . . .

'Your mother will be pleased,' he said at last. 'She's been dreaming of becoming a grandmother for ages!'

'Hold on! Not so fast! She'll have to wait a bit for that.'

True, what a stupid remark, and it really dates me! he thought. This generation can plan their children as they wish, without the slightest problem, and they don't hesitate to do so! Never mind, this great idiot wouldn't be here today telling me how happy he is if we'd behaved like that, his mother and I!

'Well, it's still a possibility in the future?' he continued. 'You won't be doing the same as your cousin Marie. Mind you, it's better that way if you're going to divorce after five years, like her!'

'Don't worry! You'll have your grandchild one day! What do you think, Béatrice is a paediatric nurse, so there!'

'Very good. Come on then, let's go straight to Coste-Roche and tell your mother. Afterwards we'll go down to the village to announce the good news to the senior Vialhes. Your grandparents will be over the moon! But go gently on them, don't tell them everything, there's no point, you understand? Introduce Béatrice as your fiancée, simply as your fiancée. Do you see what I'm trying to say? To them, that'll look better, more respectable . . .'

For the first two hours of their reunion, which had as its setting a restaurant not far from Agen, the two young people spent more time talking than eating. They had so much to say to each other! And so many lost hours to make up for!

'Are you serious, is it true? Did you tell everyone that we were engaged?' asked Béatrice, nibbling distractedly at a petit four.

'I actually boasted about it!' he assured her, lifting his forefinger to stroke one of the brown wisps which now framed the young woman's face.

In a month her hair had regrown nicely, and made her appear more graceful and feminine again. Dominique could not look at her enough, drinking in her image, engraving it on his memory. He had sought it for a month in vain and could not bear to risk forgetting it now. More, he was wondering what stupid reasons or arguments could have inspired him to wait three weeks before deciding to write to her. For his rational self obliged him to admit that she had made an impression on him from the first moment. And when he told himself, to explain his delay, that some more or less indifferent or unsuccessful experiences had no doubt counselled prudence, he was revolted by the idea of comparing Béatrice to the few silly girls he had previously known. They no longer existed, annihilated, obliterated by the young woman's blue gaze and the strength radiating from her.

'So as it stands, you've practically published the banns?' she joked.

'Almost!'

'You were so sure of yourself on the matter?'

'Yes. And of you too!'

'Why?'

'Because when you answered my card it wasn't just for the sake of starting an affair. Was I wrong to think that?'

'Of course not, stupid! Or rather, yes, you were wrong, to let me leave alone, that day at Orly!'

'Right on! I'm already cross with myself about that!'

'You know something? I really thought that you'd hardly seen me. Or rather, that you'd only seen my haircut!'

'Oh that, I must say it was rather a mistake. What on earth did you cut it with? A piece of broken glass?'

'Stop it! If you only knew! Three weeks before I came back, I woke up one morning with my head covered in lice! Ghastly! They were crawling all over the place! So, no quarter given! So, I was hideous, was I?'

'Yes, of course,' he teased her, 'and that's why I didn't say a word to you!'

She smiled at him, and crunched another petit four.

'Without getting all sentimental,' she said, 'seriously, it's great, what's happening to us, isn't it?'

'Yes,' he replied, placing his hand on hers.

'I think I should explain to you,' she said after a few moments' hesitation. 'I've had – how shall I put it, my fingers burnt. Yes, that's the right expression.'

'Me too. So we won't talk about it any more, okay? Unless you need to?'

'No.'

'So curtains, life begins from today. Does that suit you?'

'Very nicely.'

'We won't be parted again?'

'Why the question?' she said. 'Don't you dare say you were thinking of leaving without me!'

8

'YOU'RE not going out in this weather?' worried Pierre-Edouard when he saw that Mathilde, Louise and Berthe were preparing to venture out in response to the grocer's hooter.

'And why not? Didn't you go out yourself this morning?' cried Berthe, slipping on a heavy woollen coat.

'It's not the same for me!' he announced. 'I haven't got a cold like Mathilde! I don't complain constantly about my rheumatism like Louise, and I haven't got chronic bronchitis like you!' he added, totally insincerely.

'But of course, quite right,' cut in Louise, muffling herself in a huge cloak, 'you yourself are in strapping health, as everyone knows!'

'And that's why you took your normal walk this morning, despite the cold!' added Mathilde

'It's not the same for me!' he repeated. 'Besides, all I did was drink coffee at Nicole's!'

'Ah, right? Because mine wasn't hot enough, I suppose?' asked Mathilde.

'Now look at you!' he smiled. 'You tell me to go to the bistro and when I do you complain about it? Women!' he exclaimed, as he added a thick branch of hornbeam to the hearth.

Comfortably ensconsed on the fireside settle, his feet warmed by the embers, he was arguing for the sheer pleasure of annoying the three women, for he knew that nothing would prevent them from going to make their purchases and, more importantly, have a little chat.

'Wrap up well then,' he advised Mathilde. She noticed the furtive movement he made to touch his waistcoat pocket, just to reassure himself that his tobacco pouch really was there, and called to him before going out.

'And don't you dare smoke like a fireman while I'm away!'

He shrugged, retreated into the seclusion of his corner by the fire and took out his pipe.

They can say what they like, it's no weather for going to chat in the church square! he thought, looking out of the window.

Driven by the wind which had just strengthened, the fine hail mixed with wet snow, which had been falling in showers since the morning, was beating on the windowpanes. The weather had taken a turn for the worse in the last two days, and whilst 1975 had begun gently in January and February, March was coming in with hoar frost, fog and half-melted snow.

Well, better now than in three weeks' time, he thought, drawing a brand from the fire. He lit his pipe, threw the spill into the flames. Yes, that'll curb the growth a bit and maybe prevent everything being frozen! But all the same, it's still awful weather! And since it's started like this it'll hold for the entire month, even if that doesn't suit the chatterboxes on the telly!

Although his son and son-in-law, and even his grandson, had explained to him that the weather forecasts were based on sound scientific data, he considered them extremely suspect, possibly misleading, ever since one of the lady announcers had laughed one evening when speaking about the moon. It had, according to that flibbertigibbet, no influence on the weather. To Pierre-Edouard, that was almost blasphemy! For if you not only violated it by walking on it, but also began to doubt its power, that boded no good! In a little while they would be saying that it did not affect the germination or growth of plants! Meanwhile, since the full moon, it had been cold enough to bring the wolves out!

'Aren't you all a bit mad to be out in this weather!' protested Yvette, as soon as she saw the three ladies from the Vialhe house struggling against the wind to reach the grocer's van. 'No, really! It's not very sensible of you!' she added. 'Especially you, with your cold!' she called to her sister-in-law.

'You're not going to take over from Pierre now?' said

Mathilde. 'Good morning, I won't kiss you because of my cold.'

'Tell me what you three want, I'll get it for you. Go and shelter in the car,' suggested Yvette; 'the motor's running, it's warm.'

'Look at these young people!' joked Louise. 'Not even seventy years old and taking the car to go two hundred metres!'

'Exactly, and I'm not ashamed of it!' said Yvette. 'Go on, get in, all three of you, and we'll go and have coffee at the château afterwards.'

'In that case, we will!' said Berthe. 'I know your coffee is always good. Come on,' she said, pulling Louise and Mathilde along. 'The girl's right,' she added more quietly, 'it's not very warm, and besides, I'm sure a little company would do her good.'

Since she had been widowed, Yvette was living alone in the château. A Portuguese neighbour, who had moved into the village seven years ago, went up every morning to do a little cooking and housework in the three rooms still open. Louis came from time to time, but rarely, very busy, he assured her, with his work in Limoges. So Yvette was happy at each opportunity to break her loneliness.

She therefore hastened to make her purchases, joined the three women waiting in the car, and drove her DS up the track towards the château.

'As soon as we're up there, we'll give Pierre a call; it wouldn't do to worry him,' she said.

'Pierre, worry?' Mathilde was amused. 'I'm sure he'll have guessed where we're going already! Well, you're right, we'll still telephone, then he won't have to hurry so to finish his pipe!'

It was always with a slight twinge of sorrow that Mathilde returned to the château. To her it had previously represented the power, wealth and luxury in which the former lords of the manor lived. Those people inaccessible to her, whom she saw passing in the village when, as a child, she lived in a long-vanished hovel at the end of one of the seven lanes in Saint-Libéral.

99

Then everything had gradually deteriorated. After financial reverses had hit its owners, the château had responded with a rain of slates which slid the length of the roof before smashing to the ground; with pointing which crumbled, the ivy invading in its place; with shutters which rotted and leaking gutters which spilled their water over the walls. Then for a while, it had become really dilapidated. And finally, thanks to Léon – to the desire for revenge which had inspired him since his childhood, and above all, thanks to his fortune – the château, the park and the whole property had come to life again.

And Mathilde still remembered her feelings when she had first set foot within the walls which henceforth belonged to her brother. So now that he was gone, she always felt nostalgic when she returned. A little sad too, for Léon's laugh was no longer there to welcome her; because Pierre-Edouard had not set foot in the château since his brother-in-law's death; and because all those closed shutters on the rooms which now smelled of mildew and dust were enough to break your heart.

'Come into the kitchen, it's warmer there,' suggested Yvette, 'and sit by the fire. And you, Mathilde, phone Pierre.'

'It's lovely and warm here,' confirmed Berthe, taking off her heavy coat.

'Yes, it's all right. But it upsets me to heat everything when no one's living in it. But I don't want it to freeze, so I set the heating at the minimum, except in my bedroom and in here.'

'Yes, it's lovely,' repeated Berthe, sitting down in front of the hearth.

'And how's Louis?' asked Mathilde whilst dialling the number. She noticed her sister-in-law's worried look, was about to continue, and then heard Pierre-Edouard: 'It's me,' she said, 'yes, we're at Yvette's, she's making coffee for us. You expected as much? I know! See you soon. And stop smoking! What's that, I'm talking nonsense? I can smell it from here!'

She hung up with a laugh, and went to sit down by the fire.

'Now, what about Louis?' she insisted.

'I'm worried about him,' admitted Yvette.

'His problems aren't getting any better?' asked Berthe.

'No, just the opposite,' said Yvette, putting out the cups and a tin of biscuits.

She had no need to say more, for she knew that her guests had long been aware of the matter which was giving her so much anxiety at the moment.

'But really, what an idea to embark on something like that!' said Louise.

'He believed in it,' Yvette apologised for him. 'And then, it might have worked . . .'

But it hadn't worked and it wasn't going to! It was true that Louis had been dogged by ill luck. True, too, that his desire to distance himself a little from his father had driven him to take a route which he considered more honourable. For although he too was inspired by a desire to make money, he had always rather despised the trade which had allowed his father to amass so much of it. He had considered the label estate agent more respectable than that of livestock dealer. He had therefore not believed his father when he, whilst helping to set him up, had assured him that there were probably more rogues and swindlers in suits and ties than in market traders' overalls; and that the dung of the market places surely stank less than certain offices. He had quickly realised that his father was not wrong, but he liked the business and some smells did not worry him too much . . .

He had therefore made progress, attempted and succeeded in several good deals, and acquired a taste for large-scale operations. The first ones turned out to be as profitable as one could wish, the subsequent ones a little less so. As for the latest, begun more than two years ago, it was promising to be a catastrophe. For although he had been shrewd to bank on the expansion of a town like Limoges, and therefore to buy the maximum available land in the outer suburbs, he had been very unwise to mount such an operation with an associate not overburdened with scruples; a man who did not even know the word existed!

Then also unwise to invest deeply in preparing the plots, developing them, laying on services. For now that everything was poised to begin, not only were clients not rushing in, but it was raining bills thick and fast, sometimes overwhelmingly. As for the associate, he had departed without leaving an address, but not without money, the moment there was any question of sharing the costs of settling with the contractors, the surveyors, the architects, the suppliers . . .

And already, Louis knew, some kind souls were whispering here and there that he was running out of steam, that the bankers were jibbing at supporting him any further and his debts were approaching five hundred million . . . It was true, and even if it had only referred to centimes, Louis was aware he would be unable to raise them in a hurry.

In order to do that, he needed to be given time, and most of all for the rumours about his bankruptcy to cease, not to mention those about his imminent indictment for embezzlement and various frauds. Those were not true, but stories still circulated, and the creditors were growing more insistent.

He had been able to placate them so far by distributing the proceeds from the sale of some buildings he owned in Brive, and the money which his mother had given him as soon as she got wind of his difficulties. He had therefore tossed a few hundred thousand francs to right and left, a few morsels to quieten the loudest, the most dangerous.

But now he had nothing left. Nothing more which he could quickly convert into cash, for it was impossible to sell the forty-odd hectares of arable and pasture land scattered around Saint-Libéral and the plains of Varetz and Larche on favourable conditions. And if he had to sell them off cutprice, the exercise would serve no purpose. Besides, they were rented out, which lowered their value considerably. And then it was to be feared that the Land Development Agency would intervene and drag the business out.

As for the château, it was unthinkable to negotiate over it in a hurry. First of all because he could not come to terms with the idea of driving his mother out, and secondly because it represented too large a sum to find a cash client within a few weeks.

Since he had considered the problem from every angle, he now envisaged the moment when he would have to open his mind to certain propositions. They were abhorrent, but went beyond the stage of rumour, for one of the bankers had dropped a few words to him, just like that, without any apparent significance, to sound out the mood of the prey.

The solution was very simple, obvious even! As he could not settle with the businesses contracted to create the estate, others could do it in his place! On condition, naturally, that they took his place completely; that is to say, by becoming owners of the plots. Having agreed that and settled all his accounts, he would be left with nothing but a damp hanky and a ruined reputation, at least in this region.

In fact he could not see himself starting from scratch again: creating a new agency, restarting the discussions which would perhaps allow him to deal in seedy affairs for equally wretched clients. He was too accustomed to the comfort of plenty of money, to all it provided, to the happy trips to Paris accompanied by a one-night stand, or a one-month stand, those pretty girls always ready to help him empty a jar of caviare and a few bottles of Dom Perignon. Always ready to share a fortnight in Acapulco with him too, or more modestly in Monaco.

So to give up all that was unthinkable! Any more than it was possible to start driving a 2CV instead of a Porsche, to buy off the peg and not made to measure, to replace the Davidoffs with Gitane fags! And yet that was what was in store for him if he did not find a solution in the shortest possible time. He had not painted such a sombre picture to his mother during their last telephone conversation, but at least he had given her to understand that all was not going well.

'And yet it might have worked out,' repeated Yvette, as she served the coffee. She placed a plate of biscuits on the low table, passed round the sugar bowl, and sat down next to Berthe.

'So he has no financial reserves left at all?' asked the latter.

'You know, since he's been selling things all over the place . . . Léon was well off, and me too, but everything has its limit . . . You'll be telling me there's still a bit of land, the château . . .'

'You're not going to put that at risk?' protested Berthe. 'Look, you've still got plenty of years to live! You don't want to end up in a home, do you? You must be careful, my dear! I know how things go in business. When it gets difficult, it's often the fault of those who are in charge, and in that case, it's always too late to recover from the mistakes!'

'Listen, what if Louis needs me?' protested Yvette.

'I understand,' said Berthe, 'but do watch out, don't part with everything, or sign anything! Besides, believe me, the little you could do wouldn't be any use . . .'

'How do you know? Has Louis talked to you? Has he written?'

'Of course not!' said Berthe with a shrug. 'It's at least three months since I've seen your son! And he hasn't written to me either! It's my nose that tells me. But, trust me, before you do anything, promise you'll discuss it with me. And above all don't sign anything! Promise me?'

'No,' said Yvette, 'and I'm sure you're hiding something from me.'

'No, I'm not,' Berthe assured her. 'I assure you, it's my instinct guiding me. You know, my dear, if the house of Claire Diamond has branches all over Europe and the United States, that's down to me, because I knew at what point to do such and such a thing. Well, with what you've been telling us for some months about Louis' business, you don't have to be very talented to understand that he's not getting on well. That's all. So be careful.'

'I'll help Louis as much as I can!' insisted Yvette. 'Anyway, I don't need much to live on any more!'

'All right, you do as you wish, but at least you've been warned.'

'By the way, did you know that young Jo has sent some proper news?' Mathilde interrupted, for she now regretted having started a painful discussion which was embarrassing her sister-in-law.

'Little Jo?' continued Yvette.

'Yes, I saw Mauricette this morning. She had a letter in the post, a long one full of details. And what's more, she's given her address at last. That's good news, isn't it? But really, you could say she's given us a few grey hairs, that one!'

*

'Do you think it's going as badly as all that for Louis?' Mathilde asked Berthe that same evening.

She had waited until Pierre-Edouard had gone to bed, and was now in a hurry to hear why her sister-in-law had seen fit to be so frank with Yvette.

'Yes, I know it's going very badly. Louis is nearly finished, with a lot of debt. I was hoping he still had some substantial reserves, but since his mother assures us it isn't so ...' explained Berthe, lighting a Gauloise. 'Do you remember, already last Wednesday Yvette was even more thoughtful than usual, so I made a few phone calls ...'

'You did that?' Louise interrupted.

She was always surprised by her sister's way of managing problems. She faced up to them, threw herself into the thick of the fray; you had to admire her pugnacity.

'Yes, I did,' said Berthe, 'and I was right to. I'm very fond of Yvette, I'd hate to see her ruined by her son's mistakes.'

'Can you sort out Louis' affairs, do you have the means?' asked Mathilde, full of hope.

'You're joking? You know very well that I made over most of my business to Gérard, and he's in partnership himself now anyway! No, no, my income won't run to that sort of rescue plan, but that's no reason to leave poor Yvette in the lurch!'

'You said you made several phone calls. Who to?' asked Louise, who could not begin to understand how her sister could know so much about Louis without leaving Saint-Libéral.

'Oh, easy. I asked Gérard to pretend to be a prospective purchaser of some plots advertised by Louis. So his lawyer sought the information. Two or three calls to Louis' bankers were enough. The business is rotten, they're bound to foreclose before long. They didn't say as much, of course, but as I explained to Yvette, I've got an infallible nose for that sort of thing.'

'How can you be so sure?' insisted Mathilde. Ever optimistic, she was still thinking and hoping that her sister-in-law was painting a blacker picture than necessary.

'It's very simple. When someone who should be delighted to see the sale of a plot gives you to understand that it's vital to wait, that's because he's hoping to bring off a better deal later on . . . That, roughly speaking, was the bankers' response!'

'But what about Louis, then?' insisted Mathilde.

'It's sure to be bad. It must involve a very large sum. I didn't say all I knew to Yvette, I didn't want to put her in a panic, she's quite capable of doing something silly. You saw for yourself, she's ready to put the château up for sale! So we need to watch out that she doesn't find herself penniless without achieving anything. Because Léon would never forgive us for that!'

Since the evening which Dominique and Béatrice had spent with Guy just before leaving for Cayenne, Jean felt strengthened in his position and vocation.

First of all he was still under the spell cast by the young woman's eyes; he dreamed about her, and felt all weak at the knees when he thought of her. And it was not only her gaze which had affected him; he found Béatrice completely amazing! But apart from the satisfaction of having such a woman almost as his cousin, he had particularly noticed that Dominique's arguments had influenced his mother. Of course she still felt a certain reserve, not to say hostility, towards her son's plans, and had not despaired of seeing him change his mind. Despite that she had given in on several points, and it was now possible to discuss the matter without antagonising her.

Unfortunately the same could not be said for his father; with him it was like a brick wall. The more he was chatty and pleased when Jean told him of his marks and triumphs in class, the more he closed up like a clam as soon as his son talked of his future studies. At Grignon, the National Agricultural Institute, if all went well.

'We haven't got that far yet,' he grumbled; 'you're too young to know what you'll really be doing. For the moment keep working, and don't get carried away with crazy ideas, those are only dreams.'

'Dominique's not dreaming!'

'Don't worry about your cousin! Besides, I don't know whether his job is as good as he claims, or his salary as high!' threw in Guy, quite unfairly.

Doesn't matter, it's jolly interesting what he's doing in Guyana!'

'I don't think! All he'll bring back from his stay over there will be the runs and malaria! And all that for the pleasure of developing rice and sugar cane crops which cost the taxpayer an arm and a leg! Or trying to introduce some hare-brained cross between a humped Zebu bull and a Charolais whose offspring will die in the first epidemic that comes along, or be eaten by the alligators!'

'Its still interesting!' cried Jean. Then he changed the subject, for he did not yet feel strong enough to stand up to his father for any length of time. But he did not doubt that the day would come when he would have the intellectual ability and the courage to do so.

Jean did not like hunting much, especially not the sort practised by his father and his friends. However he was now of an age to take out a licence, and could have persuaded his parents to give him a gun. But he was much too independent and solitary to enjoy roving the countryside with the hunters who accompanied his father when he came to Brenne.

Jean despised those men. He found them inept, snobbish and, (an unforgivable fault in his eyes) worse than useless when they talked about birds, game or nature. They passed remarks which drove him mad, being the result of so much pretentious ignorance. And although Félix smiled, and sometimes even laughed out loud when he related some howler delivered by one of the party, he himself could not accept their conceit. He was not the right age to make allowances or be tolerant.

And when, to please his father and carry the game, he followed the valiant sportsmen for an afternoon, the account he gave of the expedition was never dull.

'You can't imagine it,' he said to Félix. 'Listen, the fat one, you know, the creep who's always sweating! The one with a Tyrolean hat and an over-and-under shotgun, you've seen him? The one who's always complaining that there aren't any women here! Well, at the Three Oaks crossroads we chanced on the track of a fallow deer. Magnificent, a beautiful hoofprint, sure to be a big second-year stag! You won't believe what he comes out with, the pretentious great wally, sounding like a professor of philosophy: "Look! It's a boar weighing at least eighty kilos!" With a bit of encouragement he would have told us its age. Well, even Monsieur Charles – yes, the banker, you know, the fool who nine times out of ten can't tell a hen pheasant from a cock! The one who fires at coots to keep his hand in – even he was embarrassed, listening to such stupidity! Rubbish, that's what they are! Rubbish! People as moronic as that ought to be barred from the countryside!'

'Let them talk. The main thing is that you know better,' Félix pacified him.

But at the age of just sixteen Jean was not inclined to be charitable. He therefore avoided going out with his father and his friends as much as possible.

On the other hand, through contact with Félix, besides an excellent understanding of nature, he had discovered and grown to like the art of fishing. And on this last Sunday in March, while Guy and his companions were hunting pigeons on the game reserve, Félix and he were fishing with live bait on the little pool at Souchet.

It was a lovely patch, three hectares of water and bulrushes, lying a few hundred metres from Félix's house. It was there, one terrible night in October thirty-eight years earlier, that Pierre-Edouard had joined Félix. But Jean knew almost nothing of that business, and it was better so.

'If you want my opinion, we won't get anything this morning,' said Félix after an unproductive half hour.

He had only come here to please his second cousin, for experience told him that the fishing would be poor, not to say hopeless. A light north wind had got up, which ruffled the water. The sun was not clear, but constantly played hide and seek behind the fat gloomy cumulo-nimbus clouds which were swelling for the next shower. The pool was as grey as a winter sky and even the water birds, the coots and grebes hiding in the rushes and sedge, seemed dull and somnolent, disinclined to be at all active.

'Nothing doing,' murmured Félix, nonetheless casting his

lure towards an old willow stump rotting on the edge of the pool.

'I know what you're going to tell me,' let out Jean. '"North wind blows, sport all goes, fish will doze"! But that still has to be proved! And then why not wake them up? Look, that stupid thing's dead!' he observed, looking at the tiny carp which he had impaled on the end of his line. He reeled in again, removed the hook from the bait and threw it into the bulrushes.

'So shall we stop?' he asked.

'Come on, let's try one last cast,' Félix relented, holding out a fresh fish as bait. 'Take care!' he cautioned.

An unneccessary warning: Jean had known for a long time just how wicked the dorsal fin of a perch was. He neatly mounted the victim on the end of his casting-rod and resumed fishing.

'You know what I've decided?' he said after a few moment's silence.

'No.'

'I'm going to spend the whole of my summer holidays in Saint-Libéral, to help Uncle Jacques. It seems his back isn't getting any better.'

'Has your father agreed?'

'He doesn't know yet!'

'Oh, I see . . .' said Félix.

He was aware of Guy's attitude, and did not feel he had the right to stoke the flames of a dispute which he knew was about to flare up.

'What's that supposed to mean: "Oh I see"?' demanded Jean with a touch of belligerence.

'Nothing.'

'You don't think it's a good idea?'

'I didn't say anything of the kind!'

'But that doesn't stop you thinking it!'

'Don't get in such a state! I didn't say you were wrong! But is Jacques in fact aware of this?'

'No, not yet. But I don't see what the problem is,' pronounced Jean, casting his bait back out towards the middle of the pool. 'Anyway, Papa couldn't possibly say anything,' he decided confidently.

'Well now, and why not?'

'Because I'm going to finish up top of the class again, and that's an impregnable position as far as he's concerned! What do you expect him to say to me? You haven't worked hard enough, so you don't deserve a holiday? Impossible! So I'll go to Saint-Libéral. I've already worked it out, I'll arrive at the end of the haymaking, just before they tackle the harvest!'

'Still, it might be as well to mention it to the people concerned, don't you think?'

'Yes, I'll think about it! In any case, down there I've got one ally. You know what Dominique said to me when he came by our house?'

'Yes of course, you've already told me. He said your grandfather is on your side!'

'Exactly! And that's bloody important to me!' cried Jean slightly annoyed, for he felt he detected a tinge of sarcasm in his cousin's voice: 'Yes, it's important,' he insisted, 'however much you laugh – you are laughing, I can see it. But I don't care if you do laugh, that doesn't stop grandfather being somebody! He knows what he's talking about, he does!' he finished in a fury.

'In the first place I'm not laughing. Secondly, I agree absolutely when you say your grandfather is somebody! More than that, he's a great man. You'll find out more about that one day. But in the meantime, believe me, instead of driving your father into a corner, why not try to convince him that it's very healthy for a Parisian boy to spend his holidays working in the open air!'

'Yes, maybe. But to him, working on the land, it's degrading. You'd never believe he was born there!'

'Now don't go saying stupid things like that, damned pigheaded Vialhe! It's exactly because he was born there, lived and slaved away there, that he knows what he's talking about! Never forget that in his day, even if you were a good scholar – and he was – the holidays were spent in the fields. And if your grandparents weren't poor, they were still a long way from being rich, and they had to work hard! You have no idea how they worked! It's the memory of that which makes your father so difficult to persuade when you talk to him about agronomy. He managed to leave the land and create a very good position for himself, and it wasn't easy, believe me. For him, it's true, the land is a step backward. So it depresses him to see that one of his sons wants nothing more than to return to it!'

9

DOMINIQUE slid his hand under the mosquito net and caught hold of the bath towel hanging over the back of the chair. It was as wet as a dishcloth, but he still passed it over his chest to sponge off the sweat which was streaming down. He had been in bed for half an hour but already felt the need to get up again and take another shower to refresh himself a little and, above all, to rid himself of the sticky moisture which covered his body. He looked at Béatrice, lying beside him, and envied her ability to sleep so peacefully.

Naked, stretched out on her stomach, her arm curved above her head, she seemed impervious to the sweltering heat pervading the room. Nevertheless, perspiration stood in droplets all over her body, and he was almost tempted to wipe it. But he was afraid of waking her, and made do with using his fingertips to brush lightly the little dimples in the hollow of her back.

Never a day passed without him wondering how he could have survived at Bellevue without her – for after six months in Guyana, he sometimes caught himself counting the months to his return home. He who had almost felt annoyance at the contract sending him abroad for one year – he was ready to sign up for double that! – now rejoiced at his employers' caution.

It was not that his work was uninteresting, far from it. The responsibilities he took on delighted him, and there was no lack of variety. The several trial stations established by Mondiagri were scattered in different parts of the territory, the handful of coastal regions where it was possible to attempt to clear the ground without running into swamps or impenetrable jungle.

His main residence was on the experimental farm Bellevue Scree. Situated at the foot of Kaw mountain, some fifty kilometres south-east of Cayenne, it was aptly named, for the surrounding countryside was magnificent.

There, besides new varieties of sugar cane, of maize and pineapple, they measured the hardiness and productivity of a herd of cattle consisting partly of Zebu-Charolais crosses. As a loyal native of the Corrèze, Dominique was convinced that the Limousin breed could adapt very well to the land, and he was endeavouring to persuade his employers of this.

So it was not his occupation which weighed heavy. In contrast, he had a great deal of difficulty in adapting to the climate. For a start he did not appreciate the sense of humour of the geographer who had one day decided that there were two rainy seasons: the small rains from December to March and the great rains from April to July! To him, great or small, it was all water which poured down in torrents! And as he had not had time to experience what was supposedly the dry season, he was prepared to find it just as streaming wet as the previous ones!

After two years spent in the Sahara, where the smallest drop of water was of incalculable worth and was welcomed with joy and respect, the permanent hot, sticky humidity which he endured night and day tired him, wore him out.

Added to that were all the crawling, flying, stinging or poisonous creatures which swarmed on every side. The revolting babalous which proliferated in the marshes; the fat spiders, mosquitos and flies present everywhere; not forgetting the leeches, lizards, reptiles, amphibians and other creepy-crawlies which one always had to watch out for. So he did not conceal from his associates that he would not be spending one day extra in Guyana at the end of his contract. Fortunately he had Béatrice.

She bore the climate much better than he did, and was a marvel at making him forget the disadvantages of the country. It was difficult not to share her enthusiasm when she went into raptures at the beauty of a picturesque site, the luxuriance of the cattleyas or epidendrum (orchids), at a shimmering toucan or macaw. Despite the fact that he was called upon to travel during the week, she encouraged him to make weekend trips into the countryside, for the pleasure of it. As they had quickly found that, apart from the bizarre Palmists Square, Cayenne held no interest and oozed melancholy, and that the other conurbations were still worse, they plunged into the jungle, at least as far as the tracks and water courses allowed.

Since Béatrice contrived to make their bungalow as pleasant as possible, and knew how to change his mood when he was overwhelmed by bad temper – he had difficulty in coming to terms with the grinning nonchalance of the employees – in all fairness he was forced to recognise that he was the happiest of men; if it were not for this damned climate!

He sponged his chest once more and smiled as he looked at the young woman. She had just turned over and was in the process of snuggling up to him, without breaking her sleep.

Regretfully, he moved away. It really was too hot and humid to spend the night wrapped around each other.

If she could have been sure of finding another job, Josyane would have immediately abandoned the agency where she had been working now for six months. But she did not want to chase after shadows, and she still felt obliged to her employer. The woman had offered her work when she had exhausted all possibilities; she was grateful to her.

As she had predicted, the director of the travel agency had not given in to the Chinese girl who had turned her husband's head, and had dismissed her a few weeks after her attempted take-over. She had then kept her promise and engaged Josyane as guide and interpreter.

The first excursions filled her with enthusiasm. In fact she was not the sort of person to pretend to be blasé, and she still remained thunderstruck at the splendour of the countryside. Of all the atolls and islands the clients wanted to visit, it was difficult to say which was the most heavenly, the most beautiful! Difficult to choose between the vast beaches of white sand on Bora, the warm water and incomparable clarity of the lagoon on Rangiroa, or the breathtaking sites of the bays on Cook and of Opunohu on Moorea. Difficult to say where it was better to stay, for a few days. Only for a few days. For she now began to feel a weariness due to the enforced and repeated revisiting of places which ended up irritating by their perfection. Finally and above all, she became more and more allergic to the tourists in her charge.

The Americans most of all rubbed her up the wrong way, made her almost xenophobic! She had discovered most of them were a detestable variety of human. The sort who having paid, and extremely dearly, believed they had the right to demand everything, do everything, say anything, complain about anything, at opportune and inopportune moments.

Confident in the wads of dollars they had paid out, some were even sincerely convinced that she was part of the package, and it was therefore permissible to pat her bottom! As for the matrons who served as wives to these louts, she found them monstrous, fat as sows and much stupider. It was they who, in the middle of the night on Bora or Tetiaroa, began to bellow when they discovered an inoffensive grey lizard in their hut. They again who refused to touch the succulent grilled fish and coconut milk during some excursion into the enchanting motus, and loudly demanded hamburgers and Cola!

On top of all that, these people were blatantly mean. And since she had to serve as their interpreter when they wanted to buy a few souvenirs, she could not forgive them for the shame she felt when they asked her to haggle over a block of coral, a pareo or some shell knick-knacks.

Stingy to the very last day; they still had purses as fat as sea-urchins when the time came to say goodbye. But they accepted without apparent difficulty the Tahitian custom which maintains that all tipping is offensive, and pretended to believe that Josyane was a native.

But it is true to say that her satisfaction on seeing them depart was such that it compensated for the lack of gratuties and restored her good humour. Until the next batch saw her at the foot of the airline steps, with her little sign OROHENA TOUR AGENCY, around which her set of clients collected, while the airport rang with the welcoming songs of various swaying, beflowered Polynesians, paid for by the Tahitian Office of Tourism.

As a result, after six months she was dreaming of some less tedious work. But she did not want to take the risk of finding herself without a job again. Above all she was careful not to break into her savings, which would one day allow her to buy a one-way ticket to Paris. She was hoping now that it would be as early as possible.

As time passed, she became more aware of her isolation, and of the kind of prison Tahiti had become the moment she lacked the financial resources to escape it. A luxurious prison, certainly, full of flowers, birds and sun; without jailers, but nonetheless weighing on her because it was so deceptively soothing. A place of exile where it was tempting to let yourself slip into the prevailing mood of indifference. It was frightening, and she was as wary of it as of a drug.

So when the solitude and the distance weighed too heavily, she forced herself not to sink into that sort of somnolence in which the island dwellers took refuge when they were 'fed up'. She feared her senses would be dulled in that complacent and restful carelessness where any willpower, any desire to act was weakened, any impulse to escape even! She did wish to leave. That was her aim and she would have already quit the island long since if the possibility had existed.

But as she did not want to send out a cry for help to her parents – she would have felt ashamed of that – as she hesitated to sell the Leica donated by Gilles and her own Nikon, for she saw them as the ultimate insurance to be preserved come what may, she had no choice but to save month by month towards the price of her ticket home.

Thus, once she had decided to put an end to her peregrinations and return to the fold, her desire to see France again became ever stronger. And often, some evenings, she took to thinking with nostalgia and vague melancholy of Saint-Libéral. To remembering her childhood there, the adventures on the peaks with her sisters, the taste of the greengages in July, the chestnuts roasted in the open fire. To conjure up the picture of her parents, her grandmother Mathilde's welcoming lap, her grandfather's comfortable knees, and his rather rough cheeks which she liked to rasp under her fingers.

And, one evening, when the sun was dipping behind

Moorea, forming a halo of fire around Mount Tohiea, whilst the group of Texans she was looking after were dutifully wallowing in rum and coke and trying to dance the tamouré, she had felt the need to write to her family; a proper letter, which begged for nothing but was nevertheless a cry for help. And it was without hesitation that she had given them her address. It was the first time since her departure. And as soon as the letter was posted, completely illogically, for she knew the time mail took, she began to expect the reply.

When Dominique had introduced Béatrice to them, to Michèle and himself, Jacques had hoped that the date of their wedding would at least be mentioned. There had been no sign of it. So he was a little embarrassed when his mother asked him for news of the couple. He knew that she was a stickler for morals and had a very low opinion of a situation which to her was not correct. It was not that she openly criticised Dominique's attitude, but he guessed she was distressed by it, as she was distressed by the behaviour of Mauricette's daughters.

He was also aware that his father did not think much of the eldest Viahle grandson living with his partner without marrying. That was not done, even on the other side of the ocean.

'I know very well that I'm out of date,' he had said to Jacques. 'You understand, I'm from the time when a girl who showed her calves was considered fast! Well, it's enough to see all those kids on the telly, or even here, showing their bottoms to everyone in their miniskirts, as you say, to know that I'm old-fashioned. That's obvious. So, all right, things change. But the boy shouldn't upset his grandmother. It grieves her, all that. So I don't like it!'

'I know. But what do you want me to do? Dominique's twenty-eight!'

'Well, yes. But you know, in my time, even at that age we wouldn't have dared carry on openly like that. What I meant to say was, amongst people you knew, in the village, for instance! I'm not saying in the town . . .'

'Dominique is several thousand kilometres from here!

Where he is, the people don't care! Anyway, I'm sure they don't know he's not married!'

'Your mother knows, that's enough for me!'

As for Michèle, Jacques knew that she felt in rather an awkward position with regard to her friends and neighbours in the village. For they had all had the opportunity to see Dominique and Béatrice strolling about, very much in love, during their visit to Saint-Libéral. And because Michèle had immediately announced that they were engaged, there were now certain good souls who expressed feigned amazement that the date for the wedding was not yet fixed!

Those gossips were often the ones whose daughters had begun to look at the wrong side of the sheets the year they got their school certificate, and sometimes even earlier with the more precocious ones . . . The same ones whose sons pawed the ground like billy goats when they spotted anything in a skirt! But it was still embarrassing to be within an ace of being lectured by them, embarrassing to be reduced to defending herself!

So Jacques was very happy to read the first lines of the letter Dominique sent. He had realised it was important even before he knew what it was, for Michèle had brought it to him whilst he was sowing maize for fodder in the Malides field.

First of all it announced that Dominique and Béatrice would be returning to France at the beginning of December, and that in itself was very good. Then, and this was even better, that they had chosen Saturday, 20 December as the date for their wedding.

'Wonderful!' he murmured. 'I know two people who'll be over the moon! Yes,' he added, seeing that Michèle did not quite understand, 'my parents were married on the twenty-first of December! That was in 1918! That will be fifty-seven years! What a celebration we'll have!'

'Probably less than you were hoping for, read what follows.'

'What do you mean?' he said, starting to read again. 'Oh damn!' he groaned at last. 'Just can't do anything like everyone else, those two!'

'I think myself that it's quite honest of the girl,' said Michèle.

'Yes, you're right. If she doesn't believe in God or the Devil, she's sticking to her principles. But I'm thinking of my parents. You know very well that for them there's no such thing as a civil wedding, it has no meaning.'

'They're not the only ones. Finish reading . . .'

'What else is there?' he worried. 'All right then! As I understand it, young Béatrice wants only a registry office marriage, because she doesn't believe in the church, and her mother, who is a religious bigot, refuses to hear of the registry office unless it's followed by a church ceremony! That should make for a cosy atmosphere!'

'You haven't finished reading. It won't make anything! They're going to get married in Paris, a quiet civil wedding.'

'I see,' he said, folding up the letter. 'But that doesn't matter, it's still a bit of good news! And I'm going to announce it at home. After all, if the young people do it in Paris, my parents definitely won't go up for it. So why tell them everything, eh? Come on, I'll pop down before lunch. It'll make them so pleased, I don't want to wait. In any case, *we'll* be there in Paris.'

Delighted and touched when Dominique had presented him with his Ami 6, Jacques had immediately traded in his old Aronde. Despite the pathetic state of the vehicle he had received an unexpectedly good price for it. But he had soon realised that his son's present was not without its drawbacks. However comfortable and convenient, the little car was totally unsuited to pull the big stock trailer, loaded with one or two calves or four pigs, which the wheezing old Simca used to drag, jogging along in a cloud of smoke, all the way to the market in Brive or Objat. So since then Jacques had been obliged to resort to Brousse and his trailer to go and sell his calves or pigs. It was embarrassing, for he did not like to abuse his neighbours' kindness.

That being so, apart from this inconvenience, he was absolutely delighted with his new car and took the wheel with real pleasure. And since Dominique's letter had put him in an excellent mood, he whistled as he covered the three kilometres which separated Coste-Roche from Saint-Libéral.

He was still whistling when he drew up in front of the Vialhe house.

His cheerfulness waned as soon as he recognised the big muddy Peugeot belonging to Doctor Martel; when needs must, the doctor never hesitated to drive up the roughest country tracks to go and see some patient, and therefore considered it pointless to clean his car.

Worried, ready to hear the worst, for he could not forget that the youngest person living there was after all seventy-five, he pushed open the door and went in. On seeing his aunts Berthe and Louise in the hallway, he immediately thought his father was having problems with his heart. That surprised him a little, for he had seen him in top form, for him, the previous evening. But he was eighty-six and anything was possible . . .

'What's happening? Who's ill?' he asked.

'Your mother,' said Berthe in a low voice.

'What! Maman!' he protested. It seemed to him inconceivable, not to say outrageous, that his mother should be ill. She had never been ill in her life and was only seventy-five! 'What's the matter with her?'

'She felt faint a short while ago, she couldn't stand up at all. But don't worry, it's probably nothing,' said Berthe.

'Where's Papa?'

'With her, he doesn't want to leave her. Even the doctor didn't manage to stop him going in to the bedroom with him.'

'Well, this is a fine mess!' he said. 'But why didn't you phone right away?'

'We did, several times, but there was no answer,' said Berthe.

'Ah, that's right, Michèle had come up to see me on the Malides.' He almost said why, but decided that his parents should be the first to hear the news.

'Has the doctor been here long?' he continued.

'Getting on for half an hour,' said Berthe. 'We were lucky, he was near Perpezac. And as he has a telephone in his car . . . Whatever people may say about it, it's extremely practical!'

'Yes, yes,' he said distractedly.

'Don't you want to tell Michèle?' asked Berthe.

'I'd like to know a bit more first.' He heard the door of the bedroom squeak, turned, and saw his father. He felt sorry for him, he looked so worried, so lost: 'Well?' he asked.

'The doctor will explain it to you, it seems it's not serious. But those sort of people are nothing but liars!' said Pierre-Edouard, sitting down.

Jacques noticed that he was clumsily buttoning up his shirt.

'He listened to your chest too? Are you ill?'

'No, but it kept your mother happy, so . . .' Pierre-Edouard sighed as he tried to push the buttons through with a hand which trembled too much, far too much.

'Would you like me to help you?' suggested Louise, who was also worried about the old man's condition.

'I'll manage,' he assured her. 'And you, instead of fussing over me, go and see your mother, that'll please her,' he said to his son.

'Of course,' agreed Jacques, turning towards the bedroom. He moved aside to allow Doctor Martel to emerge, and greeted him. 'Don't leave without seeing me!' he requested, and went into the room.

It was a shock to see his mother in bed. He hoped his feelings did not show, that his face did not betray him at all, for he realised in a flash that the last time he had seen his mother in bed was at the birth of Guy, in 1932! He had been twelve years old then, and it had made a deep impression.

Since then he had never seen his mother other than upright, in sound health, for she had always considered that any attacks of flu or exhaustion she suffered were to be treated with contempt. What was more, in his memory there remained the picture of a woman still young, a little weary but blooming, happy, her breasts heavy with milk, smiling as she invited him, and Paul as well, to come and admire their little brother. Discovering that reddish doll, squealing and crumpled, lying at her side; whilst Mauricette, upset and feeling neglected, clung to her.

And now, forty-three years later, in place of the serene and beautiful young woman he remembered came the pitiful image of a little old lady; all thin, her body withered, her hands deformed, their skin transparent and speckled with brown marks, her face lined with wrinkles and fatigue. But still smiling.

'You're here already?' she murmured. 'It's good of you to come so quickly.'

'Are you feeling better?' he asked, kissing her.

'Yes, of course, it's nothing. My blood pressure is a little high, it's nothing to fuss about. I'll be up tomorrow.'

'Certainly not! You must rest!' he said.

'Don't worry about me, better to look after your father. You've seen him, he's feeling quite lost . . .'

'Okay, okay,' he said, 'don't get worked up. And right now, think about taking care of yourself. Would you like Michèle to come and look after you?'

'Of course not! Berthe and Louise can manage perfectly well, I don't want to cause any inconvenience to anyone. By the way, do you have any news of the children?'

'Yes. Françoise phoned last night, she's well. She'll be here in July. As for Dominique and Béatrice . . . Ah, I'd have liked Papa to be here! Anyway, I'll tell him in a minute, well . . .'

'They're going to get married?' she interrupted, full of hope.

'Yes,' he smiled. He noticed that his mother's gaze grew misty, but out of consideration and embarrassment he pretended to see nothing, and added: 'Yes, they're getting married, almost the same day as Papa and you, Saturday the twentieth of December.'

'Oh! That's good, that's very, very good,' she murmured, closing her eyes. 'They'll be having the ceremony at the girl's parents, of course,' she added. 'That's normal, eh? That's how it's done. Oh, we probably won't go ourselves. I mean your father and I. It's too far for him, it would be too tiring for him, I think . . . But it would please him so much, too . . . Well, we'll see. And then it doesn't really matter, the main thing is, it's great to hear. Go quickly and tell your father. Go on, I must rest anyway. Go and tell him the good news!'

'I'll come by again this evening,' he promised, kissing her. 'Look after yourself, and have a good rest.'

*

'So what exactly's wrong with her?' asked Jacques as he accompanied Doctor Martel to his car.

'I really can't say, exactly. Some tests will have to be done. At first sight it looks like no more than a bad attack of high blood pressure. Logically speaking, everything ought to return to normal quickly. But she must be made to rest.'

'Easier said than done!' replied Jacques, shrugging his shoulders. 'She insists on doing her vegetable garden, feeding her ducks and geese, looking after I don't know how many rabbits, hens and chicks, and even fattening two pigs! I ask you! Up there at Coste-Roche I raise more than eighty a year myself! But it seems they're worthless! Because of the meal I give them; nothing but chemicals, my mother says! And my father does nothing to convince her otherwise!'

'To be honest, he must be careful too, even more than her. I took advantage of my visit to listen to his heart . . .'

'I saw that, and so?'

'So it's absolutely essential that he sticks to his course of treatment! His heart is very weak, and it won't do just to muddle along! And besides, you saw what sort of a state he got into over the little fright your mother's just given us?'

'Yes.'

'Good. So for your father, it's the same old story. No excitement, no strain, and above all he must take his medicines. And as for your mother, I'll visit again tomorrow. But what about you for that matter, your back?'

'Don't talk about that,' Jacques cut him off. 'There's enough trouble as it is for today!'

'Please yourself,' smiled Doctor Martel, climbing into his car, 'but while I was here I could have done a third consultation! Go on then, till tomorrow. And watch your father, he's the one I'm most worried about.'

Pierre-Edouard came out on to the door step as soon as he heard the doctor's car drive off.

'Right, what did he say?' he asked Jacques, 'I don't believe a word of what he told me myself!'

'Well, for once you're wrong.'

'You're starting to lie to me like the others,' Pierre-Edouard reproached him as he filled his pipe. Jacques noticed that his hands were trembling less, and was happy about that.

'Don't go smoking right under Maman's nose, you know what she thinks of it,' he said.

'Mind your own business! It'd be better if you told me what that bloody quack said about your mother. I'm sure he's hiding something from me.'

'No, no, I give you my word. Maman has high blood pressure. Fine, that can be treated. They'll need to have some tests done to be quite sure, but it's nothing!'

'Tests?' Pierre-Edouard was worried.

'Well, yes, you know! Like you when you had your heart problem. It's nothing to make a fuss about, is it?'

'Oh, right,' said Pierre-Edouard. He lit his pipe, tamped down the tobacco with his thumb: 'Oh right, he's not going to put her into hospital then?'

'Of course not! Who put that idea into your head?'

'Good, that's very good,' said Pierre-Edouard. 'You know, they played that trick on poor Léon, and it did for him. And it didn't do me any good. So if your mother ever had to go, I'm sure I wouldn't hold out, this time . . .'

'Don't give it a moment's thought. Come and offer me a drink instead. I've some very good news for you, in spite of all this . . .'

'Really? News which will please your mother too?'

'She already knows it. I've just told her, and I'm convinced that hearing it almost put her on her feet again.'

'Ah! I bet I know what it is!' murmured Pierre-Edouard, sucking at his pipe. 'Let me tell you something,' he added with a smile. 'There are only two really important pieces of news she's expecting. First that young Jo has decided to come back from the ends of the earth, from her island over there! And then that your son stops this business of living together, it's uncivilised!'

'Don't get excited, it's not good for you!'

'I'm not getting excited! Your good news, I know what it is. I know from Berthe that young Jo's not on the way back yet. She's writing now, that's one good thing. So since it isn't to do with her, it must be my grandson who's finally decided to

10

SEATED side by side in the shade of a plum tree laden with fruit which was filling the air with fragrance and driving the wasps crazy, Pierre-Edouard and Mathilde watched the huge blue combine-harvester rumbling and grumbling as it swallowed the barley on the Long Field.

As expected, the yield was superb, dense and tightly packed. The grain, nourished by the humus and nitrogen of the old lucerne, was heavy, rich. It flowed thick and fast into the trailer which followed the contractor's vehicle.

And Pierre-Edouard's happiness, already great on account of the fine harvest, redoubled when his eyes fell on the driver of the tractor. The young man who, concentrating as if handling a dangerous weapon, was steering the tractor exactly parallel to the combine.

For Jean Vialhe had been there a week. He did not begrudge his time or energy, proud to be of really practical use. Happy as well to prove to his Uncle Jacques, to his grandparents and all the people of Saint-Libéral, that he knew what to do and was capable of working like a proper man of the soil. Like someone whom neither city life nor education could divorce from his roots, who was instinctively rediscovering the behaviour and precise movements appropriate to each allotted task. For besides expertly driving the old Massey-Ferguson, you had only to see him grasp a pitchfork and handle the sheaves to understand the peasant stock working within him.

Pierre-Edouard smiled with happiness. And his joy was really complete. For just behind the combine harvester, there where the bales of straw fell out, more or less well tied by the small compresser, walked Françoise. In shorts, her loose blouse open over a nicely-filled, little blue bikini top, already bronzed like a peach, she looked magnificent. She was piling the bales into heaps of ten or twelve, and seemed to take a mischievous pleasure in moving faster than her mother and more especially her father, always hampered by his back.

'You know, they're simply fantastic, those kids,' said Pierre-Edouard. 'You see how beautiful the girl is? She looks like you, once upon a time . . .'

'Maybe, but I would never have dared walk about dressed like that!' Mathilde assured him.

'Not in the fields of course, but at home, you should have seen yourself . . .' he teased her.

She shrugged, but smiled conspiratorially and rested her head on his shoulder.

'Don't you want to go back?' she suggested, 'aren't you tired?'

'No, what about you?'

'I'm all right, quite all right now.'

It was true. After her lassitude had dragged on for several weeks, Mathilde had gradually got the better of it. Her blood pressure had returned to normal and her spirits revived, for all the tests were reassuring. But this was the first time, on this harvest day, that she had undertaken such a long walk.

'You're sure you're okay?' he insisted. 'If you like I'll tell Jacques to take you back; his car's down there.'

'No, no, we'll walk back quietly, we've plenty of time.'

He agreed absentmindedly, once more distracted by his grandchildren, and repeated:

'Yes, they're simply fantastic, those kids. I'm so pleased about them. You know, I'm wondering whether their fathers, at that age . . .'

'But of course they did!' she protested forcefully. 'You're forgetting! Remember Jacques! The year he took his bac, in 1937, he helped us through the whole harvest! You remember that, surely!'

'You're right,' he murmured, after considering the matter for few moments. 'It was that year my father gave him a watch. Yes, we had a fine harvest and Jacques was there . . . And your brother paid for his trip to Paris . . . Dear Lord, Léon would be happy today too, if he could see this, poor old Léon . . .'

'Come on, don't think about it,' she said, sorry now that she had involuntarily reopened an old wound. She attempted to divert him from his sad thoughts and continued: 'And look! Think of Dominique! Whenever he could he came to help his father! And you said yourself he learned more in a month here than in a year at his college!'

He shook himself out of it and smiled. 'You're right. Anyway, if Léon were still here, he'd say the same as me!'

'What's that then?'

'That machine, that so-called combine may be very efficient, but it doesn't do such a good job as our old reaper!'

'Oh yes it does!' she teasingly contradicted him. 'I know your opinion! That machine makes a noise and lots of dust; it crushes the grain, it loses some, it doesn't cut off all the straw cleanly, and so on and so forth! If you go on like that you'll end up rambling on like your poor father! I can still hear him saying the scythe was better than the reaper! And it wouldn't have taken much to get him to declare that nothing was as fine as a good sickle!'

'Oh you! Give you half a chance and you're trying to settle old scores with my father!' he teased.

'That's not the point. Look, shall I tell you something? If there weren't all these machines, your grandchildren wouldn't be here either! I don't think they'd have left Paris and gone without holidays to break their backs and blister their fingers tying up sheaves by hand, like we used to. And be honest, you know very well that it wasn't all roses!'

Still quite deafened by the noise of the combine, grey with dust, weary to exhaustion, but happy with their day's work, Françoise and Jean set off towards Coste-Roche by a short cut.

Darkness had fallen, filled with the cries of insects and chirping of crickets, heavy with sweet fragrances, mingling the scent of greengages, flowering clover and still warm straw. A balmy night, illuminated by an almost full moon, glowing radiantly creamy-white. In the distance, moving along the track which cut across the plateau, bounced the yellow headlight beams of the tractor steered by Jacques.

'Go a bit further to the left, otherwise we'll run into Brousse's fencing,' warned Françoise.

'Towards the trees over there?' asked Jean. He was slightly lost, and would have had difficulty in reaching Coste-Roche by himself.

'Yes, those are the plum trees on the Perrier field, on our land, you know. After that we'll pass round the top of the mine cutting, going on into Delmond's meadow. Then we'll be on Mathilde's fields, and after that comes Coste-Roche. You'll see, we'll be there before Papa!'

'You're lucky,' he said. 'You know it all like the back of your hand!'

'That's nothing special. You know, we used to have some great games up on the plateau, with Dominique. Our cousins joined us and believe me, it was good fun! Watch out, you've got a ditch over there, along the side of Delpeyroux's land.'

'You know the owner of every plot and its boundaries too?'

'Just as well! Look, don't forget that my brother and I often had to drive the animals out to graze. It wouldn't have done to make a mistake!'

'Of course not,' he agreed.

He was full of admiration for his cousin. In the first place he found her breathtakingly beautiful. Disturbingly so; he hardly dared even look at her for fear of blushing when, to be more comfortable in her work and cool down, she un-buttoned her shirt and let it hang loose, thus revealing the charming spectacle of the little cups which barely covered her breasts. As for her cut-off denim shorts which clung to her bottom and set off her bronzed thighs, they were enough to drive you mad; especially when she bent down to pick up the sheaves – a stunning sight.

So to blot out and try to stifle the fantasies which threatened to overwhelm him, he kept telling himself that Françoise was his first cousin, almost his sister. Besides, she intimidated him. She was eight years older than him, with the maturity and confidence of a grown woman; he still wavered in adolescent confusion, full of doubts and uncertainties. To be sure he ran a razor over his cheeks at least once a week, but even his voice still betrayed him when it jumped suddenly into sharps more suited to a little boy; and that was always when he wanted it to be deep!

Finally, Françoise was confident in her Corrèze childhood which filled her memory. Confident in being at home there, on the land where she had taken her first steps and which was so familiar that she knew the ownership of each tree, each bush.

It was not that his own memories were unpleasant, far from it! They were different; he considered them less stimulating, more ordinary. For although it might have been very entertaining to criss-cross the avenues of the Tuileries Gardens on roller-skates, or to sail your boat on the pool in the Jardin du Luxembourg, it was still less exciting than playing hide and seek in the caves of the mine cutting. Munching the neighbours' cherries, pears or strawberries for the sheer pleasure of scrumping, since there was no shortage of them on the farm! And then, despite it being forbidden, or maybe because it was, soaking your legs in the freezing water at the source of the Diamond.

Dominique, Françoise and his other cousins, Marie, Chantal, Josyane, had done all this. He had not. His visits to Saint-Liberal had always been too brief and the age difference too great, even with his closest cousins, Francoise and Josyane.

But now he was going to make up for that, properly explore Saint-Liberal, its fields, woods and views, create his own set of memories. And soon he would be confident, not only in the knowledge needed by young townies – especially those in the big cities – but would have in addition all that Jacques and the whole Vialhe family were eager to instil.

For his choice had been made. His holidays were going to be spent here, in the village and at Coste-Roche. And that was what he would tell his parents when they came, in a week's time. Inform them that he had better things to do than waste three weeks in Spain. Explain to them that the beach at Blanes held no attractions for him, neither did walks in the heart of Spain, nor the corrida, the flamenco or paella! Prove to them that his Uncle Jacques needed him on the farm, that his grandfather was counting on his help to bring in some wood and his grandmother was hoping he would pull up the two rows of Belles de Fontenay onions she had planted at the bottom of the garden. In short, that everyone was counting on him.

'To the right now: we'll cut across the land that's called At Mathilde's,' said Françoise. 'Just look, Papa has put in beets everywhere,' she remarked.

She had not been there since the beginning of her holidays, but recognized the broad leaves shining in the moonlight.

They were in the middle of the field when suddenly a bird flushed from a few steps in front of them, circled and then disappeared. Surprised, Françoise gave a little cry, then began to laugh.

'That stupid owl startled me!'

'That wasn't an owl,' he assured her, pleased by his expertise and also by this chance encounter, which he considered symbolic.

'Not an owl? Go on!'

'It was a nightjar! See, there it is again! Look! Look!' he whispered.

Dashing low over the ground, then swooping up vertically to swallow some noctuid moths, the bird skimmed past them, emitted a brief low churring, then disappeared.

'Super,' she said. 'So that's a nightjar? I've often seen them here, you know, especially when we bring in the cows in the evening, but I thought it was a sort of owl. Have to admit I'm not very up on birds. But you, how come you know them? Have you been observing them on the terrace at Les Invalides?'

'Yeah, sure! No, it was Félix who showed them to me. Hey, that'll be a year ago this month, we were at his place, in Brenne.'

'That's right, you often go there, don't you?'

'Yes. Félix is great!'

He was tempted to relate what his father's cousin had told him about nightjars, and the comparison he had made between them and Vialhes. But he feared his cousin would misunderstand and laugh at him. He simply said:

'They're migratory birds, they travel a long way, as far as south-east Africa. But they always return to where they were born, like swallows. Great isn't it?'

*

On condition that his stay was brief, Guy always found great pleasure in returning to Saint-Libéral. First of all because he loved to see his parents and aunts again. Then because he enjoyed meeting his former neighbours, and even some of the men and women with whom he had learned to read on the benches of the same village school. The school now threatened with closure for lack of numbers, which had previously, in the 1940s, welcomed in fifty children each morning.

Finally he was happy to view his childhood haunts, even if they had changed. Even if, here and there, punctuating the countryside, new houses with unfamiliar tenants were appearing.

Despite all this, he never lingered long, especially in summer. He soon felt embarrassed at being there doing nothing, an idle stroller, whilst the last farmers of the village toiled from dawn to dusk. And as he was no longer fit nor keen enough to help his elder brother with the work in the fields, he always had the feeling of being an intruder there. Besides, the family home was too cramped to house him with Colette and the children; he was therefore obliged to move into Combes-Nègres, Louise's house. Now, although his aunt assured him that she was delighted to open her doors to him, he knew very well that she only maintained her home for Félix and for his son and family. He was therefore always worried lest his own offspring break a window, damage the furniture or trample the flower beds.

All these little considerations did not go so far as to spoil his pleasure. They simply encouraged him to take to the road after three or four days, before the social relationships, nature and way of life became too burdensome.

But during his visit, it was a real holiday – gargantuan feasts at his parents' and Mauricette's homes; evenings at Coste-Roche; excursions into the surrounding area, for the pleasure of introducing Colette and his children to all the rich diversity of his native land.

'And how do you find the parents?' Jacques asked him on the second evening of his vacation, when he and Colette had come up to dine at Coste-Roche.

The night was beautiful, warm, full of stars. So they had seated themselves outside, under the tunnel of vines, to round off the evening. Françoise had borrowed her father's car and gone to the cinema in Brive, with Jean, not a little proud to be accompanying such a beautiful girl! As for the children, Marc, Evelyne and Renaud, they were dozing in front of the television.

'Maman's aged a lot all of a sudden, hasn't she?' continued Jacques.

'Yes, but I was prepared for worse,' said Guy. 'She looks well and seems to be in good shape. Papa too, what's more.'

'If you think so,' said Jacques. 'I find he tires very quickly now . . .'

'It's his age, there's nothing to be done about it,' said Guy with a shrug.

He savoured the aroma from the little glass of plum brandy served by his brother, tasted it and nodded his head in approval.

'My hat off to you! Nothing in the best restaurants in Paris can compare with this!'

'Twenty-nine years old, that's what does it,' said Jacques. 'Do you remember? The still belonged to old Pa Gaillard. He set it up on the path to the Combes, just below the source of the Diamond. That's from the first barrel of plums I had distilled after returning from Germany. Do you recall it?' he asked Michèle.

'That was barely two months after we were married, we were still living down there with my parents.'

'Old Gaillard?' said Guy. 'Wasn't he the one who had a young fellow with a northern accent helping him? Papa always warned us to beware of him when we went to mind the cows on Combes-Nègres!'

'That's right!' agreed Jacques. 'He was a young fellow who'd had problems after the Liberation and who was under "resident supervision" in the Corrèze, as old Gaillard put it!'

He was about to continue with his reminiscences, then saw that his brother suddenly seemed rather preoccupied, rather worried, and feared that Jean was the reason for it. His nephew had announced the day before that he intended to spend his vacation working on the farm. Jacques surmised that his brother was not particularly pleased.

'You're looking worried, got problems?' he ventured to ask.

'Me? No. But you were talking about our parents' state of health; have you seen the way Aunt Yvette is?'

'Oh that! All the worry has aged her,' said Jacques. He sighed, shrugged his shoulders: 'Well as to that, you know what's going on with Louis!'

'Do I know what's going on?' replied Guy scornfully. 'Are you kidding or what? There's not a week passes but Louis spends an hour on the phone to me! And that's been going on for more than six months!'

'So you're dealing with his problems?'

'No way! I'm a lawyer, not a businessman. All I can tell him is that he's got himself into a dreadful mess!'

'I was well aware of that!'

'He is too, but he's pussyfooting around! He's just got to give up everything and start again from scratch. And not in the Limousin, he's blown it here, finished. If he wants to start another estate agency, I would advise him to go to the Dunkirk or Calais area! And yet, it may turn out that even up there they've heard of the crash . . .'

'Is it that bad?'

'Yes. He must settle all his debts and set up again elsewhere. If he doesn't, he'll really be needing a very good barrister to extricate him from all the lawsuits hanging over him!'

'He owes a lot?'

'You bet! What with the overdrafts, the unpaid interest mounting up, the bankers with their so-called "help", the loans to pay off other loans, he'll be owing not far off seven million!'

'What?' said Michèle, 'you mean to say seven hundred million old francs? Is that it?' she asked Jacques.

He nodded in agreement. He too was rather stunned at the vastness of the sum. Accustomed to managing a budget so small and fragile that it caused him many a worry, he had difficulty in grasping that an intelligent, capable man like his cousin could get himself into such a situation.

'Seven hundred million!' he repeated, 'But how the devil did he manage that?'

'Oh, it's easy! A slightly over-inflated idea of himself, lots of sharks around him, and then . . .' Guy stopped, made sure the children were still in front of the television: 'And then women, old chap,' he continued, 'he's been on a fantastic binge for years, you have no idea!'

'Is that really so?' said Jacques.

He could not come to terms with it. Certainly he had no doubt that his cousin rarely slept alone, but even so! There was a difference between chasing after a bit of skirt and living it up until you ruin yourself!

'Believe me,' Guy assured him. 'Look, ask Colette. To thank me for having won a case for them, some clients feel obliged to drag me around those stupid nightclubs where the more disgusting the champagne and whisky, the more they cost! So believe me, the girls you find there are exorbitantly priced too! Well, just think, we've often seen cousin Louis in that sort of bordello, as Papa would say. And Louis was never with one cutie, always with two or three! Isn't that right, Colette?'

'It's true,' she confirmed. 'It can't have helped his finances.'

'Ah well, now I understand better why poor Aunt Yvette looks so sad,' said Jacques pouring himself a nip of brandy.

'Don't tell me this is all news to you?'

'As far as the living it up goes, yes, but the rest, no, of course not. Aunt Berthe alerted me to it a long time ago, and Maman too. But I didn't think it was that bad! What can he do? Do you think he'll sell his land? Or the château?'

'You've got it in one! Just imagine, he offered it to me, to keep it in the family!'

'Seriously? The château and the land?'

'Yes.'

'What could I do with it? In the first place I don't want to get into debt buying property I have no use for. In any case, even supposing I were rich enough to pick up the tab, that wouldn't save him. He's really up to his neck in it. I told him as much on our way here.'

'You've seen him?'

'Yes, yesterday morning, on our way through Limoges.'

'And?'

'Well, he'll have to give up his whole business, that will pay it off. Christ, he won't have a single sou left afterwards, but that's better than landing up in the nick, isn't it? If he does that, I've promised to refer some prospective buyers for the château to him. I know a fair number of people who could come up with a million, no problem. The château's not worth more than that, you know. And even at that price, he'll be lucky to sell.'

'Well, well, I have to say it's a fine tale you're telling me,' murmured Jacques. 'And where does Aunt Yvette come in to all this?'

'Ah, there you have me! . . . She'll have to live somewhere. Or rather, he'll have to find her somewhere to live. You know he's already made her sell all the houses in Brive?'

'All of them? Are you sure?'

'All of them. There it is, now you know everything.'

'Yes,' said Jacques pensively, 'yes, but it's not going to help me sleep better tonight . . . First of all, as mayor I'm annoyed about the château, you never know who might appear. But that's not the worst part. No. For God's sake, Louis is our cousin, and for me he's the son of my godfather. Believe me, it really upsets me not to be able to help him! My God, you end up thinking poor Uncle Léon was lucky to be out of it and not see the carnage!'

'So it's true then, you're leaving the the boy with us for the whole of August?' Pierre-Edouard insisted on knowing as he stopped to catch his breath.

He had asked Guy to accompany him on his walk, and was glad to have done so. He felt rather weary, short of breath and with a weakness in his legs. But still he felt reassured, for he had a strong arm close at hand which he could hold on to if need be.

'You know,' he said, 'this path up to the plateau, it's not far off eighty-five years I've been using it, and believe me, I've a feeling it's getting steeper all the time!'

'We can go back down if you like,' suggested Guy.

'No, no, let's sit down a while instead. Look, over there,' suggested Pierre-Edouard, pointing to a large oak stump. Guy helped him to sit, noticing how stiff and unsure of himself he had grown, and remained standing.

'Sit down, you make me feel dizzy,' said Pierre-Edouard, taking out his pipe. He stuffed it with a few strands of coarse tobacco, lit it, and pensively contemplated the countryside spread out before them.

Nearest to them, at their feet, lay Saint-Libéral with its slate roofs shining in the morning sun. A peaceful village, silent, sleepy. A village slumbering in an apathetic coma which owed nothing to the early August heat.

And then, around it, the fields and meadows. Mostly meadows, for the arable land was gradually giving way to grass. The last farmers in the village no longer had the time to sink the plough into each plot. That was obvious, for even some of the plum orchards were half abandoned, not sprayed or pruned, with dead branches dangling and suckers feeding on their roots. Nor did the walnut plantations escape the men's loss of heart. Tortured by a torrent of hail on 3 August 1971, they were dying quietly, weeping a sticky sap which seeped from the stump of each branch broken by the wind. And on their calloused trunks parasites grew unchecked.

Fortunately, so long as the eye wandered and did not linger over details close at hand, the beauty of the countryside opened out before them, the sweetness of the fresh, green valleys, the harmonious curve of the hills worn down over thousands of years. And, yet further still, the uplifting immensity of the soft blue horizon stretching as far as the eye could see, climbing up towards the Auvergne and Cantal.

'You haven't given me an answer,' Pierre-Edouard reproached him.

'To what?'

'Young Jean, you're leaving him here . . . Is that right?'

'I said yes, that means yes!' Guy assured him, chewing a tender stalk of cocksfoot grass.

'It doesn't seem to give you much pleasure . . .'

'Of course it does! Well, his mother and brothers and

sister would have preferred him to come on holiday with us
. . . And me too! But okay, since he's chosen to work . . .'

'Why don't you admit you're not pleased that he loves the
land?'

'Don't let's discuss that again, you know my opinion.'

'Yes, you're hoping he'll abandon the idea of copying
Dominique.'

'We'll see . . .' said Guy, evasively.

He had no wish to quarrel with his father. No wish to tell
him that he did not believe in the future of farming. No wish
to explain to him that from all the evidence – and some studies
proved it – it would have been much more economical for
consumers to buy everything from the United States! That he
was not the only person to work this out, far from it, and that
one day, probably soon according to the specialists, only a
few regions would remain predominantly agricultural; the
Corrèze was not about to become one of them!

Nor did he wish to tell him that it was enough to see how
hard Jacques worked and what he earned to be against his
own son embarking on a similar treadmill!

'But *miladiou!*' cried out Pierre-Edouard, as if he had read
his thought. 'You're exaggerating, farmers and agronomists
will always be needed! Look in front of you, look all around,
look at the fallow land gaining ground and the brambles
spreading everywhere! That's because there's no one to
control them! Do you think it should continue? If we go on
fooling around like that, you'll see, one day our grandchildren will be dying of hunger! Is that what you want, up
there in Paris? Or on the other hand, you know, with a
summer like we've had this year, it'll all be shrivelled up!'

'It hasn't come to that! Come on, don't get in a state about
nothing!'

'It isn't nothing! It's because it grieves me to see land going
to waste when it's begging to produce something!'

11

JEAN untied the calf. With one hand gripping the halter, the other its tail, he led it out of the van driven by Henri Brousse and waited.

All around them, locked in an indescribable jam, dozens of vehicles were unloading calves haphazardly on to the pavements and roadway.

Calmly, deaf to the gibes and insults flying around, a policeman was trying to convince the owner of a rusty 4L pick-up truck battered about by its cargo, that he could not possibly have any excuse for continuing to paralyse the entire road system. But it was obvious that he was not for one moment expecting to be heeded; the other man had better things to do!

Streaming with perspiration, brick red, close to apoplexy, his beret over his eyes, emitting long streams of Bloody-Hells and God's-Teeth and various allusions to some brothel with a divine manager, the man, kneeling in the back of the van, was trying to dislodge his calf, which was jammed across the box.

'Give it a push up the backside! Hey! You can see he's bracing himself against the door!' cried one spectator.

'Better to pull his head! That'll make him jump!' advised another.

'Shut yer mouths, dammit!' grumbled the owner, wiping his forehead with the back of his hand.

He did not seem prepared for conversation. His cord trousers were covered in urine and dung and his shirt was wringing wet.

'Right, now you must move on or I'll book you!' threatened the officer, waving his notebook.

The man shrugged, plunged back into the van, seized the calf's neck with both arms and twisted as it bellowed in terror. Free at last, the animal sprang on to the tarmac, charged towards the representative of the law, but swerved at the last moment, and stopped dead.

'Did you see that: animals don't harm their own kind!' called out a disappointed wag.

'Come on, move along now! Move, I said!' the policeman's tone was growing desperate.

A foolish hope: given the situation, it was obvious that no vehicle would shift a hand's breadth for at least half an hour if they were lucky!

'See you later at Pierrot's for a snack,' said Jacques to Brousse, who was still sitting at the wheel and philosophically reading his newspaper with the engine switched off. 'And you, don't let go of that calf!' he advised Jean.

Thiers Square was teeming with people and animals. And the din – a mixture of motor horns, rumbling engines, mooing, shouts, calls, swearing and laughter – was such that you needed to shout to make yourself heard. Already all the restaurants and bistros were full, their terraces black with famished customers; the air smelled of noodle soup, fortified bouillon, steak, camembert, wine and the cowshed. And on all sides the happy cries of neighbours or friends rang out, as they met and greeted each other with hearty backslapping.

'And make sure you hold on to that calf,' repeated Jacques. He was a little worried, for however strong his nephew might be, the calf was pushing a hundred and eighty kilos and had a tendency to pull on the tether. You needed a firm hand to control it, to lead it along the chains where several hundred animals were lined up, and to find it a space. But Jacques had been in such pain with his back for the last two days that he felt unable to hold the animal if it took it into its head to jump about.

It was a very fine Limousin bull calf of four months, top grade. Fed exclusively on its mother's milk since birth, kept in the quiet in the half-light of a box, it had knotted shoulders, a broad back and enlarged hind quarters. Moreover it would provide pale pink meat, as one could tell from the pallor of the mucous membrances in its mouth, the insides of its eyelids and its coat called 'leveret's fur', a pale covering speckled with greyish tufts.

'Shall we put it here?' suggested Jean, pointing to a place between two fine-looking animals.

'No, further down will be better,' decided Jacques, catching hold of the calf's halter.

Jean frowned but complied. He did not understand why his uncle was choosing a position in full sunshine, when the other spot had the benefit of the deep shade of one of the plane trees on the market place.

'We'll die of heat,' he said.

'Come on now!' Jacques smiled as he tied up the calf. 'Don't tell me you don't understand why I didn't want to stay where you were suggesting?'

'Well, no . . . we would've been in the shade at least, whereas here!'

'You've still got a few things to learn!' continued Jacques. 'I see you don't know the most important principle which your Uncle Léon never failed to apply: "Always present your produce as the finest at the market!" Do you get it?'

'Yes. Well no, not exactly . . .'

'Look where we are: there are nothing but "moles" all around us. Yes, Limousin-Friesian crosses. Not bad of their sort, but you know, next to ours they're real runts! Now, see how they sets ours off!'

'That's true,' admitted Jean.

'Up where you wanted to stop, we'd have been surrounded by animals just as good as him, so he'd look more ordinary.'

'I see . . . .' Jean agreed. He was discovering previously unknown side to his uncle, and it was very entertaining. 'And you try to do that every time?' he continued.

'Yes.'

'The same for the pigs?'

'Exactly. But you know, to be frank, it doesn't make much difference in the end; it's almost a game. The buyers aren't stupid, they know the system. And it's always the prices on the day which determine the outcome.'

'So we could've stayed in the shade!'

'Oh no! You must always work on the principle that you might chance on some young lad who doesn't know all the tricks . . . Hey! Cheers!' Jacques called to a man who was shouldering his way roughly through the throng of sellers.

'Cheers! Is this yours?' asked the man pointing to the calf, but not touching it. 'Ten-fifty when the bell goes' he said.

'You'd better be quiet!' replied Jacques. 'It's not open yet, so I haven't heard anything.'

'Ten-fifty on the bell!' repeated the fellow as he moved off.

'What was all that nonsense?' Jean was astonished.

'That was one of the scouts for old Jalinac, one of the biggest wholesalers in the area. As the market isn't open yet, he hasn't any right to buy. So he's making the rounds to pick out the best animals and prepare the ground. Your great uncle Léon began by doing that job. But he didn't stop at that.'

'Are you going to let it go at that price?'

'Of course not! And look here, if Jalinac is already deploying his troops, that means the Italians are here. Oh yes!' he explained, seeing his nephew's astonished expression, 'the Eyeties come as far up as here, or even further, into Haute-Vienne, to pick up anything they can. They fill their lorries up with calves; three or four hundred animals don't worry them. So you can imagine the dealers in this area are interested in keeping an eye on them. I myself don't trust them anyway, their cheques often bounce . . .'

'This is absolutely amazing,' said Jean. 'All they talk about is the common market, modern farming and economics and all that, and you're still selling like in the Middle Ages, it's crazy!'

'You're right, but I don't very well see how else it could be done. There is an agricultural intervention board in the département, but it doesn't operate at the top of the market, far from it! It works at the bottom end, picking up the unsold stuff and rejects! So here we are, myself and plenty of others, at the mercy of the wholesalers. You're dead right, the system's damnably out of date.'

'And what's more you're screwing up the whole town with this mess! All right, it's good fun, but for the tourist trying to get across Brive, it's bloody awful!'

'The mess will soon be sorted out at least. In six months' time the markets'll be held elsewhere, near the airfield, you know, on the road to Bordeaux. It'll be more efficient, but definitely not as pleasant . . .'

'Why not?'

'Because all the bistros you see around this square aren't going to be moving, are they? So I'm wondering where we'll be able to sit down with a glass of something, talk to our friends, mix some wine with our soup and have a bite to eat . . .'

Louis considered that he had payed dearly for the right to show off, to make those three louts who were ruining him believe he wasn't washed up yet. So it was with a firm hand that he initialled and signed each page of the deeds which discharged his debts, but which also divested him of his last centime, or almost. He even pretended not to notice the satisfied smiles of the new owners of his estate agency, and of the land in the process of being divided into plots where the construction work had forced him to capitulate – although, God knows, there was money to be made out of those lots!

The three crooks who had got the better of him, who had brought him to his knees, certainly knew that! They were going to triple their outlay in a few years and, whilst he was chewing over his humiliation and grovelling in poverty, those wretches would be making a packet at his expense! It was enough to drive you to murder!

Even the solicitor had an expression which incited homicide. He radiated contentment and seemed in such a hurry to see everything settled that his hand shook as he turned the pages of the dossier one by one.

Admittedly the operation was lucrative for him. And although he seemed as conceited and boastful as a turkey cock, it was obvious that he did not deal with matters of such importance every day. His expression betrayed him, showing just how much he was enjoying finishing a reputedly bleak month with such a lucrative session. It was well worth the trouble of working during August!

For that too was heart-breaking for Louis. The weather was wonderful, warm. A time for holidays, just right for lounging beside the water, a young thing with very little clothing or inhibitions in one hand and a scotch on the rocks in the other!

Instead of which he was shut up in this dark office which smelled of old dog, as cheerful as a dentist's waiting room, its walls covered in ugly grey paper in no way enlivened by the badly framed, incompetent scrawls of some depressed dauber. And worst of all, he was there to be legally stripped of everything. To sign his own extirpation and hand over what represented twenty-five years of his life, his business, to three sharks who were growing happier by the minute.

'Fine, right, that's it? Can we see the end of all this paperwork?' he said irritably. 'I have other things to do besides this, you know!'

'Nearly done. But you realise everything must be done according to the rules!' the lawyer assured him in a smooth tone. 'Here, initials there and there, and your signature to complete it,' he added with a smile. He had revolting, yellow, rat-like teeth and stank of tobacco. 'And there we are,' he said, carefully pressing a blotter over the signature, 'yes, the matter is settled.'

'Right, then we have nothing further to say to each other,' declared Louis, heading for the door.

'I hope you'll be our guest this evening, a nice little supper among friends,' suggested one of the buyers.

'Friends? What in hell's name do you think I'd be doing there! Keep your snacks, I can still afford to buy myself a proper meal!' cried Louis.

He ignored the outstretched hands, went out and slammed the door.

Louis spent the afternoon tidying his small flat in the Place Jourdan and piling his belongings into a corner of the corridor. He was no longer at home, for even these four rooms were included in the sale. Magnanimously, the purchasers had allowed him a month to sort himself out and move. But where to go, and more urgently what to do? He no longer owned anything or was anybody. And worst of all, he no longer had the will to fight on.

Fight for what, anyway? He had no child to feed, no

woman worth making an effort for. His last mistress had dropped him at the beginning of July, when she had suddenly realised that he was virtually ruined. She had left for Saint-Tropez on the arm of a young man whose family were in kaolin and prided themselves on owning a twelve-metre yacht. Louis wished him a speedy shipwreck!

It was while emptying a drawer that he discovered an old photo of his father posing boastfully in front of the château of Saint-Libéral. He then realised to what extent he had failed, wasted it all, undervalued what had been entrusted to him. And he had been given a great deal, for fear that he should lack for anything!

His father had started with nothing, absolutely nothing, and had nevertheless succeeded in reversing his fortunes. At the age of twelve he had only disadvantages and not a sou to his name. But he had a compelling need to forget that body hanging in the barn, which he had bumped into one January evening in 1900, on 16 January . . .

Never had anyone in the family spoken of this episode to Louis. But he had learned by degrees, by putting two and two together. In Saint-Libéral, even after thirty-five years, the shared recollections were still alive. And the children in the village school were quite ready to make fun of the grandson of the man who hanged himself, to cut him down to size! A little matter of making him understand that his opulent leather satchel, his boots – an insult to all the clogs in the class – and his expensive clothes would never erase the memory of the contorted face and purple tongue of Emile hanging from the cross beam . . .

And even if a few sharp blows had silenced the slanderers, the gossips and the envious, he had forgotten nothing. Forgotten nothing particularly of the way his father had tried to eradicate that stain, that fault. He had fought, all the time, all his life. He had succeeded.

And me, I've really made a mess of it, from beginning to end, he thought with a shrug. I couldn't even be bothered to give Maman some grandchildren! That's all the poor woman was waiting for, she always believed that I'd do the same as Papa, that I'd marry late! Poor old thing, she hasn't even had the pleasure of cuddling a grandson! But it has to be said that of all the tarts I tumbled with, not one of them ever asked me to give her a child. They'd have preferred to get rid of it I bet! Well, to the devil with all that, he told himself, putting down the photo, you can't undo what's done, and at my age you can't wipe it all away and start again!

Louis dined alone in an establishment which he had frequented for a long time, where the cuisine was refined and the cellar respectable. The owner was almost a friend. Not quite, however; for some time Louis had felt him more reserved than previously, less ready to put on one side the bills which he settled at the end of the month. But this evening he was welcoming, there were very few customers.

'So, now you're going off on short holiday?' he asked as he offered Louis a vintage brandy on the house.

'Yes, I really need one.'

'You're going to the coast, I expect?'

'No, home, to the Corrèze, to Saint-Libéral.'

'Ah?' said the man, savouring the aroma from his balloon glass. 'By the way, how's business?' he asked carelessly.

'Very funny!' said Louis with a shrug. 'You know very well how I'm placed! Yes you do! Yes, you know, like everyone in this town with its stinking rumours! Never mind, I'll have the last word yet. That's what counts, isn't it?'

'Of course, anyway, I'm sure I . . .'

'Look here, give me my bill, yes, the month's total.'

'There's a little more than that . . .'

'Right, that's fine.'

'Um, . . . I'd prefer cash if you have it,' said the owner, seeing Louis take out his cheque book. 'Because of the tax, you understand . . .' he said, lowering his voice.

'Of course, no problem,' Louis assured him, guessing that the tax was only an excuse: That evil-minded squirt is just worried I might pass him a dud cheque! When I think of all the dough he's had off me over the years!

He left the restaurant at half past twelve and took the road to Brive. It was at the top of the long slope leading down to Pierre-Buffière, which ends in the fearsome hairpin bend plunging down beyond the railway line where the crossing gates were always closed, that he made the decision. It all became so simple then, easy, no problems.

Suddenly relaxed, as he had not felt for months, perhaps even for years, he built up speed in his Porsche. Accelerator to the floor and engine running flat out, he hurtled down the hill at more than two hundred kilometres an hour, and launched himself against the broad metal posts which supported the level-crossing barrier on the Paris-Toulouse line. His neck broken clean through, Louis Dupeuch was already dead when the steering wheel crushed his thorax . . .

It was with a knot of fear in the pit of his stomach that Jacques lifted the receiver. It was barely three o'clock in the morning and that piercing ringing which frayed his nerves boded no good.

So, thinking that one of his aunts or his mother was ringing to tell him that his father had taken a turn for the worse, he raised the receiver to his ear.

'This is Sergeant Chastang, of the Ayen police. Is that Monsieur Viahle's house?'

'Yes.'

'Ah! Am I speaking to the mayor?'

'Of course, for God's sake! What's happened?' he asked, more and more worried and surprised.

'A problem, a big problem, sir . . . We've been trying to call Monsieur Dupeuch's house, in Limoges, hoping that maybe someone . . . but there's no reply, so . . .'

'So what? Explain yourself, in God's name!'

'Well, we thought we'd better tell you first, you . . . Our colleagues in Pierre-Buffière informed us as soon as they were able to read the documents . . . So I thought that Madame Dupeuch being old, and that . . . that . . . There it is, it'll have to be broken gently to her . . . She is your aunt, isn't she?'

My God, he thought, I bet Louis has done the same as Grandpa Dupeuch! That's all we need!

But still he asked: 'Break what to her?'

'An accident, a terrible accident . . .'

'My cousin is dead, is that it?'

'Yes. He must have fallen asleep at the wheel, and as he hadn't done up his seat belt . . . Oh anyway, the speed he was going . . .'

'I see . . .' murmured Jacques, thinking selfishly that it would be a little easier to announce to his aunt that Louis had had a car accident. He could not see himself telling her he had blown out his brains with a shotgun or hanged himself, like their maternal grandfather. Then he realised that the gendarme was still talking.

'Well, he's been taken to Limoges, but . . .'

'Very good, you've done what's needed. Listen, if you would be so kind as to come to the mairie tomorrow, I'll be there at first light. We'll see about the details then, all right?'

'Very well, sir. But you will undertake to inform Madame Dupeuch, won't you?'

'Yes indeed. Until tomorrow.'

He replaced the receiver, turned round and saw Michèle standing in the bedroom doorway.

'Did you hear that?' he asked.

She shook her head and he realised she would be convinced that it was Dominique or Françoise who had had an accident. There had been no news from Dominique for almost a month, while Françoise had been back in Paris for a week.

'Is it serious?' she murmured.

'It's Louis . . .'

He noticed that she seemed relieved, but did not blame her at all. He too had felt less distressed on discovering that it was neither his son nor his daughter, but his cousin who had suffered an accident.

'Louis?' she prompted.

'Yes. A car accident. Killed outright . . .'

'Lord!' she whispered, closing her eyes. 'Poor Aunt Yvette . . . Does she know?'

'Not yet.'

'And it's you who's going . . .'

'Yes, someone has to do it.'

'And how are we to tell your father?'

'Oh that,' he sighed. 'It's not the sort of news that'll do him any good. Nor Maman either . . . Bloody hell, what a stupid mess! No, no, it's such a mess!'

He was simultaneously bitter and furious. Bitter because it was all too senseless. Because the death of a man in the prime of life was a shameful nonsense, gross stupidity! Furious because he could not forget that his own first reaction had been to believe that Louis had deliberately destroyed himself, and he still believed it. Furious, because he knew that he would never be rid of that idea, since it fitted in so well with his cousin's desperate situation.

For one thing was certain, if it was true that Louis loved to drive fast, and Jacques knew a bit about that as he had sometimes been to Brive with him, he was not the sort to leave his seat belt undone, and much less to fall asleep at the wheel. So . . .

My God! he suddenly thought, what's going to become of poor Aunt Yvette with all Louis' business to sort out? Well, it's a good thing Guy is back from his holiday; we'll certainly need his skills . . .

'With your father,' went on Michèle, 'it'll have to be Aunt Berthe who tells him, she'll find the words to say it, she knows . . .'

'You're right. But how can I get to her in the morning without bumping into my father?'

'I'll go, if you like. And you, while I do that, you go and see Aunt Yvette . . .'

'All right,' he sighed. He suddenly frowned and glanced towards Jean's room. 'I think we've woken him. You'd better put something on,' he said.

She was barely covered by her thin short nightdress, for the night was humid, without a breath of air. She slipped quickly into the bathroom and came out pulling on a dressing gown, as Jean emerged from his room looking dazed.

'Hey, what's going on?' he asked uncomprehendingly.

'I'm afraid the last days of your holday are turning out badly. Your cousin Louis has just killed himself in his car . . .'

'Oh merde!' murmured Jean.

If he felt sad, it was more to do with the state Jacques and Michèle were in, and their distress, than any thought for

Louis. He had met him no more than three or four times in his life, and he was rarely mentioned at home.

'Can you look after the animals for me tomorrow?' asked Jacques.

'Of course.'

'I'm going to have a rough day, and your aunt as well. So if you could possibly . . .'

'I'll manage, don't worry. But tell me, does Aunt Yvette know?' He was just appreciating how fond he was of the old lady. She was charming, always pleasant, gentle and concerned about everyone. He thought of the pain she was going to suffer and tears welled up in his eyes. 'And Grandfather? And Grandmother? Do they know?' he asked, forcing himself to control his voice.

'Nobody knows anything yet, except us three,' said Jacques, pretending not to notice his distress. He moved towards his nephew, grasped his shoulder and shook it:

'Don't worry, we'll tell them gently. Very carefully. One tragedy is enough.'

Contrary to what Jacques had feared, it was not his father who reacted most strongly, but his mother. To her, Louis was her only nephew bearing the Dupeuch name, her own name. With him gone, the Dupeuch branch of the family was extinguished for ever. Furthermore, Louis greatly resembled his father physically, and she saw in him a reflection of Léon whose disappearance had already deeply hurt her.

So this new trial affected her severely. And although she knew how to put on a brave face, she remained wounded, vulnerable. Less than her sister-in-law Yvette, of course, who seemed to age ten years in a few hours. And her bewildered, lost look worried Mathilde, Louise and Berthe so much that the three ladies decided to move her in to the Vialhe house on their return from the cemetery. They made up a bed for her in Louise's room, and Yvette, distant, sealed in her sorrow, let it be done without saying a word. Without even crying, that was the worst. For everyone who saw her realised that the flood of tears which refused to flow was eating into her from within, like an acid, wearing her down, suffocating her.

'You know, you're going to have to find something to jog poor Yvette out of it. And to cheer up Mathilde too,' said Pierre-Edouard to Berthe a week after the funeral.

As every morning, he had asked his sister to accompany him on his daily walk, but it was the first time since Louis' death that he had broached this subject.

The announcement of his nephew's death had given him a shock, but much less than that of his brother-in-law three years earlier. In fact he had never been overly fond of Louis. He liked him well enough, but had little in common with him. Besides, Louis had built his life far away from Saint-Libéral, and his mode of existence and business had never drawn him closer to his uncle.

After all, Pierre-Edouard had reached an age where his memory was so full of the faces of those who had disappeared, and his heart so wrung by many a loss, that he came to the point where he no longer railed against death when it struck someone who, although not a stranger, was not very close to him either.

'Here, help me sit down,' he asked as they arrived at the old oak stump where he now rested during every walk. 'Yes,' he continued, taking out his pipe, 'you'll have to do something.'

'And what would you have me do?'

'How should I know! But you have to pull Yvette out of it, and Mathilde too,' he sighed. 'Poor old Léon,' he said after a few moments' silence, 'good thing he's not here any longer. What a mess! By the way, were you able to find out? Were Louis' affairs sorted out?'

'Yes, there's nothing outstanding. He'd signed everything the day before his death.'

'So why did he kill himself, the little fool!' He was suddenly angry. 'Because he did mean to kill himself, I know it! I'd swear to it! And that's what's eating at Mathilde, because she suspects as much!'

'Don't get worked up, you can't be sure of anything.'

'Sure I'm sure! He did the same as his grandfather Emile, that's what he did! And you know it's true too. Admit it!'

'What's the point?' she said with a shrug. 'Me, I believe what the gendarmes said . . .'

'All right,' he said calmly, 'all right, believe it if suits you. But in that case, try to persuade Mathilde! You see, she never knew her father, but she knows all about him . . . So she makes the connection with Louis.'

'There's no reason for it,' suggested Berthe. She herself was convinced of Louis' suicide, but did not consider it helpful or sensible to talk about it. Louis had chosen and that was his business, even if his decision was abominable.

'Right, fine, don't let's talk about it any more,' he said. He puffed slowly on his pipe, spat between his feet. 'You see,' he continued,' Grandfather was right . . .'

'Grandfather Edouard?'

'Yes. Do you remember what he always said to encourage us to be careful, so that we learned economical habits?'

'Yes, I've never forgotten that,' she smiled.

'"It only takes two generations to go from clogs to clogs"!' he recited. 'It's horribly true! Old father Dupeuch was the poorest man in the village, and it was touch and go whether he had enough to buy himself a pair of clogs. You hardly knew him, but I remember Emile well!'

'I do though. I was seven when . . . when he died.'

'Yes. Well there he was, so poor, but had a son who made his fortune! And then along comes Louis and devours the lot. Gobbles it all up. And it may turn out that he had barely enough to pay for a pair of clogs . . . And that's surely why . . .'

'Don't rehash all that, there's no point. Would you like to go back?' she asked.

'Not straight away, we'll walk a bit further. I want to hear you say that you'll look after Yvette. And Mathilde too. Because I don't know what to do any more, and it's tormenting me.'

PART THREE
In Memory of Léon

12

It was with a shrinking heart that Jean turned round and cast a last glance in the direction of Saint-Libéral. He fixed the image of the village in his mind as it lay bathed in sunshine, nestling up there on the side of the hill, then pretended to be interested in the road which curved away towards Brive.

He did not regret the last days of his holidays, although they had been disrupted by Louis' death. Firstly, because he had several times found himself alone at Coste-Roche, and so in charge of the farm, and he had managed that extremely well. Secondly, because his cousin's funeral had given him the opportunity to establish himself as a grandson worthy of the Vialhes.

Indeed, he had found himself the sole representative of all the Vialhe grandchildren, for Françoise had not been able to come down. As for the others . . . And he had also represented his parents, detained in Paris by pressing obligations. So he was proud to see that in the eyes of those who had come to the cemetery, he was recognised as a Vialhe, and that it was therefore right for him to be present beside his grandparents, uncles and aunts, to support the old lady with dry eyes standing rigidly by the open grave.

'Don't you worry,' said Jacques, seeing him look at his watch, 'you'll be there in plenty of time.'

'Oh, I'm not worried! Anyway, there are other trains!'

'Hey! No messing about! I told your parents you'd be arriving shortly after six o'clock, so . . . Considering you should have been in Paris at least three days ago! Seems you've done nothing to prepare for school and you haven't even anything to wear! Well, that's what your mother says.'

'Bah, I'll be ready the day after tomorrow, that's the main thing,' said Jean with a shrug.

He had not a single worry about the start of the academic

year. He was not changing schools, would meet up with lots of teachers and mates he already knew, was not concerned about the course work to come and was even keen to tackle it. In fact, all would have been well if Saint-Libéral had not been five hundred kilometres from Paris! And if, instead of running senselessly round the cinder track in the stadium once a week to get some fresh air, he could have climbed each day amongst the stones of the White Peak, knocked down the walnuts on the Long Piece and led the animals out to graze!

Anyway, he thought to comfort himself, I'll go and see Félix as often as I can. And then who knows, maybe the parents would be happy to let me come down at Christmas . . .

He dreamed of seeing the village in winter, of exploring the bare landscape, walking on the ground hardened by frost, then plunging happily into the stable which had the chill taken off it by the animals, or warming himself up again beside the hearth, deep in the chimney corner.

But he made sure he did not speak about all that. He was aware that these wishes were the ones which strengthened his father's arguments. The ones which justified him in maintaining that it all arose from a rather affected sentimentalism, from a vision of the land as idealised as it was false. For daily life in the country, especially at minus ten or fifteen degrees or in persistent rain, was quite unlike a page from Giono, however sublime his romantic descriptions might be! And his father was speaking from experience.

Never mind, he thought, looking at his calloused palms these are also the beginning of experience! Because Papa may say what he likes, I worked till my hands bled in the first week at Coste-Roche, but it didn't put me off or make me give up!

'You've got real farmer's hands!' teased Jacques.

'Bah, they'll soon go.'

'There's nothing wrong with them!'

'That's not what I meant, just the opposite!' he said, reddening a little, for he was rather annoyed that his uncle had misunderstood his reaction. 'I'd prefer to keep them as they are; but you know, in Paris it's difficult to get hold of a pitchfork!'

'There's a time for everything. You'll see, in a little while you'll be glad not to be holding a fork to earn your living! Come on, young Vialhe, don't make such a face, and think about your bac! Any fool can have callouses on his hands, but not everyone has the luck to be born with academic abilities! Don't waste that! You see, you can even tell your father I gave you some good advice! Right?' joked Jacques.

'Yes, you're almost as smooth a talker as him! But it won't make any difference. First I'm going to do the same as Dominique, and then I'm going to be a stock-breeder! I don't know how or where, but I will be one day.'

Despite her age, Berthe refused to regard herself as an old lady, at least as far as mind and spirit were concerned. She was sufficiently intelligent and honest with herself to admit that her body, ravaged by the years and weakened by adversity, was that of an old person, which could betray her from one moment to the next. But she used all her willpower to think and act without allowing for the passage of time; as if no physical weakness should remind her that she was eighty- two.

So she quickly understood that Pierre-Edouard was right to be worried, and that it was vital to help Yvette regain her equilibrium. Without it Louis' mother, who was after all her junior by almost fifteen years, would sink into senility long before her!

It was as she made her way towards the grocer's van, as she did each Wednesday, accompanied by Louise and Mathilde, that she launched her campaign.

'Pierre-Edouard's right,' she said out of the blue, stopping in the middle of the pavement, and speaking quite loudly so as to be heard by Louise.

'What on earth's got into you?' replied a worried Louise.

'He's right!' she repeated. 'You're letting yourself go a bit,' she reproached Mathilde; 'and as for Yvette, she's on the way to turning into a real zombie. Yes, a sort of ghost of herself, if you like,' she explained, seeing that her sister-in-law had difficulty in understanding. 'We'll have to shake ourselves out of it, we'll have to give her a shake!'

'Easy to say, if you think it's amusing,' responded Mathilde.

'It's not a matter of amusing or sad! We must do something, that's all! And the first thing is to stop whining!'

'But we're not whining!' protested Louise.

'Yes you are! You're complaining! Secretly you're complaining! I know it!' Berthe was suddenly quite cross. 'With Yvette you spend your time shuffling through your worst memories, shaking the skeletons, like three little old ladies competing to see who's the unhappiest! Poor Louis is just an excuse to bring out all your old sorrows!'

'You have no right to speak like that!' protested Mathilde angrily. She had tears in her eyes, for the image of Paul was threatening to overwhelm her, the image of the vanished son whose presence had been felt more keenly since Louis' death. But to say that he was being used as a pretext! 'I forbid you to say such things!' she cried furiously. 'You have no right!'

'Let me finish!' said Berthe, her voice suddenly trembling. 'On that subject I have a right to speak as I think fit! I have the right because I should have been dead thirty years ago, I've had a suspended sentence for thirty years! Yes, I have the right! I have the right because I've seen more friends and colleagues die than you can ever imagine! All my sisters in the labour camps, all those who have gone before me, are telling me to say it! And I'm not going to betray them by not doing it!'

It was so unusual for her to evoke the months of hell spent in Ravensbrück that Mathilde and Louise were left speechless. Overcome by the incredible strength and determination radiating from this little old lady, so frail, so tiny, but whose voice was disturbing, appealing, and irrefutable. A voice full of life, spirit, hope.

'Yes,' she continued, 'all those I've seen go up in smoke – and there were some who were barely fifteen – give me the right to say that life is too short to be wasted on being unhappy! Too short to live with a cemetery in your head and a coffin on your back!'

She fell silent, shook herself and smiled:

'I'm sorry, it's stupid isn't it, to lose your temper. But it's true, you know! We must act! Even if it's not easy – especially when it's not easy! Are you cross with me?' she asked Mathilde.

'Of course not. Get away, I know you,' smiled Mathilde. 'You've always been the same.'

She could not forget that in earlier times, for months on end, her sister-in-law had helped her not to succumb, not to sink into a boundless sorrow; Berthe's strength had supported her then.

'And you, are you cross with me?' Berthe asked Louise.

'No. But you are hard on us, all the same . . .'

'Well I'm sorry. Forgive me, both of you,' she said, walking on. She smiled a greeting at one of their neighbours, Germaine Coste, who looked quite embarrassed to have witnessed the altercation.

'Don't worry,' she called to her, 'we were just exchanging a recipe! Well, are you coming? We'll miss the grocer!'

On the way back, after having devoted time to the traditional chat with friends, Berthe renewed her campaign.

'You're going to help me,' she decided. 'Yes, both of you, it'll buck you up, yes it will! And I'll ask Pierre-Edouard too, and Jacques and Michèle, to join in.'

'Help you with what?' asked Louise.

'We're going to take up Léonie Malpeyre's idea . . .'

'What?' Mathilde gasped. 'You want to launch a senior citizens' club in Saint-Libéral? You? But you always did your best to see it never happened! What a turn-up!'

'It's true,' added Louise, 'Léonie Malpeyre had organised everything with Julie and Fernande. It was all prepared. And you, you convinced us that it was ridiculous, silly, that it was something for doddery old people! It's true, even Pierre-Edouard joined in poking fun at the project! And now you want to . . . Well I never!'

'Exactly! I was right to oppose it. With Léonie, Julie and Fernande, it was a club for old women! And I don't want anything like that!'

'But she was younger than me by almost ten years!' Mathilde reminded her, amazed at her sister-in-law's nerve.

'With them, it would have been an old folks' club,' repeated Berthe. 'The proof is Julie and Fernande are dead and Léonie is senile!' she added completely unconvincingly. 'Fine, may their souls rest in peace. We'll revive the idea and arrange it so that Yvette is in the chair. That's the important thing! You see, that will force her to stir herself, to make plans, to organise excursions, visits to museums or châteaux, card sessions or knitting competitions, all those silly things, you know!'

'And what if she refuses?' ventured Louise.

'If we manage it properly she won't refuse,' Berthe was sure. 'First I'll begin by asking a favour of her, because that will drag her out of the dumps . . .'

'A favour?' persisted Mathilde.

'Yes. I don't have a car any more, and anyway I don't want to drive. On the other hand it's a bore and it tires me out taking the train when I go to Paris. Yvette has a car and she's a good driver, so . . .'

'And if she refuses?' reiterated Louise.

'Then we'll have to change our tactics until she agrees! But you're going to help me convince her that I must go to Paris at the end of the month, without fail!'

'Is it true? Do you really need to go there?' asked Mathilde, impressed by her sister-in-law's confidence.

'No, I have nothing to do there. And to be quite frank with you, the car tires me more than the train, but don't tell Yvette that!'

Yvette was not deceived for one moment. She understood immediately that the entire Vialhe household had decided to support her at whatever cost.

Her first reaction was to protest, to tell them that she had the right to remain imprisoned by her grief. And if she wished to bear it alone, nobody should interfere. But the whole family's ploy was so heart-warming, so comforting, that she gave in, whilst pretending to see nothing so as not to embarrass anyone. She played the game and thus allowed her circle to share her burden, to help her carry it; she did not off-load it on to them, but it nevertheless seemed lighter, less painful to bear.

And little by little the game became a reality. Although she was secretly convinced that Berthe had no reason to go to

Paris, she agreed to get her DS out of the garage and set off in the direction of Limoges. Attentive to every detail, Berthe made sure that they took Saint-Yrieix road and did not rejoin the RN 20 before Limoges. In this way they avoided passing the place where Louis had killed himself several weeks earlier.

It was on their return, after three days spent in Paris, where Berthe, helped by Colette and Chantal, walked her from restaurant to boutique and from department store to museum, that Yvette agreed to become the advocate, and most importantly, the organiser, of this senior citizens' club which it seemed was needed in Saint-Libéral.

'You understand, everyone feels the same, you can't refuse!' maintained Berthe. 'You can't refuse, in memory of Léon . . .'

'In memory of Léon?'

'Yes. He was a very good mayor for almost thirty years and in very difficult times. So now you must do your bit to carry on after him . . . Anyway, if he were here, that's what he'd be telling you to do!'

'Yes, maybe . . .'

'And if you want my opinion,' continued Berthe hypocritically, "senior citizens' club" isn't a very nice name, it smells of mothballs, it smacks of an old folks' home . . . If I were you, I'd call it something different. For instance . . . I don't know. The Léon Dupeuch Association . . . That has a fine ring to it, doesn't it? In any case it would be logical, because we'll really need a big room to meet in and it seems to me that the château has plenty of those . . .'

'You've worked it all out, haven't you?'

'No, not all of it. For example, I haven't prepared for the fact that you might refuse. If you'd said no, there wouldn't have been much else to be done for you . . .'

Yvette became chairwoman of the Léon Dupeuch Association two months later. Almost forty-five people from the village joined enthusiastically, happy to get together, looking forward to outings, excursions, meetings, games and meals.

If Jacques, as mayor, was pleased to see the village a little more animated, he did not cruelly draw attention to the fact that there were not enough young people in Saint-Libéral to form a football team, but the over-sixties could gather by the four dozen to fill their spare time ... And even then they weren't all there, far from it!

Although she was beginning to get to know him, Béatrice was still amazed by some of Dominique's reactions. So she quickly noticed that he would not tolerate work being poorly executed by the agricultural staff. No deed was too small to escape his criticism if it concerned the land, the animals or the various experimental plantations for which he was responsible.

For example, one morning she had seen him vault over the bars of a pen, where two mulattos were unsuccessfully trying to control a three-hundred-kilo steer needing treatment against parasites.

Swearing like a trooper, he had sprung in front of the animal. Then, with his thumb and forefinger pinched in the bullock's nose, the other hand on its horn, he had subdued it and immobilised it in a corner, then had called to the two men:

'And now get a move on! Are you going to pull that head rope tight, or do damn all? I'm not going to hold on for ten years! That injection, is it coming? Have to do it all myself here!'

On another occasion, when visiting a cowshed with him, she had witnessed one of his more memorable tantrums. A cow was lying down, labouring to the limits of her strength, legs outstretched with the effort, in the process of calving. Or more accurately, in the process of trying, for her bulging, crazed eyes and her hoarse breathing showed how badly things were going.

Gripping a shiny, mucus-covered rope which disappeared beneath the animal's tail, two men were trying to extricate the calf. Surprised, for this was the first time she had witnessed such a scene, Béatrice had not at first understood what Dominique had shouted to her as he stripped to the waist.

'I bet you they haven't even checked!'

Then everything had happened very fast.

'Did you examine her internally before pulling like crazy?'

164

'Well, no, boss. Usually you pull and it comes of its own accord. The calf's big, that's the trouble!'

'For heaven's sake stop!' he had yelled.

On his knees in the soiled straw, he had plunged his arm into the animal, felt around, assessed the condition and position of the calf.

'Bloody imbeciles! You deserve to have *your* guts pulled out like that! And when I say your guts . . .'

'Why's that, boss?'

'Shut your face! The calf has its head folded back on itself, so you could pull forever!'

'Well, we saw the hoof sticking out a bit and as it didn't keep coming . . .'

'Idiots!'

His face contorted with effort, he had inserted his arm still further. And cursing them all the while, he had begun to push the calf back, to manipulate the neck into a normal position.

'And I'll knock the block off anyone who pulls before I tell him to!' he had threatened. 'My God, this is difficult . . . I can't manage it! Ah? Ah, yes I can! That's it! Pull, now. Not so hard, by God! They're cretins, these guys! There, gently. That's fine.'

And before Béatrice's fascinated eyes, more accustomed to childbirth than calving, the calf slid softly onto the bed of litter.

'And it isn't even big!' Dominique had ascertained as he cleaned his chest and arms with a handful of straw. 'Has nobody ever told you that you should never pull without knowing what's what?'

'Well, no, boss. We don't know much about it . . . That's what you're here for, after all!' one of the men had said with a good-natured laugh.

'These fellows drive me crazy!' he had shouted. But his temper had now cooled and he had politely asked for a bucket of water to wash himself.

After that performance Béatrice was no longer surprised when she saw him return to the bungalow covered in mud or dust. So that Friday afternoon, as Dominique and she sped down the track towards Route Nationale 2 which would lead them to Cayenne, Béatrice was not disconcerted when he suddenly stopped the Landrover on the edge of a field. Not far from them, rumbling smoothly, a huge John Deer pulling a three-share plough was opening furrows in the red soil.

'For God's sake tell me it's not true!' he muttered as he jumped from the vehicle. 'No, no, who's the bloody moron at the wheel?' He turned round, calling her to witness it: 'Do you see what I see?'

'Er . . . No,' she admitted. But she already suspected that her errands in Cayenne were in jeopardy, at least for the morning.

'But don't you notice anything?' he said as he took off his shoes. He dispatched his loafers to the back of the car, seized his boots and pulled them on. 'That fellow's ploughing without fixing the plough properly,' he explained as he stepped onto the turned strip and marched to the front of the tractor.

'Stop!' he yelled at the driver as soon as he drew level with him. 'Now come on, what sort of shambles do you think this is? Have you had a look at what you're doing, eh? What kind of work is this?'

'Well, it's ploughing, boss! It's going on fine!'

'Are you serious? So it doesn't worry you that you're ploughing three furrows thirty centimetres deep in one direction and fifteen deep in the other! And what's more the widths are all over the place! Now come on, it looks like a roller-coaster! You're not on a collective farm here, where anything goes! Come down from there!'

'Bah, it doesn't matter, boss!' said the driver, jumping onto the ploughed land. 'It's good soil, it'll grow fine crops! For sure, believe me!' he asserted with a broad smile.

'Matter! It matters to me! I don't like sloppy work, I'm paid to see it doesn't happen! Go on, get out your tool box . . . It won't take me long,' he reassured Béatrice who had just joined him, walking carefully across the stubble: she had no boots and did not want to spoil her town shoes. She smiled resignedly, for she already knew that he was going to get his hands covered in grease. Doubtless he would also dirty his trousers and shirt, and possibly even make a few serious tears in them!

'You've got some overalls in the car, do you want them?' she suggested.

He considered the work to be done, and shook his head.

'No it's not worth it, it'll only take five minutes,' he assured her. 'And you,' he said to the driver, 'hold that nut tight so that I can loosen the regulator. No, no! Not with that 22 spanner, it's at least 28! And you should be interested in learning how to adjust the hydraulic lifting system and how to use it! It's not just there for ornament, this lever! Nor to hang your lunch bag on!'

He busied himself with it for a few moments, judged it correctly adjusted, and climbed on to the tractor.

'Must test it . . .' he explained to Beatrice.

'Fine,' she agreed, 'I'll wait for you in the car.'

'No, stay there! You'll see the difference! Look what a properly balanced plough can produce!'

He engaged the gears, manipulated the hydraulic lifting system and started it rolling . . . He covered a dozen metres, made a face and stopped.

'It's not quite right,' he said, looking at his workmanship. 'Oh, it won't take much. The spanner!' he called to the driver, who was waiting patiently, sitting in the shade and smoking a small, bent-looking, foul-smelling, black cigar.

It was only after a further ten minutes that he considered himself satisfied. Then, for the sheer pleasure of ploughing, for the joy of leaving perfectly regular furrows in his wake in straight, shining, beautiful rows, he made three further trips up and down. He was almost sorry to return to Béatrice, who was reading in the car while she waited.

'It took a little time, but it was worth the trouble,' he assured her.

'A little time? That's your opinion!' she said, looking at her watch. 'It was only an hour and a half! Well, luckily I've got a good book!' she smiled, as she closed the latest historical novel by Troyat.

She saw that he was looking ashamed of himself, especially as he was so dirty that a return to the bungalow was imperative. 'It doesn't matter,' she comforted him, stroking his cheek with the back of her hand. 'You go and get changed.

We'll go into town this afternoon. Or tomorrow . . .' she added.

Wisely, she realised that he could not help stopping the car if he chanced to notice some work which required him to intervene.

It was after returning from Cayenne, late in the evening, that Béatrice wanted to know. She wished to understand. Already bathed and refreshed, she had slipped under the mosquito net. She waited until he came out of the shower and called out:

'You'll really have to explain it to me, one day . . .'

'What's that?'

'Why you chose this profession?'

'You're joking?' he suggested, pouring himself a measure of rum punch which he diluted with sparkling water. 'Why I chose this profession? Because I like it! I even love certain aspects of it. But you're well aware of that! So you're teasing me?'

'Not at all. You know, I've been watching what you're doing, it'll be about ten months we've been here, that gives me time to notice things, doesn't it?'

'Of course. And so, did you come to the conclusion that I wasn't enjoying what I was doing?'

'No way! But I did notice that you're only really happy when you're hands on!'

'Explain.'

'It's obvious, isn't it? Well, tell me if I'm wrong: your job is to supervise the experiments, do the tests, analyses, reports, is that right?'

'Yes, what's the problem?'

'I haven't got one. It's you I'm talking about. I'll say it again, you're only really happy when you're on the land, like this morning on your machine. I saw you when you were ploughing; if I didn't know you well, it would almost have made me jealous!'

'But are you cray or what?' he said, lifting the mosquito net to see her better. He took the opportunity to stroke her breasts, and she gently slapped his fingers.

'Let down the net, I'll be eaten alive! That's exactly it, while you were ploughing, not only did you completely forget me, but it was almost as if you were involved with a woman!' she teased. 'To cut it short, I'm just trying to tell you that I'm worried,' she said, becoming serious again.

'But what's got into you?'

'We're going back to France in two months' time and you still don't know where your employers will be sending you. So, suppose they stick you in a purely administrative area, or even a laboratory, for example, what would you do?'

'I'd tell them to take two running jumps!'

'I expect you would. You need to be on the land, don't you?' she asked again.

'Yes.'

'So why aren't you working for yourslf on a farm? On your own farm, for instance?'

He was just taking a drink and she thought he would choke, he gave such a start. Then he let out a great laugh.

'On the farm? At Coste-Roche with Papa? That's the best thing I've heard this evening! No, that's impossible, my dear! For one thing the Vialhes have never succeeded in working together on the same farm! That's how we are, we each have our own ideas. I know it, Papa always said to me he couldn't have stayed long at Saint-Libéral with Grandfather. That's why he and Maman went and moved to Coste-Roche, for peace and quiet. And most of all so that they could be their own masters. And in my grandfather's time, I know that he didn't come back until my great-grandfather, Jean-Edouard, gave him a free hand. So you see why!'

'Possibly. But the main thing I see is that you might become impossible to live with if you happen to find yourself in an office one day!'

'Yes, maybe. But we haven't got to that yet! But tell me,' he asked suddenly, 'would you like to live on a farm?'

'You are fantastic, you know!' she said, smiling. 'What do you think we've been doing for the last ten months? And what's more, here it's not only full of creepy-crawlies and mosquitoes, but the farm and the land don't even belong to you!'

'All right,' he conceded after a few moments' thought. 'But

you know, it's not really the same at all! Here, I have everything that's needed to conduct the experiments properly. I'm not saying that the purse is bottomless, but in the short term the profitability of the trials is not the chief problem. And what's more, here, even if it's often wayward, I have a considerable workforce at my disposal, and for free, at least to me!'

'That doesn't alter the fact that, in spite of your workforce, you're not happy unless you can get your hands dirty!'

'Agreed. And that's the best bit about the job! But it's not the most important part. Here, I'm on a salary and well paid. Thanks to which I can consider supporting a family. And I imagine it'll be the same as long as I'm with Mondiagri or any other company of the same sort.'

'You're trying to say that you'd die of hunger on a proper farm?'

'It would all depend on the farm. Anyway, I don't own one, and I haven't got the means to buy one either! And you know, even supposing – it's an incredible idea – that I set up with my father on the land in Saint-Libéral, it couldn't feed all of us! But I've already told you that.'

'Yes, but you still haven't told me what you'll do if one day you can't get your hands on a cow. Or, like this morning, jump on a tractor and enjoy some ploughing, even if it does mean forgetting me.'

'I haven't the faintest idea,' he spoke flippantly as he slipped under the mosquito net. 'Now while we're waiting for that unlikely day, I know what I'm going to do right away, so that you'll forgive me for forgetting you this morning.'

13

AFTER her painful experience with Gilles, Josyane vowed she would not let herself be fooled by smooth talkers again, especially if they suggested she go round the world with them!

Having burnt her fingers, she remained wisely on the defensive towards the males she steered from atoll to atoll. Although her steadily maintained reserve deterred the unwelcome, it brought her other surprises.

For instance, seeing her unresponsive towards men, a bisexual German woman with wandering hands invited her to share her hut. Another time, a Canadian woman shaped like a grizzly bear made her a direct offer, to 'set up home together' and come and move in with her at Fort Providence, on the shores of the Great Slave Lake! Josyane had not yet come to that.

Although she did not dislike her new way of life, she still found that on some days the loneliness was hard to bear. It was then that she caught herself re-reading all the letters which her parents were now sending regularly. Thanks to them she identified again with the life of the Viahle family in Saint-Libéral. And she realised just how important those ties of blood had become when, two months ago now, her heart sank as she read the first sentence of a letter from her mother:

My dear Jo,
    It is very sad news that I have for you today . . .

Mad with worry, she had immediately prepared herself to learn of the death of her grandfather or grandmother in Saint-Libéral. Her sorrow had almost prevented her from reading on, for she avowed a great love for the old couple who were so indestructible; to fear that this partnership might be broken was awful.

She had therefore felt somewhat ashamed at the relief she experienced shortly afterwards. For although the news was sad, Louis' death affected her less than the one she had dreaded. Not that she had ever disliked her cousin, but he was much older than her and did not live in Saint-Libéral. Besides, she had not seen him for years.

On the other hand, like Jean, she had been distressed to think of her Great-aunt Yvette, and was almost cross with herself for being so far away and unable to express all her affection. She had sent her a few lines, fearing they would have little effect on her sorrow.

But not all the letters were so tragic. Those from her Grandmother Mathilde for instance, were delightful, full of anecdotes, flavours of the Corrèze, titbits of news which it was nice to know. She spoke of the family, the neighbours, the fields and woods, the little crop of mushrooms brought on by the last rains, the walnuts which were beginning to drop. She also advised caution, rectitude, honesty. In short it was all evocative of times past, with an undercurrent of hope that she would soon be returning . . .

As for those from her Aunt Berthe, they were always full of spice, of advice which was never dogmatic, of humour and even slightly ironic asides on the advantages and disadvantages of celibacy! According to her, it was good to avoid shutting yourself away in solitude which might quickly become a burden. Equally good, after sowing your wild oats, going round the world, trying a little of everything, testing your character and trying your strength, not to forget that youth passes quickly and the time was coming when it would be important not to chop and change any more . . .

Josyane was increasingly convinced of this, and would have asked nothing better than to go and settle down at last in some corner of France. But her savings would not yet permit her to buy a ticket home.

She had been so pleased to find work in the Orohena Tour Agency that she had not even queried her salary, and besides, she had not been in a position to do so. It was low, for her employers reckoned that she was housed and fed by them during each trip. True enough, she had her bed and board on all the atolls the clients visited. By contrast she had to pay an exorbitant price to rent a hut, and also to feed herself, when she was staying in Papeete between two excursions; as a result there was not much left at the end of the month. She was therefore eyeing the two cameras more frequently, for selling them would probably allow her to fly off to France, so long as she did not let them go to the first Chinaman to come along!

On this particular day, resting between two waves of tourists, she was actually calculating the price she might get for them when someone knocked on the door. Thinking that her young Tahitian neighbour was making her customary visit – the teenager came for a chat as soon as she knew she was home – Josyane opened the door and almost bumped into a Bronica, the most beautiful camera in existence!

That gem is worth a fortune! she thought, before even looking at its owner. Then she realised there was a man, that he had a camera, and was immediately on her guard. The ghost of Gilles walked again!

'Are you Josyane Fleyssac?' asked the visitor.

She observed him without replying, found him very attractive, and decided to be still more cautious.

This fellow looks far too much like Paul Newman to be honest, she thought, without lowering her eyes. She was not going to let herself be influenced by this stranger's piercing blue gaze! She had seen others like it!

'Are you Jo?' he asked again.

'Josyane Fleyssac, yes,' she replied. 'Why?'

'I'm calling on behalf of your sister . . .'

This was increasingly incredible, and therefore dangerous. 'Which one?'

'Chantal, the one who works at Claire Diamond . . .'

'Chantal?' she murmured.

She suddenly felt very embarrassed, for there were tears in her eyes as she thought of her sister. She had not seen her for years and had not even written to her, except for two or three very bland postcards. Naturally she had news of her via Aunt Berthe, but it was overwhelming to discover that her sister was thinking of her to the extent of sending a messenger.

'A letter?' she stammered, forcing a smile to cover her disquiet.

'Yes,' he said, fumbling in his camera bag. She noticed an assortment of lenses, a Pentax, some boxes of film and the letter.

'I left Roissy airport last night,' he explained, holding out the envelope. 'With all the time changes, it's a dreadfully long journey!'

'Twenty-one hours, with a stopover in San Francisco,' she heard herself replying as she broke open the missive. 'Excuse me.'

'Of course.'

She sensed that he was watching her and was embarrassed yet again, for she had the feeling she was making a spectacle of herself.

'Sit down,' she suggested. 'And help yourself,' she said, giving him a glass and pointing out the bottle of fruit juice which was on the table. She needed him to stop watching her so that she could read in peace. She made sure he was no longer paying attention, and read:

My dear Jo,
  According to Aunt Berthe, you're too hard up to return to the fold and too much a Vialhe to ask for help. Maybe Aunt Berthe is wrong, but I'd be surprised if she were, she has a nose for things, even at a distance. So, if you're fed up with playing the Tahitian maiden and dancing the tamouré, don't hesitate to cash the enclosed cheque. It will cover the journey. And don't be so stupid as to refuse. You can pay me back later. Try to be there for Dominique's wedding, we must make sure he celebrates it properly! See you soon.
  Love and kisses,
  Chantal.

P. S. Christian is an old friend, nothing more. I told him you could show him the good areas to get in the can. But don't bother if it's a nuisance, or if you really think he's an ugly pain in the neck.

Amazed, biting her lips so as not to cry for joy, she took the cheque out of the envelope. It was large enough to allow her to leave as soon as she chose. She noticed that her visitor was openly observing her, thought he looked mocking, and almost took a swipe at him.

But she was suddenly so relieved, so happy at the thought of her impending departure, that she crossed the three paces separating them and kissed him on both cheeks.

'To thank the postman! I'm so happy!' she gave as her excuse.

'So it would seem.'

'Do you know what was in the letter?'

'Some of it. From what your sister said, you must have been starting to find it a long haul. I have the impression that she's not far off the mark!'

'No, she's right.'

'At first sight it's hardly tough going here.' he said, indicating the garden full of flowers and birds.

'At first, no,' she admitted. 'And then . . . and then don't let's talk about it!' she decided. 'Are you a photographer?' she asked, suddenly remembering that she ought to be careful.

'Yes. That's why I'm here. I have an assignment to do on Mururoa. But beforehand I have time to cast an eye over Tahiti and a few of the atolls. They're worth seeing, aren't they? Your sister said you could maybe . . .'

'Of course. But it all depends what you want to see and what you can afford. Anyway, how do you know Chantal?'

'I take fashion photos too, I do everything!'

'Even porn I bet, you look the type!' she challenged him, remembering that Gilles had once told her it paid well. She had then advised him in no uncertain terms not to count on her as a model!

'No, not porn,' he said, amused. 'It's funny, your sister warned me, but you caught me out! Yes, she said: "Watch out; of the three of us, Jo's the one who's quickest on the draw; like Butch Cassidy! You never know what she's going to come out with, or when!" '

'Do you know Gilles Martin?'

'No. Why, should I?'

'He's a photographer.'

'Which agency?'

'None, he works independently.'

'Gilles Martin?' he repeated. 'No, never heard of him. Although I've been almost fifteen years in the business, I don't think . . .'

'That doesn't surprise me, he's useless!'

'Well, if he's useless . . .'

'You just said that you've been a photographer for fifteen years?' she persisted.

She estimated that he must be older than he looked, and it was therefore important to be even more wary. For if, as well as looking like Paul Newman, he misled people about his age, he could be real trouble!

'Yes, I began in 1960, I was eighteen.'

'That's exactly what I was thinking . . .'

'Oh, right? I look that ancient, do I?'

'No, not at all! Well, yes! I mean . . . it doesn't matter. Eighteen, you say?'

'Yes, during the Algerian War. I enlisted. I was in the Army Film Unit. Photographer for the magazine *Le Bled*. I'm not making it up! Impressive, eh?' he joked.

'Well, in 1960 I was much younger.'

'I know. Your sister told me you're younger than her.'

'Oh, right. So Christian's your first name?'

'Yes, Christian Leyrac.'

'May I invite you to dinner? I owe you that much for the letter. We'll discuss what you want to see, okay?'

'Okay.'

'Which hotel are you at?'

'At the Taharaa.'

'Is that all? Every luxury!'

'What's the problem? My agency's paying!'

'So you must be a real photographer,' she decided. She examined him, nodded her head, realised that he wouldn't understand a thing she was about to say, but remarked all the same:

'Yes, a real photographer, that'll be a nice change!'

Jacques made sure that the ink had properly dried, closed the Civil Register and shrugged resignedly. There were periods like this when everything conspired to undermine your morale.

For one thing his back was hurting, and even though that had become the norm it did not relieve the pain.

Then, yesterday evening, he had again clashed violently with Peyrafaure and those on the council who pretended not to understand that the village lacked money. He had nothing against them wanting to liven Saint-Libéral up a little, but he could not keep up with their schemes. For, following the tennis court, they were now proposing to compete with Ayen and create a holiday village on the plateau, no less.

In fact, Jacques knew for certain that Peyrafaure had his eye on his post as mayor. He was proposing an abundance of projects simply in order to be able to say, when the moment came: 'I myself suggested this and that which would have roused the community from its stupor, Vialhe rejected everything, he's incompetent!'

That loudmouth Peyrafaure is forgetting just one thing: the elections don't take place for another two years, and between now and then . . . And after all, the way things are going, there won't be many electors left! he thought, leafing through the Civil Register.

For it was not Peyrafaure and his babblings which worried him, nor his supporters; all of them would one day see that the Vialhes still had some backing and plenty of friends! No, the time had not come for Peyrafaure to don the sash of office. But what did it matter who was mayor if you were managing a cemetery!

That was the root of the problem. For the second time since the beginning of November, he had returned from escorting one of his electors to the grave. Two deaths in less than a fortnight, nine since the beginning of the year, without even counting poor Louis. It was getting frightening, worrying. And all the more so because there was not a single birth to inscribe in the register, and would not be in the whole of 1975. Given this situation, he looked a bit silly, Peyrafaure, with his tennis court and holiday village!

'He'd do better to start a funeral parlour, the fool!' he muttered as he rose.

177

He saw that his sister was regarding him with incomprehension.

'Don't worry, I'm rambling out loud!' he said.

Since her husband, who held the title of secretary, could not be there all the time on account of the twelve children attending the school, Mauricette acted as town clerk. She did not earn a sou for it, but found it more interesting to spend her time filling in a variety of administrative bumf or answering the telephone than to waste it by staying at home in front of the television. She dreaded inactivity and boredom in equal measures.

'What's the matter with you?' she asked. 'Is it your back?'

'Among other things. But if that were all! No, what gets me down is spending my life walking behind the hearse! I'm fed up with it, do you understand?'

'Of course, but maybe things will change!'

He nearly retorted roundly that she didn't know what she was talking about! That on the contrary, all the signs were that the situation would soon deteriorate, and if it continued in the same way, Saint-Libéral would be a ghost village in twenty years time! To tell her he was exasperated by the haughty indifference with which the public authorities left villages like Saint-Libéral to wither away, all over France! To share with her the bitterness which gripped him each time he had to write: *Deceased, on the* . . . beside the name of a friend, a neighbour, an old acquaintance! To admit to her just how tired and demoralised he was, overseeing a community where the only really viable activity was the senior citizens' club! But he remained silent, for he did not want to spoil his sister's happiness.

During the last week, Mauricette had regained her *joie de vivre*, and so had Jean-Pierre. Their happiness since Josyane had announced her return was a delight to see. That was really good news for the whole family. It had elicited a gentle laugh from Berthe, lent Mathilde new energy, given Pierre-Edouard the excuse to pour himself a small glass of plum brandy, made Louise say that she knew young Jo would come back one day and roused Yvette to a real smile. A smile reaching her eyes which, for an instant, brought a little balm to the scar she bore on her heart.

'Yes, yes, maybe things will change,' he said, noticing once more just how much younger his sister looked.

'That reminds me,' she said, holding out a letter to him. 'You didn't tell me you'd been chasing up the Ayen police: it arrived this morning . . .'

'Ah? They replied?' he said, taking the document. He read it and shrugged: 'You can close the file, like the enquiry . . .'

'Surely that's not what they're saying!'

'No, but it comes to the same . . .'

'Did you write to them?'

'No, but I met the new inspector, the one responsible for the whole sector. He was at Objat the other day when Chastang received his Order of Merit for Agriculture. He was preening himself and boasting of all the cases he and his colleagues had chalked up for speeding or careless driving. You know, they had a special campaign on throughout the département. The great buffoon was really pleased to have trapped I don't know how many guys on the N89 road, and even on the 901!'

'I know,' she agreed. 'Marie-Louise Vergne got caught coming back from Terrasson: it made her really sick!'

'Exactly, he was irritating me, the fat sheep! So I told him that handing out fines was simpler and less tiring than finding church robbers!'

'You said it to him just like that?'

'Why shouldn't I! And can you imagine it, that nitwit wasn't even aware of what had happened! He listened to me, believe you me! The funny thing was, he didn't even know who I was. The sergeant from Ayen was killing himself laughing! He must have got a bawling-out later on. That'll be why he thought he'd better write. But you can close the file since it says *The enquiry is continuing* – It's hopeless, we'll never see poor old Saint Eutrope again!'

'Maman just can't accept that.'

'I know. But as we're talking of her, do you think she suspects anything?' he asked.

'About the wedding?'

'Yes. Do you think she's fooled?'

The closer it came to 20 December, the more afraid he was that his mother would discover there was to be no religious ceremony. He knew it was the sort of news which could ruin her happiness, and for a long time to come. And he had even written to Dominique conveying this. Not so that he would try to persuade Béatrice differently – he respected her opinion – but to warn him not to put his foot in it in front of his grandparents.

'Maman?' said Mauricette. 'Yes, I think she believes this story of a civil wedding in Paris on the nineteenth and the church one at Draguignan on the twentieth. But Papa, I wouldn't swear to it . . . I get the impression that he knows very well we're doing all we can to prevent either him or Maman being at the wedding!'

In truth, to avoid a fuss and having to explain to his parents why they could not possibly be at the wedding, since the journey was too long and tiring for his father, and therefore dangerous, Jacques had constructed one of those huge lies which would have left him blushing for the rest of his life, if he had not had the excuse of doing it all in a good cause. In collusion with Berthe, whom he really had to confide in as she had every intention of attending the wedding, he had explained that Béatrice had been born in the Midi, at her grandmother's, that the whole family were from there and it was therefore quite natural for her to marry there . . . As for the civil ceremony, since Béatrice was resident in Paris, it was logical to . . .

'Yes,' he said, 'I wouldn't bet my right hand that Papa is swallowing the story . . . I have the feeling that he knows much more about it than he's saying, and that goes for a lot of things!'

'But do you think he'd deny himself the pleasure of setting us straight?'

'No, of course not. But he keeps quiet for Maman's sake; well, that's what I believe.'

As soon as she had her ticket, and her seat booked on the flight on Thursday, 4 December, Josyane began to rediscover the bountiful charms of Tahiti. She no longer felt herself a prisoner, so life there became very pleasant again.

After informing her employers at the Orohena Tour

Agency that she was leaving, she gave herself a few days' holiday. And, without dropping the guard she had sworn to maintain as far as Christian was concerned – this was not the moment to be ensnared by a photographer, even a real one – she agreed to show him the most beautiful parts of Tahiti.

It was on the evening of the second day, when he had invited her to dinner, that she agreed to accompany him to Moorea the next day. It was only ten minutes by plane or an hour by ferry.

'All right, that will let me make a last little pilgrimage, and of course it's so beautiful! But don't count on me after that. You're old enough to explore the other atolls on your own! Anyway, in three days' time it'll be adieu Polynesia for me!'

'I shall be bored!'

'I'd be very surprised! And I thought you were supposed to go to Mururoa.'

'Yes, that's the plan. But I'm waiting for my journalist friend. He's arriving at the end of the week, via Nouméa. So if you drop me tomorrow evening, I'll be at a loose end for three days, and that's the truth!'

'You're kidding! You don't look the sort who gets bored, wherever you might be!'

'I thought I was the sort who took pornographic photos!' he teased.

'Don't change the subject! Joking apart, if it's a girl you're after, you only have to say the word! That sort of person is quickly found in Papeete! And what's more, they love to be of service and give pleasure!'

'That's not what I meant,' he assured her.

'Yeah, that's what you say, but I don't believe a word of it!'

'Are you always as sharp as this?'

'Always!'

'Then I don't believe a word of it either! Anyway, that's your problem. Right, tomorrow we're going across to Moorea?'

'Yes, you'll see, it's worth the trip. Having said that it's like all the islands; you soon end up being bored by them.'

'Not as good as the Corrèze, eh?'

'No comparison,' she said with a shrug, 'and why do you say that, anyway?'

'Because of Chantal. She talks non-stop about that God-forsaken dump!'

'It's not a dump!' She cut in drily. She suddenly realised that he was teasing her, and smiled. 'It amuses you to make me lose my temper?'

'Aha! It's the same with Chantal; on that subject you can set her off in a trice, it's a real treat.'

'Do you know it?'

'What?'

'The Corrèze?'

'No. Well, yes, I've had to drive through, like everyone. But I must admit that I didn't notice anything special. Except perhaps that there are lots of bends!'

'You're a real berk, if that's all you're capable of remembering!' she shrugged dismissively.

'Don't get annoyed,' he said, placing his hand on hers, 'I was joking. I've promised myself I'll explore your region as soon as I can. Do you know why?'

'Because Chantal talked to you about it.'

'Yes, but not only that. Now I'm not joking when I tell you this next bit. My great-grandfather was born in the Brive area, but I don't know where.'

'Ah, that's where the name Leyrac comes from, then?'

'Probably. My mother told me that he was supposed to have owned a tiny farm south of Brive, not far from the River Lot. She didn't know anything else about it. She had that from my paternal grandfather.'

'And you've never tried to find out any more?'

'Well, no. I have to admit it's not that simple,' he said evasively.

She saw that he was hesitant about speaking, as if he feared to bore her with family stories.

'Come on then, tell me! That is, if you want to. After all, it's a free country! We can just as well talk about cooking or photography!'

'Oh, there's no secret,' he said. 'I don't know very much, because there's no one left to tell me about it, that's all.'

'Oh, I see . . .'

'Yes, my mother died five years ago, and she was the only one left who knew anything.'

'And your father?' she ventured to ask.

'He died in Dachau, in July '44.'

'Oh! I'm so sorry,' she murmured, placing her hand in turn on his. She drew it away as if she had burned herself: 'Excuse me,' she added.

'It's not your fault! I was just explaining. If he had lived, I'd have known where my ancestor came from. All my mother told me was that he went off to Chile, in the 1870s I believe. To seek his fortune! Can you imagine it? They had big ideas, those fellows then! But it worked! To prove it, it seems he ended up owning a hacienda of I don't know how many thousands of hectares! And he'd also earned a fair bit by going up to work on the Panama Canal! In short, that allowed him to pay for my grandfather's education. He was born out there. He came to France and left again as a qualified agricultural engineer, to take charge of the estate.'

'Oh, him as well!'

'Why him as well?'

'Because one of my cousins is an ag type, that's all. But why are you here, then? You should be Chilean!'

'Logically, yes. But would you believe it, my grandfather wanted to return to France to take part in the war in 1914! I'm telling you, they had grand ideas, those old people! He could have stayed out of trouble on his hacienda, but no: at the first shot from the guns, he reappeared! With my grandmother in tow. He set her up in Bordeaux and left to enlist, at the age of forty-two!'

'Maybe he knew my grandfather from Saint-Libéral,' she smiled. 'He served right through the war too. And then?'

'My father was born in 1915. My grandmother died of the Spanish 'flu, in 1918, in Bordeaux. As I understand it, my grandfather found a job as steward of some vineyard, one of the best vintages, I don't know where. That's it.'

'And he didn't leave anything behind, any documents?'

'No. I have to say he didn't like it much when my mother remarried in '48. He broke off all connection with her . . . Anyway, with my mother and her husband, we were living in

Paris and he was in Bordeaux! He died in 1950, I was eight and I hardly remember it. Pity, he could at least have told me which corner of the Corrèze the Leyracs came from! And my father, too, would have told me . . .'

'It's funny, all that,' she murmured. 'Oh, I beg you pardon!' she continued. 'That's not what I meant.'

'I know,' he reassured her.

'Yes, I meant to say: it's strange, families. We, on the Vialhe side, can trace our ancestors back through several centuries. We're all from the same area. On my father's side it's almost the same. When I'm over there, I'm really at home, on our land. What I'm saying is a bit pretentious, but it's true, whereas you . . .'

'Yes, but it's no big deal! I was born in Paris, like my mother, as for the rest . . . I certainly don't lose any sleep over it! But all the same, it's interesting that we're here in Papeete, in the French Antipodes, busy discussing the area the Leyracs come from, which I don't even know!'

Engrossed in her happiness at returning to France, Josyane decided that Christian's absence at Faaa airport was of no importance. Besides she really had done everything to prevent him feeling obliged to come and say goodbye before she left.

Obviously it was a little remiss on his part. He could at least have stirred himself to thank her once more for having introduced him to Tahiti and Moorea much better than he could have done it by himself. But his absence proved that he was just the creep she had thought, and that she had been right to mistrust him. Her instinct had not betrayed her; all was well.

Having checked in her baggage, she turned towards the boarding gate and was about to go through when she changed her mind. After all, maybe he hadn't been able to find a taxi?

But no, that was silly. He had hired a car. So he had no excuse. She looked at the huge clock in the hall, hesitated, then smiled suddenly as she spied him coming towards her with a fistful of shell necklaces.

'According to what I've been told, that's the custom here, when someone leaves!' he said, placing the garlands around her neck.

'Yes, that's the custom,' she murmured, blushing.

She was furious with herself. Furious for having waited for him and especially about the fuss he was making which, she felt, must be noticed by all the people there.

'It was high time,' she forced herself to say, 'I was just going to go through passport control.'

'I would have regretted it for the rest of my life!' he said, camping it up. 'No, but joking apart, I hate long goodbyes. So I always arrive at the last moment. Even if it means lying in wait in a corner and launching myself on my quarry at the last second!' he added, laughing.

'You're quite capable of doing a thing like that! But this really is the last minute! Listen: they're calling us for boarding.'

'Very good. But you'll still give me a kiss?' She did not have time to move and he placed a kiss on each cheek: 'And thank you again for the guided tour, it was perfect. Talking of which, if I come to the Corrèze and you happen to be there, will you act as my guide again? Yes?'

'In the Corrèze?' she murmured. 'If I'm there? Okay.' She fingered the necklaces adorning her: 'And thank you for these,' she said.

She gave a little wave of her hand, and walked away without looking back.

14

'DON'T you catch cold on me!' warned Pierre-Edouard, lifting his nose out of his newspaper. He made sure Mathilde was wrapping up warmly before going out to feed the ducks and geese, and called to Louise: 'And you too, wrap up well! My God! It's cold this morning, the pond is covered in ice. You're going to get frozen, both of you!'

'Don't worry so! We're not made of sugar!' Louise reassured him.

'Wrap up warm, I tell you!' he persisted. 'What an idea, to have such a flock to feed up!'

'Oh stop it! You don't say that when you take seconds of confit de canard or foie gras! Even though you're not allowed either because of your cholesterol!' said Mathilde, grasping the bucket of steeped maize which was warming not far from the hearth.

'The doctor's an ass!' he declared, immersing himself once more in his reading.

He waited until the two women had gone out, and glanced towards Berthe. Absorbed in doing her crossword puzzle, she did not seem to have heard him. That annoyed him and aggravated his ill humour. He had been very low for some time.

To begin with he had a cold, and Doctor Martel had forbidden him to go out, and also to smoke! He took no notice of that and, to get some peace and not hear the women's scolding, he went out in the courtyard whenever he felt the urge to smoke a pipe.

But the fact that he was unable to take his daily walk annoyed him a great deal. He missed his short hour of exercise, as well as the conversations with any neighbour he met and especially the confidences exchanged with Berthe. But she was complying with Doctor Martel's orders, and had refused to accompany him for three weeks now. It was infuriating, for he did indeed feel rather too weak to venture all alone up the steep path to the plateau.

'The doctor's an ass!' he repeated, impatiently folding his newspaper. He threw it on the table, immediately in front of his sister: 'Do you hear what I say? The doctor's an ass!'

'Yes, and so what? You say that twenty times a day. That won't start him braying, luckily!'

'And, what's more, all of you, you treat me like an ass too!' he shouted, getting up. He moved over to the window, checked that Mathilde and Louise were indeed in the barn, busy force-feeding the ducks: 'Like an ass! Absolutely! Are you listening to me, eh?'

For it was that in particular which was spoiling his temper; the near-certainty that something was being hidden from him, that someone was trying to deceive him.

It was Jacques and Mauricette especially who had started him thinking. Both of them were too eager to divert certain topics of conversation, to dodge his questions. At the same time they were also almost too cheery to be true. Certainly they had every reason to be happy. First little Jo was expected daily, and Dominique and his fiancée would be there in a week.

Despite that, Pierre-Edouard felt there was something mysterious going on, and he did not like it. Even Yvette seemed to have joined in hoodwinking him. She was feeling better, Yvette, that was very good: she had returned to the château, and spent a lot of time on the Friends of Léon Dupeuch. Yes, she was getting better. But that was no excuse for siding with those who wanted to take him for a ride. For he was almost certain that they were trying to fool him. And the worst of it was that even Berthe had gone over to the enemy, the guardians of the secret!

'I was speaking to you,' he said, seeing that she had returned to her crossword. 'Why do you take me for an ass?'

She sighed, smiled, and lit a cigarette.

'You know, you're a dreadful bore!' she said. 'Come on, make the most of my smoking to fill a little pipe, Mathilde won't be back for a while.'

'What a stupid idea, all those animals to force-feed! Now you answer me, right? I know you're hiding something from me. Is it so serious?' he asked as he lit his pipe. 'Is it so serious? Answer me, for God's sake!'

'No, no, it's not serious! That's exactly why I didn't tell you anything . . .'

'I really don't like that! Not at all! Who's got problems? Young Jo? She's not coming back? She's set off again for Patagonia or somewhere?'

'Not at all, she's landing tomorrow evening at Roissy.'

'So she's expecting a baby and the father has run off, is that it?'

'My poor Pierre,' she said, bursting into laughter, 'for donkey's years young people have only had the children they want! Even in my time all you needed was a bit of skill . . . So think of it now, them with their pill! No, she's not pregnant. Well, I don't think so. No, that's not it. All right then, it's not you they're trying to protect, it's Mathilde.'

'Mathilde? Come on then, it's that serious?'

'Mmm, it all depends how important you think these things are . . .'

'Right then, tell me straight out, that's enough beating about the bush!'

'It's to do with the young people's wedding. It's this – they're only getting married at the registry office, that's all.'

'Ah, I see,' he said, nodding his head. He meditated for a while, moved nearer to the fire to spit: 'That's why you don't want us to go to it, I understand! So okay, you're right. Mathilde mustn't know, it would depress her too much! And what about Louise?'

'The same, she doesn't know.'

'All right. Let's hope it lasts. But why are they doing that, the young people? Does it embarrass them to go into a church?'

'The girl doesn't believe in it, you can't force her!'

'Of course not,' he murmured. 'But Mathilde absolutely mustn't find out that they're marrying like heathens. It would spoil all her pleasure, you understand?'

'You're telling me, why do you think we're taking so much trouble to keep it from her!'

189

'True, true. But me, you could have told me!'

'Don't pretend it doesn't hurt you a bit!'

'Well yes,' he admitted, 'but all the same, I'd have preferred to know.'

It was true. Of course he was saddened to discover that his eldest grandson was not following in the Vialhe tradition. This held that men should go to church at least twice a year, celebrate their first Communion there, marry there, have their children baptised and be buried there. Everyone had abided by this until now, and with good grace. And here for the first time was a Vialhe breaking with custom; it was distressing. Despite that, he did feel in a better mood after his sister had told him. He considered he still had the right, and even the duty, to know everything concerning his family, even if it was not always very good for his heart . . . He drew a last puff, tapped his pipe on the top of the andiron, and subsided onto the settle.

'While you're at it, have you anything else to tell me?' he continued.

'No, isn't that enough for you?'

'Yes, it is.' He reflected, and then suddenly realised: 'But then, as I understand it, you're only going to Paris, not to the Midi?'

'Yes. Anyway, there's nothing happening in the Midi. When we talked of Draguignan, it was because that would be too long a journey for you. Paris is too near, you'd have wanted to go there, and as there'll only be a civil ceremony . . .'

'Well, well, you're a fine pack of liars! Oh, you villains! But who had the idea of this wedding miles away?'

'Jacques and Mauricette . . .'

'I see. Ye Gods! Such big liars, they get that from their mother! It's the Dupeuch side coming out! Yes it is! Léon was like that too. Ooh, the wretches! Right, not a word, Mathilde's coming,' he said, hearing the sound of feet on the steps outside.

'You were right, it's terribly cold,' she said as she came in. She shook herself, took off her coat and moved over to the fire to warm her hands. 'You, you've been smoking,' she said abruptly.

'Me? No, no! I give you my word! It was Berthe. Eh, it was you, wasn't it Berthe?'

'You know very well that Doctor Martel forbade it!'

'Martel is an ass,' he cut in.

He winked at Berthe and began to laugh quietly.

It was always with a certain regret, an underlying sadness, that Dominique left his work in progress. Already in the Sahara, fifteen months earlier, it was with a feeling of frustration that he had left to others the observation of his experiments and the trouble of continuing them properly. And yet over there he had had the time to watch the development of the crops and the growth of a flock, to test the validity of his plans, the accuracy of his predictions. He had been able to establish that his work was useful. But here, in Guyana, he had hardly had time to get used to the climate, the way of life, the mentality of the inhabitants. As for getting to know the land, its reactions and capabilities, it was impossible to discover its secrets in twelve months; he had barely even glimpsed them. It was annoying.

'You must understand, I do like to see the results of my work,' he explained to Béatrice whilst helping her pack. 'It's true, isn't it? What's the good of sowing if you can't reap it! And that's what's happening. What's more, my successor may chuck all my work away!'

'All the same, you need to sort out what you want,' she said. 'I don't think two days have passed without me hearing you moaning about this wretched country, the rain, the mud, the creepy-crawlies, just about everything!'

'Granted, I must say I've adjusted pretty badly to this dump,' he admitted. 'But you, I take my hat off to you! I've never heard you complain!'

'You know, after the bush clinic where I was working in Upper Volta, this is paradise!'

'So you've often told me. Well I hope there's a less humid paradise than this one waiting for us!'

'It'll soon be sorted out now.'

'Let's hope so!' he sighed.

That too did not improve his temper. He had a horror of

uncertainty. For, despite his letters to Mondiagri's Paris office, it was still impossible to find out where he was to be sent. And as the firm had branches throughout the world, apart from the Eastern Bloc . . .

'They'll have to tell you something, won't they?' she said.

'Of course. But I've already explained to you, the annoying thing about these big companies is that they feel obliged to use a system which softens up the managers, by leaving them to stew without knowing where they're going! Okay, we're well paid, but that's not my style! And if they rub me up the wrong way any longer, they'll see what a Vialhe temper is like!'

'You know, I believe they couldn't care less! Come on, be a good boy, stop grumbling and help me close this trunk instead, I can't manage it.'

He came to her aid, pressed down their things and closed the lid.

'That's that job done!' he said, then walked out on to the terrace of the bungalow.

Night was about to fall, but he could still make out the huge man-made prairie in front of him, where a herd of cattle were grazing. And over to one side, the illuminated cowshed hummed with the motors of the milking-machines. Still further off the jungle pulsed, rustling with the animals and insects which wake at night. He sensed that Béatrice had joined him, and drew her close.

'You see,' he said, 'if it weren't for this damned climate, all this rain and those mosquitoes, it would be fine here. The soil is good and there's some good work to be done, isn't there? Look how beautiful that herd is!'

'Come on now! You're not going to regret leaving at this point?'

'No. What I regret is going away without having finished what I began . . .'

'If you stay with Mondiagri, that'll happen to you a few more times!'

'Bound to. But it's hard to come to terms with it, it's not in my nature.'

'Your peasant nature?' she joked. 'Yes, I've known you

were really a peasant at heart for a long time now. Lots of qualifications, but still a peasant!'

'Probably. But I hope that won't stop you marrying me? Well, you can still reconsider!'

'Bah, look how I've compromised myself with you!' she teased, pressing against him. 'Besides, I want to. Yes, I'm really very pleased to be marrying someone whose expression and voice change when he talks of the land, it's reassuring.'

Josyane had felt cold for two days. Barely out of Roissy, in penetrating drizzle driven by a bitter wind, she had realised just how pleasant it was to wear light clothing and live in a climate which was always equable. The cold had taken hold of her and would not release its grip.

Even the comfortable two-room flat in the Rue de Berri where Chantal lived had seemed to her badly heated, which was far from being the case. Nevertheless, it had needed all her sister's warmth and welcome to bring her out of her shivering numbness, to revive her cheerful energy.

And yet their first contact had felt rather strange. Without immediately admitting it, they were neither of them as they remembered each other.

Josyane preserved the memory of Chantal as a tall dark girl with hardly any make-up, long hair, and sometimes a slightly timid appearance. She discovered a very beautiful woman, extremely soignée, with short blonde hair, impressively elegant, sure of herself. As for Josyane, Chantal had seen her leave almost four years earlier, still rather childlike and gauche. She returned radiating self-confidence, tanned, determined, very beautiful too, although dressed like nothing on earth.

'I don't know if I'd have recognised you in the street,' Chantal had eventually admitted.

'The same goes for me! You're blonde now, and what style!'

'And you, you used to be rather skinny and pale, you're so brown it shouldn't be allowed, especially in December. And just look at your figure!'

That evening, after telephoning their parents, the two

sisters had chatted away until long past midnight. They had so much to tell each other, to hear about each other. Only tiredness due to the journey and the time change had overcome Josyane and stemmed the flow of her questions. On meeting her sister again she had discovered with emotion that her family ties were much stronger than before her departure. She had wanted to break them by going off on impulse one day, in order to liberate herself, to assert herself. She did not regret a moment of it, but realised now that some roots could not be torn up, and that was as it should be.

'Are you settling down or going off again?' her sister asked her the following evening.

Exhausted, Josyane had slept fifteen hours without a break and although she felt much better she was still permanently cold.

'No, I'm not going off again.'

'It was rather crazy, you know, to stay away so long, you gave our parents some grey hairs . . .'

'Sure . . . But you know, you need to be able to come back . . . You say they've aged a lot?'

'That's putting it mildly. But don't blame yourself, I played a part in it, and so did Marie . . .'

'That's true. I heard from Aunt Berthe. You know, I'd never have believed it, I'd have thought Patrick pleasant. But of course, I didn't know him very well.'

'Yes. And as Aunt Berthe says, it's not you who's involved with him! Poor Marie, she didn't deserve such a jerk! Dead boring, that guy!'

'I'd never have believed it . . .'

'But just imagine it! He spent the evenings counting up his retirement credits. "In thirty-two years I'll opt out!" he used to say. Stick-in-the-mud, that guy was, snoring away. And what's more, depressing, a real kill-joy! Well what can you say, an economics teacher!'

'You're exaggerating!'

'No I'm not! Heavens, I'm sure he thought of his retirement even when he was in bed. Marie had good reason to dump him! I wouldn't have put up with him for a weekend! But all the fuss didn't suit our parents. And as I contrived to upset them as well . . .'

'You? How?'

'Oh! Enough of that! I don't have to draw you a diagram, do I? To our parents I'm a loose woman, end of story. As Grandfather said to Aunt Berthe one day, it was she who reported it to me: "That Chantal, she needs a good hobble!"'

'Oh yes!' Josyane was amused. 'That enormous log that was hung from the cows' necks to prevent them jumping the fences!'

'That's it. Anyway, you've come back, that's the main thing.'

'Talking of which, I'm going to pay you back two-thirds of the fare right away, and if you can wait a bit for the rest . . .'

'I can wait for the lot. Pay me back when you have a job. But do you have any ideas about that?'

'Not a lot. Of course I could try to find a job in a travel agency, I've got to the stage where I know enough . . . After all, I could give the customers information about a fair number of countries . . .'

'That's not very exciting!'

'Or I could launch into photography. I have some quite beautiful and original photos, I think. Well, I say that, but you have to find magazines or agencies who might be interested, and there . . .'

'Is it Christian who gave you that idea?'

'Not at all! I didn't wait for him to teach me how to hold a camera!'

'Don't be so touchy! Come on, admit at least that he's an attractive man.'

'Yes, rather too much so! And then he's old!'

'Old? Well . . . But he's nice, isn't he?'

'At first sight, yes. But I know him less well than you. I took him around a bit in Tahiti like you asked me to, that's all. Look, would you have a slightly warmer top, I'm freezing.'

And now that she was dozing on the train travelling towards Brive, Josyane wondered what had made her change the subject. At times she was almost annoyed with herself for having wasted a good opportunity to learn a little more about

Christian. But on balance she was still quite proud of having kept to the code of conduct she had decided on – discretion.

When he had announced the date of his wedding and warned his parents that there would be only a civil ceremony, Dominique had also thought that it would be a small one. He was a little upset about it; if the decision had been his alone, he would have happily led Béatrice to the altar and invited the whole family to the celebration afterwards.

However, as he saw in his fiancée's decision proof of her honesty and her rejection of hypocrisy – she could have submitted to a religious ceremony and pretended to be as reverent as a child making her first Communion – he had not tried to talk her into it. Actually, he had been amazed to discover that she was more outspoken than him on many issues. In any case, it was not the concept of God she was rejecting, but the way men manipulated Him.

'When I was a girl,' she had told him, 'I already had great difficulty in accepting the moral precepts imposed on us. All right, I was already a troublemaker, but I always saw them as an expression of hypocrisy rather than faith. So I'm not about to support those sort of rituals now!'

She had understood that he was a little disappointed, and had continued: 'And now, be honest! You know very well we're living in fornicaton and sin in the eyes of those who've established the rules which I reject. And you're a damned liar if you dare say you regret it!'

'I don't regret anything. It's just that I think a religious ceremony which seals a promise is more serious than a boring administrative procedure, recorded by any old deputy mayor who doesn't give a damn about us, or we about him!'

. 'Possibly. But I prefer that to deceit; yes, deceit! If I believe my catechism, which is yours too, and if my memory serves me, to get married in church we'd need to attend confession. Well I've no desire to lie by going to tell some priest, preferably a deaf one, that I repent of cohabiting with you for a year, that I'm sorry I was in seventh heaven in your company without the approval of some father of the church! Count me out of that sort of masquerade!'

'Okay. All right, put like that, you're right.'

'So, what's the problem?'

'There's no problem. I'm thinking of my grandparents, that's all. They'll never understand your arguments. Well, my grandmother especially, and as I love her dearly . . .'

'Don't worry, they won't know anything about it ever.'

'And your parents?'

'My father doesn't care. As for my mother, she's considered me a tool of Satan since she discovered I was living in the sin of the flesh, that is, for ages now! But I don't bear a grude against her. I'm sure that my position allows her to indulge her devotions even more and to pass for a saint, not to say a martyr, in the eyes of her friends! She's always enjoyed that sort of role, she adores spiritual improvement! So why deny her that pleasure!'

'Right, fine. But I hope you don't still want a wedding with all the trimmings?'

'No. As quiet as possible would be best. On condition, of course, that I don't deprive you of the pleasure of giving me a beautiful ring and a honeymoon worth the name!'

It was after this discussion that he had written to his parents and proposed that they alone should travel up to be present at the exchange of vows. So he was very surprised and moved when he discovered, on the morning of 20 December, that his Aunt Berthe, with the co-operation of Guy and Colette, had organised everything for a proper family celebration, fitting for the wedding of the eldest Vialhe grandson.

That added to his happiness and good humour. He had at last found out, two days earlier, that Mondiagri was sending him for three years to one of the experimental farms they owned in Tunisia. And that was a piece of good news.

Mathilde thought that the little saint looked rather ugly, and she turned him slightly to hide his injuries. He had a chipped nose, his right hand was cut off at the edge of the sleeve and his paint was flaking off. He was almost frightening, which was not his raison d'être!

With his arms raised to the sky showing amazement, and his angelic smile, he stood spellbound in ecstasy in front of the crib. In order to encourage all the faithful to imitate him. To invite them to worship the plump-cheeked doll which in four days' time would be lying on the straw, between the ox with only three legs left and the donkey minus an ear and a tail!

'Our crib is really like our parish: it's pathetic,' murmured Mathilde, arranging a few tufts of moss at the feet of the Virgin Mary.

Even she looked a little sad, for her colour had long vanished, allowing reddish patches of the terracotta she was made of to show through here and there. Only Saint Joseph, two shepherds and three sheep were presentable. On condition that they were never placed side by side. They were not to the same scale, and the good carpenter would be transformed into a dwarf and the lambs into fat curly calves as soon as they got near each other.

'And for goodness sake don't put down too much straw, you know what'll happen!' Louise reminded her.

'Don't talk of calamities!' interrupted Mathilde as she delicately dusted a shepherd's brown robe.

She had not forgotten. Twelve years earlier, the unfortunate fall of a candle had almost transformed the crèche into a blazing inferno. Luckily the fire had broken out during Midnight Mass and, as chance would have it, the large font was also full. The volunteer firemen had the blaze under control before it reached the big lumps of wrapping paper which were supposed to represent the rocks of Palestine.

However, the incident had completely disrupted the service and the children had taken the opportunity to run wild. As for old Julienne Lacroix, who had just entered her ninetieth year, she had been so frightened that she had to be put to bed immediately after the consecration of the host! Her robust constitution had quickly recovered from this, but she had nevertheless decided not to attend such a dangerous church any more. She had kept to her resolution until her burial four years later!

'Here, pass me the miller,' requested Louise.

'But my dear, you know that the kids in the catechism class broke him last year!' Mathilde reminded her, raising her voice, for her sister's deafness was not improving.

'Oh, that's right. The longer it goes on the smaller it gets. When I think of what it was like once upon a time . . .,' murmured Louise, contemplating the whole crèche with sadness.

For almost twenty years now she and Mathilde had taken responsibility for arranging the crib each year. They knew that the children would be impatiently waiting for it to appear, even if there were fewer and fewer of them grouped around it for the Christmas Mass.

And the last few parishioners also liked to meditate in front of the figures. For even if they were a little damaged, a little lame and always sparser on the ground, they were still the ones which they had marvelled at sixty or eighty years earlier, in the days when, in the crowded church, the Limousin Carol rang out at the end of the third Mass at midnight: *Awake you shepherds, leave your flocks to go to Bethlehem . . .*

Now only a few old ladies still remembered the words. But they did not dare even to hum them; they feared the priest would not understand.

And yet Father Soliers, who had served the parish for five years now, was a good man. To be sure, he celebrated Sunday Mass on a Saturday, began the midnight service at eight-thirty in the evening and completed it at nine-fifteen! He dispatched the burials and marriages at breathtaking speed. But at least he had never objected to the crib.

He was not like that clergyman who had turned up in the village in the mid 1960s. Certainly he had the excuse of being young, of having everything to learn about country ways and being responsible for six or seven other parishes. Very concerned to revitalise his flock and to announce to them that the moment for changes and reforms having come at last, he considered it necessary to sweep away a whole heap of antiquated customs . . .

But that was not sufficient reason to dress like a tramp and feel obliged to have two or three drinks at Nicole's, with the sole aim, he assured them, of meeting the men in their normal suurroundings! No reason either to launch into long tirades of coarse language, and even some swearwords, when his little red motor-bike refused to start! No reason, in particular, to dare tell Mathilde and Louise one December day that he did not want a crib because it was a childish form of a faith forever gone, and smacked somewhat of fetishism, not to say superstition. True faith was expressed through involvement and action in the world, not through narrow-minded and repetitive devotions in front of plaster figurines, whose ugliness was rivalled only by their sickly sentimentality!

On that day Mathilde had seen red, as she had thirty years before, when Father Delclos had thought fit to meddle in matters which she considered private.

'I'm sixty-six years old! There has always been a crib in this church for me to see, here at the foot of our Lady of Lourdes. I've been arranging it for years! And neither you nor anyone else will prevent me from doing so! And if necessary, I shall call on all the men of the parish! They'll come and help me to install the crib, every single one of them!'

He had mumbled some vague comments about latent paganism still prevalent in the countryside, but he had not dared demolish the crèche when he had returned a week later. He had simply avenged himself meanly in his sermon by insinuating that Vatican II had come at the opportune moment, to sweep away all the retrograde and outdated practices which certain people confused with faith and felt obliged to perpetuate . . .

Luckily this reformer in grimy jeans and unbuttoned shirt had not lasted long in the area. He had disappeared one day, and nobody had been sorry.

Three years later Mathilde had happened to learn that he had married a girl of eighteen. She had been deeply distressed by this. God be praised, she had not had any further problems with his successors! Even if Father Soliers did not come often and kept strange hours, he had not objected to the crib any more than to the angelus bell or reciting the rosary; that at least was something!

Mathilde positioned a last tuft of moss and stood back to admire the crèche. All the little figures were in place, turned towards the empty, peaceful manger, which would soon be occupied by the Infant Jesus.

'Seen from a distance it's still beautiful,' she said.

'If you think so . . . But there aren't enough figures. Tell me, do you think we can use the sky again? It's all torn!' asked Louise, bringing out of the cupboard a large, dusty, dark-blue board sprinkled with stars.

'Of course! We'll clean it, and with a bit of sticky paper it will do!' Mathilde assured her optimistically.

Since the beginning of the month she had recovered her good humour and joie de vivre. It was enough for Jo to arrive one evening and come to kiss her, for happiness to reign once more in the household. For Jean-Pierre and Mauricette to shed their worried expressions, for Pierre to grumble a little less, and smiles to flourish again amongst all the Vialhes.

And the wonder was that it had all happened without any acrimony or bitterness, as if no one held it against Josyane for having stayed away so long. She was back, that was the main thing. The rest was no longer important, reproaches were no longer in order.

Admittedly she was so changed, so mature, that all the reprimands prepared and rehearsed over more than three years had become obsolete. The criticism which had built up was aimed at a girl who had left on the spur of the moment. It could no longer be applied to the returning adult. To want to do that would have been just as ridiculous and silly as scolding her for having pinched some jam fifteen years earlier!

Pierre-Edouard had immediately understood. And yet, if anyone was prepared to tell the prodigal that she had over-stepped the mark, it was he. He had seen how her disappearance had affected Mathilde, and normally he could not bear her to be hurt. And he could not tolerate either that his daughter should have suffered such a long and demoralising wait.

Despite that, since he had guessed in an instant that his granddaughter had already learned her lesson long ago, he had suppressed the choice sentences of biting irony which he had resolved to fire off as soon as he saw her. And it was without anger, but still with gravity, that he had welcomed her.

'So there you are, my girl? You certainly took your time on your little walk, didn't you?'

'Well yes, grand-père, it took me further than I thought . . .'

'But you didn't get lost because here you are. That's good. You know, there's nothing to stop you going a long way away, but the important thing is to find the road home again . . . And now come and kiss me. You've grown so beautiful and you look so much like your grandmother that I feel sixty years younger!'

Mathilde had been relieved that it all passed off in this way, and added to the happiness of having seen Josyane come back there was the delight in Dominique's return.

Naturally she would have been even happier if she could have attended his wedding. But that was really impossible, too far and too tiring. Besides, it did not matter whether she and Pierre-Edouard were at the celebration. What counted was that on that very day, 20 December 1975, fifty-seven years after his grandparents and twenty-nine years after his parents, Dominique Vialhe was finally marrying the companion he had chosen to accompany him on life's journey and perpetuate the Vialhe name. God willing!

15

WITH the arrival of spring, very early, Pierre-Edouard had recovered a dynamic energy which amazed him. Admittedly he had passed an excellent winter, without even a cold, and his spirits were in good shape. During the last fortnight, he had therefore resumed his daily walks all by himself. Wisely, he ventured much less far than previously, hardly strayed from the well-used paths, hesitated to step beyond the edge of the woods, and stopped frequently to catch his breath. But he then took the opportunity to revel in the scenery.

On this last Sunday in March the countryside was magnificent, ready to unfold, to embark on an orgy of greenery and flowers. Already the birds, deceived by the warmth of a balmy sun, were calling from bushes and groves, attempting trills and cantatas, showing off. Even the cuckoos and the hoopoes, which had arrived in the last two days, were competing with oft-repeated calls which echoed throughout the woods, spreading the news far and wide that spring was really here.

On all sides, in gentle touches which grew day by day, the tender green of the buds, sticky with sap, were prevailing over the pearl grey of the still leafless branches. And here and there, in the hollows of the little valleys, on the edge of the pools, or along the winding course of the Diamond, fat clumps of pale yellow willow shoots were bursting out, all bordered with catkins. Even the poplars were attempting some colour and holding up to the sun the slim and trembling fingers of their opalescent flowers.

Humming busily and as if confused by all the scents emanating from all sides, thousands of bees were launching an attack on the corollas, forcing them open sometimes, then slipping in to reach the stamens and feast on the constantly renewed supply of nectar.

'Tiens! Even they've arrived!' Pierre-Edouard smiled as his

eyes followed the dizzy arabesques of a red-throated swallow. Then he watched a bee frantically trampling over a broad dandelion flower which had opened like the August sun. Already two fat balls of orange pollen sticking to its back legs were weighing it down, making its search rather clumsy.

He thought that he was going to have to ask Jacques for a hand to visit the hives, clean them out, mend some of the frames and maybe feed them a little if the brood cells were too numerous. With such an early, warm spring, there was the danger that the queens might have already started intensive egg-laying, so that if by ill-luck the cold should return . . .

'Because you can never be sure of anything until the Ice Saints' Days!' he always said.

So whilst happy to enjoy the mild temperatures and magnificent weather, he could not help fearing some damaging cold spells. The moon would be reappearing on the thirtieth, and if it took it into its head to play up, that would be a catastrophe.

Mustn't forget we're in a year with thirteen moons, and that's never great shakes! Still, when the cranes come over it's usually rather a good sign!

He had heard them passing over four nights earlier. A huge flight, without a doubt, which must have stretched over several hundred metres, for the harsh calls of the birds had echoed above the village for some minutes. He was not asleep, and could not help thinking of the old superstition formerly associated with the flocks of migrating birds which called them the *chasse volante* – the Wild Hunt. His grandmother and mother were terrified by them, attributed all sorts of evil charms to them, and brought out their rosaries at the slightest sign of one.

It's incredible what the old people could believe, and what nonsense they repeated! I hope I talk less of it than them . . . he thought as he resumed his walk.

He had decided to climb as far as the plateau, to rest there a while, then go back down without hurrying. By that time it would be half past eleven and Mathilde would not have time to get worried, that was the main thing.

*

Pierre-Edouard had barely covered fifty metres when he heard behind him, rising from the village, the deep tone of the church bell marking the hours. He counted out of habit, frowned at the twelfth stroke, and waited attentively for the second peal, meanwhile consulting his own watch. It indicated two minutes past eleven.

'Ten . . . eleven . . . twelve . . .,' he murmured. 'All right then! It's that stupid electric clock, gone and done it again! They work when they feel like it, these modern machines! And yet it cost hundreds and thousands! Old Fernand would never have got the hour wrong! Even drunk as a pig, he could still count!'

He sighed at the memory of the old sacristan, dead for many years, and continued his walk towards the plateau. It was then he suddenly remembered that Jacques had warned him the day before that the clocks were going to be changed. He had understood nothing of what his son had explained, but had declared that, in any case, the sun and he had no truck with anything decided by those morons in Paris!

'Change the clocks?' he had cried. 'And what next? They'll be asking the moon to rise in the west while they're at it, those asses! Don't expect me to accept such a stupid idea!'

'It's true, it's a load of rubbish!' he muttered, looking once more at his watch. Then he observed the sun again and was reassured. It was indeed five past eleven, no more.

And yet the church clock had struck twelve strokes . . .

'Ah, merde alors!' he exclaimed suddenly, understanding at last what Jacques had told him. 'Oh the buggers! They've foisted German time on us again! Why not say so straight off! But then, if it's midday, Mathilde must be getting worried! Oh, the buggers!'

Crossly, he turned on his heel and hurried as fast as he could towards the village.

'Couldn't you have said that it was today, the German time?' was his reproach the moment he entered the room where the three women were waiting for him.

'Where's your head, then? You only listen to what interests you! You were told yesterday, and this morning too!'

Mathilde reminded him. 'Well, it doesn't matter, we guessed that you had forgotten.'

'I'll say I forgot!' he grumbled. 'I'm not going to clutter up my brain with all those nonsenses! No, it's true, it really is! You have to be crazy to dream up something like that!' he exclaimed, calling on his sisters to agree with him.

'Oh! They've already thought up plenty of others, worse ones! And I'm not even mentioning the stupidity of giving kids their majority when they're still sucklings!' cried Berthe angrily. 'No! But listen, remember the eighth of May last year!'

This she had never forgotten or forgiven. That they should dare to abolish the anniversary of a victory over absolute evil had disgusted her, wounded her. And she, the Resistance worker, the Gaullist, a former deportee, had insisted on going alone on the morning of 8 May to lay a huge bunch of wild flowers on the memorial to the dead of Saint-Libéral.

Nobody had mocked the frail silhouette, motionless in front of the stone pillar topped by a mossy old cock crushing a lichen-covered, spiked helmet. No one had laughed to see this old lady crying silently, who refused to forget and who, for the first time since the end of the war, had pinned her medals onto her white blouse.

It had taken this event for many people, even some of her own family, to discover that she was an officer of the Legion of Honour, decorated for her part in the Resistance; that she also had the cross for a volunteer in the Resistance and the medal for deportation and internment.

And nobody had seen her solitary demonstration as any condemnation of a people. The oldest inhabitants of Saint-Libéral knew that she had nothing against Germans, far from it! She had loved one and was preparing to marry him when the Nazis had assassinated him. And Gérard, her adopted son, had been born in Germany, to German parents. No, it was not a people nor a race that she had fought against in 1940. It was a system, a way of thinking, the Nazi order. And to learn that they were intending to court base popularity, out of stupidity therefore, to wipe away the date which commemorated the crushing of the swastika, had revolted her. Since then she regarded all those who had agreed to, not to mention applauded, this gesture, with extreme suspicion. As for the man who had instigated it, she despised him.

'Yes,' she reiterated to her brother, 'don't delude yourself, you can expect anything from that kind of people! And they'll do more!'

'I know. They don't know what else to dream up to annoy folks! But miladiou! I'd like to be told what the point is of changing the clocks?'

'It seems that it makes for savings . . .' suggested Mathilde.

'Savings? What sort of savings?' he shouted.

'You know very well, it's because of the oil, they say we won't have enough!'

'Well then, they only have to bring back ration tickets, same as during the war. And those who don't like it can walk, that'll stop them wrapping themselves round the plane trees!'

'Come on now, don't get in a state, it's not good for you,' ventured Mathilde.

'As for savings,' he continued, 'shall I tell you something? You could make some fine ones by hanging all bureaucrats in the ministries! All those officious little squirts! And while they're at it they could even hang a few ministers and deputies! Oh, by God, I wouldn't go into mourning!'

'Now, now, don't get worked up like that,' said Mathilde. 'And after all, you know, nobody's forcing us to change the clocks!'

'That's true,' he admitted. 'I don't want anything to do with German time, that's a collaborator's idea! Well, we'll stick to the old one. Besides, it seems it's past midday, but I'm not hungry! Right, that's decided, we won't bother with that Parisian notion.'

This decision calmed him. And it was in good spirits, laughing at the idea of underlining his independence, that he went to take a turn in the village during the afternoon, just to find out a little of what people thought of the new time. He returned to the house delighted, for all the people he had met were of his opinion and were preparing to take absolutely no notice of the official time, especially those who had animals to look after.

But he howled with rage and disappointment that same

evening on realising that he had missed the television news and the beginning of a film he was looking forward to seeing. For if his watch and the light outside actually indicated eight o'clock, it was no less than nine o'clock official time. And that could not be helped.

'Well yes, my dear, whether you like it or not, if you want to watch the telly, you'll have to live on German time!' cried Berthe. 'I'm telling you, it's what you can expect from people like that! I think they're more stupid than wicked, but that's no excuse!'

Immersed in his accounts, which were far from pleasing, Jacques found the furious and incessant barking of the dogs increasingly irritating. The two mongrels were nice enough, but often barked merely for the pleasure of listening to themselves. Or again, when the wind carried the sound, they loved to answer their fellows giving voice three kilometres away in the alleys of Saint-Libéral, particularly as night fell.

'For pity's sake, shut up those yappers!' he begged Michèle. 'I'd like at least to finish my estimated balance in peace!'

The results were not inspiring. Since 1973, following an absurd decision by the public authorities, the prices for all cattle had fallen by twenty-five to thirty percent and were not about to rise again tomorrow! In fact France was importing beef from the Argentine and central Europe by the hundreds of thousands of tons. It was obvious that those responsible for such a ridiculous and pernicious commercial policy could not care less about the French breeders' situation. On the electoral level their influence was growing ever weaker, so there was no need to pander to them, let alone listen to them.

Jacques knew all that was normal. As normal as the collapse in the price of pigs. As normal as the huge question mark which rounded off his provisional accounts; everything was negative and forced them, Michèle and himself, to cut down on anything which was not absolutely essential. It was to be hoped things would go better soon, when Françoise had finally completed her studies . . .

'Good God! What's got into those mutts?' he asked.

'There's a car coming up,' warned Michèle after looking out of the window.

'At this time of night? You'll be telling me it's only seven o'clock by the sun, but with this dratted summer time!'

'It's Aunt Yvette,' announced Michèle, recognising the DS.

'Oh yes! She said to me this morning she'd be coming by! I'd completely forgotten,' he reproached himself as he closed his account book and filed away his bills. He rose and went to meet her.

'I hope I'm not disturbing you?' asked Yvette after greeting her niece.

'Not at all,' he assured her. Nevertheless he was a little curious, almost worried, for the ghost of Louis hovered not far off . . .

'Shall I make you a herb tea?' suggested Michèle.

'That would be nice,' said Yvette, sitting down. 'I wanted to come and see you here rather than at the Mairie, it's simpler and more discreet,' she explained.

'Is it the mayor or your nephew you want to see?' he asked. He was now really worried, for he did not understand his aunt's actions at all.

'The mayor and former regional councillor.'

'Would it perhaps be better if I left you two alone?' proposed Michèle.

'No, no! Don't be silly, go and make your tea and come back. Are the children all right, then?' inquired Yvette.

'Fine,' he said. 'Dominique and Béatrice seem to like it out there. Dominique has a job he's interested in and Béatrice has found something to keep her busy at a maternity hospital. As for Françoise, she's okay. She'll be here in two months, towards the middle of July. Right, you've got something to say to me? You know I always get straight to the point.'

'Yes, that's in the family! Right, this is it, I'm tired of being alone in the château, fed up . . . So I want to get rid of it . . .'

'Oh, I see . . .'

'I'd be very surprised if you did!'

'Have you found a buyer?' asked Michèle from the kitchen.

'No, I haven't looked for one yet. And it all depends on you,' she said to Jacques. 'Yes, on you, monsieur le maire!'

'I don't quite see how . . .'

'The château, you're going to take it over.'

'You're crazy! I wouldn't even have enough to pay for the upkeep!'

'I'm talking to the mayor,' she explained. 'This château, I don't need it. I'm bored to tears in it, I certainly don't have to sell it to live comfortably for the rest of my days. So I've decided to give it to the community, in memory of Léon. There, that's all.'

'Ah? That's all?' he stammered after a few seconds. He was flabbergasted. 'But where will you live?' he asked eventually.

'After Louis' death your mother told me there was a room free at their place. I get on so well with your parents and aunts. I'll be fine there. And then I'll look after them a bit, they're getting on, you know . . .'

'Yes, yes. But it can't be done just like that!' he continued. 'In the first place, even if it could be done, the village hasn't the means to take responsibility for a building like that. Then, more importantly, Léon has nephews . . . and don't misinterpret this: I'm not talking about Guy, Mauricette and myself, you know that! But what about the others? Look, I know of at least one. Yes, I've never told you this, but Paul and I made him drunk on your wedding day . . . Well, I'm sorry, but legally, he's Léon heir before you!'

'Go on with you!' she said, amused. 'You know, Léon taught me only to speak when I was sure of myself. The other nephews have no say in this matter. Besides, believe me, if they had hoped to pick up something, they would have come to his funeral. And to Louis' . . .'

'That's true, they didn't have the courtesy, but . . .'

'But nothing!' interrupted Yvette. 'The château is mine alone. Yes, when Léon bought it, in '46, it was as much with his money as mine. However, he absolutely insisted that it be in my name. In my name alone. And when we were married he wanted us to keep to the system of separate property . . .'

'Good heavens! I'd have happily bet the château was left to Louis!'

'You're right, it was really for him that we bought it, but he was too young at the time. And anyway, Léon didn't want it.

He said to me: "If he believes he's lord of the manor at fifteen, it might go to his head, he'll think that money grows on trees . . ." Poor Léon, poor Louis . . .'

'Hey! Is that lime-tea coming?' called Jacques to Michèle, seeing that his aunt was about to succumb to tears. 'Right, fine, the château is yours, but you can't give it away like that!'

'Give it or sell it for a token franc, what's to stop me? Well, what does the mayor think of that?'

'We'll have to see . . . I can't take the decision all alone, it's a weighty matter that you're putting to the community!'

'But you're interested?'

'Indeed! My goodness!' he exclaimed, 'I'll have to bring the chief executive of the council in on this, and we'll get together to look for some influential group to support the whole business. Just imagine, if we had the château, we could instal, look, I don't know, . . . a children's holiday home! Or something like that! Good God, that would liven up this dying community a bit. That would at least bring in some young people for three months of the year!'

'That's what I'm hoping,' smiled Yvette. 'You know, it's often depressing to be president of a senior citizens' club, even when it's called after Léon Dupeuch . . . So I'd really love to see some children running about in the park . . .'

'Fantastic,' he murmured, already lost in plans filled with children's songs, activities, life. 'Tomorrow I shall call a meeting of the council, and as soon as I have their agreement, we'll get going! But you've definitely decided? You're sure you won't regret it?'

'Certain. For several months I could have told you what I said tonight.'

'It'll be wonderful for the village if it works,' said Michele, coming back with the lime-tea.

'Yes, but we'll need to pull all the stops out to do it,' he said. 'Just imagine! Now we'll really need a tennis court, and a swimming pool as well! And there, it will at least be used by someone! I can't wait for tomorrow evening, I'm dying to see the faces that moaner Peyrafaure and his mates are going to pull!'

*

After pondering far into the night the best method of realising their plan, Jacques awoke feeling a little less enthusiastic. He knew very well what difficulties he would have to surmount, what procedures to set in train, in order to transform the huge château into a building which could accommodate people.

First of all, there were administrative problems to resolve. Then, capital would have to be found to enable the château to be provided with all the infrastructure of a hotel. Finally, it was vital to interest a large firm in it by promoting the premises, activities, and a site which children would be happy to visit. None of that would be easy, and for the first time in many years he regretted that he was no longer a regional councillor. That would probably have enabled him to speed up the process. But he pushed aside the various pessimistic thoughts which assailed him when he considered all the work awaiting him, jumped in his car and set off to inform all the town councillors. He told them that the meeting would take place that very evening, that it was a matter of extreme importance and everyone should be present.

Then he went to visit his parents, but restrained himself from telling them of Yvette's visit. He had decided in conjunction with her to say nothing to anyone before the council meeting. Its members should be informed before anyone else, otherwise some of them might be annoyed and become fierce opponents, out of pure spite.

Right from the beginning of the meeting Jacques was glad that he had kept the secret, for it was obvious that some of them were in a black mood.

'I hope you haven't inconvenienced us for some trifle!' Peyrafaure went into the attack.

'Do I usually?'

'No, but there's a first time for everything! But maybe you're going to announce that you're resigning? That would be good news!' cried Castellac, in a tone which was intended to be pleasant and humorous but which still betrayed a latent animosity.

'Hey! Have you eaten somethings that's got stuck?' joked Jacques.

'You could look at it like that,' remarked Peyrafaure drily.

'Dammit! Speak your mind!' burst out Jacques.

'Don't get upset,' Coste explained to him with a laugh, 'with this meeting you're doing them out of a rugby match on the telly, and a great one too! So you can imagine how much they love you!'

'Oh, you should have said straight away! Well, I'm sorry gentlemen, but what I have to tell you seems to me more important than a match. I believe it is, anyway. It's this; my aunt, Madame Yvette Dupeuch, my aunt,' he repeated, 'has decided to part with her château . . .'

'It was only to be expected,' groaned Delmas, 'but we can't do anything about it, can we? Right, so what's the problem? If there is one, let's sort it out, and if we get on with it, we'll see the second half!'

'You're beginning to get on my wick with your game!' declared Jacques. 'There is no problem! My aunt has decided to give, I emphasise give, her château to the commune. I need your opinion before accepting.'

'Give? Well I'll be blowed!' whistled Martin. 'But why? She's losing by it!'

'That's right, on the face of it she's losing!' admitted Jacques.

'So what's the catch?' demanded Peyrafaure.

'There's no catch.'

'I don't believe it!' insisted Peyrafaure. 'You don't give away, just like that, a building worth perhaps . . . I don't know, at least . . .'

'More than that!' interrupted Jacques, who could feel his anger rising. 'I tell you there's no hidden snag, nothing! All we have to say is: yes, madame: thank you, madame! Dammit, it's clear enough! And it's free! Free!'

'Well, except for the taxes to be paid, and they won't be very small,' warned Peyrafaure.

'With a good lawyer that won't be a problem,' Jacques assured him.

'Granted,' said Martin, 'but what's the village going to do with that vast barrack of a place? Firstly it'll cost us a fortune to maintain and then, we've got nothing to put in it, so what's the point?'

'Firstly, I would reply to that you should never look a gift horse in the mouth,' said Jacques. 'Next, I shall make every effort to get the support of the sub-prefect to obtain favourable loans from the FAELG.'

'The Fa what?' rejoined Delmond.

'The fund to aid the equipment of local groups,' explained Jacques. 'And if that's not enough, we'll turn to the Crédit Agricole. In addition, I would expect to pick up a few grants here and there. Well yes, Monsieur Peyrafaure, it can be helpful to have friends in the right places . . .'

'If you don't mind going begging . . . And then, it's very fine, all that, but what purpose will your refurbished château serve?'

'Very simply, I hope to be able, not this summer but the next, to open it as a holiday home for children. And now, if you want to see the end of your match, we'll vote to accept my aunt's gift and you're released!'

'Why a holiday home?' persisted Castillac.

'Are you against it?'

'Bah . . . Not for it, particularly. Well yes, I am against it! It'll bring in a flock of kids! And kids make a noise and break everything!'

'Oh, right?' cried Jacques. 'You'd prefer a retirement home, maybe? An old people's home? They make less noise, old people! That's true! But don't you think we've got enough of those in Saint-Libéral? Eh? Our own aren't enough for you?'

'Castellac, my old friend, you're talking rubbish,' Peyrafaure intervened gravely. 'Monsieur le maire is right, for once. It's true, kids make a noise and break things, but at least they sing and shout and laugh, they're alive! I vote for the project!' he said, raising his hand.

He had scarcely completed the movement before every hand was raised, except Castellac's.

'Passed unanimously, minus one vote,' said Jacques. 'Gentlemen, I propose that tomorrow we immediately pay a visit to my aunt to thank her and to tell her that the château, whatever it's ultimate use, will be called The Léon Dupeuch

214

Foundation. But of course, we will understand if the opposing party is absent . . .'

He looked at his watch, happy to ascertain that the meeting had not lasted long and that he had time to go and announce to his parents that Saint-Libéral would perhaps live again.

Dominique had felt at ease as soon as he arrived in Tunisia. Here, unlike in Guyana, there was no need for acclimatisation. It was more or less what he had known in the north of Algeria. And that also applied to some of the scenery, methods of cultivation and mentality of the local inhabitants.

The great difference was that he was working on much more fertile, productive land than that of the oases. He was not complaining about this. Established in the Mejerda valley, south of Beja and above the town of Bab el-Raba, he was, as in Guyana, in charge of an experimental unit. But the greatest change from his previous assignment was in the modest area of the operation. Here, it was obvious that Mondiagri had experienced difficulty in negotiating with the government to install an experimental farm.

In the 1960s, the management of the group had been out of step with theories applied by supporters of agricultural reform prevailing in the country. Although it was now obvious that this had ended in a resounding disaster which endangered the economy, certain of the work habits had persisted. For example, some people thought of the land, crops, flocks and the tools as collective property, and so did not bother to treat them well.

However, since the farm was small and the workers few in number, Dominique did not have too much difficulty in making them understand the importance of agricultural research and interesting them in it.

As he was not overburdened with work, and Beatrice's duties at the maternity hospital in Beja also left her with some free time, they filled this by setting off to explore the countryside. It had also been a great pleasure to meet with Ali again. He had turned up as soon as he had learned of his friend's arrival, and the two men had embraced each other, with a great deal of back-slapping, before Béatrice's astonished eyes.

'Don't worry, it's our old bond as Saharan veterans,' Dominique had explained to her. 'We had such a rough time together on that bloody useless land in the oases! And you can't imagine what a merry dance he led me too, this rogue! A bigger coward than him doesn't exist! Didn't want to get his hands dirty, or to bend down, the lazy devil!'

'You bastard! Still just as colonialist and racist! Well, they were good times, after all . . .'

'Isn't it going well? Are you having problems?'

'Your successor is a little squirt and a boot-licker! He implements the plans and directives from our technical advisors down to the very last letter. Oh yes, we have that sort of scum amongst our lot too! So I'll leave it to you to imagine the results! With those types around you're heading straight for famine! Come on, let's talk about something different. So you finally got married!'

'Yes, a real gem!'

'And brave as well!'

'Wretch! Right, come and have some lunch. You're going to discover a cordon bleu cook who trained in the foie gras region!'

Since this reunion, Dominique was waiting for the opportunity to go and visit Ali. He was also looking forward to the idea of seeing once more the country in which he had spent four years of his life, and certainly not the worst ones.

Besides practising a profession which he enjoyed, accompanied by a very loving and attentive wife, he also greatly appreciated being close to France. Not that he was homesick, but he found it comforting to be only a few hours from Saint-Libéral, from his family. To be able to pop over to France if the fancy took them, for him and Béatrice to go and spend a weekend at Coste-Roche, or even in Paris.

He was delighted when a letter from his father informed him that the commune was now the owner of the château. That château encompassed his childhood and he was sentimentally attached to it, as were all the people of the village. And, like them, he caught himself saying 'our château'! It was there, solid, firmly planted above the village. And it belonged to everyone, like the wash-house, the church or the countryside. So to learn that from now on it really *was* theirs gave great satisfaction.

'And now, you'll see,' he said to Béatrice, 'it'll give my father a taste for the fight again. It's a good idea, a children's holiday home, isn't it?'

'Excellent. Your grandparents must be pleased as well!'

'You bet! And doubly so since Yvette has moved in with them. It's really funny, she must be in her seventies, but with her there's a bit of youth coming into the house!'

'I hardly know her, but she's obviously a very kind lady, so thoughtful.'

'That's true, but on that score she's nowhere near beating you,' he said, pulling her to him and holding her against his shoulder.

He knew that he would never forget the proof she had given him; he still felt quite moved by it. And proud too, to have a wife of such moral strength. Immediately after their marriage, on the afternoon of 20 December, he had not the faintest idea where she was dragging him off to when they had emerged from the town hall of the Sixth Arrondissement in Paris.

'A short visit to pay, and then we'll rejoin you at Guy's,' she had told her brother and sister-in-law (the only representatives of her family) and the much more numerous Vialhes. Then she had dragged him into a taxi.

'Stop in front of the Préfecture of Police,' she had requested. As he understood nothing, but particularly wanted to avoid giving the driver the chance to start a conversation, he had remained silent until they arrived there.

'Do you want to bring charges of assault and battery already?' he had joked. 'No, joking apart, what are you playing at?'

'Nothing. Come on, we're going to visit Notre-Dame, it will make me feel young again. I often used to come here to listen to organ recitals.'

'*You* are asking *me* to go into Notre-Dame?'

'Why not? It's one of the most beautiful cathedrals, isn't it? Listen, you know how I hate lying, I just can't help it. I'm aware of the act your parents have had to put on to conceal our decision from your grandparents.'

217

'And you disapprove?'

'Not at all. But if one day I have to answer a question from your grandparents about it, I want to be able to say to them "Yes, we went to the church." Maybe it's a play on words, but by doing that I'm lying much less than if I'd agreed to accept a religious ceremony. And then, apart from that, knowing you as I do, I'm sure you're very happy to make a short visit to this place, on this day, with me . . .'

Afterwards, he knew that he would always remember that visit to Notre-Dame.

16

JOSYANE went back up to Paris to look for work after spending a month in Saint-Libéral. She was aware that her parents would have preferred to see her settle locally. But although her urge to roam the world had now waned, the idea of accepting some modest job in the Corrèze was not immediately inspiring. She was twenty-five and already had a fair experience of life: she intended to make use of it.

'I could suggest that you work for the Maison de Couture,' Chantal said to her, 'Aunt Berthe and Gérard would be delighted, but frankly, I have the feeling that it's not quite your style ... From what I know about you, you'll be snapping at the first old bore who appears, and as they form ninety-five per cent of our clientele, we'd get straight into a nasty incident, or bankruptcy!'

'Yes, I wonder how you can resist the temptation!'

'Very easily; I have no contact with them! My job is to organise and promote the Claire Diamond collections, in France and in Europe. But in that area, I really don't see what I can offer you either.'

'Don't struggle. Your rig-outs, even with the Claire Diamond label, are just not my kind of thing.'

'That's plain to see,' said Chantal sweetly: 'I'm coming to believe that your total wardrobe consists of one pair of jeans!'

'Almost! In any case, it's not work I'm asking you for, it's simply if I can sleep at your place, just until I find a room that's not too expensive. But if that'd put you out, say so. Well, I mean to say, perhaps you've got someone it might upset ...'

'No problem,' Chantal said, amused, 'I never entertain men at my place. You see, if you do that, they soon start calling for their slippers the moment they arrive! So my flat is out of bounds, as a matter of principle. Out of bounds except to you, naturally.'

'Thanks, I hope I won't be in your way for too long.'

'Have you any ideas about work?'

'Yes, still the same thing. I'm going to begin by going round all the travel and press agencies. And if that doesn't produce anything, I'll look for something on the secretarial side; after all, I am trilingual, that may be some use!'

'Definitely. Look, as a matter of fact, someone's been asking after you . . .'

Josyane guessed that 'someone' had blue eyes and resembled Paul Newman, but she carefully avoided showing any reaction.

'Oh yes? Who?' she replied.

'Don't play hard to get with me, if you don't mind,' teased Chantal. 'You know very well who I'm talking about. I thought he was in a very strange state, poor old Christian, what did you do to him in Tahiti?'

'Absolutely nothing, I promise you!'

'Yes, that must be why he looked so ill. With your good little girl act combined with top-notch bodywork, you just turned him on and then slipped away!'

'I don't turn anyone on, that's not my style!'

'Thanks very much!' said Chantal with a laugh. 'All right, it doesn't matter. The fact remains it's Christian who asked me for news of you. That's nice, isn't it? Oh yes, and he also said that one of his projects was to explore the Corrèze. If I remember rightly, he once told me that his great-grandfather was from Brive, or nearby. You knew that, did you, did he mention it to you?'

'Vaguely,' Josyane replied evasively, 'but I didn't understand his story at all!'

It was a barefaced lie, but she expressed it with great élan.

'Oh, right. Well briefly, he's in Paris at the moment, if you feel like thanking him for playing postman . . .'

'No, that's already been done!'

'Golly, you do look fierce. Well, we won't talk about it any more if it annoys you. But if I were you, making the rounds of the press agencies I'd prefer to be recommended by someone from the profession, and someone well known! But you do as you think best . . .'

'Exactly! I shall manage by myself!' declared Josyane. She was suddenly in an extremely bad temper, for she knew this was not the best way of finding employment.

Exhausted by a testing and complex case, Guy decided to go and get some fresh air during the Whitsun weekend. Although he felt himself to be very Parisian and enjoyed living in the capital, he often needed to go and tread something other than asphalt. Needed to feel the earth beneath his feet, to breathe in the fragrance of the forests, to enjoy the greenery, and oxygen which did not stink of exhaust gases. Consequently, even when it was the close season for hunting, he did not think twice about going to spend twenty-four hours at Félix's. Down there he would forget his files, his clients and the smell of the courts.

In contrast to his eldest son, he was not very keen on fishing; got bored if the fish were slow to bite, often snagged his line in the branches of the willows and his hook in the roots of the water-lilies. But that did not prevent him from keeping Félix company when he decided to put buttered pike on the menu. For even if Guy was often left empty-handed, the Souchet pool was so beautiful, so calm, that two hours spent on its banks was a real treat, a joy.

All the more so since Félix's conversation was never dull. He read a great deal, kept abreast of everything. Without feeling the need to give his opinion here there and everywhere, his judgement was sound when one requested it. What was more, as he was fascinating and inexhaustible when it came to questions about nature, it was a pleasure for Guy lead him onto that subject. It made a change from the futile and trivial conversations he was often forced to endure on his evenings in Paris.

However, this morning the two men turned their steps towards the Souchet pool in silence. Nature was so beautiful, so rich, and the chorus of birds so captivating, that it seemed sacrilege to interrupt it. It burst forth on all sides, amazing in its strength and variety. The raucous, repetitive call of pheasants was answered by thin piping from great tits, and the harsh drumming of greater spotted woodpeckers drilling into hollow trunks alternated with the singing exercises of lesser whitethroats and chiffchaffs.

The forest, still all damp with dew, was resplendent. The light was streaming in, and the oak groves, in the rich unfurling of their delicate, tender, spring greenery, drank in the sun in long draughts, gorged themselves on it.

'What a treat this morning,' whispered Guy as they arrived without a sound at the edge of the pool.

There, where a few wisps of creamy mist hovered over the grey-blue water, grebe and coot, moorhen, teal and mallard were preening and flapping, diving, calling, quacking. And amongst the rushes, cat's tails and reeds, enlivened by delicate touches of pale yellow flag, the sedge, reed and Cetti's warblers trilled with open throats.

Standing sentinel over them all, perched on a dead branch of an old, worm-eaten alder, a dignified purple heron kept an eye on the two men as they approached.

'We'll stay here, this is a good spot, and it would be a pity to disturb such a beautiful party,' said Félix, laying his equipment on the grass.

'Yes,' he continued shortly afterwards, 'you see, I know him, this heron, it's almost like a game between us. If we move forward another ten metres, he'll take off. Then it's goodbye to the ducks, moorhens and the rest. Everything will hide! Look, try this spinner, it's a new model, Pierre told me it was good.'

'He's well?'

'Very well. You should have arrived earlier yesterday, you'd have seen him. He was here with Jeanette and the children.'

Pierre Flaviens kept a small shop for fishing and hunting tackle in Buzançais. He often asked his father to test some new article.

'They're coming down to Saint-Libéral this summer?'

'Of course! If they missed it again this year my mother would be upset, poor woman! With the children's measles keeping them here last year, it was a tragedy for her! Well, almost.'

'And you, you'll be coming?'

'Probably; it will please your father, and my mother as well.'

'You can say that again! Oh blast!' Guy, suddenly irritated, passed his rod to his cousin. 'Fix this thing for me, I don't know how it's supposed to be attached!'

'Calmly,' joked Félix, as he deftly knotted the spinner on to the end of the line: 'There, and now no more playing around if you want to eat fish for lunch!'

It was Guy who made the first catch. After twenty minutes of struggling under Félix's direction, he succeeded in landing a pike of almost eight pounds on the bank, a magnificent, plump beast with the mouth of a killer.

'You can take that one away with you!' He's much too big for us two,' said Félix. 'My goodness, a fine beast! But if you'd lost him, your son would have had a good go at you!'

'I wouldn't have told him!'

'But I would have,' teased Felix. 'Joking apart, he's well?'

'Yes, he's swotting for his bac.'

'But that's no problem?'

'No, not unless he breaks his legs the morning of the exam. Dammit, help me! I'll never manage to unhook this monster!'

'Yes, you're well on the way to losing your fingers!' advised Félix, deftly slipping his thumb and forefinger into the pike's gills. He retrieved the spinner and stunned the fish. 'And next year?' he asked, resuming his fishing.

'Oh ho! Don't you play games with me, if you don't mind! You know very well how the land lies!'

'Dammit! To listen to you, you'd think he wanted to become a guru in the foothills of Nepal or manager of a brothel! Seriously, there's nothing so dreadful about wanting to study agriculture!'

'He hasn't got that far yet! But the little wretch has already succeeded in extracting my permission to register for the preparatory course! And just imagine, he's turning his nose up at the holiday I was offering him too, for passing his bac. Yes sir! I suggested a trip to England, but oh no!'

'I know,' said Félix, 'he'd rather go and work with Jacques.'

'He told you so?'

'No, not this year, but I'm guessing. Okay, that's no big deal!'

'I didn't say it was! I'm simply saying that, gifted as he is, it's wasting his talent to want to launch into such a wretched profession!'

'Dominique's earning a crust or two!'

'Yes, I know. But Jean wants to be a stock-breeder, I ask you, a breeder! No less!'

'He has time to change his mind! Once he's an agricultural engineer, he could develop a career like his cousin.'

'He's so pigheaded, it would surprise me! Because you may know that monsieur has his own little plan for breeding. Indeed he does. And Dominique agrees with it, he may even be the inspiration! Oh yes! I was watching them at Dominique's wedding, they spent a whole evening chatting together!'

'That's rather a good sign, isn't it? That proves he's gathering information!'

'Oh Lord yes, the little devil! And monsieur isn't going for the economy model! Breeder yes, but in style!'

'How's that, in style?' asked Félix. He felt a bite, struck briskly. 'Look, there's our lunch,' he said as he reeled in. 'Shouldn't be too big, soon have it out . . . You say he's doing it in style?' he continued as he played with the reel-drag to tire his catch.

'Exactly! Monsieur wants to produce pedigree animals, registered Limousins, championship beasts. The finest of the fine, for export, right! And Dominique approves of it, or is advising him, hard to tell which! He says his father should have got into this a long time ago and he would have made a much better living from it!'

'That's not so stupid.'

'Get away! You're agreeing with Jean, as always!'

'No, no, quite the opposite! When he comes I spend my time calming him down. Here, get the landing net ready, judging by the way he swallowed the hook, he won't slip off by himself. Are you ready?'

Félix pulled the pike dexterously to the edge of the bank, guided it into the net.

'That's good,' said Guy.

'It's a young one, no more than three pounds,' estimated Félix. 'So, you were saying he wanted to go in for top class breeding?'

'Yes.'

'That's not so stupid,' repeated Félix. 'No, it isn't: Oh, I know what you're thinking: if our economists and politicians go on the way they've started, they'll kill farming – well, our sort, the middling enterprises; the little ones are already dead! I see it clearly, the Brenne area isn't particularly rich anyway, but it's going from bad to worse. And it's the same in the Corrèze! That's our fault, we've left control to the eggheads who've never set foot out of the cities, except to go skiing or to the beach! So to them the country is just a bunch of yokels!'

'Well now, if after all that you have the cheek to tell me I'm wrong to worry about my son . . .!'

'Yes, you're wrong. I'd understand you turning grey if he wanted to work the way Jacques does at Coste-Roche. And yet he's a good fellow, is Jacques! But he was in the forefront thirty years ago . . .'

'There, that's exactly what I'm saying! Jean's going there this summer!'

'But not to do the same as him! Listen, the way things are going, you need to aim for the exceptional, the top of the range, as they say. There'll always be customers for the unusual. So for the dilettante, why not pedigree animals? After all, it was by developing into haute couture that Aunt Berthe raised her fashion house to where it is. It wasn't by selling aprons, blue overalls or tea towels that she created Claire Diamond.'

'Certainly. But right at the beginning I have to state that I have no land, not a square metre! You know that we came to an arrangement in the family and our parents left all the land to Jacques. That meant he had to take out a loan to compensate Mauricette. All right. I'll get the family home one day, but as for land, apart from the patch of garden . . . I've no complaints, it's fine like that. But really what I'm trying to say is, I've no desire to ruin myself now by buying a farm for my son. So, him and his cows, you get my drift!'

'If you look at it like that . . . But shall I tell you something? I'm not worried about Jean. After all, maybe his years in agriculture will teach him that there are other things besides stock-breeding.'

'Let's hope the gods hear you! You must admit the boy isn't choosing the easiest course!'

'Have you ever seen a Vialhe choose the easy way? I never have!' joked Félix. 'Come on, let's go back, we'll let this beast cook while we're taking an aperitif. What would you actually have liked him to be? A lawyer, like you?'

'Why not? It's not so bad. Or the ENA civil service college.'

'Why? Don't you think there are enough thick-heads coming out of there? I tell you, I'd prefer Jean to be interested in the land and stock-breeding. It's much less run of the mill, times being what they are. And what's more, less risky than having ambitions to govern the lives of the hoi-polloi like you and me, who don't want it anyway.'

'Maybe. But it has to be said, you're bloody subversive! I could be listening to my father!'

'Well yes, that's a Vialhe trait too, you have to live with it. Right, let's go, and don't forget your catch. For once you'll be able to impress your son!'

'Do you think so? Knowing him, he'll never believe I caught it all by myself!'

'I'll make you a certificate!' promised Félix, bursting into laughter.

Jacques had been worried for almost two months. He had felt that the month of April was abnormal – too beautiful, too sunny and in particular, too dry and hot. He had never forgotten the saying that his grandfather Jean-Edouard used to trot out whenever Paul and he had the audacity to complain about a wet April spoiling their Easter holidays:

'This month has only thirty days, but if it rained for thirty-one it wouldn't have rained enough!' the old man would declare.

Since then, Jacques had learned that he was right. April was when the last significant reserves of water filtered down into the subsoil before the hot summer days. When the plough-land, meadows and pastures drank it in, when the fodder crop was assured.

But the month had come to an end without heavy rainfall. And the new moon on the twenty-ninth had not brought any change. As for May, it was radiant: too much so, for the few stormy showers had hardly settled the dust.

Already the beets and maize had germinated poorly, and were wilting in patches. As for the man-made pasture, it was possible to discern, at the foot of the clovers and grasses, the granules of ammonium nitrate which had been spread at the beginning of the month and were still not dissolved.

By now, going on for mid-June, it was obvious that the fodder cut would be meagre, not to say non-existent on some plots. Even the cereals were suffering. They were already yellowing, and the ears of corn remained desperately empty, flat. Some of the fruit trees were also beginning to show distress, and to drop a few green, dry fruits which had shrivelled onto their kernels.

This morning of the 10 June, Pierre-Edouard felt he had the heart to walk up and cast an eye over the plateau. There, spotting Jacques reaping the lucerne crop on the Malides field, he pressed on, just to see what the cut was producing.

'If we have no thunderstorms in the next week, to unsettle the weather, you'll soon get the rest of your haymaking done!' he predicted. 'It's not up to much, is it?' he added, bending down to pick up a handful of fodder already wilted by the blazing sun.

'No, even the lucerne is sparse! As for the rest . . .'

'I've seen,' said Pierre-Edouard. 'It might be worth your while cutting it all straight away and, if it ever gets round to raining a little, you'd have a second cut.'

'I thought about it, but the density is still so poor! Mind you, we'll have to do something if this blasted weather stays stuck the way it is!'

'It reminds me of 1943,' said Pierre-Edouard. He reflected a moment, hesitated: 'Yes, it was '43. That was the year the reaper let us down. Yes, I took Guy to Brive to order another. What did I want to say now? Oh yes! We got the hay made quickly that year! You'll be telling me I had less stock to manage than you!'

'Well yes, I soon won't know where to graze them.'

'Have you got any hay left from last year?'

'Hardly any, maybe eight or ten tons, no more, that won't go far . . .'

'You're right,' sighed Pierre-Edouard. He suddenly felt very tired, and went to lean against the trunk of a plum tree.

'Are you not feeling well?' Jacques worried, and climbed down from the tractor. His back was hurting and he limped up to his father: 'Are you not well?' he asked again.

'Fine, I'm puffing a bit, that's all,' Pierre-Edouard assured him.

He observed his son who was pulling a face as he massaged his back, and laughed ironically:

'We're a fine pair, us two! You can hardly drag yourself along and I . . . Well I've got the excuse that I'm old, but we could do with someone to take over!'

'You shouldn't have come such a long way,' Jacques scolded, 'it's not sensible!'

'I know, but the devil with being sensible! I enjoyed seeing the plateau again.'

'I'm going to take you on the tractor as far as Coste-Roche. Then Michèle will drive you down in the car.'

'No, no, that'll be a waste of your time,' protested Pierre-Edouard without great conviction.

He was by now rather breathless and would gladly have sat down, for his legs felt heavy; but he hesitated to do so on the bare ground. It was so far down, and so difficult to crouch down without lying flat out. And then, afterwards, you needed to get up again . . .

'Come on, I'll help you climb onto the tractor. You can hold onto the mudguard, right? Can you get a grip?'

'Let me have a breather. I'll go back down by myself on foot, it's not far!' said Pierre-Edouard.

He felt unable to heave himself onto the tractor, and in particular to balance himself against the mudguard as far as Coste-Roche. But he would not admit it, not for anything in the world.

'Yes it is a long way! Too far for you!' insisted Jacques. 'Right,' he decided, 'don't move from there: I'll slip off to fetch the car and take you back down.'

'Well, all right, have it your way,' Pierre-Edouard gave in after a moment's hesitation. 'But promise me one thing; you'll drop me at the edge of the village. Promise, otherwise I'm going to walk.'

'But why?'

'Promise!' he said, making as if to set off.

'Right, okay.'

'It's for your mother's sake,' he explained, resuming his support against the gnarled trunk of the plum tree. 'Yes, if she sees me coming down in the car, she'll be worried. That'll make a whole lot of trouble, she'll want to get Martel, all that rigmarole, you know!'

'And she'll be right!'

'Get away with you!' said Pierre-Edouard irritably, before continuing: 'Whereas if I arrive on foot, thanks to you I'll be in plenty of time and she won't suspect anything. She's sensitive, you know, she doesn't show it but I know her. You have to be careful, worry isn't good for her. Go on then, go and fetch your car. You're right, I'm a bit tired now . . .'

Jacques kept his word and deposited his father on the edge of Saint-Libéral. But before returning to Coste-Roche, he wanted to be sure the old man was feeling better and decided to wait until he reached the main square.

Satisfied to see him walking away at a good pace, he nevertheless resolved to tell Aunt Berthe to keep an eye on his jaunts. For if, in addition to the weather conditions, his father joined in to complicate his life, things were going to get difficult!

He comforted himself by considering that Pierre-Edouard had some reason to be tired. After all, not content with climbing to the plateau – and the slope was steep! – he had pushed on as far as the Malides field, all under a lethal sun. That made more than three kilometres, a fine achievement for a man of eighty-seven with a weak heart.

And he was ready to return on foot, he thought admiringly.

I wouldn't bet on doing as much at the same age, if I get there . . .

He waited until his father had disappeared at the end of the main street, and returned up the track to Coste-Roche. After all that, he had not finished cutting the lucerne. It was not critical, as, unfortunately, the weather was not threatening to break.

Some mornings, when she returned exhausted to her room in the attics of the Rue de l'Ouest, Josyane came close to thinking that independence was very dearly bought.

As she had forecast to Chantal, she had found a job. It was reasonably paid, and had therefore allowed her to reimburse her sister for the plane ticket and also to move into a little studio flat under the eaves. The only problem was that her duties corresponded very little with what she had expected. Certainly she was working in a travel agency. However, instead of welcoming clients and informing them about the charms of the Seychelles, the Carribean, Acapulco or any other supposedly enchanting spot, then organising their itinerary, she found herself forced to pilot groups of foreigners around the capital.

It was bearable when her stint was during the day, but very unpleasant when she had to guide some Japanese or Americans for an evening trip, from the Moulin-Rouge to the Lido, with a detour to the Eiffel Tower, Place de la Concorde and Notre-Dame for the illuminations, a 'typical' bistro and back to Pigalle! It was not only exhausting, but also devoid of any interest. What was more, as in Tahiti, she often needed to convince certain clients that she was not part of the 'Paris by night' package! Consequently she began to think Chantal had been right when she had tried to persuade her not to accept that sort of job.

Annoyed at first by her sister's remarks, she now considered them increasingly sensible, especially when tiredness forced her to collapse fully clothed on her bed at a time when normal people were beginning their day.

'I hope you're not crazy enough to accept that idiotic job!' Chantal had commented to her.

'It's the only one being offered to me at the moment! And, besides, there's no such thing as idiotic work! I have to earn my living, that's the bottom line!'

'But not like that! It's ridiculous. You deserve better! And why don't you want to ask Uncle Guy to help you? He suggested it. Good God, with the people he knows, I'm sure he'd find you a job in no time! And then, look, as soon as Gérard gets back from the United States, I'll mention it to him, if you like?'

'Certainly not! I won't ask anything of Uncle Guy, nor Gérard, nor anyone in the family!'

'But that's absurd! Then what's the point of having a family, in your opinion? We're there to hold together, to support each other, to help each other! Look, do you think Uncle Jacques hesitated before getting his brother in on the search for a firm which might be interested in the château? That's the way to do it, and no other way. Only fools don't grasp that!'

'That's your opinion. Listen to me: I set off one day for the ends of the earth to cut the cord, okay? So today I don't want to tie it up again, do I make myself clear? That's why I'm not asking anything of uncle Guy, nor anyone else in the family!'

'Shall I tell you something? On the pretext of wanting to manage all by yourself and distinguish yourself from your family, you're behaving like a shopgirl! It's absurd! What are you playing at? A photo-romance in 'Nous Deux'? I was hoping your years of roving around would have knocked a bit of sense into your brain; I was wrong!'

'Don't you worry about my brain! Anyway, what's the problem? I've just found a job for now. That doesn't mean I'm going to devote my life to it!'

'Fine. Then let me at least ask Christian to put in a word for you with the press agencies, he's not part of the family, is he?'

'I forbid you to bring him into this, of all people! I made the rounds of all the agencies; none of them wanted anything to do with my photos! So there's no question of lowering myself now by getting your pal to intervene!'

'Well, my dear, I think you're going about things the wrong way! You seem to be looking for a hard time. In fact you probably came back from Tahiti too soon!'

The two sisters parted very angrily, and Josyane waited more than two weeks before going back to see Chantal. Then, as always, they made it up.

And now, after three months of work, Josyane was beginning to think that her elder sister was right and the time had come to show some sense. Already she was contemplating swallowing her pride and going, as a first step, to ask her Uncle Guy's advice. But she still hesitated and deferred the decision. As she remained a little cool towards her sister as well, that did not improve her temper. For she was cross with Chantal, not for being sensible and realistic about her work, but for being incapable, until now, of bringing her together with Christian by one means or another.

And as there was no question of demeaning herself by requesting such a service, this fit of sulking with her sister was in danger of lasting, and even of getting worse if the situation did not resolve itself.

Josyane consulted her watch, calculated that she had four more hours of work before being able to sleep, and picked up the microphone again:

'. . . And on your right, you see the obelisk from Luxor. It was erected in 1836, in the reign of Louis-Philippe. At the same time the two fountains were built which . . .'

'And where are the Folies-Bergère?' interrupted a joker who was creating a rumpus at the back of the bus.

'. . . You can also see the eight statues which each represent a town in France: Lyon, Marseille, Bordeaux . . .' she attempted to continue.

Then she realised that no one was listening because, probably as a result of a dirty joke, the whole herd of Americans were guffawing and slapping their thighs.

'Give it a rest,' the driver advised her. 'They don't give a damn about your commentary. They're already as pissed as newts! If you want my opinion, we should drive them straight over to see the strippers: then they'll give us some peace for a while!'

She acquiesced. Exhausted by four sleepless nights – she had agreed to stand in for a sick colleague – she struggled manfully against encroaching slumber and forced herself to remain standing in order not to succumb. Despite that, she was not far from falling asleep, she was so tired, lulled by the gentle rocking of the coach, and she swayed as she gripped the support bar.

In good form after four brown ales, three cognacs, an armagnac and three glasses of champagne – a dreadful demi-sec which Josyane would not even have used to clean out her casseroles! – William B. Barlow, of Miles City, Montana, was fascinated by the rump undulating in front of him, within hand's reach. He found it so beautiful, exciting and graceful, squeezed as it was into the little blue skirt which accentuated its contours, that he could contain himself no longer. Alerting his neighbour with a knowing nudge of the elbow, he made the attempt. Not slyly or furtively, but openly, with cheerful vulgarity, burning to touch the soft warm skin he expected to find, between her thighs. He did not get far, barely above the hem.

'Filthy pig! Think you're on your ranch?' growled Josyane, turning round. And her hand shot out, like lightning; struck first one cheek then the other, before the culprit even had time to attempt a defensive movement.

'And you think that's funny, do you, you clot from Kansas?' she shouted at his neighbour, a gross, adipose redhead who was laughing fit to bust.

He too got the slap of a lifetime, but continued to choke with laughter just the same.

'Bunch of louts!' she exploded, going to sit on the little folding seat beside the driver.

'Now, now! If you start hitting the customers . . .' he murmured. He had heard it all and understood it all: 'Look, if they ever complain about you, you've had it!'

'Don't care, wish the buggers were dead! I'm getting out at the next red light!'

'Oh no! You can't leave the coach! Oh no! You're responsible for this horde of barbarians!'

'Don't give a damn! I resign, I have every justification! It's not stipulated anywhere that I have to let myself be pawed by drunkards!'

'Listen, let me at least drive them to the cabaret. After that you can do what you like. I'll take them back to the hotel all right by myself. Do that for me. Come on, be a good girl!'

'Okay, but as soon as they're off getting an eyeful, I'm leaving,' she vowed. And she took up the microphone again to announce: 'And here you see the Arc de Triomphe on the Place de l'Etoile. Begun in 1806, it was completed in 1836. Here lies the . . .'

'That's great, love, you'll see, you'll get used to it!' the driver encouraged her.

'Don't count on it!'

After sleeping like a log for half the day, she made for the house of Claire Diamond, located in the Faubourg-Saint-Honoré. She was anxious that Chantal should be the first to know of her decision to leave the agency.

PART FOUR

*Held to ransom by the
Fallow land*

17

If it had not been for the drought, now catastrophic and tormenting, for there was no sign of an end to it, Jacques would have had every reason to be happy.

First of all, Françoise had been there for a week. She had succeeded brilliantly in her final year at veterinary college, and with her thesis. For a few weeks, before beginning work in the laboratories of the National Institute for Agricultural Research, she was free, and planning to spend part of her holidays at Coste-Roche.

Dominique and Béatrice were also keeping well. They wrote frequently, always sent good news, and even envisaged a trip to the Corrèze in September.

Another pleasant interlude: Félix had spent ten days in Saint-Libéral with his son, daughter-in-law and grandchildren. Thanks to all of them, there was no lack of entertainment within the family.

Added to that was the imminent arrival of Jean. As expected, he had passed his bac without any problem, and he was due at the end of July. He had eventually accepted his father's offer and set off to explore England. And there again, Jacques was pleased about this, for it was he who had, by telephone, begged him not to make an ass of himself and to take advantage of the offered visit.

'Besides, with the drought, there's nothing to do here! I promise you, it's true,' he assured him. 'So go and find out whether English food is as bad as people say. And don't think you have to bring back an English girl, your parents wouldn't appreciate that very much!'

Finally, another reason to be content: good, reliable tenants had at last been found for the château of Saint-Libéral, thanks to Guy. From July 1977, it would welcome children of the employees of the Franco-Belgian wireworking firm Lierson and Meulen. This was a large industrial group which produced thousands of kilometres of fencing wire in its factories, and was also involved in ironmongery. One of the directors was a friend of Guy's and went hunting with him at Brenne.

Lierson and Meulen's decision was excellent news, for with the children would come the support personnel; male and female group leaders, administrators. Jacques had undertaken to find a couple of caretakers who would live there permanently and maintain the château. It would therefore remain open and ready to receive guests. For the firm also planned to organise, in peace and quiet and during the off-season, some seminars for their representatives and salesmen. All this would give a great boost to Saint-Libéral. Already in the plans was the tennis court so eagerly demanded by Peyrafaure, and also a swimming-pool, without which the Lierson and Meulen group would have refused the lease.

Of course, all these developments brought enormous costs which the community was unable to meet alone. Jacques had had to knock on many doors to obtain subsidies, and in particular, long-term loans at very favourable rates. He knew that the management of the entire operation would not be easy, but never regretted for a moment that he had launched into this venture. For it was really cheering to see his friends, neighbours and fellow citizens preparing to join in the rebirth of Saint-Libéral.

Already, Brousse was planning to develop his market garden to supply everything the château kitchen was obviously going to require. As for Delpeyroux and Delmond, they were proposing to provide all the milk, cheese, eggs and poultry the residents might need. Even Coste was mulling over the idea of investing in the purchase of a few ponies and horses which the young people, and not just those in the holiday home, would be delighted to mount. He even saw himself opening a sort of ranch, with refreshments, various games, and pony trekking around the local lanes.

'All he needs is to hire a few Red Indians and arm himself with a Colt pistol and it'll be the Wild West!' commented Pierre-Edouard sarcastically on learning of the project. He did not regard the transformation of Coste into a sheriff very favourably, and dreaded seeing the track he followed for his daily walk invaded by hordes of riders, with or without bows!

'I shall bring out my twelve-bore again, the day that happens! And not just for the Redskins!' he had warned.

Despite reservations and comments of this kind, Jacques, as mayor, could only rejoice to see his community reviving.

Josyane almost did an about-turn when she saw, even before entering, that the Claire Diamond salon did not look as it normally did. She thought it was arranged for a fashion parade: nothing was in its customary place, and spotlights were standing ready to illuminate the grand staircase. Conscious that her threadbare jeans and rather faded T-shirt were likely to be out of place amongst the couture house's choice products, she was about to take to her heels when Chantal caught sight of her, and beckoned her in.

'Look, have you seen my outfit?' asked Josyane after kissing her.

'And? What's the problem? It's Monday, there are no customers!'

'Monday?' she calculated. As a result of going to bed in the early hours, she occasionally lost count of the days: 'Well what do you know, I hadn't realised yesterday was Sunday.'

'You don't look very well, you know?'

'That'll soon change, I'm stopping work with the agency.'

'Ah! That's good news!'

'Maybe, but I've no other work. Tell me, what's all this fuss going on here?' she said, with a nod in the direction of the spotlights.

'That? Just the photos for our winter collections. But guess who's upstairs? Yes! Our friend Christian! He must be busy flirting with Karine!'

'Idiot!' said Josyane, blushing a little, but also smiling, for she was suddenly very happy to have come. 'In the first place your Karine is called Josette! What's more she's as flat as a lemon sole, and I'd be very surprised if he were interested in a stick like that! And besides, she's sure to be a dyke!'

'Ah, right! You wouldn't happen to be a mite jealous?' Chantal was amused.

'And why would I be? And on what grounds? Your Christian, I haven't seen him since I was in Tahiti!' she said with a scowl.

'Well, go and say hello to him! He'll be delighted, he asked me again for news of you. You know the building, go up.'

'No. I'll wait here!'

She had decided once and for all that she would not take the first step, and intended to stick to the principle.

'As you like, nobody's forcing you!'

'Just as well! By the way, have you any news of the family?' she asked, simply to change the subject for she had received a letter from her mother three days earlier.

'Yes, last night on the phone. Everyone's fine. But it seems they're suffering terribly from the drought. Just imagine, the Diamond has stopped flowing and the spring has almost dried up. When I think that we're delighted with this super weather!'

'That's true, it's very pleasant,' said Josyane absent-mindedly as she glanced covertly towards the staircase.

'Are you sure you don't want to go up?' her sister teased.

She was highly amused, for, without her lifting a finger, everything was happening the way she would have organised it if she had wanted to intervene. She had known for months that Christian was not indifferent to her sister's indisputable charms and that he had not forgotten her. But she knew too that Josyane was still smarting from her previous experience. Consequently, so as not to spoil or rush things, she had decided to leave it to fate. And today, 26 July, fate seemed at last to be taking a hand.

'All right, then, come and have a drink in the office,' she suggested. 'In the meantime he'll probably come down . . .'

'Oh! Don't make so much of it, please!' smiled Josyane, who knew very well that her sister had guessed her secret long ago. 'And don't imagine I'm going to throw myself around his neck! What an idea!'

'I'm not imagining anything. So you've finally decided to stop your silly job?'

'Yes, it was really getting a bit much. And then, it was a killer!'

'And what will you do now?'

'Not the slightest idea,' said Josyane, placing herself in the doorway to watch the staircase. It was then that she saw him coming down, his Bronica in his hand.

He in turn noticed her, stopped, smiled. Then, as a professional reaction, because the young woman's outfit and her style were a magnificent challenge in this stuffy, affected, posh salon, he lined her up with his camera.

'Do you mind?' he said at the same time. And, without waiting for the answer, he photographed her three times.

'That's mean!' she said without moving. Then she waited for him to approach and exclaimed: 'You took your time coming back from Polynesia. Were you held up by one of the local girls?'

'One? You can't be serious! More like twelve! Anyway, don't tell me you've been waiting for me, I wouldn't believe it,' he joked. Then he noticed she was wearing one of the shell necklaces he had hung around her neck the morning of her departure from Tahiti. 'That's nice, you still have that trinket,' he said.

'Oh! It wasn't easy! I've already had to restring it twice, the shells cut through the thread,' she explained. Then she realised that she had just given the game away, and burst into laughter.

Motionless in the shade of the huge chestnut trees which encircled the pasture, where the reddish earth was cracking open day by day under the sun, the animals were waiting. Exhausted by the heat, debilitated by thirst and hunger, irritated by clouds of horseflies which attacked them incessantly, they were lowing pitifully whilst listening anxiously for the rumble of the tractor which would bring them water.

For more than a week now the spring which fed their pool had almost stopped flowing, although according to the old folk it was supposed to be inexhaustible. Now, on the bottom, baked by the heatwave, a blackish, stinking mud was thickening and hardening. Jacques was therefore forced to fill his tank every evening at Coste-Roche, where water was not yet scarce, and to cover the four kilometres which separated his farm from the fields and meadows of the Heath.

Despite all the time this wasted, he did not regret having taken his herd over there. For although the drought was just as dreadful as on the plateau at Saint-Libéral, there were woods and thickets here, where the cows could shelter from the sun. They succeeded in stilling their hunger a little by browsing on the lower leaves, the ling and a few dried grasses in the undergrowth, for there was nothing left on the pastures. Shorn and dusty, they no longer retained the slightest traces of greenery. As for the fields where tobacco, beet and maize should have grown, in the heatwave they revealed only the shrivelled skeletons of dead plants. It was a desolate spectacle.

And the worst of it was that there seemed to be no indication of rain. For the leaden blue sky was not relieved by the shadow of a cloud. And the sumptuously luminous sunsets were followed by sunrises all just as sparkling, harbingers of warmth and fine weather. The holiday-makers were delighted: the pools, lakes and river banks of the area were packed, thronged by the masses who had every reason to feel happy and lively.

But in Saint-Libéral and throughout the countryside there echoed the monotonous bellowing of thirsty cows. Every-where too, from the break of day, taking up the response, the strident call of chainsaws and the heavy blows of axes sprang from echo to echo, as the oaks were pruned around which the cows and sheep crowded to snatch leaves and still tender twigs. Wisely, all the farmers were deferring the moment when they would have to broach their meagre stocks of hay. For if feeding had to start in August, what would be left in the lofts when February came? And yet it was essential that the animals were fed and watered!

Driven by thirst and hunger some of them, although quiet and peaceable until then, jumped the fences or crushed them. Then, mooing to their last gasp, cutting through by the shortest route, they bounded down to the bottom of the valleys where a semblance of greenery still clung to life. Or alternatively, and more seriously, they settled among the first vines they reached and nibbled them down to the stock. In the same way, attracted by the orchards, they pounced on and guzzled the leaves and fruit, at the risk of choking by swallowing big mouthfuls of green apples too quickly. Or again, guided by the smell of the little kitchen gardens which were watered somehow or other after a fashion, for they lay close to the houses, they gorged themselves on cabbages, carrots and beans. And even the strong, cloying smell of the tomato leaves did not deter them.

Fortunately Jacques' animals had not indulged in this sort of escapade. He really did not need that to take up his time. In fact, victims of the fierce heat prevailing in the piggery, three pigs weighing about a hundred kilos had succumbed, laid low by heat-stroke. Two sows, also within inches of apoplexy, had been saved in the nick of time by Françoise's initiative; she had performed a life-preserving bloodletting on each of them, then sprayed them thoroughly with cool water.

Since then, Jacques, Michèle, Françoise and Jean, who had arrived ten days earlier, took turns in the piggery, where the temperature was unbearable, to sprinkle all the occupants periodically. Jacques was very much afraid that water might now be cut off, rationed. Such an eventuality was quite probable and very worrying. For besides the pigs, he had to water his thirty-five cattle every day. With the heatwave, they each swallowed their fifty litres without difficulty. Now if, besides being underfed, they were to be short of water . . .

'You're right, those cows are hungry,' said Jacques to his nephew when he entered the enclosure that afternoon.

Busy with contractors' problems - the work on the château had begun a fortnight ago, but slowly because many of the workmen were on holiday – he had not had time to come the previous day and had left to Jean the task of driving the tank with its two thousand litres of water. He now had complete confidence in his nephew.

In one year Jean had changed a great deal; broadened out, grown seven or eight centimetres and acquired the build of a lumberjack. He had hands like carpet-beaters, shaved from necessity and not to be like the grown-ups, and had a fine voice, firmly fixed in the bass register. And above all he had become less impulsive, less dogmatic. He was prepared to accept arguments, no longer jibbed like a mule, and even went so far as to acknowledge that he could be mistaken.

Given that, he was still just as determined about his plans. With, however, one change which delighted his father. Although the idea of being a stock-breeder still gripped him, he admitted now that it would probably take several years before he could set up on his own account. And although he really hoped to achieve this one day, at least he declared himself prepared, for a while, to do the same as his cousin Dominique. On condition, of course, that it would be to manage a fine herd of pedigree animals. Jacques did not have the heart to tell him that such work was not so easy to find as he thought. He guessed his nephew would realise this for himself.

'You're right,' he repeated, climbing down painfully from the tractor, 'those beasts are hungry! Good God, look at that one there, how she's faded away! I know full well it's her calf killing her, but all the same!'

'We should at least bring them a few sacks of granules.'

'Hey, hang on! It's easy enough for you to say that! Do you know what they cost? And once you start . . . No, we're going to do the same as our neighbours; luckily there's no shortage of oaks here!'

'Where do we start?' asked Jean, catching hold of the axe which he had tucked in alongside the mudguard of the tractor.

'Remind me to bring the ladder tomorrow. But in the meantime let's tidy up this tree. You know how to climb, okay? Just leave the crown right at the top and prune as you come down. But mind you don't break your neck!'

'What an idea!' said Jean with a dismissive shrug. He slid the axe under his belt, sized up the tree, and climbed nimbly to the top.

The cows rushed over as soon as the first branch tumbled down. And it was such a pleasure to see them greedily swallowing the leaves and budding acorns that Jean stopped for a moment in order to watch them better.

244

'That looks great! They make me feel hungry!' he called to his uncle.

'Don't let me stop you! Look, tomorrow, remind me to bring them two or three blocks of salt as well. They've finished it all, natural in his heat.'

'Hey!' cried Jean, suddenly stretching out his arm. 'Have you seen over there? It's burning!'

'Where?' said Jacques looking in the direction he was pointing. 'Oh! Bloody Hell! My God, that's on the far side of the plateau, at the foot of the peaks, it's our place! Come on down, we'd better get over there, with this drought the whole plateau might go up, and the woods with it!' he said, quickly unhitching the tank. He waited while Jean climbed up beside him, and charged towards the black smoke which was already darkening a section of sky.

Starting from the edge of the track which wound towards the White Peak, the fire, driven by a hot east wind, leapt first on the bushes which covered the slope climbing up to the plateau. There you could make out the regular pattern of the little walls and boundary furrows which had formerly criss-crossed it, in the times when it was cultivated.

Well exposed to the spring sunshine, with an open aspect to the south, the plots which clung on there were rich with a soil suited to the spade; deep, easy to work, generous. Here, some sixty years earlier, succulent spring vegetables used to grow: the first extra fine peas, of an incomparable flavour, new potatoes with tender delicate flesh, juicy spring carrots, garlic and white onions, top quality green beans and even early season strawberries with a heady scent.

From there came the baskets and crates full of all that exceptional produce for which the wholesalers of Objat or Brive competed and paid the asking price, certain of making a great profit from the grand restaurateurs of Paris.

But for lack of manpower, and because the slope was much too steep to be cultivated mechanically, the gardens had been abandoned one after another. Then, very quickly covered by weeds, fleabane, broad-leaved dock and rye grass, they had subsequently provided a welcome for the first roots of bramble and dog rose. Encouraged by the richness of the soil, all the parasitic plants and shrubs had flourished, gaining on all sides, invading in giant strides with rhizomes, suckers and seeds, covering the land with an impenetrable barrier of thorns, spikes and creepers.

From a spark, the fire leapt to attack such a feast. Snapping up the blackthorn, brambles and bracken with crackling greed, it swelled up, spread out. And the red tongues, increasingly voracious, quick and long, swallowed in an instant the network of thorny brushwood, guelder rose, old man's beard and shrubs which emitted the sinister whine of boiling sap and splitting bark.

Its appetite whetted, strengthened by its first victims, it threw itself on the meadow spread out before it. This belonged to Yvette, but Jacques had rented it for years. Dry as gunpowder, it offered no resistance to the flames which darted now like grass snakes, jumped, flitted, busied themselves creeping in the layers of bent grass and the withered grey tufts of creeping soft grass.

Driven by the wind, fanned by its own force, the conflagration gained ground, spread across the plateau like a shifting blanket. And it was with the strength of a front which covered more than a hundred metres that the inferno, having crossed the Meeting field, attacked the White Peak. Eating into its flanks, with sudden high torches of flame it reduced to ashes the fragrant junipers, the twisted box trees, almost a hundred years old, and the great broom bushes which colonised the arid soil. The blaze then became terrifying. And its roar was so violent at the edges that it drowned the call of the bell in Saint-Libéral, at last tolling the alarm.

Monotonous, dismal, resounding from hill to hill, it appealed for help, begged all fit men to hurry along to try to control the wildfire up there, now encircling the White Peak with a moving crown, as stifling and evil as a stream of lava. And already, growing drunk on the stubble fields, feasting on the dead stalks of maize defeated by the drought, the fire grazed avidly on the plateau, homing in on the nut trees and plum orchards.

*

When Jacques and Jean finally arrived in the area of the blaze, a few villagers were already in position, trying to hold back the fire's progress on to the plateau fields. That was the only place where it could still be approached; for there, although the flames were lively and fast-moving, they were low. That was not the case with the ones devastating the peaks, which only tons of water might be able to control.

'Where are the others?' called Jacques.

'They're sure to come,' explained Delpeyroux. 'Us lot, and Valade, it happened while we were pruning the oaks on the slopes; so when we saw the smoke, you can imagine how we ran!'

'Bloody hell, we'll never stop it like this,' declared Jacques, observing how rapidly the fire was advancing, despite the furious, and exhausting, shovel blows which Valade, Delmond and Delpeyroux were dealing out to the flames devouring the stubble and dry grasses.

'And the fire brigade?' asked Jacques.

'Have been alerted!' said Bernical without stopping hitting. 'I did that myself, but by the time they get here from Ayen and especially from Objat! And then I gathered they had a job before this one behind Saint-Robert, towards Segonzac . . .'

He was already streaming with perspiration and tears, for the thick, acrid smoke was swirling all around, stinging the eyes, burning the mucous membranes.

'Right, can you manage to attach the rotavator?' decided Jacques, turning to his nephew. 'Then run and fetch it. Get Françoise to help you and come back as quickly as possible. Bring all the shovels you can find and remember, tell your cousin and aunt that women wouldn't be in the way, if we want to stop this inferno before it moves down to the village! Go on, hurry up! But mind you don't overturn the tractor!'

He did not wait for Jean to set off, but picked up one of the shovels brought by Bernical and rejoined his companions.

'Need to all get together,' he decided. 'And try to hold this corner, for the sake of the walnut trees. Because if it gets over there and takes a hold on the slope . . .'

The slope was the one descending towards Saint-Libéral. It was covered in wood, scrub, undergrowth. But above all, it was there that the roofs of houses showed above the treetops, the ones built in the mid-sixties, on the land which had then belonged to Léon and which Louis had sold as building plots.

'You're right,' admitted Valade, 'need to all get together in the same area.'

Elbow to elbow, trying to beat rhythmically to stifle the flames at the same moment, the men threw themselves head on at the blazing mass. Soon joined by ten, twenty, thirty volunteers, they had almost succeeded in controlling that small section of the fire when the wind veered, turned suddenly from east to north. It was only a brief change of direction, maybe a whirlwind created by the furnace roaring over the peaks. But however brief, the gust was so violent that it revived the blaze, renewed the flames' vigour and forced the men to retreat. Already, on their left a long flickering, red tongue was stretching towards Brousse's walnut plantation.

'My God! What are the fire brigade playing at? And where's Jean?' cried Jacques.

Like his companions, he was already crushed by exhaustion and on his face, now brick red under a mask of ashes, sweat and tears were tracing grey furrows.

'It's turning on us!' yelled Bernical suddenly. 'Over here, you lot! Over here! It's going into Duverger's tobacco! Dammit! We'll never hold it! Never.'

They rushed to the glowing front which was now attacking the tobacco, roaring like a wild beast. The plants, still green but withered by the drought, flared up, shrivelling and crackling. The smell of the smoke changed.

It was now half an hour since Jean had left for Coste-Roche to fetch the rotavator, and Jacques was worrying that he hadn't returned when he finally caught sight of him. He watched him and nodded his head in approval. Jean was doing the best possible thing.

Engine and clutch full out, he was moving parallel to the wall of flames, a few metres from them. And behind him, raising a cloud of red dust, the machine, its gearwheels humming as fast as they could go, was opening the ground, digging it up and, most importantly, scraping it thoroughly and burying the stubble. And the flames were suffocated and weakened on arriving at this band of almost bare earth; a few blows of the shovel finished them off.

'With him, we'll maybe hold it, at least on the plateau,' rasped Delmond in a hoarse voice. His mouth was so parched and coated that he could not even spit out the half-burnt cinders and dust which swirled around the men, choking them, burning their eyes, drying their throats and noses.

Almost a quarter of the tobacco was destroyed by the time Jean finally reached it. He stopped at the edge of the field, hesitated.

'Go on, boy, dig it up!' Duverger encouraged him. 'But my God, what a waste . . .!

Leaning on the handle of his shovel, exhausted, he was disheartened, battered. This ruined, ravaged tobacco was a loss of thousands of francs. The drought had already greatly reduced the value of the expected harvest; the conflagration was wiping it out.

'Go on!' he repeated, 'dig, boy, don't think of the tobacco, dig! We've just got to stop this bloody fire!'

'Hey, listen!' said Jacques suddenly, 'here's the fire engine at last. I'd better go over there to find out how we should organise ourselves now. Make sure you tell Jean to go across a second time and watch the fire doesn't jump.' He delivered a last blow with his shovel to the sparks sputtering at his feet and moved off.

He could barely stand, his back was hurting him so much, and he was bent double as he walked towards the red truck which he could make out on the edge of the plateau, outlined against the high flames devastating the peaks. For the Caput Peak was also ablaze now, like an enormous pine torch . . .

'Right, if you don't drive me up there straight away I'm going on foot!' threatened Pierre-Edouard.

Standing in the doorway, his eyes fixed on the heavy, black layer boiling up wildly above the plateau, he was fidgeting impatiently. Furious at being there, stuck at home, powerless, he was commenting continuously on the advance of the fire. He knew the peaks and plateau so well that he could almost say, to within a metre or so, where the inferno was and on which bush or tree it was feeding.

He had wanted to dash up there the moment he had caught sight of the smoke, just after the first peals of the alarm bell. However, Yvette had unfortunately gone shopping in Objat, and as she owned the only car in the family . . .

He had then tried to get a place in Peyrafaure's old 403, as he was also going up to the fire. But his car was already filled with men still young and strong. Men who were needed up there, who were awaited.

So, because he knew perfectly well that he could do nothing, that he would be of no assistance in the battle, he had let Peyrafaure go without insisting. Conscious of his uselessness, he had not signalled any of the vehicles flying past towards the inferno. They too were full of men, women and even children who would be much more effective than him. And he had waited, seething with rage, his gaze fixed on the big cloud of smoke which was growing denser and larger by the minute.

At last, Yvette had arrived. But now Mathilde, Louise and even Berthe wanted to dissuade him from setting off.

'Be reasonable. You can't do anything, you're not going to go and get in the way of the ones who are working!' Mathilde had begged.

'I won't get in anyone's way! Bloody hell, those are our fields going up in flames! Our trees! Our hills! I have a right to be there. It's still my property, hell and damnation! And you, Yvette, if you don't take me up there straight away, I'm leaving on foot!'

And as she knew very well that he would do it, and that nothing could hold him any longer, Mathilde shrugged her shoulders:

'Fine, then, if it amuses you to make yourself ill!' she said. 'But don't come complaining afterwards!'

'Right, let's go, we've wasted enough time!' he said to Yvette as he marched towards the car. He was about to get in when he changed his mind: 'By God! I may not be able to take a shovel to bash the flames, but I've certainly still got the strength to carry a drink to those who are fighting! And you're going to help me, you women, because even at your age, you can still do that!'

'Why not,' agreed Louise.

'Yes indeed . . .' said Berthe, moving towards the sink.

'If you think . . .' said Yvette.

'You're right!' said Mathilde.

'Then fill the bottles, all the bottles, a quarter wine, the rest water. And the same in the jerrycan! Come on, get a move on! They're thirsty up there, I know it. They're waiting for us!'

18

Encircled on the plateau as night fell, the fire, having reduced everything to ashes on the White and Caput Peaks, launched itself into the woods and scrub leading down to Fonts Perdus. There stood three-hundred-year-old chestnuts, enormous, bulbous trees, often hollow but still living; they flared up like so much cotton waste. And the oaks, acacias, Scots pine and brushwood blazed in their turn in gigantic and billowing whorls of smoke, roaring like a stormy wind.

Broken with exhaustion, the men who had struggled to prevent the whole plateau being destroyed felt increasingly discouraged when they realised just how dangerous, not to say impossible, it would be to check the advance of the inferno. Settling like an enormous, red, fluid octopus into the woods which covered the dizzy slope plunging towards the valley, the blaze was unapproachable.

Even the firemen from Objat and Terrasson, finally arriving as reinforcements, did not really seem to know how to attack it. They feared, quite rightly, to venture into the gullies and amongst the fallen rocks, to be cut off there if the wind veered again. It had strengthened since sunset and remained changeable, unpredictable. It blew now from the east, now from the north, stirred the seat of the fire and, sometimes seizing in flight the highest flames, hurled them twenty or thirty metres further into the tops of the pines which then seemed to explode in enormous crackling firework displays. And the pine cones, shooting out like grenades, flew in all directions and lit new brushfires.

'Do you know which way we could get down there?' the leading firemen asked Jacques.

Dead on his feet, with his back aching all over, Jacques was seated on the mudguard of a Jeep and felt incapable of moving, barely able to speak. He looked at the firemen who were training their hoses at full force but without great result; at the volunteers, now almost powerless, for there was no question of extinguishing fifteen-metre flames with shovel blows, and shrugged his shoulders.

'I don't really know,' he murmured eventually.

'Yes, yes!' exclaimed Pierre-Edouard suddenly. 'You'll have to go and block it at Calvary Coombe, it's heading straight over there!'

'Ah! you're still here,' said Jacques.

He had not seen his father for more than an hour, and thought he had gone back down to the village. He had noticed him handing out drinks to everyone and even, for a few moments, taking a shovel from a boy's hands and attacking the flames; just to prove that he could still be of some use.

'Can you direct us there?' the leading firemen asked Jacques.

'Yes, if you help me to stand up and get into your Jeep,' said Jacques with a sad smile. 'But you,' he emphasised to his father, 'get someone to take you down to the house; it's irresponsible being here at this hour, Maman will be worried.'

'No, no,' said Pierre-Edouard, 'she's still over there, on the plateau, not far away with Yvette. You do as you think fit,' he told the fireman, 'but at Calvary Coombe you should cut down a swathe of trees and perhaps make a fire-break, or else don't stint with the water . . .'

'We'll see,' said the officer, stepping up briskly to support Jacques, who was staggering. 'Hey now, mayor, you're not in very good shape!'

'It'll pass,' Jacques assured him as he climbed in beside the driver. 'Come on, let's go. We'll cut through over there,' he decided, pointing to a grove of trees half way up the slope towards which the flames were extending. 'There's an old track which is just about passable,' he explained, seeing the driver hesitate a moment, 'the trucks will be able to get through there, but they mustn't hang about.'

'Don't be afraid to cut the trees, over there!' Pierre-Edouard shouted to them as they were already moving off. 'If you don't stop it there, it'll spread into Villac forest, and then . . . And mind you take care, there's enough damage done as it is . . .' he murmured, turning towards the plateau where the hissing skeletons of fruit trees were still glowing here and there.

If I'd been told I'd one day see that! he thought as he contemplated the extent of the damage. Despite the darkness, he could sense it all around him, for on all sides, on the peaks and the plateau, he could still make out a few men extinguishing the last small fires. He approached the group of women who were talking beside the cars, and noticed Mathilde and Yvette.

'You're still there,' he said.

'We were waiting for you,' said Mathilde. 'Do you think they'll stop it?'

'I hope so! They've gone off to wait for it at Calvary Coombe. That's the only place they might be able to block it. Well, well, so you're here?' he called out as he recognised the pair of gendarmes from Ayen.

'Oh yes, Monsieur Vialhe, for the investigation,' explained one of the officers.

'Investigation? What do you hope to find? Everything's gone up in smoke!'

'One never knows,' the gendarme assured him. 'In this case, as the fire only originated in one place, I don't think it was due to criminal activity, more likely a walker's cigarette-end. It seems that some hikers did pass through the village this afternoon. They even visited the church before taking the path to the peaks, it seems . . .'

'They get the blame then, your hikers!' scoffed Pierre-Edouard. 'In my time, it needed more than a fag-end to light an inferno! Yes, in my time, there where it started there were nothing but gardens full of green vegetables! Nothing for the fire to devour, right! And the edges of the track were trimmed! You never saw a blackberry bush! You could sit down there without pricking your bum on the thorns! Yes sir! And there was no risk of fire catching hold!'

'Come along now, calm down,' said Mathilde, laying a hand on his arm.

But he was so miserable and angry that he could no longer remain silent, nor hide his pain.

'But now, with all these fields lying fallow, it's burning! And it'll burn again! And it's in the process of wiping out a chestnut plantation more than three hundred years old, and hundred-and-fifty-year-old oaks!' he said in a voice trembling with emotion. 'And do you want me to tell you why it's gone up in smoke? Because there's nobody left any more to stop the brambles taking over! No one to maintain the steepest hillsides any more! No one to prevent the brambles spreading and the undergrowth gobbling us up! But nobody gives a damn about that! And when you say someone should be looking after the land, you're treated like an old fool! Then the fire has all the cards stacked on its side! Oh Lord yes! Fine state it's in, our country. There they go, strutting about on the moon and leaving our countryside to go up in smoke! And this is only the start!'

'Come on, let's go,' insisted Mathilde, pulling him away. 'It's late, you know, we must go back down. You'll end up catching something on me!'

'The start!' he repeated. Then he shrugged his shoulders, climbed into the car and waited until nobody was watching him to wipe his eyes furtively . . .

As Pierre-Edouard had predicted, it was on the edges of Calvary Coombe that the men finally succeeded in mastering the fire. Drowned under torrents of water, encircled on either side and, above all, suddenly deprived of combustible material, it lost its arrogance, grew tame, then crept low and died with a prolonged damp hissing.

Stunned, dazed, hands and faces stinging, the men looked at each other at first without recognition, they were so dirty, covered in ash, stained with charcoal. In addition they had such dry mouths and throats, and lips so baked by the furnace heat, that each word was painful to articulate.

But unexpectedly, coming from one or other of the trucks, bottles of water made the rounds. Then, gradually, the men emerged from their stupor and became aware of the all-enveloping exhaustion which was almost paralysing them. Already, veiled by the layers of smoke, pale glimmers of the sunrise could be discerned in the east, beyond the black petrified trunks.

Starting out twelve hours earlier from the other side of the plateau, the fire had covered almost two kilometres in its longest thrust forward. Behind it, more than eighty hectares of ravaged woods, scrub, fields and meadows were still smoking . . .

Since she had found Christian again, Josyane was living in a state of bliss. She could not get over the fact that such happiness could exist, and was almost beginning to convince herself that her situation was unique, just as Christian was unique.

For even when she sought to reason with herself, to return to a semblance of objectivity, she was forced to admit that no other man she had ever known before would bear comparison with him. In the first place, she well realised, they were all kids. And the more they tried to play at being grown up, the more they made themselves look ridiculous.

In any case all of them, without exception, only thought of one thing, getting her into their beds as quickly as possible; the rest did not interest them. The worst had been poor Gilles, and she no longer understood now how she could have stayed such a long time with such a failure. She blushed at the memory! For she reckoned that Christian, next to all those pretentious little brats, was like an oak amongst saplings, a strength and certainty in the face of frailty, doubts and mediocrity.

'Right, go on, say straight away that he's the only man in the world, unique, the handsomest, tallest, cleverest, and let's not talk about it any more!' joked Chantal when her sister gave vent in front of her to impassioned hymns of praise.

'You don't understand!' she said dismissively.

But she was too intelligent not to recognise, in her heart of hearts, that her reply was stupid. When it came to men, Chantal had great experience, and she never hesitated to extend it! But that was no reason to underestimate Christian!

In the first place, he was reliable and always even-tempered, which was a great comfort, and very restful. What was more, even after searching thoroughly, she just could not find the slightest fault in him, which had the happy result of reducing her sister to tears of laughter.

'No faults, Christian? You're joking, surely? He's stuffed full of them – yes, and a good thing too! I know of nothing worse than men who try to be perfect! They're feeble, feeble in every respect!' Chantal assured her. She knew very well at the same time that Christian was someone on whom one could rely, hard-working, with not an ounce of boastfulness, honest, and also a very handsome man. But she so loved to hear her younger sister arguing that she took a mischievous pleasure in making her angry; with Christian as the target, it was really too easy!

'You can say what you like,' Josyane exclaimed in the end, 'Christian's not like the others . . .'

She would say no more about that, it was her secret. Nor about what made Christian so special, so different from the other more-or-less adult males with whom she had dallied, sometimes not without pleasure, but always without excitement. And she almost cried with happiness at the memory of the evening of their reunion during which, having invited her to an excellent restaurant, he had taken her for a stroll along the embankment, not far from the Ile de la Cité.

'There, now at last we can talk to each other a bit,' he had said as he leant his elbows on a parapet. 'There was too much of a crowd in the restaurant, and our neighbour was obviously ready to join in our conversation.'

'Yes, I saw that.'

'I wanted to ask: could we perhaps stop saying 'vous'? It seems a bit stiff, doesn't it?'

'Yes, rather, but it was you who began it!'

'Well, yes, I'm from another generation! But considering you nearly chucked me out of your hut the first time we met, what would you have done if I'd addressed you as 'tu'? Right, we'll say 'tu'?'

'Okay.'

'That's that. It's a bit crazy, what I want to say to you,' he had explained as he took her hand, 'but, if you want it as well, I'd like us to go a little way together. How do you feel about that?'

'I'm ready for that, but . . . How do you see it, this way?'

'As it should be. Just because I've waited till I'm almost thirty-five, it doesn't mean I don't believe in marriage.'

'Oh? Marriage? Straight off . . . well now . . .'

She had been taken completely by surprise. Firstly, because it was the first time in her life that such a proposal had been made to her. Secondly, because she had always thought whoever made it would use customary form and procedure. Yet Christian had neither wrapped up nor gradually introduced his remarks. His offer was clear, frank, straightforward; it was typical of him.

'Are you against marriage?' he had continued.

'No, but I didn't envisage things going in this direction so quickly.'

'There comes a time when decisions have to be made, a time to act. To prove to yourself, and prove to everybody, that you're changing course, changing your life even.'

'We hardly know each other . . .'

'And so, who's to stop us getting to know each other? I didn't say I wanted to marry you next week!'

'If you're so sure of yourself, to the point of announcing it to me this evening, when we've only just met up again, why did you wait so long before trying to see me? You could have got my address from Chantal!'

'I've had it since the day you moved! What are you thinking of, do you take me for a child?'

'And you did nothing? Why?'

'To be absolutely certain. Certain that I wanted to see you again, in a serious way, not for one of those easy affairs which everyone gets fed up with in the end.'

'And what's more, I might not have agreed to that sort of thing!'

'Exactly, I didn't want to spoil anything.'

'Oh, right . . . And what if we hadn't met again? And I'd thrown myself into the arms of someone else?'

'Rubbish! I knew very well you were waiting as well!'

'You knew it?'

'Of course, ever since I put that twopenny-halfpenny necklace round your neck. Ever since I saw you walking off towards the aeroplane, one morning, in Tahiti.'

'And you waited patiently for such a long time?'

'Is that a reproach?'

'No, but why so long?'

'Because Chantal told me that you needed to find your feet, on your own.'

'Oh? She's in on this, big sis?'

'No, no further than that. But she guessed it all, naturally. She's bright, your sister, you know!'

'And what if we hadn't met again at my aunt's just now?'

'I'd given myself until August the fifteenth before going to look for you! There it is, you know everything. So now it's up to you to decide.'

Her gaze fixed on the Notre-Dame illuminations, she had reflected for a long time before replying. It was not that she was hesitating, but she wanted to allow the seriousness of the situation to sink in. To grasp the idea that her life was about to change, in every way, irrevocably, and that she was mad with joy.

'Yes, I'd love us to make our way together, and for that way to be long – and very, very long!' she had said eventually.

'Then, our agreement should be sealed?'

'Of course.'

And she had thrown herself into his arms under the amused eyes of the walkers who were enjoying the sweetness of that summer evening, and its calm, for already Paris was on holiday.

Later on, when he had accompanied her back to the Rue de l'Ouest, she had once again got the measure of his real seriousness, his strength, his honesty too.

'Here you are, home. It is here, isn't it?' he had asked as he stopped his car below the block of flats.

'Yes; I see you really do know my address.'

'Did you doubt it?'

'Not for a second. Right, here we are . . . Do you want to come up?'

'No.'

'Why?'

'You know very well.'

Touched, she had smiled, then continued: 'Yes, I think I know, but I want to hear you say it. Go on, explain to me why you don't want to come up! I'm so ugly? I'm not your type? You think I'm frigid?'

'Oh yes, just like a furnace at white heat,' he had said, pulling her close to him. 'Ugly? Good Heavens no, you're almost as beautiful as my last conquest! Hey, don't pinch me so hard, you're making marks! No,' he had said, becoming serious, solemn, 'I won't come up this evening, nor tomorrow. After a while perhaps, yes, but not this evening. This evening must be marked out as different. It's not an affair we're starting. Or rather it is, but it begins with a capital letter. And if we don't want this one to be broken off, we'd better not manage it like others. So there it is, a nice kiss and we'll part until tomorrow, okay?'

He had placed a fleeting kiss on her lips, then leant over to open the door for her.

'Go on, go quickly, before I change my mind . . .'

She had got out of the car and almost run to the door of her flat, so as not to be tempted to make him go back on his decision.

It was all this that she could not explain to her sister; it was her secret, a huge part of her happiness. To know that Christian, in contrast to the posers she had met, was capable of waiting. Capable of patience, to prove to her that he considered her different from all the others, that she was to him unique.

After all the effort he had put into fighting the fire, Jacques could no longer climb onto his tractor, nor even take on very strenuous physical work; his back was torturing him. So, taking advantage of the presence of Françoise and Jean, he tried not to exacerbate the pains in the small of his back and only undertook the administrative chores at the mairie and those of the conversion work at the château. And there, it was not as easy as all that!

A dormitory, refectory and showers needed to be provided. Also bedrooms for the group leaders and a large kitchen: in short, the means to accommodate the sixty children whom the Lierson and Meulen company would be sending in two batches spread over July and August 1977.

But because the conglomerate had also announced that a week-long seminar would take place in April, it was essential to check that the various skilled workers were present each morning on the building site. That was not always the case, and as the project manager they had hired had other things besides the château to supervise, Jacques had then to fill in for him. A few telephone calls were sometimes enough to round up the absentees. But he was very often obliged to jump into his car to go in search of some craftsman or other, supposedly detained elsewhere by some urgent repair work.

Nevertheless, despite these additional tasks, he was happy to note how lively Saint-Libéral was in comparison to the preceding years. For not only did the workmen lend animation, but more, there were numerous inquisitive holiday-makers who came to take a look at this village which the whole region was talking about. And the fire had increased their number.

Now, the ravaged hills had become a place to take a walk. Jacques thought you really needed morbid taste to come and gaze on such desolation like that. For what with the drought which would not end, the plateau had turned into a lunar landscape. So appalling that even Pierre-Edouard did not wish to go up there any more.

'I'll go back there when it's rained,' he stated. 'Besides, I don't like all those walkers who come to gaze on our misfortune: I might say something rude to them . . .'

Jacques knew that the old man had, fortunately, other sources of satisfaction. Firstly, in July he had spent a good while with Félix. Now he was eagerly awaiting the arrival of Dominique and Béatrice. They had confirmed that they would be coming over in mid-September and everyone was happy about that. But at the moment, he was preparing in particular to welcome his granddaughter Josyane and her fiancé. For this was the great news in the family. Twelve days ago, that is on the day after the fire, Josyane had telephoned to announce her engagement to one Christian Leyrac. Mauricette and Jean-Pierre were deliriously happy. Truth to tell their youngest daughter had given them enough to worry about; now they had the right to relax a little. For according to Chantal, the suitor was really nice, serious, exactly what Jo needed. Only Mathilde was a little anxious. Jo was her favourite granddaughter and she had frowned on discovering that her fiancé was almost ten years older than her.

'Well, there, you've got a nerve!' Pierre-Edouard had exclaimed. 'And what about us then?'

'How do you mean, us?'

'So I'm not eleven years older than you, by any chance?'

'Yes. But in our time, it was quite different!' she had interrupted peremptorily. 'And you were only twenty-nine when you married me. And you would have done it earlier if it hadn't been for the war ... This fellow, that'll make him almost thirty-six! If he's waited until now and he's not a widower, he must be a terrible fast-liver!'

'That's a fine thing to say about Léon!' Yvette had then joked. 'He was forty-three at our wedding!'

Disconcerted, Mathilde had blushed and then shrugged. She had no wish, especially in front of her sister-in-law, to support her arguments by citing her brother; until his marriage, Léon had never aspired to any award for virtue ...

'All right, I haven't said a word,' she had concluded, 'but I'm dying to see this fellow. And if I believe he's not right for my little Jo, I shall let him know it; he'll be hearing from me!'

'You'll do nothing of the sort!' Pierre-Edouard had cut in. 'We know very well that Jo's your favourite, she's so like you! But that's no reason to interfere in her affairs! Anyway, don't forget she managed perfectly well all by herself for the three years she stayed away! So don't you go playing at mother-in-law, it'll be enough with your daughter in that role!'

'It's because I'd like so much for her to be happy ...'

In fact, although she never mentioned it, Mathilde was still affected by Marie's divorce, and feared that Josyane might one day seek the same remedy if her choice turned out to be disastrous, like her sister's. She was therefore anticipating the visit of her granddaughter and fiancé with some anxiety. They had said they would be arriving on 28 August. That was in another two days, and she found it still a very long time!

Too busy watching a sky that was still a delight to sun-worshippers, Jacques paid little attention to the change of government which marked the last week of August. For a long time, anyway, political jousting, from whichever side it came, had barely interested him. At the very most he merely smiled on realising that his father and Aunt Berthe were going to miss a chance to comment wickedly on the television news when they caught sight of the former Premier on it.

'When you've had the good fortune to make your début with the General you shouldn't team up with a Judas!' grumbled Pierre-Edouard, who could not forgive the head of state's treachery in April 1969.

'You can say that again,' added Berthe, who had not forgotten the suppression of the 8 May memorial service. 'I really don't understand how a man who appears to be intelligent could have associated with that other chap, the accordion player, Giscard d'Estaing. What's more, he plays like a pig!'

However if all this was mere trifling, the drought was no such thing. Now the damage had been done, the maize was lost, the tobacco dry before being ripe, the potatoes so ridiculously small and shrivelled as to be pitiful. In any case, the ground was so hard that it was impossible to lift them.

And the worst thing now was seeing the cows grow thinner day by day. Under-fed, thirsty, they had already acquired an ugly-looking, coarse, lifeless coat. As for their calves, even by buffeting fiercely with their heads, they barely succeeded in extracting from the udders, flabby as empty goatskins, a quarter of the milk they needed to put on weight. They looked like bean-poles, and there was absolutely no need to be interested in stock-breeding to understand that they would never regain those missing kilos. Like all animals for the butcher's trade, they were unsaleable anyway, for the market was now overloaded with stock which the breeders had got rid of in the hope that the sacrifice of one animal in three would enable them to maintain the rest. The calculation might have been valid if it had finally begun to rain.

But the sky was still superb, for holiday-makers and town-dwellers. Magnificent in its purity, it was full of promises of bathing in the coming days, of refreshing siestas, picnics at the water's edge, lovely, long, mild evenings in the garden, filled with the rustle of chirping crickets quite undisturbed by the chime of ice-cubes clinking in glasses misted with condensation.

But to those watching for clouds, to those awaiting the providential storm, the sky seemed so unmercifully set on drought day after day, that it became agonising, almost frightening, since there was no longer any hope of some development towards a change for the better.

So on this account as well, this desolation which afflicted the countryside and was so painful to contemplate, Jacques did not complain too much at being forced to take care of his back and not go out into the fields any more. But this was only temporary; Françoise and Jean would be leaving again before the week was out. At that point, fit or not, he would certainly have to look after his animals, go each day to lop oak trees for them and take them water. And whether he liked it or not, his back would have to hold out!

'And you say he was from the Brive area, in the south?' persisted Pierre-Edouard.

'Yes, that's what I've been told,' confirmed Christian, politely refusing another portion of *conflit d'oie* with mushrooms and sauté potatoes offered to him by Mathilde.

He could not eat another morsel! And he was amazed that they could dine on such luxurious produce without appearing to be aware how lucky they were to be able to take their fill like this of foie gras, cep mushrooms, *conflit d'oie*, omelettes with chanterelles, guinea-fowl and real farmyard chickens!

During the three days he had been in Saint-Libéral, he had swallowed more foie gras and other regional specialities than in the rest of his entire life! As a result he was beginning to wish for a plain lettuce leaf as his whole dinner. But that was unthinkable. As Pierre-Edouard had said to him at the outset, handing him a plate of succulent, delicious-smelling smoked ham:

'You haven't come here to die of hunger! Tuck in! After that there's nothing much . . .'

Christian did not believe a word of it, but had felt obliged to serve himself a slice as thick as a hand. After that had come rillettes, then a joint of veal with green beans. And now he was absolutely unable to take more *conflit d'oie*; it was beyond his strength.

'No, really and truly. It's excellent, but . . . I'm not used to it, you see?' he said, passing the dish to Josyane.

She was seated beside him, and smiled at him. He guessed her thoughts and knew that she was happy to see him there, at her grandparents' table, with Mathilde on his left, Pierre-Edouard opposite him and the three aunts who were also observing him, weighing him up, watching his behaviour, reactions, remarks.

'If I understand things right, you're going to put me through one hell of an examination,' he had said to Josyane just before arriving in Saint-Libéral, three days earlier. She had painted a portrait of the whole family in detail, which did not make it sound at all reassuring, since it was obvious that nobody there lacked character and they would be checking that he had one as well . . .

'And then, you'll see, my grandmother Mathilde, I adore her. I'm supposed to look like her.'

'Then we'll get on very well, she and I.'

'But watch out. She's never at a loss for a quick retort either! And what's more she has sharp eyes, almost as bad as my grandfather!'

'They're not going to eat me alive, are they?'

'No, no, and besides you've got inner resources!'

Resources, without a doubt, but much less appetite than he should have had to do the meals the justice they deserved.

Apart from this drawback, obvious proof of lack of practice, everything had run very smoothly. First of all because he had immediately got on well with his future parents-in-law. Then because he had won over Mathilde from the first day. For it was indeed true that Josyane greatly resembled her; she had that same dark, piercing gaze, that same shape of face, with a small, slightly tilted nose and a very sweet smile.

So, without thinking, because he was moved to discover in that elderly, rather shy but smiling lady what Josyane would probably one day become, he had retained her hand in his and said exactly the right thing, just like that, in all sincerity:

'Jo said she looked a lot like you. It's true, I'd have recognised you anywhere!'

And the old lady's smile and eyes had told him that he was part of the family from now on, and very welcome.

'And you've never tried to find out more about him?' persisted Pierre-Edouard. He was extremely interested by what Christian had told them about his great-grandfather.

'No, it wasn't so easy.'

'I can imagine that,' said Pierre-Edouard, to whom Josyane had spoken of Christian's family, and especially about his father in the Resistance, who had died in the camp where Berthe's fiancé had disappeared, during the winter of 1939.

'I'll tell you a funny thing,' Louise intervened. 'On the railway workings here, in 1908, there was an old man who had worked in Panama too, on the canal. Yes, I remember it well,' she murmured, with signs of emotion. 'Octave often spoke to me about it . . . Don't you remember?' she asked her brother.

He reflected, then shrugged his shoulders with some irritation. He did not like to be made to lose the thread of his remarks.

'Not particularly, no. But it doesn't matter, it's interesting all the same that you have Corrézien blood in you. Usually it's not bad stuff. And you say your profession is taking photos? Just that?'

'Well, yes.'

'And that provides enough to feed a man?'

'That depends on the man!' affirmed Josyane, placing her hand on Christian's.

'For me, at present it does provide enough and I hope it'll continue to,' he said, cutting himself a minute slice of Cantal cheese, in order not to offend the lady of the house.

He noticed that Pierre-Edouard suddenly seemed absent-minded, distant, and almost jumped when he shouted at Louise:

'What was that you were saying, you, about Panama?'

She repeated the story to him, brought it all to mind again.

'Miladiou! Yes! Of course I remember that old man!' he said at last. 'He quite likely knew your forebear. There's a funny thing! Yes, I remember, he talked to us about the Americas, every evening at the Chanlats'. My father didn't really like me hanging around the inn, but when he'd gone to bed . . .'

He fell silent, became thoughtful again, lost in his memories.

'I see you don't like cheese, you haven't taken any!' he said suddenly to Christian, disconcerting him with his changes of subject. 'Now then, why don't you do the rounds of the solicitors? They'd be able to tell you!' he said, returning to his original idea. 'Why yes!' he continued, seeing that nobody understood. 'To find out where your ancestor lived! he's bound to have bought or sold something, that fellow, either him or his father! All that , it's written down somewhere! Or else in the christening registers . . .'

'I hadn't thought of that,' admitted Christian. 'Well, if I have the time, one day I'll try to find out which village Antoine Leyrac came from.'

'And you'll be right to do it,' said Pierre-Edouard. 'It's important to know where you come from, that gives you your roots. And say what you like, roots allow you to stand tall, and to withstand storms properly too! Ask young Jo: if she remembers what her grandmother taught her, she can tell you about the Vialhes as far back as my great-grandfather. That's not bad for a start, is it?'

19

WHEN Christian and Josyane embarked on the exploration of the Corrèze, it was for pleasure and not to discover possible traces of his ancestors. For despite the drought which disfigured it, lending its hills and slopes the russet tints of autumn's end, it remained beautiful in the valleys, harmonious. Bewitching, too, with its little blue-roofed villages nestling amongst the chestnut groves, its romanesque churches with their moss-covered stones, and remnants of castles, hidden by ivy, but still impressive, clinging fiercely to their crags.

Hand in hand, Christian and Josyane set out each morning and did not return till nightfall, exhausted but happy, their heads full of memories and country scenes.

But it was on visiting Saint-Libéral, lane by lane, that Christian had an idea he considered realistic enough to communicate to Jacques.

The evening before, Jacques and Michèle had come down to eat dinner with Josyane's parents. They were feeling rather low, for Françoise had gone away that same morning, while Jean had returned to Paris two days earlier. His absence was already being felt, for even though Jacques was improving slightly, his back was still making him wretched. Probably rather disheartened at finding himself alone again, he had fallen to doubting whether the château's new function would be sufficient to breathe fresh life into Saint-Libéral.

'You've got to understand: the kids will be great, but from the commercial point of view, I don't think they'll encourage shopkeepers to come and open up. What we need are adults. Even for three months, that would at least be something. Because we have to see things as they are; it's never going to be farmers who'll make the village live again, might as well look to holiday-makers right away. But how to attract them?'

'I thought you'd planned a swimming-pool and even a tennis court!' Josyane had said to him.

'Yes, but I doubt whether that'll be enough. And then, God willing, there'll be rainy summers too, so the pool and the tennis court . . .'

'Your uncle's right. Your village lacks excitement, life. Look at that boarded-up inn, it's so sad! And that lifeless grocery store! It's really off-putting to tourists!' said Christian as he dragged Josyane into the little road which led to the village hall.

'Look, they've refurbished it a bit,' confirmed Josyane after pushing open the door. 'Ah, I see . . .' she said, reading the plaques which adorned the walls.

In fact, for lack of young people to fill it, and since the château was no longer available, it was there that the Léon Dupeuch Association met, none of its members less than sixty-five years old . . .

'Not bad, this building,' said Christian, having made a tour of it. 'But, my goodness, it's gloomy! It already feels like an old people's home!'

'Yes, like the whole village. And when you see it in winter . . . It's frightful, I swear, dire.'

'I believe you. But there's sure to be something that can be done. Where the countryside is so beautiful, so welcoming, and where one eats so well, far too much but so well, you can't just stand by and wait for the village to die.'

'Easy to say! If you think that my uncle hasn't said all this to himself already, a long time before you!'

'Probably, but all the same I have a little idea. He can make of it what he will. We could go and give it to him straight away, if you like.'

'An idea? A sensible one?'

'I think so . . .'

'Come on, tell!'

'This!' he said, miming the movements of a photographer. All the time he had been on holiday he had not touched his cameras, and she did not immediately understand.

'How, that?'

'Well now, here you have the premises, the countryside, as

many subjects as you like! I think, if there were , in the summer, a permanent exhibition of the best photos by amateurs, that would bring in a few people. It should be aimed at holiday-makers. There are plenty round about; the problem is to entice them here. And as they all see themselves as first-rate photographers, they need to be flattered . . . All right, lots of them are actually rotten, but what of it, nothing venture nothing gain! Right then, with a bit of publicity, a few displays, a small lab, several joint first prizes, things like baskets full of local delicacies, that should attract the crowds. And, what's more, it would provide a good pastime for the kids in the holiday home! Come on, let's go and see your uncle. Your dying village is getting me down!'

'It's not so stupid, your idea,' said Jacques, 'but the trouble is, I know nothing about photography myself, nothing at all!'

Christian and Josyane had found him at Coste-Roche, filling the water tank for the cows still confined in the woods at Heath Farm. As he continued to have great difficulty in driving his tractor, it was Michèle who was going to transport it.

However, whilst waiting for the tank to fill, Jacques, Christian and Josyane, seated in the shade of the porch, were refreshing themselves with a well-chilled beer, it was only four in the afternoon according to the sun, six by the clock, and the heat was suffocating.

'Yes,' repeated Jacques, 'I don't think I've taken twenty photos in my life!'

'It's not you who'll be taking them,' Josyane said, amused, 'so where's the problem?'

'The best ones will still need to be judged, the ones to be exhibited!'

'If that's all, we'll come and lend a hand,' promised Christian. 'All it takes, at the start, is to launch the idea. Afterwards it should run of its own accord. But to begin with, in my opinion, you need a specific subject which attracts people here, to the community. For example, the best photos of the village, the church or the old houses.'

'Not so stupid,' murmured Jacques. 'That would oblige the

tourists to come. But they'd better not think they're in a zoo and take us for zebras. I have a few electors, among them my father, who would *not* appreciate that! And nor would I!'

'Easy', interrupted Christian. 'You stipulate in the rules that any photo including any person or group of people will be automatically eliminated, and there's an end of it; you have peace!'

'You know, young Jo,' smiled Jacques, 'I have the impression that you've found a resourceful fellow!'

'Yes, I feel it was worth the trouble of going to wait for him in Tahiti,' she joked.

'Enough flattery,' interrupted Christian. 'One essential is missing in this business.'

'Oh, what?' asked Jacques.

'Food!'

'How's that?'

'Yes, the people who come here must find something to eat. I'm amazed that nobody's thought to open a farm guest-house or something of that sort. They do it in other areas.'

'Easier said than done! You can't become a cook just like that!' retorted Jacques.

'Go on! We've been here eight days, and I've already put on at least four kilos! That's the sort of cooking to offer the summer visitors; real, solid stuff made with good local produce. You don't realise, but I know people who would make a detour of fifty kilometres to eat the way you eat at home at your sister's, or your grandparents, so there!'

'You don't imagine that I'm going to open a guest-house here?' Jacques smiled. 'As it is I never reach the end of all my work!'

'No, but there's an inn in the village and it's a real shame that it's closed. That's where something should be set up!'

'And why not . . .' murmured Jacques reflectively. 'After all, poor old Suzanne's daughter might be pleased to be able to rent out that barn of a place. It's been for sale since Suzanne closed down. That was in . . . I don't know any more, she died shortly afterwards, it must be more than ten years . . . Yes, for sale, but nobody's interested. Bloody hell, your ideas are worth looking into, and I'm annoyed with myself for not having thought of them before! I must be too old . . .'

'Not at all. You know, it's not always from close up that you take the best photos,' said Christian. 'You see too many of the irritating details and not enough of the subject as a whole. Personally, I like to step back a bit. As for your village, don't give me the credit, it's just that I see it from the outside, with all the necessary detachment.'

'Well then, I hope you'll come back often, to help me to stand back,' said Jacques. 'I'm bloody well in need of it. Or else, I'm too old.'

That morning, 4 September, Mathilde seized her chance while Christian was in conversation with Berthe – they were discussing the next catalogue for the House of Claire Diamond – to drag Josyane out to the kitchen garden. For a long time she had wanted to see her granddaughter alone, but had not yet found the opportunity.

'Look, isn't it miserable, all dried up, all dying,' she said, stepping into the little enclosure full of vegetables. 'What wrongs we must have done the good Lord, that he should send us weather like this!'

'It's more a question of an anticyclone,' smiled Josyane, 'but then, why not the good Lord as well!'

'I wanted to see you alone,' said Mathilde, instinctively lowering her voice. 'Here, help me pick the tomatoes, at least they benefit from the sun. Yes, I wanted to say to you first of all: I'm very, very pleased with your fiancé, I like him a lot.'

'Yes, I'm extremely lucky . . .'

'Definitely. Listen, I don't know how you . . . That is, how you two are living; that's not my problem. For a long time now I've understood that you, you young people, don't behave as we did in my time. We, you know, before we were married, well . . .'

'I know,' interrupted Josyane, a little confused and embarrassed to hear her grandmother tackling such a subject, 'but you mustn't worry!'

'I'm not worried! You know, Jo dear, I didn't wait for you,

273

after all, to find out how good it is to be in the arms of the man you love! So I'm saying to you, you do as you like, as you see fit. I don't know whether it's better or worse than before, that's not my business. Anyway, it wasn't that I wanted to talk to you about. I simply want you to make me a promise, just one.'

'Right away, if I can!'

'Promise me you'll get married. I'm not even asking you to wear white, because . . . But promise me you'll get married!'

'Of course! Christian is set on it, and so am I!'

'No, you misunderstand me. Really marry,' said Mathilde, lowering her voice. 'Marry properly, not like Dominique and Béatrice . . .'

'But what are you talking about!' attempted Josyane, guessing that she was preparing to lie to no avail. 'Why do you say that?'

'Come on, don't take me for an idiot,' said Mathilde, with a trace of sadness in her voice. 'You know, you're the first and only person I've spoken to about this. And when you've promised me you won't do the same as your cousin, I'll never speak about it again, to anyone!'

'So you were in the know about Dominique?'

'No, I realised afterwards. But I didn't say anything, on account of your grandfather. If he knew, he'd be so unhappy, it would disappoint him so . . . Yes, it was afterwards I realised.'

'How?'

'Simple. When you marry in church, you always have the photos taken in front of it, in the doorway, with the whole family . . . I didn't see any photos in front of the church, none. There were only some photos taken at Guy's . . .'

'And that was enough for you to understand everything?' asked Josyane.

She was filled with admiration. And above all, overflowing with affection for her grandmother, now quite tiny, but still so strong, so clear-thinking. And above all so discreet, who suffered in silence because her grandson had not followed the normal course for a Vialhe. Who suffered but remained silent, so as not to distress her aged partner.

'It was enough for me to realise that Berthe was a bad liar ... So I want you to promise me that you'll get married in church, and I want to see the photos!'

'Listen, bonne-maman, listen carefully,' said Josyane, stepping nearer and placing her hands on her grandmother's shoulders. 'You won't need photos to be sure. We're going to get married here, in Saint-Libéral, and you'll be in the place of honour, with grandfather, both of you beside us. There, are you happy?'

'When?' murmured Mathilde, whose eyes had grown a little misty.

'Very soon,' promised Josyane. 'We haven't fixed the date yet, but very soon. Perhaps before the end of the year. Oh, you're not going to cry, are you?'

'It's nothing, it doesn't matter,' said Mathilde, turning away, 'I'll say I was peeling onions ... But why did Dominique do that?' she continued.

'Not say anything? That was on account of you two. Yes, grandfather and you, he didn't want to upset you. He knows you well, you see. And then, you can't make people believe! And Béatrice didn't want to play the hypocrite. The proof is, you must have seen it, she didn't have a white dress. There you are; personally I think that proves she's honest.'

'That's true,' admitted Mathilde. 'She wasn't in white, she's honest. And you say it was to avoid upsetting us that they said nothing?'

'Yes, the only reason.'

'Then they were right,' said Mathilde after a moment's reflection. 'Yes, it wouldn't have done for your grandfather to find out about that. You must have seen, he's growing old, poor thing, he's growing smaller, he complains. Sometimes he loses his memory a bit too. So, it's especially important not to upset him, he doesn't deserve it ... Right, now we won't speak of this matter again, of this ... this set-up, never again. And now, give me a kiss. I'm so pleased about what you've told me, so pleased! May I tell your grandfather?'

'Certainly, but it might be best if I tell Christian first!' said Josyane, placing two big kisses on her cheeks.

'He doesn't know?' Mathilde looked anxious.

'That he's going to marry me? Oh yes! It was he who brought it up first, he'd better not have changed his mind! But we hadn't decided yet to do it here. Now, it's definite, you can get the church ready!'

'Are you sure, really and truly?'

'Sure, Christian has no reason to deny me that. Come on, we'll go and ask him straight away.'

As they had both foreseen from the beginning, it was without forethought or calculation that Christian and Josyane put an end to the kind of test which they had voluntarily imposed on themselves on the evening of their reunion, almost two months earlier.

Since then they had never gone beyond the limits they had set themselves. Thanks to this, they had discovered the charms of tenderness and consideration, of suspense. And it was with amusement, on the evening of their arrival in Saint-Libéral, that Josyane had observed her mother's astonished expression when she had requested two rooms, without further explanation. Obviously her mother did not expect such prudishness on the part of a girl who had left on an impulse to travel the world on the arm of a boyfriend, not even her first! But she had asked no questions, and had taken two pairs of sheets out of the cupboard.

Since then, each evening, Christian and Josyane parted sweetly at their thresholds after several embraces which never went so far as to force an inevitable conclusion. Yet they were expecting it; it was just that each day they had made a sort of game of repeatedly putting it off.

It was two days before their return to Paris that everything moved on in a calm and logical progression. Before even admitting it to each other, they each deduced that the moment had come to begin a new stage, that the imposed period of waiting no longer served any purpose.

Less than an hour earlier, neither of them had planned that their walk should lead them to the other end of the plateau, away from the peaks, there where the fire had not penetrated. And neither of them had planned to go and sit in the shade of the pines bordering the field called Léon's Letters. Rather breathless from the hike, for the heat was oppressive, Josyane stretched herself out with a sigh at the foot of a pine, on a carpet of moss so dry that it rustled beneath her weight.

'What a heatwave! I'm sweating like a crock of water in the sun!' she said, peeling her soaked T-shirt away from her body.

He regarded her, smiling, and found her more beautiful than ever. He appreciated once again the firmness of the small round breasts, their swelling nipples pointed under the material, the flat stomach which ran down sweetly to the gentle mound of the pubis, shapely under the skirt clinging with perspiration. A skirt rucked up far enough above the knees to reveal honey-coloured, lithe, exciting thighs.

She hummed as she stretched herself out, propping her head in her hands linked in a cradle behind her neck.

'It feels so good, here! You see,' she explained, 'here, we're at home! Well, at the Vialhes'. That's called Léon's Letters, I'll tell you why one day. When I was little, during the summer holidays, I used to come here with my sisters. We often met up with Dominique and Françoise, we used to make shelters. What fun we had! And in season, every now and then we went to scrump a bit from the neighbours' plum trees and even their apples! The apples were still sour; it sets my teeth on edge just to think of it!'

He sat down at her side and drew her to him.

'What I'd really like to do now is to eat you,' he said, placing a hand on her hip.

'Really eat me up?' she whispered.

He smiled, assented, and settled her head in the crook of his arm as she curled towards him.

'It's true, in the end it gets boring, this being sensible,' he murmured.

'Yes, very boring.'

'So shall we decide we've played long enough at the-first-to-give-in's-the-loser?' he continued.

'Yes. But there won't be any loser, quite the opposite,' she said. She briskly stripped off her T-shirt then unhooked her skirt fastenings:

'And now, don't waste any more time,' she breathed. 'And be very, very loving. This evening, now, I can tell you I've wanted you since the first day I saw you in Tahiti; that's ten months I've been waiting.'

'Me too, and it's been a very long time.'

The sun had just set when they came to their senses again, but the sky remained brilliantly radiant, still almost dazzling, so deep was the azure. Leaning over her, he saw that she was about to speak, and placed his forefinger on her lips.

'Ssh!' he smiled. 'You know what they say: the first one to talk after making love always says something foolish!'

'That's why you wanted to speak first?'

'Of course, to take responsibility for the folly.'

'That wasn't foolish,' she said, stroking his chest. 'And even if you've made me a beautiful baby, it wouldn't be! You know, I really hope you have created one! Yes, I do! I'd very much like to have your baby, straight away! Well, in nine months! After all, you did all that was needed, I think?'

'Well, I certainly didn't do anything to prevent . . . But you know, if it didn't work, don't get in a state, I'll be glad to try again whenever you like! Tell me, what's that?' he asked, placing his forefinger on a small brown mark which adorned her left breast. A little crescent-shaped mark which seemed to support the areola. 'What is it?' he insisted. 'A surprise present? It's absolutely delightful!'

'Oh, that?' she said, laughing. 'That's the family hallmark, seal of quality. It really is, it seems that my grandmother has one in exactly the same place! It was she who told me, when I was little. And it's because I take after her that I have a right to it. My sisters haven't got one. You have no idea how I used to infuriate them with it, when we were girls. I managed to make them believe it was they who had something wrong with them! Right, perhaps we should be thinking of going back?'

'Yes,' he said.

He gazed at her with tenderness, placed a kiss on the tip of each of her breasts, then helped her to slip on her T-shirt and remove a few scraps of moss from her skirt.

They walked down towards Saint-Libéral hand in hand. On their right, shining like a mirror, not yet full but already rounded, the moon was rising above the blue horizon.

Jacques turned the knob of the radio so forcefully that it almost came off in his fingers. For him, nothing was going as it should.

In the first place, the weather forecasts were all announcing the continuation of what the ignoramuses on the radio called the fine spell! He felt ready to put on a demonstration for them of this fine weather! Ready to invite them to come right here and see what things looked like – an orchard dying of drought, cows which could no longer bellow, they were so hungry and thirsty, and soil now grey, crazed, cracking open.

And, as if the weather forecasts were not enough to depress his spirits, the news had got in on the act. Now the commentators tried to outdo each other in finding fault with the farmers – those moaners who, not satisfied with evading taxes, were going to get money from the honest taxpayers, made to pay for the fine weather – perhaps it had lasted a little too long, but it was certainly less catastrophic than was being made out! And to support this type of clumsy lie, they had even produced some pedant who baldly stated on the airwaves that the peasants' tales of woe were without foundation! As proof, he maintained, France comprised one million three hundred thousand farmers who were the owners of one million three hundred thousand tractors! Well, if you knew the price of a tractor, did you not have the right to question the alleged poverty of the land-owning classes?

There again, Jacques was ready to issue an invitation to this loudmouth, just to let him see the reality of this luxury implied in his proof. In particular to let him know that many farms north of the Loire each owned half a dozen machines, or even more, which negated his theory.

Unfortunately, this fine orator was not the only one to spout. In fact it was open house to whoever could pour most scorn on those moaning farmers who were always complaining about everything and constantly demanding subsidies!

'Naturally, the moment there was the chance to muck things up, the morons governing us jumped in feet first! You couldn't find anything more pathetic than those technocrats!' he railed, each time that the television or radio news maliciously drew attention to the tax which some inordinately stupid, incurable halfwits had thought fit to impose; and christen the drought tax!

Like all his neighbours and friends, like all farmers, he felt it as a slap in the face each time a commentator mounted that hobby-horse again and attacked, repeating those two words: drought tax.

'For heaven's sake! The townies already turn up their noses at us, despise us because we're peasants; what'll happen now! But they're doing it deliberately, up in Paris, there's no other explanation! And for a start, they're perfectly able to help us without touching the taxpayers! Who does this bloody useless government think is going to believe they've got no more money? They know very well where to find it when it comes to bailing out the Renault Corporation!'

And as if all that were not enough to sap his morale, Dominique had informed them that he was deferring his arrival for at least a fortnight. Before coming it seemed he had to host several big noises from Mondiagri on a fact-finding tour. This change was obviously not a tragedy, but still, it was annoying. Just as it was extremely annoying that Michèle had to go out each afternoon to drive to Perpezac and take care of her mother.

The poor woman had slipped in one of the alleyways of the village and broken her hip. Without believing that she had deliberately stepped on a banana skin – it was difficult to imagine black ice! – Jacques could not prevent himself from grumbling whenever he thought of her. During the thirty years that he had known her, he could not remember a month having passed without her complaining of some bronchitis, flu, assorted aches, pains in the head, stomach, teeth, or ears, which obliged Michèle to step up her visits to Perpezac.

'You'll see,' he had often said to his wife, 'You'll see, just to muck us about, she'll break a leg one of these days!'

That was virtually what had happened! And, of course, Michèle was saddled with the work, as usual!

Since she no longer had the time to drive the tanker to Heath Farm, he had then been forced to mount the tractor again, despite the terrible pains that this induced. But as there was no question of constantly calling on his neighbours, and no question either of allowing the cows to die of thirst, he heaved himself onto his old Massey-Ferguson every evening and set off towards the woods at the Heath.

Very relieved to be rid of his visitors at last, Dominique did not even wait until their plane had taken off to climb into his car and take the road to Tunis.

If all went well, once he had got through the town, he would still have two full hours of driving before reaching Béja. Once there, he would collect Béatrice from the maternity hospital and return with her to their villa nestling amongst the date palms, tamarisks and oleanders of Bab el-Raba.

He felt much better since he had seen his visitors disappear into the embarkation hall. Not that the four men – a German, an American and two Frenchmen – were unpleasant, but they stank too much of greed, self-interest and ambition for him to wish to make friends of them. Very competent, no doubt – otherwise they would not have occupied the positions they held – they thought only of revenue, profitability, international markets, exchange rates.

When he had signed his employment contract with Mondiagri, Dominique certainly suspected that the word philanthropy was not part of the current vocabulary in the multinational company. The aim of the firm was not to teach the peons of Peru or Mexico better ways to cultivate their maize-plots. It was not to instruct the peasants of Black Africa how to avoid transforming their countries into deserts of beaten earth, nor the Egyptian fellaheen to irrigate better, or the unfortunates wading in the Indian rice-fields to protect their meagre harvests from rats.

Dominique knew all that. However, whilst he was in Guyana, that situation did not worry him because it it did not apply – or applied in a less obvious way – on French territory.

On the other hand, since he had been in Tunisia, his judgement had matured, and his critical abilities as well. He had therefore more and more difficulty in not bucking the system, such was his disapproval of the policies pursued by the brains of Mondiagri.

'It can only be one of two things,' Béatrice told him when he started talking to her about it, 'either you're incredibly naïve, or you were aware of it and didn't care when you signed the contract with them!'

'I didn't think it would reach such a level of hypocrisy. And then, admit it, in Guyana it wasn't so apparent!'

'No, of course not! But the fact is that you were working with equipment and techniques suited to all the Amazonian types of areas! By which I mean to say that everything you were developing on the technical side will be exported to northern Brazil, to Colombia – to Central America, and I don't know where else!'

'Stop! I'll begin to regret my job in Algeria. With Ali, at least we were genuinely working to help his mates feed themselves better, to make progress! But here!'

In fact, he knew very well now that the aim of the sharks managing Mondiagri was to increase their hold over the Third World. To set up research units almost everywhere, committed to creating or testing new varieties of seeds, animal hybrids, chemicals, to promote healthy plants and even equipment adapted to each soil, to each climate.

Next, and the faster the better, it was vital to persuade the governments to specialise in new forms of production and cultivation. As if by chance, Mondiagri would then suggest the selected seeds, the fertilisers, the animal feeds, the equipment and even the technicians to be responsible for setting everything up. Then, still paternally, the vultures of Mondiagri would also guarantee the purchase and export of the crops, at the lowest prices and after deducting various expenses, naturally!

Always ready to be of service, these same good Samaritans went so far as to sell back some of the provisions to those same countries, in order to allow them to feed themselves a little . . .

It was against all this that Dominique was rebelling. And yet he himself was only the advance guard, the reconnaissance scout, the pilot fish, the one testing the terrain. When his work was done the bulk of the troops would arrive, the lucrative government contracts, countless promises, bribes too. And

282

always poverty. With as a bonus, for many peasant-farmers, the neglect or abandonment – if not the destruction – of their traditional agriculture which, however poor it was, still prevented them from dying of hunger one day out of two.

And the four mercenaries from Mondiagri whom he had just accompanied to the plane had come for just that. To make contacts, pave the way, to demonstrate, with the help of the experimental farm, that such and such a crop was exactly what the country needed. And to crown it all, they would no doubt be believed and even thanked, as saviours.

He avoided, at the last second, an absolutely decrepit Peugeot 203 taxi which had just shot out suddenly from the right. He hooted in rage, overtook the wreck and even cut him up. He was not in the mood to be intimidated by anyone. And especially not by a ruin of a taxi which smoked like a threshing machine and stank like an oil tanker.

'You look tired,' said Dominique, kissing his wife. He wrinkled his nostrils, for she smelled somewhat of ether and the delivery room: 'Have you been busy?'

'Yes, two births this morning and this afternoon a vaccination clinic. I won't describe the results, the mothers were wailing more than the kids! And how about you, is that it, have you sent off your VIPs?'

'Them, they can go to the devil! Anyway, they thank you for your hospitality, so welcoming, so French, in short, all that nonsense! But when I think that you served them foie gras from Coste-Roche! Those rogues didn't deserve that!' he said, turning on to the road which climbed towards Bab el-Raba.

'I was thinking of your promotion!' she joked.

'With foie gras like that, it's already settled! You'll be able to tell my mother, that'll make her happy.'

'Oh by the way, the post from France arrived this morning, just after you left.'

'And what's new?'

'I bet you'll never guess!'

He shrugged his shoulders, and changed down a gear because the slope was steep.

'So tell me?'

'Jo's going to get married, on the fourth of December, in Saint-Libéral . . .'

'What?' he exclaimed, laughing. 'Jo? Getting married? Is this a joke? Well, well, if anyone had tried to tell me! But who's the poor devil chancing his arm?'

'A photographer, a friend of Chantal's.'

'That's not very reassuring! Between Chantal and Jo, it would be difficult to say which has wreaked the most havoc! He's brave, that bloke! And what's more he'd better be in good health, because with Jo he'll need to deliver the goods . . .'

'Don't be unkind, Jo's very nice.'

'I'm not being unkind. I love her, you know that. But you're not kidding? She's getting married for real?'

'Yes.'

'Then that's absolutely the best news of the day! Well, we'll soon get some details.'

'Yes. You know, I'm thrilled we can leave at last. Even for a week, it'll cheer us up. And then maybe it'll put you in a better temper,' she added, seeing that he had resumed his sombre expression. 'Are you still thinking about your visitors?'

'No. Well, yes, I'm thinking particularly about the report they asked for; it seems it's urgent. And as we're leaving in three days . . .'

'They can wait! You're not going to take work home, are you? Your parents wouldn't like it! And nor would I, which is more important!'

'We'll see . . .' he replied vaguely as he drew up in front of their villa.

'If you play that trick on me, I can tell you it'll be bad news for you!' she warned, getting out of the car.

'Oh yes? You'll arrange separate rooms perhaps?'

'Right on!'

'Fine,' he said, moving aside to let her pass, 'so this evening, my only option is to get ahead beforehand. With my work, of course!' he said, patting her bottom.

Although engrossed in his work – the report which he had to prepare was long and detailed – Dominique lifted his nose from the page when Béatrice came out of the bathroom. He surveyed her from head to foot whistling softly, and nodded.

'Congratulations, lovely lady! You're magnificent! Yes, you are! And I know what I'm talking about . . .'

Still covered here and there with a few drops of water, with just a towel wrapped round her waist, which revealed one thigh to the hip, she was very attractive. He noticed once more that the semolina, frequently used in their diet, had a tendency to fatten her a little. But it was not yet a problem. Rather than thin, angular women he had always preferred the dimpled ones with rounded hips, soft to the touch.

'You're not going to work all night, I hope?' she asked, sitting down on the corner of the table.

'No; anyway, it's impossible under such dreadful conditions,' he admitted, placing one hand on her knee and lowering his eyes to the half-open towel.

'Well come on. That is if you want to get ahead in other ways than your work . . . But don't wait until I'm asleep!'

'I'm showering and coming,' he said, closing his file, 'and to hell with the report!'

He joined her shortly afterwards, and immediately forgot Mondiagri.

It was whilst he lay resting on her and they were still light-headed from their embrace that she whispered to him, her lips close to his:

'As your job seems to absorb you to the point of blindness, I'll have to point out to you that we've just been making love as a threesome . . .'

'What?' he jumped. He moved away sharply, observed her: 'Are you sure?'

'Yes. I'm way overdue now. And then, I am quite well placed to recognise the symptoms.'

'Wonderful!' he said, kissing her and hugging her once more, 'wonderful! But tell me, it must be only just? I may be absentminded and stupid, but all the same I'm not blind.'

'Yes, it's a little over a month, the baby'll be here at the beginning of May!'

'Well, what a thing . . .' he murmured, still in shock from the announcement.

Although, in the three months since Béatrice and he had decided to increase the Vialhe family, he had found time to prepare himself for the news she had just given him, he nevertheless felt strangely different from the person he had been half an hour earlier; he had altered. And his wife, suddenly also seemed changed; more solemn, more serious. Much more beautiful too, and strong.

'So that's what the semolina was . . .' he said.

'What are you burbling about?'

He stroked her hip and explained.

'Yes, I thought you'd put on a few kilos on account of the couscous,' he said, laughing and gently pinching her thigh. 'And these too, the same thing . . .' he said, passing a hand under her breasts. 'For a little while I've found them even more magnificent than usual, and that's saying something!'

'Ah? You noticed that. Naturally, whenever you can get an eyeful you do! But you didn't see that I was dead-tired every morning!'

'Er, no . . . But is that true? Are you feeling ill? Very ill?'

'No more than is normal,' she reassured him. 'And now I really must sleep, I'm tired. Are you going back to your work?'

'Oh no! Not now. This evening I'm staying with you. With both of you,' he continued, having placed a kiss on her stomach.

He turned out the light and snuggled up to her.

20

JACQUES took his foot off the accelerator, left the tarred road, and turned up the steep lane which wound towards the woods of the Heath.

A thick cloud of very fine, red dust surrounded the tank and tractor as the tyre treads bit into the dirt of the track. This had become so dry, light and powdery that it covered and tinged with ochre all the withered grass and dry thorns which colonised the edges of the way; bitter and suffocating, it made the searing breath of the solar winds even more painful.

He slowed down again and prepared to change gear. He was nearing a hogsback which needed to be approached at full speed but in second gear, otherwise the hammer blow transmitted to the tank might throw it off balance. And it was unwise to forget the weight, and especially the force of inertia, in two thousand litres of water when shaken too violently.

When it eventually rains, and the soil is less hard, I'll have to level off this hump, he thought. But in fact, when it's rained I won't need to bring water to the cows!

He began to disengage the clutch and cried out, suddenly pierced by an uncontrollable pain which started in his left buttock, tore through his loins, and immobilised him.

Paralysed by a fiery stabbing which stopped his breath, it was so agonising, unable to move his legs and still less to press on the pedal, he saw the ridge approaching.

Too fast! I'll be thrown off! he realised in a flash.

Instinctively, he pulled on the lever which cut off the fuel. But the tractor had already bounced over the obstacle. Almost at the same time, Jacques heard at his back the terrific bang made by the water as it slapped around inside the tank. Then he felt the tractor tipping, dragged by the weight of the tanker which was sliding to the left, turning over as it twisted the coupling.

I've had it! he thought, seeing the right front wheel of the tractor already more than a metre off the ground.

Then, despite the hellish pain paralysing his legs, he clutched at the wheel guards, heaved himself from the seat with the strength of his arms alone, and threw himself to the right, praying that the wheel would not drag him under the machine. It struck him violently in the stomach and flung him to the left.

He just had time to tell himself that Dominique and Béatrice, arriving the next day, would be there for his funeral. Fireworks exploded in his brain. He lost consciousness.

Michèle was not worried by her husband's absence when she returned from Perpezac. Ever since she had been obliged to go and see her mother every afternoon, Jacques had fed the pigs alone, each evening. But as he also had to take water to the cows he had brought forward the feeding-time. Nevertheless, he did not leave until late in the afternoon, and only returned at dusk.

One thing was certain, he could not delay until it was completely dark; the tractor's lights had not worked for the last two months. And even for someone who knew practically every metre of the countryside, it was not wise to drive blind.

Convinced that Jacques would not be long, for the sun had just set, she was singing as she prepared the evening meal. The knowledge that Dominique would be there next day filled her with joy. He had not been back to France since his marriage and had most probably lots to tell, and Béatrice too.

Relations between Michèle and her daughter-in-law were good, but slightly ambivalent. Without admitting it, Michèle was almost intimidated by her. In the first place, Béatrice was from the town, which gave her an ease and confidence that was sometimes rather disconcerting. In addition, she took a lot of trouble over her dress and make-up. And there again, Michèle felt at a disadvantage when she compared her work-worn hands to those of her daughter-in-law, her face, coarse and reddened by the fresh air, to that of Béatrice, always smooth and delicately made up.

Also there was no doubt that Dominique adored her, doted

on her. That was fine, but Michèle felt rather pushed aside not forgotten certainly, but a little less appreciated than before. She was intelligent enough to know that it was all quite natural, and the most important thing was for her son and daughter-in-law to be completely happy. However, even though she reasoned with herself, she still felt rather awkward in Béatrice's presence. The proof of it was that she could never manage to use the familiar 'tu' as Jacques had done from the start. That really simplified a relationship, made it less stilted.

I ought to try, from tomorrow, she promised herself, and I'll ask her to say tu to me as well; that is, if she doesn't mind . . .

She suddenly noticed that it was almost completely dark, and was surprised at her husband's lateness. Not yet very worried, but still, prompted by the need to reassure herself, she went to the doorway and listened out, hoping to hear the droning of the tractor. But only crickets were singing and bats squeaking as they chased mosquitoes.

'Now what's he up to?' she murmured to the dog stretched out in the courtyard dust. 'Hey, what are you doing here?' she asked in surprise.

Usually the animal was not tied up like its companion called 'the pointer', and enjoyed trotting along beside the tractor; it followed Jacques like a shadow. But the sun was still so hot when he left on the water run that you could understand the old mongrel's laziness.

If he leaves it any longer, he'll just have to walk back, she said to herself.

The moon was only in its first quarter: a tiny crescent quite useless for lighting the way. She took a few steps, went beyond the yard, listened again more carefully.

'No, nothing . . .' she remarked, biting her lips.

Now tormented by a little nagging fear, she tried once more to reassure herself. Then she suddenly made a decision, ran to the car and took the road to the Heath.

At first it was the smell which annoyed him. Still half-conscious, unable to understand why his bed was so hard, Jacques began to groan and wrinkled his nose. The stench of fuel and hot oil was unbearable and particularly out of place in his bedroom . . . or maybe it was the oil change he'd just done which had dirtied his hands . . .

No, no! It was more than two weeks since he'd completed that operation, he had even changed the diesel oil filter! Then why was it stinking so much, there, right under his nose, practically in his pillow which rustled as if it were stuffed with dry leaves?

He tried to turn over to resume his slumbers free from that nightmare stench, screamed in agony, and then regained consciousness completely. Gasping for breath because of the stabbing pains shooting through his back, he still took in his situation at a glance.

Above him, overturned on its side, the tractor was pouring out oil in every direction. It was flowing thick and warm from the engine and the axle, and forming a huge slimy pool which was now soaking into his shirt. And as the diesel oil had spurted out first and much more quickly, there was nothing surprising about the way he stank.

It must be at least ten minutes I've been lying here like an idiot! he reckoned, looking at the sun which was disappearing behind the trees. Then he suddenly realised how lucky he had been, felt himself pale, and thanked the Lord.

But for the big oak stump which was propping it up and had halted its spiral, the tractor would have turned over completely. As it was he lay almost underneath it, his chest against the big left wheel with part of the tread digging into his ribs.

'My goodness, I've had a close shave . . .' he murmured, gently feeling his head. He had a huge bruise above the nape of his neck, but it was not too painful. I knocked myself out as I fell, and if the tractor had continued its roll, it would have flattened me without my knowing! It could have gone up in flames, too, if I hadn't stopped the engine. Seems my time hasn't come . . . Right, I've got to get out of here.

It was then that he realised with anguish that he was incapable of getting up by himself. The moment he moved, the pain was such that he almost fainted away again. He could not even get his legs under him in order to lift himself up.

Good God, I must have bust something in my spine as I fell . . . Then he remembered that acute pain had paralysed him just before the accident: That's true, and that's why . . .

He forced himself to think it through, to reassure himself; carefully tried moving his toes, which obeyed, then his feet, which also deigned to respond.

Okay, it's probably something less serious than the spine . . . But as for getting myself upright all alone . . .

That was impossible, too agonising, beyond his strength. And yet I can't stay here with my nose in the oil! And then, good God, what if the batteries make contact, I'll be roasted like a pig!

He felt fear knotting his stomach at this thought and began to crawl, elbow over elbow, suffering the torments of the damned. It hurt so much that he was crying. Groaning and dragging his legs, he moved away from the tractor, crept through the dry leaves.

Exhausted, coiled like a foetus to try to assuage the searing waves eating into his back, he curled up at the foot of a chestnut tree. It was when he wanted to tighten his belt a notch to try to stop the ache at its source, there in his lumbar vertebrae, that he made one move too many. Overwhelmed by pain, he saw the sky revolving above him and the enormous branches of the chestnut toppling down. He thought they were going to crush him, and lost consciousness.

'Oh my God! No! No!' cried Michèle, as the headlights of the Ami 6 came to rest on the overturned tank and tractor. Her sudden braking raised a cloud of dust which whirled around in the lightbeams.

Her heart gripped in a terrible vice, she leapt from the car, rushed to the tractor and burst into sobs, convinced that Jacques could only be under the machine, since he was nowhere to be seen. And such was her relief, when she heard his voice emerging from the darkness, behind her, that her tears flowed twice as fast before ending in a nervous laugh when she understood that he was alive.

'You're there! You're there!' she said, kneeling beside him. She touched him, stroked his face, kissed him, hugged him.

'Careful, careful,' he advised. 'I can't move at all, you'll have to go and get help!'

'But I can't leave you!'

'Go and fetch help! Phone Brousse, and Doctor Martel.' And as she seemed to hesitate, he continued: 'I tell you I can't move at all. You can't carry me even to the car, after all.'

'And if I support you?'

'No. I must have some bloody thing trapped in my vertebrae, it's hurting like mad! Go quickly and fetch help. Look, I've been here more than an hour, I can wait a bit longer . . .'

'I'm going to call the emergency services.'

'Not that! That would complicate everything! And then, by the time the ambulance arrives from Brive! No, no. Anyway, I don't want to go into hospital.'

'But what if something's broken?'

'Doctor Martel will tell me. Go on, get going. Oh yes, tell Valade too: he'll have to bring our animals something to drink, otherwise they'll break everything down, you can hear them bellowing from here already . . .'

'That's all we need, for them to escape!' she said.

'Yes, go quickly. You'll do the best you can, I know. But organise it so that my parents don't get in a panic.'

'Of course,' she said, leaning down to kiss him.

He sensed that she was crying, and held on to her.

'Just remember I was very lucky. Very,' he insisted. 'As my mother would say, the good Lord was with me. At this moment you might have been a widow! So unless you're crying because you're not one, stop it and go and get help.'

'You're right.'

She gave him a last kiss and ran to the car, where the motor was still running.

Motionless in the darkness, concentrating on not moving so as not to exacerbate the gnawing pain paralysing him, Jacques stared at the few stars he could make out between the leaves. One of them, an enormous one, twinkled just above him.

That must be it, my lucky star, he thought bitterly.

He would have liked not to succumb to despondency, still less to despair. However, although he had escaped death almost by a miracle - he knew that tractor accidents were generally fatal - he did not manage to feel as pleased as he should have done at being unharmed.

And anyway, I'm not unharmed. Here I sit like a lemon, unable to move, confined to barracks. And how long for?

That was his main worry, his obsession. All would depend on the state of his back. Either it could be put right, and the accident would become just another unpleasant memory, or the damage was irreversible and would prevent any exertion. And then the farm would go to the dogs, for it was impossible for Michèle to manage it alone. And as for taking on a paid worker, you might as well hand in the keys right away. The herd, pigs and land did not bring in enough to afford such a luxury.

'It's been my fate to have really failed at everything,' he murmured, reproaching himself for voicing once more that dismal refrain.

It had lain on his mind for more than thirty years and he forced himself to banish it, to forget it, when he felt strong in health and spirits; he had a tendency to give in to it when fatigue and worries assailed him.

It's true! I wanted and was supposed to be a veterinary surgeon! That blasted war had to go and ruin everything! Six years lost, buggered up! And she makes the most of it by marrying the first little sod to come sniffing around . . .

There it was, one of his secret, painful thorns, stuck forever in a tiny corner of his memory, which sometimes sprang back to life . . .

She was called Marie-Louise, and had promised to wait for him, to marry him. And he had believed in it. No doubt she had too. But, there again, the war had come to destroy everything. Goodbye to Marie-Louise and his illusions! It was a real tear-jerker, like a magazine romance!

Bah, she was nothing compared to Michèle, he told himself, to banish the rather hazy but still touching image of a young girl before the war.

That was true. But even though Michèle had always been

an excellent wife, a good mother and a dependable partner through life, she did not have the power to suppress for ever his lost dreams.

No more than Françoise's success could make him forget that he too, one day forty years earlier, had resolved to follow the same route. And, there again, goodbye to the fine plans for the future!

And now I'm going to end up the confirmed duffer. All because the ruddy war forced me to take over a farm which was already sinking into decline . . .

On this subject, too, he knew that he was not being objective, that he blackened the picture. In fact he had made the Vialhe farm extremely productive, and had been able to live off it and raise his family there. But what made him bitter was living always on the borderline of poverty, of collapse even. Fighting a losing battle, still having, at his age, frightening loan repayments. Having to row ceaselessly against the current, so as not to be swept away, swallowed up like so many others; it was wearing, exhausting.

And now that Michèle and I were finally going to breathe a bit easier, since the children don't need us any more, my body gives up on me! My God, I'm fed up with always having to fight on, fed up with struggling . . .

He wanted to turn over a little for numbness was creeping into his legs, but groaned with pain as soon as he tried to move.

Nothing doing, it's seized up . . . And what's more, now I'm dying for a pee! Still, not going to wet myself like a baby! I already stink of fuel and oil . . .

He managed to unbutton himself, turned a little on one side and relieved himself. But the proximity of the soiled leaves and moss annoyed him straight away. So once more, despite the pain and the weight of his legs dragging behind him, he crawled a little further off.

Well, what are they waiting for? What are they up to? He no longer knew how long he had lain there, his back against the warm earth.

He felt all his black thoughts returning, all those sombre reflections which he hated. Then, to chase them away, he tried to distract himself by contemplating the sky. He even ventured to count the stars which he glimpsed through the gaps in the foliage. He thought he had checked off sixty-three when he finally heard the noise of vehicles climbing the dirt track.

'Well, bugger me, you had a bloody lucky escape!' Delpeyroux whistled as he shone his torch on the tractor.

'Oh, is that you?' said Jacques. 'You're here? And you too!' he remarked, recognising Brousse, Coste and even Peyrafaure in the light of the car headlamps.

'Of course we're here, what d'you think? Wouldn't you have come if it had been one of us in your place?' said Brousse. 'It was the doc who told us to get together and come up, so as to move you more easily. We've even thought of a ladder, as a stretcher!'

'Where's the doctor?' asked Jacques.

'He won't be long,' Brousse assured him. 'By a stroke of luck, he was in the village!'

'Who with?' asked Jacques, immediately thinking of his father.

'At Antoinette's! Seems she got sunstroke coming back from the cemetery, that'll teach her! It's true, with this heat, that sort of thing could quickly land her next to that old fright she goes to visit there!'

Jacques managed a pale ghost of a smile. Old Antoinette was one of those rather bizarre but colourful characters who provided gentle amusement for the whole of Saint-Libéral. Widow for more than fifteen years of a lewd drunkard, who had been as bad-tempered as a sick pig and beat her black and blue almost every evening, she did not let a single day pass without going to pay her respects at her deceased husband's grave. There, after stirring the soil a little, pulling a few weeds and shifting the vase of artificial flowers, she murmured a few Ave Marias, then left again, at peace. At least that was what the charitable souls asserted . . .

Those less charitable, and they were more numerous, swore that the old woman's mutterings had nothing to do with the 'Hail Marys' or any other pious recitations. In fact, if old

Antoinette made the effort to trot as far as the cemetry in all weathers, it was for the pleasure of being able to whisper over the grave: 'There you see, you old bastard, you're there, right underneath, and I'm still here, alive and kicking! And I'm trampling on you!'

'And Michèle, what's she doing?' asked Jacques suddenly.

'She's coming. She called on your sister and brother-in-law to tell them,' said Brousse. 'Now don't worry about your cows! Valade is just filling his tanker and he's taking them something to drink. Is that them I can hear bellowing like that?'

'Yes, they're waiting for the water,' said Jacques. 'Hope they don't break down the fence . . .'

'No, no, don't worry,' Delpeyroux reassured him, 'we'll take care of it all. And tomorrow, we'll come and fetch your tractor. My God, what a lucky escape you had!'

'Yes, you can say that again,' admitted Jacques. 'You know, you fellows, you're good mates, real mates.'

He was deeply moved to see his neighbours and friends around him. Touched to discover that even Peyrafaure had taken the trouble to come. And yet he had not always seen eye to eye with him.

'How did you know?' he asked him.

'Brousse told me as he went by my house,' explained Peyrafaure. 'But don't get in a state about that,' he added, anticipating Jacques' worry, 'we didn't raise a hue and cry. Your parents definitely don't know anything. There'll be plenty of time to tell them tomorrow, after you're sorted out!'

'That's it, tomorrow, and gently of course,' said Jacques.

Framed by his sister and brother-in-law, stretched completely flat on the bed, washed, clean, almost rid of the oily smell and best of all, relieved by Doctor Martel's injections, Jacques began to take a more serene view of life again. But that did not last long.

'Good, this time you can't get out of it,' the doctor told him, returning after discussing the matter with Michèle.

'Get out of what?' he asked rather curtly, for he had a premonition about the answer.

'It's the operation, or a wheelchair before very long. This time, you almost killed yourself. The next attack could come when you're in the car. And then too bad if there's a kid crossing the road when you can't brake any more . . .'

'Oh come on! You can stop that sort of argument, it's called blackmail! Look, I know my back is in shreds, but . . .'

'There's no but,' cut in Doctor Martel. 'You must be operated on as soon as possible. And as soon as possible doesn't mean in a fortnight's time! It means it's really urgent! Oh yes, just you wait till the effect of the injections wears off . . .'

'I know,' said Jacques wearily, 'I don't need you to tell me that it'll hurt! Right,' he sighed, managing a faint smile in Michèle's direction, 'how are we going to do it? I mean the farm, the cows, all that!'

'I'll cope,' she assured him.

'Come on, you know very well you won't manage all by yourself!'

'I'm telling you I'll cope with it! The neighbours have promised to come over. And Mauricette will help me, Jean-Pierre too.'

'Of course,' agreed Mauricette, 'we'll come.'

'You'll soon get tired of it! Anyway, Doctor, how long will it take after the operation?'

'Well . . . some time, yes . . . I'm not a surgeon, and . . .'

'You're a bloody hypocrite instead!' cried Jacques. 'Come on, give it to us straight, right! One month? Six months? How long?'

'It will certainly be necessary to avoid heavy work for several months, yes; but I do mean heavy work.'

'Like the tractor?'

'Oh, that! That's the worst thing for the vertebrae. So if you want a repeat of this evening . . .'

'Right,' sighed Jacques. He considered the matter, then decided. 'And where am I supposed to have the operation? If it has to be done, I'd prefer it to be by a good butcher, not one who does it with a knapped flint!'

'I know of one. Oh, I'm sorry!' the doctor corrected himself with a smile. 'Yes, I know a good specialist in Bordeaux. He's

297

an old friend, a fellow student. If you like, I'll contact him this evening. Right away even, the choice is yours.'

'As if I had any choice!' grumbled Jacques. 'Go on, I'll give you a free hand. But from now on, the quicker the better! And don't feel you have to tell me it wouldn't have come to this if I'd agreed to have an operation earlier, I know that! So don't lay it on!'

'But I'm not saying anything, am I!' the doctor defended himself. 'Yes I am: where's your telephone?'

Although informed with great care by Mauricette, Pierre-Edouard still took the news of his son's accident very badly.

Actually until then he had been so pleased to be seeing Dominique again – Béatrice and he were due to arrive that same evening – that he was totally unprepared to hear bad news. It shocked him, left him speechless for several seconds.

'And is it serious?' he asked eventually.

'But I've told you, no! There's not even a scratch on him!' Mauricette assured him. 'However, he still has to be operated on.'

'And that's what you call nothing?'

'Now listen,' Mathilde intervened, 'you know very well he should have had it done a long time ago! So now he'll have to go in. But it'll be all right!'

She endeavoured to be reassuring, calm, but was concealing her anxiety poorly. She had never undergone a single operation, and regarded clinics and hospitals as totally unhealthy, treacherous places. You knew when you were going in and what for, but as for knowing when you were coming out again and in what state . . .

'And all his animals, eh, who's going to look after them?' he queried.

'The neighbours have promised to help us,' Mauricette assured him. 'I'll go and give Michèle a hand as well. And Jean-Pierre'll come too, in the evening after school.'

'Your husband?' he said dismissively. 'He's never looked after an animal in his life. What are you rabbiting on about!'

'And so what? He can still help!' interrupted Berthe suddenly, who considered that the picture was being painted too blackly. 'It's not very difficult to feed pigs! Especially with modern equipment!'

'I'd like to see you do it!' he grumbled.

'Oh come on! Are you going crazy or what! I looked after them more often than you, our pigs!' she recalled. 'Yes sir! While you were chasing girls up near Paris, about 1910 on, I was carrying the pig-swill morning and evening! So if a teacher isn't capable of doing the same, what are we coming to!'

'Come, come,' Mathilde intervened, 'calm down, the pair of you; Mauricette's right, we'll manage.'

'You, I'm not letting you go up and work at Coste-Roche! You'd make yourself ill!' he cut in.

'Don't get so worked up! Maman won't be needed, don't worry!' said Mauricette. 'It'll all be fine. And then Dominique's arriving this evening. He's capable of helping, as well, isn't he?'

'No doubt,' he replied. 'But he's not staying very long. So afterwards, who's going to look after everything? And, what's more, in this drought, which means you have to take water to the animals! And then if Jacques has overturned, his tractor's had it! Oh my God, it all comes at once!'

He sighed and had to sit down, for he was suddenly very tired and very weary. And his heart was beating much too fiercely and too fast.

'You see, you shouldn't work yourself up into these states,' Mathilde scolded him. 'Look, don't you think we've got enough worries as it is?'

'You're right,' he admitted. 'When's Jacques leaving?'

'He's gone,' explained Mauricette, rather awkwardly. 'Yes, the ambulance was at Coste-Roche at seven o'clock this morning. Well, we thought it might frighten you to see it stop here . . . Jacques felt it was better to go without saying anything . . .'

'Of course, I understand,' he muttered. 'You wanted to hide everything from me, as usual, eh? But then who's at Coste-Roche with the animals?'

'Brousse and Valade,' confirmed Mauricette.

'Ah good, very good . . . So I can't help with anything?' he asked.

'You can help by not falling ill, that'll go a long way,' said Mathilde. 'Come on, don't worry any more, and best of all, think of this evening. Dominique and his wife should at least have the pleasure of finding you in good shape. Because if, besides their father being in the clinic, they see you with that dreadful expression, they'll be sorry they came.'

'And you say Félix has decided to come down? That's something!' said Jacques.

Operated on the previous day, and following a quite painful awakening, he was now recovering complete lucidity and even his strength. He felt in a particularly good mood, relieved. It was a relief to have it over with, and if, as the surgeon assured him, it had all gone extremely well, he would soon be back on his feet. Naturally he would have to be careful of his back for some time, but he didn't want to think about that yet. He preferred not to consider too deeply how he was going to organise things to accomplish all the work needed on the land . . .

For the time being, he wanted to be happy and show a suitably pleasant face to his son. For Dominique was there, strong and soothing, at his side. He had arrived an hour ago, and Jacques already felt quite cheered by his presence.

'Yes,' repeated Dominique, 'according to Grandma, Félix will be arriving tomorrow. But you know, I don't want to upset you, but I think he's really coming for Grandfather; this business has been a blow to him. I found him quite gloomy, worried. Félix'll cheer him up. And then together they can supervise what's going on at Coste-Roche.'

'But who told him?' asked Michèle.

She too was now relaxed, calm. She had been so frightened that she still had difficulty in believing it was all over, or almost.

'It seems it was Jean,' explained Dominique. 'According to his father, as soon as he heard about your accident he was ready to cut lessons to come and look after your animals. Luckily he's done no such thing! But it's a short step from that to suggesting Félix should pop down to Saint-Libéral . . .'

'Sure,' Jacques smiled. 'You know, he's great, that lad. He's got the bug, he believes in the land, we could do with lots like him. Which reminds me, are you staying for long?'

'Where? Here with you, or in France?'

'In France.'

'The whole week.'

'So I shan't see your wife,' said Jacques. 'I'm stuck here for longer than that . . .'

'Oh yes you will,' Dominique assured him. 'I thought it better to leave her in Saint-Libéral, she was rather tired from the plane – they gave us a fair old shaking, and she's just as frightened as ever!' he explained in a convincing tone. He did not want to announce the impending birth without Béatrice, and was anxious to find a good excuse for her absence.

'She'll be coming?'

'But of course! We'll come together next Wednesday, before catching the plane back.'

'Oh, good. That'll keep me happy.'

'I hope so!' smiled Dominique. 'Right, now you're going to explain to me what's to be done at Coste-Roche,' he asked his mother, 'I'll take charge of it, for these few days. With Brousse, there won't be any problem.'

'But I'm going there!' she protested vigorously. 'I am, right away, I'm coming back with you!'

'Out of the question!' he cut in. 'You're going to stay here with Papa. He needs you, and you'll have a chance to rest, that'll do you good, you look ghastly. Besides you can't leave; Françoise is supposed to be dropping by during the weekend, I had her on the telephone yesterday.'

'Oh, is that right?' said Michèle, delighted at the thought of seeing her daughter again. 'But as for Coste-Roche, you'll never be able to do everything!'

'That's it, say straight away that I'm incompetent, and then we don't need to talk about it any more. Fine, I'm listening, pass on the orders!'

PART FIVE
One Day in May

21

SUPPORTED by Brousse on the first day, Dominique had no problem afterwards in caring for the animals. The work even made him feel several years younger, and reminded him of all the holidays in times past spent helping his father on the smallholding.

As a bonus, on account of the unusual events which left them the sole occupants of the house, Béatrice and he spent a wonderful week at Coste-Roche. Undisturbed, they enjoyed a sort of honeymoon which left them with only fond memories, and made them understand better why Pierre-Edouard and Mathilde always spoke of Coste-Roche with such feeling.

Truly the isolated house far from the village was a haven of peace, an island on which you could pretend you were at the end of the earth, far from constraints, free. In addition, as Dominique had remarked to his wife, who was quite ready to dream of just such an idyllic existence, the drought made any cultivation of the fields impossible and thus gave the impression of a very light workload.

In fact, with the slightest bit of know-how, the pigs were quickly taken care of. That done, there remained the lopping of the oaks for the cows. Dominique spent less than an hour on it each morning. He set off there in the cool of the morning, before sunrise, and returned to find his wife still in bed, all drowsy and languid, but already happy, thinking of the beautiful, sun-drenched day to come.

As for the water run, Félix took charge of that, pleased to be able to make himself useful in a small way. Jacques' tractor had only suffered minor damage. Once set upright, its tanks refilled and batteries recharged, it had started immediately. Carefully, and taking his time about it, Félix drove it at tortoise pace, which never failed to provoke jokes from Dominique.

'To see you, anyone would swear you were leading a pair of oxen!' he called out that evening, when he saw him returning from the Heath.

'Keep talking, my lad, I've got all the time in the world! Anyway, if your father still had oxen . . .'

'Hey, stop that engine and come and have a drink, it's time for a quick one!'

The sun was plunging into the red horizon and already foretelling that the following day would be just as beautiful and hot as all the previous ones, for the last four months . . .

'So, you're about to leave?' asked Félix, returning from the shed and seeing Béatrice packing her case.

'Well, yes,' she replied. 'A week passes quickly, especially under these circumstances.'

'That's right, funny sort of holiday! Your mother's coming back tomorrow?' he asked Dominique.

'Yes, and Papa the week after. I've asked Brousse and Valade if they could come and help maman with the animals.'

'I'll still be here myself,' said Félix, diluting the anisette Dominique had just given him.

'But you're not going to stay for ever, are you?'

'Certainly not! Well, we'll see . . .'

'What's up, then?'

'First there's your grandfather. He's not at all in good shape. I told you already, I thought he'd aged a lot. And then he's eating his heart out about here, the farm . . .'

'He has some reason to . . . It worries me too. I really don't see how Papa is going to manage. Or rather, yes I do know how he could, but to convince him . . . And what else is the matter, besides all that?'

'My mother. She's aged terribly as well! She's no longer interested in anything much, doesn't talk much any more, as if it tires her to join in the conversations. Admittedly she's getting increasingly deaf. Well, that's the impression she gives. But what can you do, she's almost eighty-seven and has been through so much in her unhappy life . . . So, as I know she's pleased to have me here, I'll maybe stay a bit longer than I intended. And then that'll give your father the time to recover a bit more.'

'That would be really nice if you did that, I'd go away feeling happier. In any case, we can never thank you enough for having come straight away!'

'Bah! You're making a big thing of it! But I'll never get here as fast as your grandfather came one day to help us, your aunt and myself, in October '37 . . .' murmured Félix, suddenly thoughtful. 'Right, and then I'm retired, aren't I?' he remarked, cheering up again. 'Have to say, too, that your cousin was so unhappy at not being able to come.'

'Jean?'

'Yes. He's a real dynamo, he'll go far!'

'I hope he does. But most of all, I hope Uncle Guy will finally accept the idea of having an agricultural engineer for a son!'

'Yes, it's coming already. I believe he's given up hope of seeing Jean follow him at the bar. But it hasn't all been easy going! And you, your work, it's okay?'

'My work on the land, yes, but the rest . . .' said Dominique, with a quick grimace which did not escape his cousin.

'Oh yes? You sound mad keen!'

'I'll explain it to you one day,' promised Dominique. 'In any case, for the time being I'm under contract to Mondiagri, so I've got to make the best of it. But that doesn't mean I'm married to them for life! That's the way it is. But mind you don't talk about all this to my parents, they're so pleased that I've got a good job! Here, are you ready?' he asked Béatrice. 'Yes,' he explained, 'we're eating at my grandparents' this evening.'

'I know, so am I, and believe me, knowing your grandmother's meals, I've been fasting since yesterday! Well, almost.'

The night was so beautiful, mild and bright that Dominique and Béatrice, leaning on the windowsill, could not make up their minds to go to bed.

It was so good to cool yourself in that gentle current of air from the north. So good, as well, to listen to the songs of the night, all humming with foliage rustling in the breeze, rodents

307

pattering as they zigzagged through the dry grass, the calls of tawny and little owls, haunting as sobs; with sometimes, coming from an unseen and distant farm, the rather sad and poignant howls of dogs on leads, complaining of their chains to the moon.

'It's beautiful, admit it,' whispered Dominique. He spoke softly, so as not to break the spell and the peace of the night.

He sensed that Béatrice was agreeing, and pulled her against him.

'I think we did the right thing to speak out, it really made them happy,' he continued.

She nodded in affirmation, and he saw that she was smiling.

'You know,' she said at last, 'if you hadn't made me the baby already, it's here, in this house and this week, that I'd have liked to make it.'

'I've been aware of that,' he said. 'But it's true, it's been a really lovely week.'

He almost felt ashamed of it, for he could not forget that the peace, freedom and intimacy which he and Béatrice had enjoyed was due to his father's accident, his mother's absence.

'That proves that families should never live communally,' he said in reply to his thoughts.

'Shall we do it again?' she asked.

'What? Make a baby?'

'Sex maniac! Have a holiday like this, all alone here.'

'Yes, we could try to – send my parents on a trip, it'd be the first time they'd have taken one. But we won't be alone any longer, we two' he added, gently stroking her stomach.

'That's true,' she smiled.

'You know, I think we made them awfully happy!' he repeated.

'Definitely.'

They had not, however, consulted each other before the dinner at their grandparents. But they had suddenly realised the depth of Pierre-Edouard's melancholy and lethargy, and Mathilde's anxiety which one glance was sufficient to discern. Dominique had therefore announced:

'We wanted to tell our parents first, we'll do that tomorrow. But here goes – you're going to be great-grandparents. The next Vialhe is due in May!'

And those few words, which had suddenly softened all Mathilde's wrinkles, made Pierre-Edouard's lips tremble and blurred his gaze, had shown them that this announcement swept away everything else. It brushed aside Jacques' accident, all the worries and latent sorrow which Pierre-Edouard had been combatting less and less successfully.

'That, now, there's a piece of news, really good news,' he had eventually murmured, fingering his glass. 'You know,' he had said, smiling at Mathilde, 'that – yes, that makes me want to live a bit longer . . .'

He had got up, walked over to Béatrice, who was rather overwhelmed and did not know what to do, and had leant down to kiss her:

'And mind you don't get up, my girl,' he had said as he embraced her. 'Don't move, in your condition you've the right to stay seated in front of an old fossil like me!'

And, immediately, the lavish meal was enhanced by the smiles which sped from Pierre-Edouard to Mathilde, from Mathilde to Béatrice, already on intimate terms. By Berthe's jokes which declared that Taureans, like Gemini, were dreadful pests, of which Dominique was the proof, and that the next Vialhe born under one of those signs would surely break all records! By Félix's laugh, Louise's restored happiness, and the bottle of champagne which Yvette quietly went to fetch.

On coming to live at the Vialhes', apart from a few bits of furniture, she had brought the cellar patiently collected by Léon; Léon whose memory had unexpectedly hovered in the room.

'Maybe we should be thinking of going to bed,' suggested Béatrice, in the middle of a yawn.

'You're right. We've got to get up very early tomorrow and it'll be a long day, especially for you, 'he teased. 'Knowing how much you like aeroplanes! Well, it won't be easy for me either, I'm not sure my father will enjoy what I'm going to tell him! Let's hope the impending birth will calm him down . . .'

'That's it! You can look now, we're still alive! And don't feel you have to go on pulling off my arm!' joked Dominique, leaning towards Béatrice to kiss her.

She pinched him a bit harder, just to teach him not to make fun of her, then decided to open her eyes. The plane was already over a thousand metres and still climbing.

'Like a magazine?' he suggested to her.

'No, I think I'm going to sleep until we get to Tunis.'

'You're quite right. That way, if we explode in mid-air, you'll reach paradise without the slightest anxiety!'

'Just stop it!'

'Okay, sleep, have a rest,' he said, opening his newspaper. He skimmed through it distractedly, found it boring, closed it, and wondered yet again how his father was going to react now.

Béatrice and he had been agreeably surprised when they visited him. He looked marvellous, in very good spirits, was beginning to walk and starting to make plans again. Michèle had also seemed to them to be in much better shape, rested, relaxed. As expected, both of them had been extremely happy and proud to learn they were going to be grandparents. Already Michèle was talking of knitting the layette; as for Jacques, he pictured himself wheeling the baby right through the village, so that nobody should be unaware that the Vialhe's succession was assured.

It was a little later, when Michèle and Béatrice had left to buy a few bits and pieces which Jacques needed, that Dominique had initiated the conversation.

'I think, I'm sure even, you'll find the farm, pigs and cows in good condition. You can thank your neighbours for that, they're true friends. And Félix too. He won't be leaving before you return. But after that, how are you going to cope?'

'I don't know, have to manage . . .'

'Listen, Pa, you ought to use this accident as the opportunity to change tack completely. It's now or never to make the leap into the unknown.'

'Hah! I almost did that the other day! Once is enough, let me catch my breath, if you don't mind?'

'No. I'm not joking. I know fine that the drought makes all the fields, meadows and orchards look horrible, but still it's obvious that even then you couldn't do everything properly.

'Oh . . . It's as obvious as that, is it?'

'Yes, it's obvious. Three-quarters of the sown pastures are too old, worn out, finished, need re-doing. Your plum trees are ruined. There are brambles on the edges of the land, and they're spreading. The walnut trees are full of dead wood, the . . .'

'Stop! I know, dammit! But I'd like to see you try and do it! Do you think it's fun for me? Well, try working with a wonky back! You've seen how that ends up, haven't you?'

'. . . And there are far too many cows which should be sent for slaughter in your herd,' Dominique had continued.

He knew very well that he was hurting his father, infuriating him even, but none of what he was saying was an exaggeration. He had not even said it all! The farm was going badly; a few more years and it would collapse, for lack of energy, initiative, strength, effective care. In fact, if it foundered, Jacques and Michèle would go down with it, becoming embittered, sinking into poverty filled with resentment, with hopes and dreams dashed forever.

Dominique refused to accept this conclusion, and so did Françoise. Brother and sister had organised it by telephone. Neither of them wanted to see their father an old man before his time and their mother wizened, faded, broken by work. Dominique had therefore decided to say all that had lain in his heart for years, which he had more or less suppressed until then so as not to fall out with his father.

But from now on, staying silent bordered on cowardice, amounted almost to failure to render assistance to an endangered person; at least that was what Françoise had said. Therefore, at the risk of unleashing paternal fury, he had decided to speak, to bring matters to a head.

'So you're still dying to lecture me?' Jacques had eventually retorted. 'It's your agronomist's diploma which makes you so impertinent, eh?'

'Oh come on! Stop that! I've no wish to lecture to you. I'm simply saying that if you go on the way you are, you won't even reach retirement, or you'll be in such a state! As for Maman, if you make her go on living this way, it'll be her you'll be sending to hospital! And that's not okay by me!'

'You think I enjoy seeing her killing herself by standing in for me?'

'Right, so consider something different, for her sake and yours. Listen; you keep yourself informed as much as I do, if not more, about what's going on in Europe! Good God! The minute you not only don't squash, but actually back, the creeps whose sole aim is to make two-thirds of agriculture disappear, the sort you practise is done for, finished! And I'll take all the bets you like: one of these days, those rogues or their successors will impose a freeze on farming, fallowing the land! They're already talking about it, they're preparing the ground! And already they're slaughtering dairy cows. So you're in a fine state with your little farm, your little crops. Already nobody wants any of it!'

'Here, I wasn't waiting for you to find all that out!'

'Sure. But you haven't drawn the conclusions from it! You know, when I arrived in France, I asked myself how our politicians could have been so stupid as to launch the idea of a drought tax. I thought it was one of those silly notions they're fond of, just one more! Well no way, I believe now that it was intentional, calculated.'

'Maybe not, but all the same . . .'

'Yes it was! They need to spoil the image of the all-providing, indispensable farmer. Make people forget that he's there to produce food. Get it into the consumers' heads that it would end up cheaper for them if all our grub was bought elsewhere, from the Americans for example.'

'Yes, that story's been going around for a while now!'

'That's just the start. But soon you, yes you, the small producer, you'll be called a pariah, they'll say you're sub-sidised to the hilt! They'll even blame you for the surpluses which our pathetic administrators can't be bothered to sell. Following that, they'll break you, in the name of the great European dream. Yes, a great dream which the incompetents are busy transforming into a nightmare, and mostly into an appalling mess! A Europe of bureaucrats, but most of all a Europe with a French desert, whole areas sacrificed, all the family farms killed off! And all that so that a few twisted brains can promote their evil idea of what agriculture should be in the year 2000! And that bearded fellow, the Minister of

Agriculture, will be proved right; one day, in France, there'll be no more farming south of the Loire! So, Coste-Roche . . .'

'And after telling me all that, which doesn't teach me anything new, you want me to change tack? You think I've the heart for it? Look, do you know how old I am?'

'Fifty-six! Grandfather was over sixty when you convinced him to buy a tractor and he changed practically everything on the farm . . .'

'All right. You win there; next?'

'Next? Given that all our useless experts and other myopic futurologists, not forgetting politicians of all colours, except maybe the reds – that's the last straw – have decided to go for us, we've got to catch them on the wrong foot and refuse to play their game.'

'Easy to say! And what is their game, in your opinion?'

'That the smallest number should produce the maximum, as cheaply as possible! So we've got to do the opposite: stay in the last handful who produce less, as expensively as possible!'

'You say the first thing that comes into your head, don't you?'

'No. The aim is economic planning of production, which means second-rate from the taste point of view. Now, your milk-fed calves, which make so much work but are still the best, are in competition with the ones coming out of the factory farms. And as they're less expensive than yours and the customers have already lost their taste for fine produce, you're done for before you start if you don't switch to a higher gear. And it's the same for everything! Vegetables, chickens, eggs! And, believe me, the day will come when even the foie gras will be disgusting, like everything else. Disgusting to all those who still have any taste-buds. And those people will save you, because they'll be ready to pay very highly for quality.'

'Need to be a bit more logical, my lad! On the one hand you say it's done for, on the other, you assure me that it'll work!'

'You haven't quite got it. You need to eliminate ruthlessly all the produce which won't reach deluxe standard! Your pigs, for example, quite likely cost more than they bring in. That's to be expected, your little piggery is no match for the

313

industrial concerns, but as you produce the same rubbish as them, you get paid what they're worth! So, you need to step outside the mainstream, aim for the top, specialise. At present you're doing too much of a mixture.'

'Yes, I know, and I'm doing it badly. That's it, isn't it? Go on, say it.'

'You're not going to get more annoyed? Right, we can't discuss it all day, I've a plane to catch. So this is what Françoise and I thought.'

'Oh, your sister's in on it as well, is she? That doesn't surprise me!'

'Will you let me speak, eh? Right: firstly, starting from now, Françoise and I will be sending you a cheque each month. Let me speak, I tell you! After all, we're only reimbursing you for our education. That money will allow you, Maman and you, to take a breather. And especially you, so that you don't climb back up on your tractor too soon. Secondly, I've asked Brousse and Valade, and they're ready to plough wherever you tell them to.'

'Look, don't you feel that's going a bit too far? I think we've taken advantage of the neighbours quite enough, haven't we?'

'That's for you to say; me, I'm telling you what I know. Thirdly, and don't go through the roof, you ought to give up the pigs, you're working for practically nothing, a waste of time. You'd do better to tell Maman to start feeding up geese again, like in the past, but no more than she can fatten alone and by hand, to produce a real deluxe goose liver; that'll always sell at a very high price, because it'll taste of foie gras and not of frozen fish! Wait, it's not over yet! Fourthly, whether you like it or not, your yields on cereals and maize are too low and cost you too much. Drop all that. And as for your livestock, start making silage. You ought to sell off half your cows and begin to go into it seriously, selective breeding, pedigrees, yes . . .'

'Oh right! You've taken over from your cousin, on my word! He's dreaming of one day producing show animals, for export he says!'

'He's right, it was me who gave him the idea! There, that's all. Don't answer now, but think about it at leisure. Look at it all with Maman. Oh! Another thing, I asked Aunt Yvette not to sell or re-let her land without talking to you . . .'

'You're crazy, aren't you? As it is I can't keep up with the work, and I haven't even finished paying for the Heath! I've got that for four more years!'

'Who said you should buy it? Don't I by any chance have the right to do that, myself? Or even your brother, yes, Guy, for Jean one day . . .'

'You're serious?' Jacques had murmured after a few seconds of silence. 'Guy, at a pinch, but you? Why? Don't tell me you want to take over Coste-Roche? That would be absolutely stupid, let me tell you!'

'In the next few years, it probably would. You know, I don't see myself working with you. But in fifteen or twenty years, who knows? Perhaps I'll want to invest in some land of my own and play the nightjar! Yes, you ask Jean for the explanation, he has quite an amusing theory about it! But, joking apart, it may be that one day I'll want to start stock-breeding, the sort I mentioned to you, of course! Then I wouldn't be sorry to have a starting-point at Saint-Libéral . . .'

'Well, if anyone else had told me that . . . But you mean it?'

'Yes. But don't forget: I said in fifteen or twenty years, perhaps more even. So you'd be well advised to take care of yourself if you want to hang on until then! That said, think about setting up a stock farm which is a bit out of the ordinary. One of those that's quoted as an example when breeders are talked of. That's the sort of standard you have to produce, and you can do it, because you've got the training, the technique. Because you know. There, mull over all that, calmly. And now I wish Béatrice would come back, or we'll end up missing our plane.'

'Look, one question: would you have told me all that without this dratted accident?'

'I don't know. But I've had it in my thoughts for a long time. In any case, it would have come out one day. It's done now. It's for you to judge. But remember I'd prefer to find a going concern rather than fallow land, if one day Béatrice and I move in up there.'

'That's practically blackmail! It's just to force me to change tack!'

'Call it what you like, but don't forget anything I've said to you. Dammit, I bet you our women are chattering away in some corner! And time's running out!'

'You're coming back for Jo's wedding?'

'No.'

'Pity, it's going to be a fine do. Why not come back? Just pop over, for the weekend?'

'Because I want to keep all our leave for May. Béatrice wants to have the baby in France, and I can understand that. So, since her mother doesn't seem to be in a hurry to see us or get to know me, we thought of coming to Coste-Roche at the end of April, if it's not too much trouble for you . . .'

'You devil,' Jacques had smiled, 'you little devil! You and your wife, you're really doing all you can to wrap us round your little finger! Ah, look! Here are our wives.'

'You know what?' cried Michèle as she entered. 'Well, Béatrice and I have decided to say 'tu' to each other, it's easier, ısn't it? Well now, what's so funny about that?'

After clouding the sky for several days, hesitating and even attempting some minor sallies which were cut short, the rain finally made up its mind to return, to set in for good.

Driven by a west wind which seemed set to hold, it started to fall gently, fine, steady and mild. The whole countryside then began to smell different.

Casting aside first the dispiriting odours produced by four months' dust, it soon exhaled the slightly acid, bitter scent of humus gorged with water and the heavier, almost sensual one of the earth drinking, saturating itself, rediscovering its pliancy, its life.

From all the woods there soon rose the strong aroma of damp bark flexing, washing itself at last and emitting the perfumes of tannin, resin, sap and of foliage soaked through at last, restored to life and drawing breath. Very quickly, as if in a hurry to obliterate the huge, distressing grey and red blotches which spread their leprous scales everywhere, eating into the meadows and fields, infecting the woods, nature awoke in a sudden burst of verdure which transformed it within a few hours.

Born of each shower, a tender green, delicate as pastel strokes, crept from place to place, overflowed the valleys, flecked the pastures, dispelled the sad and earthy tints from the hills and far horizons. The first drops cleansed away the ash which enshrouded the plateau and peaks ravaged by the fire – they were the first to revive, to react by covering themselves with a carpet of minute grasses, soft as a downy quilt.

Comforting, steady, the rain fell for several days. Heavy but not violent, shower followed shower and autumn took on the colours of spring.

Overjoyed at the announcement of the imminent birth of a Vialhe boy or girl, reassured too by Jacques' homecoming to Coste-Roche and also by the weather returning to normal, Pierre-Edouard felt almost young and carefree again. Therefore, despite Mathilde's protests, he resumed his habit of going for a little walk each day.

He had not climbed back up to the plateau since the fire. The idea of seeing the ground scorched equally by flames and drought revolted him, put him in a bad mood. So he waited to take the track to the peaks until the countryside grew a little green again, became more welcoming, good to look at. And he would probably not have embarked on such a walk if Félix had not been able to accompany him. He felt safe with him; knew that his nephew, despite his sixty-six years, was still strong, sturdy, ready to help him to get up again if need be, and support him if the walk became too difficult.

That was no longer the case with Berthe for, although cheerful and lively, she no longer had the strength to steady him. She seemed to be shrinking ever smaller, like an apple which has faded and wrinkled after a winter on the straw. She was therefore unable to hold him if he faltered, or even to enable him to get up again if he felt the wish to sit down for a moment on one of the logs which punctuated his routes.

So with her he did not go beyond the last houses in the village or sometimes, when he really felt in good shape, the first two hundred metres of the track to the peaks. But with Félix, it was different. His presence was almost an invitation to adventure, to do something out of the ordinary.

'Well, you see, it's not my legs that are giving up on me, it's my breath,' he said to Félix that morning as they emerged onto the plateau.

They had, however, climbed quite slowly, without haste, stopping often to rest; and in particular for Pierre-Edouard's breathing to become less spasmodic, less wheezy.

'You're okay though?' Félix asked him. 'You know, you mustn't hesitate to say if you feel too tired. We'll wait here, quietly, and if we're not at the house by a quarter to twelve, Yvette will come up to meet us in the car, I asked her to.'

'You did that? You've got a nerve,' replied Pierre-Edouard. 'You all really think I'm on my last legs, don't you? Huh, basically you're not far wrong . . . Because frankly, it's true that it's beating a bit too hard down there,' he added patting the area of his heart with the palm of his hand. 'And don't annoy me by asking whether I'm taking my medicines, I'm taking them.'

'I didn't say a word,' Félix defended himself.

'Yeah . . . But don't think you need to repeat all this to your aunt, the poor little thing is already worried enough about me. Good heavens, what damage that fire did!' he exclaimed, surveying the countryside.

'Yes, we'll have to wait till spring for it to look better again.'

'Spring . . . That's it, spring . . .' murmured Pierre-Edouard. He slowly passed his hand across his face, then over his eyes which he massaged for a long time with his fingertips, as if to clear away some painful and irritating dust. 'Look, find me a stone to sit down on; I'm getting tired,' he said at last.

'Here,' said Félix, supporting him to a big rock.

He helped him to sit down, and noticed once more with sorrow his exhausted air, the dry and wrinkled face, and above all the stare which occasionally seemed to become vacant, to slip off into the distance, way, way beyond the horizon.

'I'm not sure it was a good idea to come up this far, it's too long a walk for you,' he said.

'No, no, don't worry! And if I don't make the most of you being here to help me! Poor Berthe can't . . . Tell me, don't you think she's getting awfully bent?'

'Berthe? Oh no, she seems to me in fine form.'

'It's true she's still young,' murmured Pierre-Edouard. 'She's only . . . wait . . . Seventy-three? No, eighty-three . . . Ah, still . . . So, you, you're off tomorrow?'

'Yes.'

'You could have stayed a few more days, your mother is going to miss you.'

'I'll come back for young Jo's wedding, and in the spring too,' promised Félix.

'That's good,' replied Pierre-Edouard, nodding his head, 'but the spring, that's a long way off . . . Well, for me . . . Listen, but don't repeat this to your aunt, sometimes I wonder whether I'll ever get to see Dominique's baby . . . It's so long till May, so long! You see, I'm frightened of the coming winter, yes I am . . .'

'Get along now! What're you thinking of! You'll see plenty more winters!'

'Not many . . . You know, at one time, I really loved the winters,' continued Pierre-Edouard. 'Mmm, especially when there was snow. Ah yes, just imagine, one year, we climbed up there onto the White Peak, me and Louise and poor old Léon, and . . .'

'I know,' cut in Félix, 'that was in '99, at Christmas! And on the way back you were frightened by the wolves which were ranging the area, you threw away your thrushes . . .'

'Oh? I've already told you that story? Oh right, I didn't realise . . . what was I talking about before that? I don't know any more . . . Oh yes, the month of May, that's it, it's a long time till May, a very long time . . .'

'Come on, don't talk rubbish, just because you've walked further than usual and you're tired, you don't have to ramble on! You're too old to talk nonsense!'

'It's not nonsense to say you won't last for ever . . .'

'All right, but would you mind talking about something else?'

'Huh, if you can't talk about yesterday at my age, nothing's sacred any more . . .' said Pierre-Edouard. He sighed, pressed his hand against his chest then rubbed his eyes once more, blinked his eyelids and stared hard at the eastern horizon.

'Miladiou! Look my boy, look!' he exclaimed in childish excitement, stretching his arm towards the hills. 'Look behind Yssandon! See how they're streaming towards Perpezac, see them! My God! What a mass! Can you see them? Oh, my goodness! It's years since I've seen such a big flight of pigeons! And look, look at the one coming behind! Can you see? And the other one after it, you see?'

'Of course,' murmured Félix after a few seconds of watching, 'they're beautiful, and so many . . . Well it's the season, it'll soon be Saint Luke's day! Yes, they're very beautiful,' he repeated, suddenly grasping why Pierre-Edouard was worried by the approach of winter and questioning whether he would ever see May again.

For in the grey sky, amongst the low, heavy clouds which foretold further showers, there was not the shadow of a pigeon, not even a tiny flock of starlings, nothing. And already, Pierre-Edouard's eyes seemed to have forgotten what he believed he had seen.

22

So as not to succumb to the temptation of climbing back on to his tractor too soon, Jacques chose to devote himself to his job as mayor. He knew that if he stayed at Coste-Roche the work which had accumulated due to the drought would push him to do something unwise, such as hitch up his Brabant and set off to plough.

Therefore, instead of biting his nails, he busied himself more than ever with village problems, and especially the refurbishment of the château. This had made good progress during his absence, and everything now pointed to the building being ready on the planned date. Besides the whole teams of artisans working on the inside, a contractor was already in the process of levelling the tennis court so dear to Peyrafaure's heart. When that was done he would tackle the excavation of the pool, then its construction.

However, the supervision of the various works and all the details to be sorted out here and there were not enough to blot out all the worries overwhelming Jacques. His father was not the least of these. Not that he was ill; he still kept on his feet and took his little walk each day with Berthe. But he had an increasing tendency to isolate himself in a deep and distant self-absorption which cut him off from the outside world. And although Jacques, unlike Félix, had not witnessed one of the delusive visions which sometimes afflicted him, that did not prevent him from dreading them. He was too accustomed to his father always being perfectly lucid not to be horrified at the thought of seeing him sink into a sort of permanent absence of mind or, worse, senility.

He still retained the memory of the last pitiful months passed by his grandfather Jean-Edouard, and constantly feared that his father might also come to such a lamentable end. And the rather unconcerned pronouncements of Doctor

Martel, who attributed all that in broad terms to the medicaments, to some sudden but transient variations in his blood pressure or urea levels, to the weakness of an ageing heart and above all to the old man's approaching eighty-eight years, were no comfort to Jacques.

So, since his main occupation kept him in the village, he called every day – and twice more often than once – at the family home. That was not very reassuring either, for unfortunately, when his father seemed to be on top form, it was his aunt Louise who gave the impression of losing ground! She was not actually ill, slept well and kept herself busy with knitting and sewing. But she was indifferent to everything, had no enthusiasm for anything. And, like her brother, she often gave the impression of being tired of finding herself faced each morning with a day which she had to endure without wishing to, like a burden, almost a duty.

Luckily, Yvette, Berthe and Mathilde were still there to help her to interact, and even to chivvy her. But Jacques preferred not to think too much about what might happen if his mother in her turn gave up the struggle, and if Berthe fell ill. Yvette could never cope with it all alone. She might well be in good health; she had still seen sixty-nine years go by.

And when you know that seven out of ten houses in the village are in roughly the same situation, it really makes you despair for the future of Saint-Libéral! he mused.

That was why he concentrated on the hope of a sort of community renaissance resulting from the conversion of the château. At the same time, he had not forgotten Christian's suggestions. Because of his spell in hospital he had not had the chance to discuss them in the town council, but he often thought of them.

After all, the people of Saint-Robert actually organise concerts, and that attracts people. So why not bring in some life with photos?

In the same way he was increasingly convinced that the opening of some sort of farm guest-house could be beneficial to the whole village. But there he ran into the problem of where it should be.

We'll need to discuss all that at the next meeting. After all,

Coste's talking about starting a ranch, he could set his wife to cooking! I'll ask Michèle what she thinks. About that and all the rest, especially the rest . . .

'The rest' was what his son had said to him about the farm. He had still not mentioned a word of it to anyone. And yet not a day elapsed without him recalling Dominique's arguments. And each passing day confirmed the notion that his son saw things clearly, that he was right, and that the survival of Coste-Roche was going to depend on the decisions he would have to take. And take quickly.

Happy to continue the experiments which interested him, Dominique was glad to return to the trial farm at Bab el-Raba. Despite that, it took him very little time to realise that he would not be remaining in the employ of Mondiagri.

'You're going to think I don't really know what I want, that I'm vacillating and cultivate as many contradictions as varieties of hybrid maize, but I'm not going to make my career in the service of Mondiagri,' he said to Béatrice one evening.

She was already in bed, reading. She put down her book and smiled:

'You're forgetting you've already told me all that! The last time was two months ago, just after the visit from your supervisors,' she reminded him. 'But why are you talking about contradictions?'

'Because my work definitely interests me, because everything I do on the land gives me pleasure. It's afterwards that it comes unstuck! Look, if you like, it would all be fine if my work served some other purpose than to enrich the Mondiagri shareholders,' he said, coming to sit down on the edge of the bed.

'And to feed your wife and your future progeny!' she joked.

'I know,' he replied, stroking her face. 'No, seriously, I'd like you to understand.'

'Come on now, don't take me for an idiot! I can see, you know! Whether it's Guyana, here, or with even better reason in Coste-Roche, you're only really happy on the land. You need something concrete, some action. Anyway, I've already said that to you. So of course, when everything is reduced to simple experiments on little plots . . .'

'If not in tanks and test-tubes . . .'

'Exactly. Deep down, what you miss is a real farm, some land, some space, is that it?'

'Probably, but I'm not so naïve as to dream of the impossible, utopia was never in my line, so . . .'

'So?' she pressed him.

'So, since we're a long way from having the means to set ourselves up on a farm, but I don't want to grow bitter working twenty-five years for people whose outlook I don't like, I think I won't be renewing my contract with Mondiagri . . .'

'Which means to say you'll be finishing with them when we come to the end of your three years here? In two years' time, right?'

'Yes.'

'And after that?'

'I'd like to devote my time to a task which is really useful and in keeping with my training. Hey, for example, the sort of work I did in Algeria, with Ali. There at least we were teaching people to grow things better so they could feed themselves better! That was certainly more interesting than slogging away to fatten up Mondiagri. All right, it's less well paid and there's not much chance of making a career, but . . .'

'But it would be less distressing for you, wouldn't it?'

'Yes.'

'Well, for me too.'

'Is that true?'

'Yes, I don't like to see you constantly railing against your employers, it's unhealthy. So if it isn't working out with them, leave them and don't let's talk about it any more! But mind you don't set sail for some obscure country on the other side of the world! Remember there'll be three of us next year, or more if you've given me twins!'

'I promise. In fact, I haven't told you yet, but I really think that in twenty years' time I'll go back to try my luck in Saint-Libéral. Yes, at home, on our land at Coste-Roche. Would that suit you? You said you liked it a lot there.'

'It would suit me very well,' she smiled, 'and all the better if it's in twenty years' time, which leaves me a little while to choose the colour of the curtains, eh?'

'But I'm not joking!' he said, bending down to kiss her.

'Neither am I,' she assured him earnestly. 'And you know, quite frankly, I bet you don't wait twenty years . . .'

Whereas the idea of organising, in the following summer, a photo competition and exhibition was received with polite interest but not much eagerness by the assembled town councillors, that of trying to breathe new life into the auberge was by contrast welcomed enthusiastically.

'I'd go so far as to say we're fools not to have thought of it earlier! It's true, it was better when we could still go to Suzanne's!' sighed Delpeyroux nostalgically.

'You can say that again! Those were good times,' agreed Duverger, as he too began to dream of the fine pre-war period when, not content with serving drinks, the comely Suzanne allowed the young men of the village to ogle her generous cleavage. Sometimes even, when curaçao proved inadequate to relieve the bouts of depression provoked by the memory of her late and heroic husbands, she even allowed a lot more. And Duverger was now growing quite sentimental, thinking with what generosity, refinement and skill she then shared her sorrows . . .

'It's true, you lot wouldn't understand!' said Coste, with a tinge of pity, to the newcomers to the community, the Martins, Lacombes and Peyrafaures and others who had only ever seen the inn closed. 'Yes,' he continued, 'when Suzanne was here, the village looked different!'

He too had been a young man in Saint-Libéral and, if he added his testimony in praise of Suzanne, it was because he owed her a great deal. It was she who, one evening in August 1945, had tenderly helped him to grow up, to cross the threshold. She was then forty-nine years old, but immensely experienced and with boundless affection, and he, at eighteen, had a great deal of enthusiasm and imagination but no experience. He still felt a debt to her generosity of old.

'Have to say that Suzanne was . . .'

'Hey! Steady on, steady on,' interrupted Jacques, seeing that Delpeyroux was preparing to divulge his memories one by one. 'It's not a question of bringing Suzanne back to life or of replacing her, but of finding out whether it's possible to make use of the auberge, to set up a sort of guest-house there, that's all! Unless you know anyone who's willing to take over the whole thing, get it all going again, with a restaurant and rooms. Not forgetting that when Suzanne closed she'd had no customers for a long time, I mean to say customers for the inn . . .'

He had never himself helped Suzanne relieve her attacks of vague yearning, but knew that a number of men in the village, between seventeen and seventy, had considered it their duty not to leave her alone during her painful and grievous phases of melancholy. It was therefore to be expected that memories of her would still be so vivid, and that some would speak of her with a little tremor in the voice!

'Right then, explain!' said Coste.

'You're still wanting to invest in buying some ponies and horses?' Jacques asked him.

'Yes. That'll be a tidy sum to come up with, but it ought to bring in a bit all the same. Anyway, if it doesn't take off, they can always be sold again for slaughter, seems there's a shortage of that sort of meat in France. I don't like it myself, but if it sells . . .'

'Exactly. You've thought about feeding the people who'll be coming to play at cowboys?'

'Oh, that, no! I'm not a restaurateur!'

'All right, but your wife knows how to make an omelette? or warm up a jar of *confit d'oie*, eh? You ought to give that some thought!'

'No, definitely not!' Coste grouched. 'In the first place Paulette wouldn't like it. As it is she's not too keen on the horses . . . And then, if she cooks, I'm sure to lose all my customers! They won't come back a second time! Well that's how it is!' he protested, raising his voice to drown out his neighbours' laughter, 'grub's not her strong point! At home, it's mother-in-law who does the cooking and she complains, although there are only three of us! Think what a welcome I'd get if I told her she'd have to work for ten or fifteen! She's too lazy, the old girl! No, no, the ranch is okay, but snacks are out!'

'Well, don't let's talk about it anymore, 'said Jacques. 'I only mentioned it because it would liven up the village a bit, attract some visitors, that's all. Right, let's go on to other things, unless anyone has any ideas on this subject?'

'It might be possible. Well, have to see . . .' said Lacombe. He rarely intervened in the discussions, so everyone fell silent in anticipation of his comments.

'Have you a suggestion to make?' pressed Jacques.

'Maybe . . . But beforehand, we'd need to make sure it's possible to rent the auberge.'

'For that we only have to ask Suzanne's daughter. But why?' asked Jacques.

'Because my brother-in-law is retiring next year,' explained Lacombe. 'Yes,' he said, with an apologetic little smile, 'he'll have a warrant officer's stipend, that's not bad, you know. And then, he's not old yet. But you see with Indochina and Algeria, that makes some bloody fine increments and a good pension at the end of the month!'

'Okay, okay, but what's all that to us?' interrupted Peyrafaure rather curtly.

As a pensioner of the SNCF railways, he did not care much for the conversation turning towards the advantages enjoyed by former servants of the state. He had long known that his situation aroused some jealousy and had no wish to be used as scapegoat, should one of the council members start up the old refrain. The one saying that state employees, not content with doing damn all, were also scandalously overpaid. It wouldn't take much for a wicked old reactionary like Delpeyroux to say that civil servants shouldn't even have the right to vote, since no change of government ever challenged their position! What's more they were all irresponsible! Indeed, Peyrafaure was aware, from working in his kitchen garden, that it was even whispered behind his back that he had had to wait until his retirement to discover how exhausting work could be.

'Yes, what are you leading up to with your sarge?' insisted Martin. He was rather annoyed that Lacombe, whom he thought a good friend, had never spoken to him of this brother-in-law in the army.

'Oh, it's simple. My sister wants to come back to this part

327

of the country,' explained Lacombe. 'Yes, like me she's a native of Terrasson. So she told me to look for something to rent in the area. And as I know my brother-in-law would like to supplement his pension a bit without overdoing it too much . . .'

'What a joke!' scoffed Martin. 'If he liked work he wouldn't be in the army!'

'You mean to say he'd be prepared to take over the inn?' Jacques intervened.

'No, not the whole thing! Certainly not the rooms, that is except for himself. But a bit of cooking in the high season. That yes, he knows how to do that, and do it well . . .'

'Hey! Is he a sarge by profession or a cook, your brother-in-law?' cried Martin.

'Both. Yes, for the last ten years he's been doing service in the officers' mess. Well, they need a manager in the kitchens!'

'Why didn't you say so!' put in Martin.

'And you think that might interest him?' continued Jacques.

'I believe so. That is if he can rent the inn. He could live there with his family and at the same time open a sort of table dot or something . . . Well, what you were saying just now.'

'Table d'hôte meals, that would be really great,' said Jacques. 'Wouldn't it?' he insisted, questioning his neighbours with a look.

They all agreed, especially those born and bred in Saint-Libéral, already happy at the idea of hearing again the bright tinkle which the little bell hanging above the door of the auberge used to make, in Suzanne's time.

'And that would give us a few people too . . .' added Lacombe.

'How's that?' asked Jacques, guessing that he had not told all.

'Well, yes, they have some little ones . . . That is, I mean their children! Six! That would be good for the school, wouldn't it?'

'What? Six kids?' gasped Castellac. He had raised one with great difficulty and was still suffering from it, so six!

'But how old are your nephews and nieces?' asked Jacques, also a little disconcerted.

'Hmm ... They go from twelve, no eleven ... I don't know, the last one's not walking yet, that must make him about seven or eight months.'

'Well, me old mate!' said Martin. 'Listen, it's not your brother-in-law who's in need of retirement, it's your sister! I understand, she wants to come back here for a rest cure! But with his pension, plus his family allowances, your brother-in-law has no need to burst a blood vessel to earn his crust! He's already done it by slipping off his pants, and jumping into bed!'

'No, seriously, do you really mean all that?' Jean-Pierre Fleyssac interrupted.

As secretary to the mairie and brother-in-law of the mayor, he had resolved as a matter of principle never to speak during council debates. His role was to take the minutes, no more. But this, six kids at one go, was a blessing for the school, postponing the closure which was discussed again each year. And for him, the teacher, a guaranteed future at Saint-Libéral until his retirement. He had to know about this!

'Yes, really, my sister has six kids,' said Lacombe. 'And she could still have more! After all, she's only thirty-four! And she likes it. Well, I mean, children ...'

'Can't turn up her nose at making them either ...' joked Martin.

'Six! Well I never,' Castellac started up again.

'But there may still be one little problem ...' continued Lacombe in some slight embarrassment.

'Ah, that wouldn't surprise me, it was all too perfect!' griped Peyrafaure.

'And what's that, the problem?' insisted Jacques.

'Hum ...' said Lacombe. He hesitated, then made up his mind: 'Have to say, I myself don't mind at all, but I know for some people ... Well, it might be a surprise, especially here, eh? Have to admit it's not very Corrézien ...'

'Come on, spit it out! We'll be here all night!' Martin urged him on.

'But make no mistake, through his father he's as French as you and me, right!' said Lacombe. 'Yes, he's French. But he's from Phnom Penh ...' he blurted out at last, with a look to Jacques and Jean-Pierre pleading for help.

'What country's that, Africa, isn't it?' asked Duverger quietly of Delmond, who wisely limited himself to pursing his lips to avoid answering.

'You mean to say he's Cambodian, is that it? What's the problem?' said Jacques.

'Well, he's a mite yellow. And the children too . . . Less than him of course. But it's still obvious they're not from Terrasson, nor Brive!'

'Ah! That's why you never talked to me about him?' said Martin in annoyance.

'No, that wasn't why! It never came up, that's all! And now, if you don't like coloured people, say so!'

'I don't give a damn!' cried Martin, 'and after all, I'm not your sister!'

'Please, gentlemen!' interrupted Jacques. 'Right, in the event that this business goes ahead, which is my earnest wish, I hope that nobody will be so crass as to hold his origins against him, this Monsieur . . . Monsieur, what's his name, anyway?'

'Defort, Pierre,' said Lacombe.

'That's not a chink name, that!' said Peyrafaure, proudly displaying his knowledge.

'I told you his father was French!' shouted Lacombe, who had begun to lose patience.

'So then, he's only half yellow, your brother-in-law?' said Martin.

'Yes! Dammit!'

'No need to get in a state! It's not your fault! It doesn't run off – well I hope not, for your sister's sake!'

'Gentlemen, please,' repeated Jacques. 'Right, it goes without saying that we shall do our best to welcome Monsieur Defort, his wife and six children and . . .'

'Be seven or eight of them by next year . . .' whispered Martin.

'Quiet, please!' said Jacques in irritation. 'What we need now is to find out whether the auberge can be rented. You'll deal with that, Monsieur Peyrafaure? Yes, you'll know the best way to negotiate all that tactfully. We're relying on you. And if by any chance Suzanne's daughter doesn't want to let it, there are other empty houses in Saint-Libéral, and we'll find one! The meeting is closed. Good night, gentlemen!'

Michèle had not gone to bed when Jacques returned to Coste-Roche, but was knitting in front of the television. He smiled to see the little white vest which she often held out at arm's length in front of her, to appreciate its appearance and progress.

'You're not taking any risks, eh?' he teased. 'Neither blue nor pink!'

'Exactly,' she smiled, 'but white's really sweet, isn't it?'

'Very.'

'That's done? You talked to them about this photo competition and exhibition?'

'Yes, yes,' he said absentmindedly, taking the top off a bottle of beer.

'It wasn't to their liking?'

'Yes, I think it was; but to be honest, I feel it seems a bit rarefied to some of them. Well, the main thing is to get it up and running. But on the other hand, if you'd seen them when I talked about the inn!'

He filled his glass and described his evening while Michèle got ready for bed.

'And there you are,' he concluded. 'Eight years ago it was the Portuguese who brought some young blood into Saint-Libéral and prevented the school from closing. And again, you remember, fewer of them came than we were hoping for: four families and thirteen kids were expected, and only two with five kids came. I still remember poor Jean-Pierre's disappointment. If I hadn't still been a regional councillor, I'm sure they'd have closed the school. Anyway, if all goes well, next year we'll have seven Cambodians and a lady from Terrasson! And they'll save the school too; at least, I hope so. With a bit of luck, they'll revive the auberge as well and bring in a bit of life. But who knows what's coming next? Turks? Arabs? Blacks?'

'And that worries you?'

'No, it even seems to me logical, quite logical. Saint-Libéral is growing emptier, the old people are disappearing and there are no births to replace them. Then, like in fields which are left fallow, the wind carries in seeds from all parts, and here, some Cambodians have turned up. It's to be expected. You know very well nature can't abide a vacuum. So long live Monsieur Pierre Defort, his wife and six children . . . for the moment, as that clown Martin said!'

Josyane twirled gracefully in front of the mirror, assumed a few deliberately suggestive poses, then poked out her tongue at her reflection and shrugged her shoulders.

'Grotesque!' she said, unfastening the dress. 'With that on my back I look like a sack of potatoes! I wonder how you find sapheads who'll buy this sort of clobber off you! It's so corny!'

'What can I say,' sighed Chantal. 'Claire Diamond's customers don't have your tastes. And a good thing too! We'd have to shut up shop! Right, try that one; in any case, you're not leaving here without choosing your wedding dress! I don't want to fall out with my future brother-in-law!'

'I know,' Josyane was amused. 'He told me he didn't want me in jeans for our wedding. But as for insisting that I come and ruin myself in one of the poshest boutiques in Paris!'

'If Aunt Berthe could hear you!'

Wisely, knowing her sister well, Chantal had waited until all the vendeuses were gone and the doors locked to begin offering her model gowns. But the evening was turning out to be difficult, Josyane not wanting a classic wedding dress.

'If I dare carry even a white accessory, Grandma will have the sulks on me!'

And she was also refusing one of those excessively formal and dressy outfits for which the couture house was renowned.

'Look, just try that one,' suggested Chantal. 'By the way, did you manage to get in touch with Marie?'

'Yes, she hasn't made up her mind about coming,' said Josyane, regarding the dress with a critical eye.

'She's stupid!'

'That's just what I think. Right, okay, from what you told me she married a cretin, but hey, anyone can make a mistake! But I think she actually feels a bit embarrassed about coming back to Saint-Libéral without him.'

'That's true. She hasn't seen our parents or grandparents since her divorce . . .'

'Well that's just it! She ought to take the opportunity of our wedding to pop down there! That's what I told her. But you should phone her too, and insist on it, you know! I'm sure it'd be a treat for our parents.'

'You're right, I'll give her a call. Right, you're trying on this dress?'

'With that on I'll look like an old tart and Christian'll be furious!' decided Josyane.

'Try it all the same, he'll be really furious if I don't find you anything! No! Stop! The sleeve is here! Here! But be careful, don't pull like a lunatic! It does up down the back, there . . .

'Oh, you look wonderful!'

'Oh yeah!' said Josyane, looking at herself in the swing mirror. She turned round, took a few steps: 'Yes, all things considered, that one might do . . .,' she admitted after a few moments. 'Yes, it would maybe do,' she repeated, tracing out a dance step, 'but how much does a rag like this cost?'

'Never you mind! I'm under orders, it's on the house!'

'Whose orders?'

'Aunt Berthe's, of course.'

'That doesn't surprise me,' smiled Josyane. 'She's really something, Aunt Berthe.'

'You don't have to tell me! Right, hurry up and take that off. You did say that Christian was coming by to pick you up here? Well if he arrives now, it would be dreadful! Oh yes,' teased Chantal, 'you know very well that the fiancé shouldn't see his wife's outfit before the wedding day! But joking apart, you come back tomorrow for the alterations. Yes, that's not my job, I don't know anything about it.'

'You think it needs altering?'

'Yes, definitely, you're a bit better padded than our usual model girls. What's making you laugh?'

'Oh, nothing.' Josyane was enjoying herself. 'Well yes, I can tell you, the alterations don't have much chance of being useful for very long . . . A good thing we're getting married in a week's time!'

'Seriously?' said Chantal, who understood immediately.

Then she burst into laughter. 'And when's this little Leyrac expected?'

'June.'

'You two didn't hang about!' replied Chantal after rapid calculations.

'Yes we did, longer than you think! Well that's it, all that to say this dress needs to be expandable if I want to have the use of it for a bit.'

'And naturally, our parents aren't in the know?'

'Oh no, not yet. And don't spill the beans, we'll announce it to them as a Christmas present. Yes, I know, at one time it would have created a scene: or rather, a premature baby of eight pounds! But as it is, I'm sure they're going to be over the moon. And tell you what, I even bet you Grandma will be quite pleased about it when she's told!' Josyane assured her. Then she thought for a moment, and smiled. 'But it's quite likely I won't have to tell her anything. She'll notice it as soon as she sees me next week!'

23

DROWNING in an icy fog which absorbed the slightest sound, veiling everything beyond ten metres, smothering the few rays of light filtering through the heart-shaped holes in the shutters, Saint-Libéral seemed as deserted as a ghost village, dead.

And the tiny black silhouette scurrying along the main street like a stray mouse was so frail, quiet and alone that she rendered still more poignant and melancholy the silence and emptiness crushing and paralysing the village.

Even the dogs held their peace. Curled deep in their kennels and barns, they had begun their slumber. For in defiance of the three strokes which were just sounding from the bell, darkness was approaching, already brought on by the fog which drowned everything in dirty cotton wool, gloomy as a dark colourwash.

And yet, despite the agonising loneliness which seeped from every corner, the deep silence and nightmarish façades of the houses distorted by the mist, Mathilde was happy. Happy because all the family would be here before the end of the evening; all except Dominique and Béatrice. Already, Josyane and her fiancé had been there since the previous day. And their shared happiness was such a pleasure to see that no one could resist the joy radiating from them.

Marie was there as well, a little embarrassed at first, for she was suddenly aware that Patrick's absence was still an oddity to her parents, her family. But Jo's liveliness was so infectious that everyone's awkwardness had quickly disappeared, melted away, engulfed in the enthusiasm of the reunion.

Besides, if black looks were due for those who had given their parents grey hairs, Chantal had also earned some sour expressions! She had not been back to Saint-Libéral for three years and had changed so much, looked so elegant and soignée, that Pierre-Edouard had not immediately recognised her; he had even felt a little shy when greeting her.

Finally, to the great pleasure of his mother and Pierre-Edouard, who seemed rejuvenated each time he saw him again, Félix was also there. As for the others, Françoise, Guy and Colette, Jean, Marc, Evelyne and Renaud, they were already in the train, the one arriving in Brive at six. Naturally, going to fetch them in this fog, Yvette and Jacques would do well to take care: the road to Brive was not going to be easy, especially on a dark night.

Oh, they'll drive slowly, that's all, thought Mathilde.

With a firm hand she pushed open the heavy door of the church. The creaking of the slightly rusty hinges echoed round the square like the wailing of a cat.

Mathilde shivered, surprised by the damp, cloying chill pervading the church. Despite the need to warm herself up as quickly as possible by sweeping up and putting the finishing touches to the arrangements before the next day's ceremony – she had come expressly for that – out of habit and courtesy she knelt down before the niche where, in former times, Saint Eutrope had smiled. A Saint Eutrope probably gone for ever, now sold to some unscrupulous heathens for whom hell would be too mild. In his place, for the empty niche was too sinister, distressing, Mathilde and Louise had installed a Saint Joseph previously relegated to a corner, on a wobbly stool next to a broom cupboard.

It is true that he was not exactly beautiful, poor man, and the years had not been kind to his plasterwork or colours, so bright and triumphant in the early 1900s, when he was young! Attacked by the damp, chipped here and there, he was a miserable specimen, for his nose, slightly broken in the middle, gave him the strange appearance of a bearded boxer.

But such as he was, Mathilde still loved him well. And since Saint Eutrope was no longer there to listen to her secrets, her wishes, Aves and also thanks, it was he who received them. And today, on Friday, 3 December, he needed to be specially thanked.

First of all, because the whole family, or almost all of them, were reunited, which was a great joy and a gift from heaven. Then, because for several weeks Pierre-Edouard had been well. To be sure, he was accepting without too much argument the new medicines prescribed by the doctor. Naturally his health was always fragile, subject to successive highs and lows which could no longer be evened out. Despite that he was in good humour, joining in the conversations in a lively and purposeful way. Moreover he was delighted to be seeing his granddaughter married the following day.

And it was important to give thanks for her, too. She had come back from so far away, little Jo! And she had been so lucky to find a man like hers, strong, able to help her, to support her when needed.

Of course, as she had chosen not to speak of it, one had to close one's eyes to her condition . . . Not to dwell on her hips, which had definitely spread since the previous summer, her much heavier breasts, already almost maternal, and her face, still smiling and youthful but now more solemn and serious. Yes, that was the way of it, she was expecting a baby before time . . .

And, all things considered, for that too thanks should be given. For according to the newspapers, radio and even the television – but should they be believed, when it was so astounding, incredible! – there was no need for Jo to keep it, this little creature! The law allowed her to cast it aside if she felt like it. And Mathilde shuddered at the thought that she might have been capable of parting with it, of killing it!

So, yes, give thanks! And too bad if a few neighbours took it into their heads to count the months . . . Besides, who paid any attention to that in the village now? Births were so rare, and were such an event, it never occurred to anyone to check on anything, not even if the father was the right one!

Her thanksgiving completed, she crossed herself and rose. She felt frozen stiff, and decided to have a good sweep to warm herself up again. Then she checked that everything was correctly in place, on the altar and in the nave, and especially that the big butane stove was working properly. To economise, it was never used except during services. But she resolved to send Félix, in the morning, to light it a good hour before the Mass, to warm the church a little and drive out that penetrating, icy damp.

And we'll put Pierre next to the stove, she planned, and Louise and Berthe as well; they mustn't catch anything on such an important day!

Pierre-Edouard tapped his empty pipe on his palm, smiled as he watched the dancing couples, and leaned towards Félix.

'Could you take me back to the house?' he asked him quietly.

'Yes, whenever you like. But is anything wrong?'

'No, no, it's just I'm getting a bit tired. And then all this wild music is too noisy, it's making me dizzy!'

He had had a hard day. It had begun at ten o'clock with the civil wedding, during which Jacques had made a very fine and moving speech. First of all reminding the young couple that if marriage – rather disparaged in recent years – had many attractions, charms and virtues, it also had duties and constraints. It was important to respect each other, if you wanted to have some chance of celebrating your Diamond Wedding one day, as the model couple here present were preparing to do, strong in their fifty-eight years of marriage. He had then described the fine qualities of Josyane's parents, and had stressed her father's enlistment in 1944 in the army of the Liberation.

After that, turning to Christian, he had also recalled his father's sacrifice of which he could be justly proud. For his battle, like that of the men and women who had chosen to fight and not accept, allowed them all to be there today, happy and free, in the Saint-Libéral mairie which had seen such a succession of Vialhes and, it was to be hoped, would see many more!

Then, in jest, he had warmly congratulated Josyane on having the wisdom, good sense, taste and intelligence to choose a man who, although a native of Paris, had his roots in the Corrèze, a guarantee of endurance, strength, courage and patience!

'And with Jo, my dear Christian, I'm telling you, you'll need plenty of all those! Take the word of her old uncle!' he had concluded amidst laughter.

338

Everyone had then set off for the church, where a beautiful and simple ceremony had been enacted. A little hurried, to be sure, for Father Soliers had a burial in Yssandon afterwards. And as they knew that he had another wedding in Perpezac that afternoon, it was understandable that his homily was kindly but brief, his blessing without embellishments and his Mass quickly dispatched. Pierre-Edouard had not complained about this for, despite the stove which blew its hot breath on his back, he was close to catching a dreadful chill on his chest; the church was as cold as the grave. Fortunately the village hall was very well heated, the meal and wines excellent, and the good humour universal.

But now, Pierre-Edouard felt weary. He had not touched the substantial cold buffet which the young people pounced on towards seven o'clock, nor the champagne. He wished for nothing more than to go and rest at home, in the peace of the chimney corner, his feet close to the warm cinders.

'I'm going to suggest to my mother that I should take her home too,' said Félix. 'Look at her, I have the impression she's in a hurry to get back as well.'

In truth, Louise, with Michèle and Mauricette on either side, seemed distant, far away, lost in some thought which made her nod her head occasionally, or smile, as if replying silently to an invisible questioner.

'Right, then we'll go,' said Pierre-Edouard. 'But the main thing is not to worry Mathilde, she must enjoy the celebration. Look how happy she is to be with her grandchildren! And did you see her dancing just now with Jacques and Christian? Like a young girl! So we won't spoil the evening for her. Just tell her that I'm going home because I feel like some soup with something in it! It's true, I miss my bouillon. And mind you say I don't need her and she shouldn't move from here. Otherwise I'll throw a fit!'

'Okay,' smiled Félix, getting up.

'Hey!' said Pierre-Edouard, holding him back by the arm. 'Tell little Jo and her husband to come and say goodbye to me as well. They're sure to be setting off on their honeymoon any moment now, so by the time I see the two of them again . . .'

*

339

A little out of breath from the last jive with his cousin Françoise – she danced like a dream! – Jean poured himself a glass of champagne and went to sit beside his uncle Jacques, who was in discussion with his father.

'Well talk of the devil . . .' said Guy.

'Oh yes?' said Jean warily.

His relationship with his father had much improved, but he wisely did nothing to provoke him. So, since his father now agreed to him following the same path as Dominique, it was really pointless to annoy him by mentioning the stock farm he hoped to own one day, later on, in several years' time; it would be soon enough to introduce that project when it needed to be financed . . .

'You were talking about me?' he asked.

'No, your father's joking, I was giving him the news of Saint-Libéral, and Coste-Roche too.'

'Oh yes, that's great! Christian told me you're going to launch a photo competition and exhibition! I'll join in, okay? Even do the presentation if need be!'

'Right, you never miss a chance to spend your summers here, do you?'

'Well, look! I love taking photos. I'll let you see the ones I took with Félix, at his place, super! And listen, I'll even bet you, if you organised photography courses, sort of improvement workshops, with processing facilities and everything, you'd get people. I have friends myself who'd like nothing better than to spend a week or two here! Especially with the swimming pool and tennis court . . . And if you found them a field to pitch their tents on as well . . .'

'So it's goodbye to helping your uncle!' joked Jacques. 'Well, too bad, I'll manage without you!'

'Oh yes,' agreed Guy joining in the game, 'goodbye to the cows, make way for the picture postcards!'

'Joking apart,' said Jacques, 'Dominique gave me some ideas concerning Coste-Roche, it happens they're the same as yours . . .'

'*What* a coincidence,' Guy said, amused. 'Yes, your uncle's going to cut the grass from under your feet, the last straw for a stock-breeder! He's thinking of going in for pedigree animals, but you know more about that than him, don't you?'

'Seriously?' said Jean, careful not to react to the final comment.

'Yes,' said Jacques. 'Well, I'm thinking of doing it gradually. Your aunt and I, it's high time we got ourselves better organised at Coste-Roche. And as I don't even know what sciatica feels like since my operation, we'd better make the most of it. Hey, go and fetch us something to drink, we're dying of thirst here!'

'No, but it's not a joke?' insisted Jean. 'It's true, Dominique managed to convince you? Bravo! When we last saw each other, just before his wedding, he told me your problem was not so much backache as stubbornness, worse than a dozen Arabian mules!'

'Ten out of ten for respect!' Jacques teased. 'Go on, you lout, go and fetch us a drink, we'll talk about it all again tomorrow, before you leave.'

'These young people have a nerve!' said Guy, watching his son move away.

'Bah! There was no shortage of that in our time either. Think, remember Paul . . .'

'That's true,' sighed Guy. 'When you recall he was hardly older than Jean when he slipped away to England!'

'Yes indeed! And if you think about it, Aunt Berthe had plenty of daring as well. And Aunt Louise, that wasn't bad either in its way. So they've got an act to follow, our kids!'

'That's for sure,' admitted Guy. 'So, you were saying we may be going to get some Cambodians?' he said, resuming the conversation interrupted by Jean.

'It's possible. Since Suzanne's daughter's not able to sell the auberge, she's quite happy to let it. So if our NCO is still agreeable, next year Jean-Pierre's school will have some young pupils with rather slanty eyes . . .'

'Incredible,' murmured Guy. 'But by the way, what does papa say about it?'

'You'll laugh, he thinks it's fantastic! "For myself," he said to me, "The Annamese" – yes he's still calling them that! –"the Annamese", I saw some of them during the war, the Great

War. They weren't cowardly or evil. So I don't see why they should have changed!'

'Incredible,' repeated Guy. 'But he's in good shape, Papa, isn't he? Well, it seems so to me.'

'Yes, at the moment, it's all right. He accepts seeing the doc from time to time and he takes his medicines properly. And Maman's well too, so what more can you ask? You know, I calculated the average age in the family home, including Yvette and she brings it down, it was over eighty! So believe me, when I go down there each morning, I always wonder whether someone's going to be missing from the roll-call. Because I know very well everything's going to fall apart any day now, without warning. Like those old chestnut trees that have stood up to the worst storms, for two or three centuries, and fall over one day, toppled by a breeze . . .'

Despite the cold, fog and especially the darkness which made their escapade almost dangerous, Christian and Josyane sneaked quietly out of the village and wandered away up the road rising towards Coste-Roche.

They suddenly felt the need for peace, privacy. The need to be alone together for a few moments, just to exchange their impressions of the day, escape the rather too powerful sound system, get some fresh air before plunging back into the celebrations for a few hours longer.

Later, towards midnight, they would slip away and escape to the Black Truffle Hotel in Brive, where Christian had booked a room. Then, for twelve days they would conform to tradition with a honeymoon in Italy.

'Okay,' Christian had said at the time of booking the tickets, 'I admit that it's very petit-bourgeois and unimaginative, but that's too bad, it's worth the journey. Especially at this time of year, when there are fewer tourists.'

'You know, I don't mind tourists, now I'm not responsible for guiding them around! So long live the Bridge of Sighs and the gondolas!'

But meanwhile, they were there, walking slowly, clinging close to each other to withstand the damp chill engulfing the village. Christian stopped, pulled her to him and kissed her. She had deliciously cool lips.

'You see,' he murmured, 'if I believed in numbers and I was betting each way, there are two I'd tick, the four and the twelve . . .'

'Boring, a whole load of suckers play their wedding dates!'

'I know. But you've certainly got a short memory!' he said, stroking her cheeks with the backs of his fingers. They were all damp from the fog, downy as a peach on the vine pearly with dew. 'Yes, you have a short memory,' he repeated. 'It's a year today that I looped some shell necklaces round your neck and watched you go off towards the aeroplane. I was already missing you!'

'Are you sure? That was the fourth of December, like today?'

'Certain.'

'Well, you took your time about deciding to marry me!' she joked.

'There's one other thing I want you to know. And there's no need to tell me, in your usual way, that I'm lapsing into daft romanticism! Yes, you've already told me that! Right, so this is it: I do love your family, very much. Until now I've never really known what a family was. It's true, for an only son it's not easy to envisage. So there it is, I want you to know that I like yours a lot. And now, we ought to go back, otherwise they'll wolf-whistle when we go in!'

'That doesn't matter,' she decided. 'Let's walk on a little. It's good to be alone. But first, give me a big, big kiss, the way I'd have liked you to a year ago today! There, you see, this evening, I'm the romantic one.'

Softened by the increasingly impenetrable fog, the lively sounds escaping from the village hall echoed around Saint-Libéral. They reminded the very oldest inhabitants of the time when, almost every Saturday evening, waltz tunes used to resound in the alleys.

Occasionally, carried by the fitful breeze which sprang up in the church square and wafted down the main street, some

343

muffled booming reached as far as the Vialhe house, right at the end of the village.

'There's nothing else I need; you can go back and join them again if you like,' Pierre-Edouard suggested to Félix.

Seated in his usual place, in the right-hand chimney corner, the old man, leaning towards the fire, gently stirred the embers with little puffs from the old bellows, its leather cracked and nozzle dented by the years.

'Don't you want to go back there? Now that your mother's in bed and I've had my soup, you can go!' he insisted, placing a few twigs on the still hesitant sparks.

'Later on, maybe,' said Félix. 'Berthe said she wouldn't be long coming back, so I'm going to wait for her.'

'I see, you're afraid to leave me alone with your mother? It's true she's not been doing so famously for some time, and I myself . . . Well, if you prefer keeping an old man company to running about with the young people . . .'

'You know, I'm like you, all that music tires me out in the end. I'm too old for all that noise.'

'Get away with you!' said Pierre-Edouard dismissively. He took his pipe from his pocket, tamped down a pinch of tobacco which he lit with a spill.

'And what do you think of the new fellow?' he asked suddenly.

'Which new fellow?'

'Young Jo's husband, I can never remember his name.'

'Christian.'

'No, I know that! His surname! It's from around here!'

'Leyrac.'

'That's it, it's a local name. What do you think of the young fellow?'

'I think he's really great, strong, just what the girl needs.'

'You saw how beautiful she is? You'd swear it was her grandmother when I married her!' smiled Pierre-Edouard. He was lost in memory for a few moments before exclaiming: 'But he'd be well advised not to torment her, like that other one with Marie . . . What, what did you think, that I wasn't in the know?' he continued.

'Well . . .' Félix said evasively.

344

He did not know exactly what the old man understood about his granddaughter's divorce, and above all did not want to have to explain anything.

'They wanted me to believe he had too much work to come to the wedding,' scoffed Pierre-Edouard. 'A teacher, too much work! Examinations, or something, they told me! Take me for an ass! Well, it's not so serious,' he sighed. 'But I pretend to swallow their stories, because I'm not sure whether Mathilde knows all about it, so I say nothing . . . You must understand, I won't be the one to tell her, poor thing, that would depress her so much!'

'You're right,' Félix approved.

He had always thought that wanting to hide anything from Pierre-Edouard or from Mathilde was a monumental error, a trap, even, for those who had chosen, out of consideration and care, to suppress certain things. This had created a delicate situation which was not easily resolved. Especially with Pierre-Edouard, who obviously took malicious pleasure in seeing his family circle tied up in knots.

'And Jacques, what do you think of him?' asked Pierre-Edouard suddenly.

'He seems to be in fine fettle. I'm pleased, his operation really was a great success.'

'Yes, maybe . . .' murmured Pierre-Edouard, suddenly pensive. He smoked in silence, and spat into the embers, which sputtered. 'Did he speak to you about his plans?'

'Yes.'

'Which ones? For Coste-Roche or for the village?'

'Both.'

'And? Do you believe they'll work, all these changes he wants to make?'

'Yes, why not?'

'Huh . . . I have my doubts,' grumbled Pierre-Edouard. 'Doesn't want to keep pigs any more, seems it no longer pays! Nor cereals, too much work for very little. Wants to pull up the plum and apple trees, there again, seems they're not worth anything any more! But then, what is worthwhile? Seems he wants to sell half his animals to replace them with better ones, talk about a mistake! And he needs to change his tractor too,

you'll be telling me, with the other one doing a pirouette . . .
And after all it's more than twelve years that he's been using
the Massey! Even so, that's all money going out with no
return!'

'He's bound to have considered everything before making
the decision,' said Félix.

'And it seems it's Dominique who put all this in his head,'
continued Pierre-Edouard without listening to Félix. 'I'm very
fond of the boy, but I tell you: too much studying and these
children end up talking nonsense! It's all very fine, education,
I'm for it, we paid for Jacques and if Paul had wanted to . . . And
then, look at Guy, and even Mauricette, we don't regret it.
Education is good, but you have to know when to stop before
you go barmy! Dominique must have gone on too long!'

'No, no, I'm sure he's right!' protested Félix.

'Bunkum! It's too many changes in one go, all that! And
then Dominique, it's not him who'll be out of pocket!'

'Now you're not being fair! You know very well he sends
his parents a cheque every month!'

'Possibly. But he's a long way from the land. He just talks,
and his father breaks his back! And then all these projects,
they're very fine, but you've seen how one lousy drought
messes up your beautiful plans, haven't you?'

'Listen, you mustn't make yourself ill over this!' cut in
Félix. 'Tell me, don't you think Jacques is old enough to know
what he should be doing? You're forgetting he's about to be a
grandfather!'

'I know fine! But all the same, all these changes worry me.
Because, you see, I realise that sometimes I'm a bit soft in the
head – yes, yes! Don't contradict me, I know it! But all the
same, when I'm all right, when my memory's there, I think it
all over. So I'm telling you, ever since Jacques has been on the
farm, I've watched him chasing after something or other!
He'll have spent his whole life haring about, poor fellow . . .
Well, if *you* tell me there's no need to worry . . .'

'Yes I do. I tell you, everything'll be fine.'

Pierre-Edouard sucked on his pipe and became absorbed in
contemplation of the fire in front of him, now hissing as it
attacked a big oak stump.

'And what about the village?' he asked suddenly.

'Now what's the problem?'

'Do you think it's good, what he wants to set up? The château, the swimming pool, the Annamese in Suzanne's place, and I don't know what else? Oh yes, there's that one who wants to make a sort of ranch! Do you think that's a good idea?'

'Oh, that, yes! I'm sure of it, that'll make the village come to life!

'Mmm . . . yes . . .,' said Pierre-Edouard sceptically. 'Come to life, you say! I've been told that before . . . Yes, when poor Louis began to sell plots of land for building. Yes, on the track leading up to the plateau. Well, at the time, Jacques said to me: "That'll give Saint-Libéral a new lease of life!" Oh yes! Now today, there are people here we don't even know! And who don't want to be known. Look at how some of them don't even say good morning! Well, if that's what a new lease of life is!'

'You mustn't let that worry you either! Look, I bet Jacques will still get through in the first round with seventy-five per cent of the votes!'

'Why are you talking about that now?'

'Hey, the vote's in three months!'

'For the municipal elections?' said Pierre-Edouard in surprise.

'Yes, of course! You know that!'

'Already the elections? Oh, miladiou! Why didn't anyone tell me? Nobody ever tells me anything round here!'

'There's been very little said about it as yet, that's why,' lied Félix, realising he had annoyed the old man by exposing his failing memory and alertness. 'But I'm telling you,' he stressed, 'Jacques'll get through in the first round, as usual, right!'

'Oh good, that's because the people really like him, because he's a good mayor,' said Pierre-Edouard rather abstractedly.

He suddenly felt tired, distant, and Félix understood that the time for rational, not to say heated, discussion was past.

'Wouldn't you like to go to bed?' he suggested to him.

'No, I would not! I'm not sleepy. And besides, if I go to bed at this hour, I won't sleep at all from three o'clock on, thank you very much. Anyway, I want to wait for Mathilde. But turn on the TV for me. It's not that I watch it, but it keeps me company. And then it's not tiring!'

After the three days of liveliness and jollity in Saint-Libéral, thanks to the wedding, the village sank back into its habitual torpor, apathy, silence.

The fog was followed by drizzle almost like fine hail, slippery, disagreeable, inducing people to shut themselves away at home, to huddle by the fireside. And when the grocer's van arrived on Wednesday, few clients were brave enough to emerge into the cold and face the easterly blast, cutting as a razor.

Therefore, as was his habit, Pierre-Edouard protested when he saw Mathilde slipping on her coat. He knew very well that she would do as she pleased whatever he said, but he would feel to blame if he did not warn her.

'You're not going out in this weather? It'll just make you ill!' he called out.

'No it won't! Anyway, I've already been out this morning to see to the animals. It's not as cold as it looks. And the forecast is for milder weather.'

'Pooh! The forecast! With them you're really well informed! Those chatterboxes must never put their noses out of doors!' he grumbled.

'Right, does anyone need anything?' she asked.

'No, no,' replied Louise and Yvette, without lifting their eyes from their knitting.

'Nor for me,' said Berthe, 'but I'd love to know what you're going to get, apart from a severe chill! Yvette did all our shopping the day before yesterday in Objat! We've got enough to keep us for a fortnight!'

'I know,' admitted Mathilde, knotting her thick woollen scarf.

'Right, so admit you're going out for your own amusement!' said Pierre-Edouard, seizing his chance.

He was in a grumpy mood, for he had been bored since Félix had gone home. So without going so far as to pick a quarrel with his wife, he still felt like crossing swords, just for something to do!

'Hey! Stop that, you two!' cried Mathilde. 'I'm going to the grocer's and that's that! Because if no one goes down when it's a bit cold, he'll end up not wanting to come, and he'll be justified!'

'That would be a great loss,' pronounced Pierre-Edouard with damning insincerity. 'He sells at ten times the price of other places!'

'All right,' she cut him off, 'but you don't say that when he fixes you up with tobacco! In any case, I really do need to go there. I haven't any spices left, and we forgot to buy any the day before yesterday. So, if you want the black pudding and grilled meat to be edible, don't waste more of my time! And you,' she threw at Pierre-Edouard, 'unless it's too tiring for you, or you don't know how to do it any more, instead of muttering, you'd do better to sharpen the knives! You should be thinking about that now, not tomorrow, when we'll be needing them!'

She impudently pulled a face at him and went out, not unhappy to have scored the last point.

24

DESPITE the pleas of her nearest and dearest, who constantly reminded her that her health could always play tricks on her again, Mathilde had not given up fattening two pigs. She also continued to feed up fifteen to twenty ducks and geese, raise half a dozen rabbits, and care for more than thirty hens and chickens.

And if Jacques happened to scold her for creating lots of work for herself, when he was very well able to supply her with eggs, chickens, ducks and pigs, she invariably retorted:

'All your animals raised on mixtures made of God knows what, they're worthless! They're only good for townies who don't know any better! Your father is much too fussy to eat just anything! And so am I! And even your aunts. Just go and ask Berthe what she thinks of your meal-fed produce! So you leave me to do as I think fit!'

And indeed, her way of fattening the two pigs destined for family consumption – and they were all beneficiaries, even those living in Paris – bore only a distant relation to the methods in use at Coste-Roche. For economic and therefore compelling reasons, Jacques was forced to aim for rapid growth. The granules, meal products, vitamins and different antibiotics which he dished out to his charges had the sole objective of making them reach optimum weight in minimum time. And the insipidity of the meat thus obtained hardly mattered. For a long time now, consumers had been accustomed to eating any old thing! They gulped down without a qualm chicken which resembled veal, veal you could take for pork, pork often mistaken for roast turkey. Not forgetting colourless eggs and fruit and vegetables without smell or taste.

Mathilde had an easy time ridiculing that sort of food. What she produced was on a different plane. So even if it did give her lots of work, she continued her varied stock-rearing.

'In any case, it keeps me busy!' she maintained.

Patiently fattened – in twice the time it took Jacques to get his battery pigs to the same weight – the piglets she cared for had the privilege of a first-class diet. A judicious mixture of steamed potatoes, barley meal and sunflower-oil cakes, with just a dash of maize flour. Not forgetting, of course, the refreshing cabbages and turnips spiced with artichoke peel. Finally, when the season came round, the happy guzzlers, already nice and plump, were entitled to succulent desserts of chestnuts, apples, beets and store carrots.

On a regime of this quality twice a day, with long and beneficial siestas and peaceful nights in the thick, soft litter of barley straw, the temporary quests developed, week by week, a succulent meat. Flesh which, when the time came, would be delicious-smelling, firm without being tough, without excess fat, just sufficiently marbled. Meat which would be fragrant in the cooking, refined, full of aroma; a treat, a delicacy.

And the hams, fillets, chops, shoulders and roasting joints, not forgetting the black puddings (made with chestnuts, apples or just plain), sausages, faggots, potted and grilled meats, the brawn, salt pork and trotters would be of such quality, and the pleasure of those who tasted them so great, that Mathilde would forget all her hours of work. And since the same went for everything she produced, since she was happy and proud to offer her family food of this value, she was not about to stop, despite the arguments and advice of her immediate circle.

What's more,' she would cry laughingly to conclude the discussions, 'if I were to take you at your word, you'd be the first to suffer! Deep down, you don't want me to stop at all!'

For a long time now Pierre-Edouard had been unable to help kill the pig. The effort required to hold the animal, which always seemed to sense the events to come, was too taxing. It needed too much strength and stamina. So he preferred to keep his distance from the sacrificial victim. He was not the only one.

To prove it, this year even Jacques refused to risk grasping one of the animal's hooves and clinging on. Even with the help of three other strong fellows, Delmond, Coste and Brousse, he no longer felt up to tossing the screaming beast on to the ladder resting on breeze-blocks, and holding it there until Delpeyroux plunged his knife into the neck and severed the carotid artery.

And that was not the end of it; for despite the torrent of blood spurting into the bowl, which Mathilde would stir after salting it, to prevent it coagulating, the beast would still have awful convulsions, spasms, snap furiously with its clashing jaws, ready to snatch at a hand and crush it.

It was only gradually that the death rattles and kicking diminished, grew more feeble, more sporadic. Then, whilst the muscles quivered with final tremors and the air bubbles, red and frothy, swelled and burst on the edge of the wound, the last rumblings sounded. Now the men could relax their efforts, wipe their hands and foreheads, then roll a cigarette.

From that moment on, Pierre-Edouard knew how to make himself useful. There was no need for great strength to run the lighted brand over the beast stretched on a temporary, crackling bonfire of straw, in order to burn off the coarsest bristles, those on the back, trotters and ears. Afterwards, when the pink skin was mottled here and there with sooty patches and the fire had become more harmful than useful. Pierre-Edouard could still scratch the hide with his knife, as the water poured by Yvette trickled over it.

'Bloody fine animal, must be about a hundred and thirty kilos!' commented Delpeyroux, passing his whetstone over his sticking knife.

Even though he did it well, always with perfect precision, he did not like this job of slaughterer very much. But the tradition was there, which had one day virtually forced him to take over from his father, who had grown too old, too debilitated to have a sure hand. As he had assisted him for years, and mastered the technique, he had agreed to replace him, to provide the service. And since then, come winter, when the bitter cold helped make the meat easy to handle, when the moon was old, and therefore favourable for preserving, he killed the pigs, without pleasure, but quickly and well.

'You say a hundred and thirty? A bit more, I think,' reckoned Pierre-Edouard. 'Must be over a hundred and thirty-five. He's heavier than his companion. But the other one's beautiful too, longer, maybe more meat on him.'

That one was destined for Mauricette and Jean-Pierre, but their daughters would have a share. And Guy and Colette as well, only too happy to enjoy a superlative ham.

'Talking of which, shall I do him straight away or begin the cutting up?'

'Straight away,' Jacques intervened. 'You know if you wait he'll get worked up, go crazy, get over-excited; it's not good for the meat.'

'Bet he's already worried,' agreed Pierre-Edouard. 'He's heard the bawling, and then the smell of the blood . . . You lot fetch him, I'll go on scraping this one; don't fuss, it's not difficult.'

He saw Mathilde coming back with the bowl, empty but still red-stained.

'They're going to do him now, I hope?' she asked.

'Of course.'

'Poor thing . . .' she murmured, for already the men were emerging once more from the shed, dragging and controlling the victim as best they could.

Wisely, Delpeyroux had muzzled the mouth with a halter. Yet the animal squealed, struggled, tried to bite, fought for its life.

'Poor thing,' she repeated.

'Hey! Come on, now,' said Pierre-Edouard, 'you don't want to keep him till he dies of old age!'

He was joking, but understood his wife's feelings very well. She had looked after and fed this pig for months, made a fuss of it every day, talked to it. So it was quite natural that she should feel a bit sorry for it. One could love black pudding without much enjoying the essential and only method of making it . . .

In front of them, the cries intensified as the men laid the beast on the ladder. Delpeyroux stepped nearer, Mathilde too. The blood spurted out.

*

Despite a still robust appetite, it was not the food which Pierre-Edouard appreciated most at the meal following the sacrifice of the pigs, but the reunion with neighbours. With those who had come to help and were invited to dine as a thank-you. And he was delighted to have around him Delmond, Coste, Brousse and Delpeyroux – whose fathers and grandfathers he had known – because it reminded him of the period when mutual help was so frequent, so normal, that not a month passed, or even a week, depending on the season, without friends meeting this way, at long and cheerful tables after work.

At that time it would never have occurred to a neighbour to refuse a favour – expecting it to be returned, naturally. That was the time when they would make up a 'troupeau' as it was called; six or eight strong, willing men who would undertake the heavy work together. Thanks to them, and at minimal cost, it was possible to tackle the deep ploughing of a fallow field, or break the subsoil of a future vineyard, the excavations and foundations for a house or barn, or set up their wooden framework; and, on the slopes inaccessible to machines, to harvest with scythes, or even sickles. And always, above all, marking out the seasons, the threshing machine, the grape-picking and the pig-killing.

But those days of work and interdependence which maintained friendly ties and united neighbours had long gone, disappeared, been forgotten even, except by the old.

Certainly, and Jacques' accident had proved it, neighbours still knew how to lend a hand to someone in need. But those were individual cases which required almost exceptional circumstances to inspire them.

In fact, because tractors had brought the possibility of decreasing the amount of work done by hand, the idea of helping each other had been eroded from lack of practice. Now only the day of the pig-killing could still unite four or five men and their wives around the same table.

On this day the house came alive again as in former times. It echoed happily with the chatter of the women as they prepared the potted meat and pâté, cooked the black pudding, cut up the hams and shoulders or watched that the heavy pots full of fat placed on the stove did not catch fire.

The house laughed too with the men, who, towards midday, came into the main room, bringing with them on their cords the smell of burnt straw and lightly-grilled crackling, absorbed around the fire. And at the tables where everyone sat together, laughter and jokes soon rang out, old stories were retold, heard a hundred times before but no less valued for that, and the past was brought to life. There, too, all the village news was commented on, ideas were exchanged, impressions of such and such an event. All that was over now, except for once a year.

So today, Pierre-Edouard was keen to play his part at the table as head of the family and he was enjoying it very much. Happy to see his neighbours, whom he met almost every day, but too fleetingly, during his walk in the village. For although he had nothing to do, that was not the case for those he greeted; it was therefore impossible to start a proper and satisfying discussion with them. It all went too fast.

'Bonjour, Père Vialhe. Lovely weather, that won't last! Right, it's not that I'm tired of your company but there's work waiting for me. Salut, Père Vialhe. And mind you look after yourself!'

Here at table it was different, one could forget the time. One could even allow oneself the luxury of some gentle teasing, and that Pierre-Edouard really loved.

After pouring a good measure of wine into a bouillon as meaty as one could wish for, and thickened with vermicelli, he turned light-heartedly to Pierre Coste, sitting next to him.

'So according to what Jacques tells me,' he said to him, 'you're planning to start up a ranch, just like that?'

'Oh, a ranch! Don't exaggerate, we're not the national stud at Pompadour, you know! What I want is just to keep some ponies for the kids coming to the château. And some horses too, for the bigger ones.'

'I see . . .' replied Pierre-Edouard. 'Here, help yourself,' he said, passing the dish of pot-au-feu. 'Some ponies and horses,' he continued. 'But do you know about these animals?'

'No, not too much,' admitted Coste. 'With me it's been mostly cows, as you know, so . . .'

'I see,' repeated Pierre-Edouard, serving himself in his turn.

'But you do know they give terrible kicks, those animals?' he said, thoughtfully contemplating a gherkin speared on the end of his fork. 'Kicks which kill you outright!' he insisted.

'My father's is always exaggerating,' interrupted Jacques with a laugh.

'What me, exaggerate? Tell me straight out I don't know a thing about horses!'

'Oh no! Nobody would dare say that, Père Vialhe,' Delpeyroux assured him. 'It's well known that you were an expert!'

He was old enough to remember the time when Pierre-Edouard had his horse and cart. He also knew just how much the old man liked to joke, and here his tone and expression were signalling a hoax.

'But Jacques says I don't know a thing about it!' said Pierre-Edouard. 'And yet, my lad, I had up to sixty horses to take care of morning and evening – yes, when I did my military service, I certainly did! Not to mention the percherons I had when I was working in the Brie area! Because I ploughed with horses, I did! To say nothing, either, about the ones which pulled our 75-millimetre cannon during the war! So, to hear that I don't know anything about it, and from my own son too!'

'The family always lets you down,' said Jacques. He knew his father well, and without guessing all the ins and outs, he saw the joke being constructed.

'Well, if I tell you that a kick from a horse can cut you in two, it's true,' said Pierre-Edouard, 'and the same with their teeth! They bite, those animals, you've no idea, worse than dogs! That's the only reason you put a bit in their mouths – and while they're chewing on it, they don't think of snapping up your arm!'

'Get away, they're not as vicious as all that!' replied Coste with a shrug. But he was nevertheless rather shaken.

'All right, but you just mind out. And if you pass behind them, allow at least . . . oh, three good metres! They can lash out as far as that,' Pierre-Edouard assured him.

'Oh no! There I don't believe you, that's a joke!' said Coste, laughing. He was relieved to have detected the trick in time.

'Okay,' admitted Pierre-Edouard, 'I'm exaggerating a bit, but it's just to make you careful.' He drank a few mouthfuls of wine, wiped his mouth before continuing: 'In any case, you'll do as you like, but on the treks, don't take the animals in the direction of Delpy's place, you know, into the valley.'

'But I'll have to go down there; the public road passes that way and it makes a very nice ride, you know that perfectly well!' said Coste. 'And anyway, why shouldn't I go there?'

'Have you thought about the pond?'

'The one Delpy had dug three years ago? Yes, and so what?'

'Any one can see you really don't know a thing about horses,' Pierre-Edouard reproached him. 'If you don't learn a bit more, you'll soon have lost half of them . . .'

'What?'

'Yes indeed! Has no one ever told you that they love to swim, those animals?

'Oh, no! But after all, even if . . . I don't see why . . .'

'And you've never been told, either, that mares shouldn't swim? Well it'll be all right if you only have geldings, but if you have mares . . .'

'Oh dear! That's right, that would be unforgivable!' commented Delpeyroux. 'It's common knowledge,' he insisted, 'a mare should never swim, never!'

'Well, how the hell can it harm them?' demanded Coste, more and more disconcerted.

'It's because they take in water, young man! Everybody knows that. All mares take in water!' said Pierre-Edouard in a tone which brooked no reply.

'And it doesn't do any good even if you hold their heads out of the water,' Delpeyroux went one better, 'because that's not the way they fill themselves up . . .'

'Huh! Now you're making fun of me, aren't you?' said Coste. But he was not really sure of anything and thought it wise to continue: 'So where does the water go in, then?'

'Tut, tut . . .' Pierre-Edouard sighed, glancing in the direction of the women at the other table, to make sure they were not listening. 'Think about it a bit, young man,' he explained, lowering his voice. 'Delpeyroux told you the water doesn't enter by the mouth, or the ears, okay? So . . .'

'Damnation . . .' murmured Coste, after a moment's consideration and an effort of imagination, 'damnation, I'd never have believed it! It's good thing you warned me! Well, well, I'd never have believed it!' he repeated.

'And yet, you need to know it,' said Pierre-Edouard, seeing that Jacques, Delpeyroux, and Delmond were about to explode with laughter. 'Yes, yes, young fellow, and I'll tell you something else – *I*'d never have believed that joke could still work!'

He had to raise his voice to make himself heard over Delmond who, his eyes filled with tears, was roaring with laughter as he delivered mighty slaps to his thighs.

'Do you know what?' continued Pierre-Edouard. 'That joke, we used it on the rookies coming from the towns, when I was only a second gunner and crew marksman in the Fifth Artillery Regiment in Besançon in 1909!'

'Good old Coste! "I'd never have believed it!" he said! The fool! The fool!' hiccuped Delpeyroux in a strangled voice. And his guffaws were so infectious, so heart-warming, that the whole table joined in.

As a result, nobody noticed that it was not laughter, but the memories of himself at twenty which now brought a few tears to Pierre-Edouard's eyes.

According to a tradition going back close on thirty years, Mathilde and Pierre-Edouard invited their children to share their midday meal on Christmas Day. And although it was exceptional for the Paris members, Guy and Colette, to be there, Jacques and Michèle, Mauricette and Jean-Pierre always kept the appointment.

Certainly the absence of young children made the celebration less boisterous, less noisy and cheerful, but everyone was still eager to forget for one day their worries, their little physical aliments, their work.

And in December 1976, nobody had need of forced jollity to bring some happiness to the Vialhe household. Mauricette made sure, during the aperitif, of cheering them with the hot news just telephoned through by Josyane and Christian: a baby was on the way for them, expected in June . . . So there it was . . .

'I knew it,' said Mathilde. 'Yes, I did, she'd changed too much all of a sudden, little Jo! Well, so it's June? All right . . . That's how it is . . .'

'Well, well!' smiled Pierre-Edouard, holding out his glass to Jacques for another drop of Banyuls wine. And, mischievously, he could not stop himself announcing: 'In our time, we weren't as smart as young people nowadays. If I remember rightly, you needed to allow at least nine months after the wedding to make a proper baby . . . But, there's progress for you, everything happens so quickly nowadays . . .'

'Stop it, will you?' Mathilde said to him; despite her pleasure, she was a little embarrassed that everything was not quite as it should be. And in particular, she was not forgetting that Jacques and Michèle had already, in their time . . .

'Oh, go on!' insisted Pierre-Edouard. 'Why shouldn't I say they've had Easter before Palm Sunday? That's how it is, we're not going to pretend to believe otherwise! In any case it's very good news: babies, you can never have enough of them!'

'Very good news,' agreed Jean-Pierre, who was bursting with pride at the idea of being a grandfather soon. 'Pity the baby's not being born here, with Dominique's; that would have made two more births in the village!'

'Yes, a hundred per cent better than this year . . . A fine feat!' said Jacques

'We'll talk about all that at table,' suggested Mathilde, 'because if you wait, the turkey will be too dry.'

It was while they were tackling the hors-d'oeuvre – a succulent home-made foie gras – with good humour and a little more good wine than usual bringing a sparkle to their eyes, that Mauricette launched the second piece of news:

'All right, Jo and Christian won't be having their baby here, but they will be having a house in the village!'

'A house? How's that? They want to have one built?' asked Jacques.

'They're not going to come and live here, are they?' said Mathilde.

'No, no,' cut in Berthe, who thought she understood, 'they only want a holiday home is that it?'

360

'Yes,' confirmed Jean-Pierre. 'They asked us just now to look for one for them; it seems that Christian feels more Corrézien than ever!'

'Do they want one in the village itself or in the parish?' asked Jacques, delighted at the idea of seeing some young people return to Saint-Libéral, if only for a few weeks a year.

'It doesn't matter to them. But Jo would like it to be on the plateau side, so not too far from the village,' said Mauricette.

'Are you going to tell me or not? I don't understand a thing!' Pierre-Edouard suddenly lost patience, and spoke with a brusqueness which surprised everyone.

He was vaguely aware of not having paid any attention to the beginning of the conversation, and was rather cross with himself. But on the other hand, it was sometimes so tiring, so exhausting just to keep track of everything being said! Especially when there was such a crowd and everyone was talking at the same time! That almost made you feel like doing the same as Louise, who no longer made the effort to listen to what was being related around her. It's true that it was often of such little interest . . .

On the other hand, not to know what people were talking about, that was annoying. Especially when you had the feeling that they were doing nothing to help you follow their discussion! That really was something to get cross about!

But there again, it was quite tiring, you always came away with the nasty impression of having fallen out over very little. For, actually, what they told you in the end, to calm you down, was of absolutely no importance, no interest at all!

But that was still no reason to leave you deliberately in ignorance of what they were saying. Because of course everyone deliberately spoke quietly, whispered, so that he heard nothing!

'It's true, by God! I never get told anything round here!' he cried in a voice filled with anger.

'Yes, yes, you do,' replied Berthe gently, placing her hand on his arm to calm the trembling. 'Right, what would you like to know?'

'Berthe's right, we'll explain everything,' said Mathilde, in a tone which barely concealed her sudden concern for Pierre-Edouard.

He seemed both exasperated and distant at the same time; the weariness which had swept over him in just a few seconds lined his features, distorted them. And at the end of his knotted fingers, all speckled with brown patches, the nails were turning purple.

'Now listen!' said Berthe. 'Jo and Christian want to buy a house in the village, to come and spend their holidays here. There, that's simple, isn't it?'

'Who wants to spend the holidays?' he asked.

'Young Jo and her husband,' explained Mathilde.

'Ah? Well, you could have said all that straight away, couldn't you? And so what's the problem?' he said, beginning to eat again.

'There's no problem,' said Jacques, noting with relief that his father seemed to be on an even keel again. 'And you know very well there's no lack of houses for sale in the area, sadly!'

'Ah yes . . .' replied Pierre-Edouard.

'And then, we'll need to know what sort of price before looking seriously,' continued Jacques.

'Not too expensive, I think,' said Mauricette.

'So that means they'll be coming here more often?' Pierre-Edouard intervened once more.

'Of course,' said Mathilde. 'It's good news, don't you think?'

'Yes, yes,' he said absentmindedly, as if all that was of no further interest. 'Yes, yes,' he repeated. And he sank into contemplation of his empty plate.

'Would you like to go and rest a while, take a little siesta?' suggested Mathilde, to try to break the awkward atmosphere which had fallen over the table.

'A siesta?' He reflected for a moment, passed his hand across his face, then frowned. 'A siesta? No, it's not time! And I want some turkey!' he said, his voice suddenly normal and firm again. He smiled at Mathilde, and continued: 'Say, if young Jo comes back more often, you'll be happy, won't you?'

'Of course,' she agreed, forcing herself to return his smile. But worry was etched on her face.

*

'No, I assure you, he's not in bad shape. Well, I mean to say, no worse than usual,' said Doctor Martel to Jacques after his visit the following day.

At the request of Mathilde, and although it was Sunday, Jacques had telephoned the doctor. But beforehand he had warned his mother that he ran the risk of finding a locum; a man whom Pierre-Edouard would not know and with whom he would have words. For he was very lucid again and less inclined to make allowances, especially for a stranger.

Luckily, Doctor Martel was on duty and had come as quickly as possible. And although Pierre-Edouard had not failed to complain that it was all being done just to annoy him, that he only wanted one thing, to be left in peace, he had let him sound his chest.

'Right, so, if we agree that he's no worse, what do we do when he seems ... how shall I put it? ... Yes, when he switches off?' asked Jacques.

'Oh, that! Only a genius could give you the answer! It's his age, and ... But I think his heart misses a bit from time to time, so the brain is poorly supplied; that could explain his periods of absentmindedness. Having said that, as you asked, I took the opportunity of my visit to examine your aunt, and there ...'

'Let's have it! I've heard worse things!' insisted Jacques.

'She's declining fast, almost quicker than your father. And, as well as her mind not being very strong, she might be hatching a nasty surprise for us in the stomach area ... You'll be telling me, at her age, it could take a long time ... Then I must remind you to watch that your mother doesn't do more than she should; she seems well, but ...'

'I know,' sighed Jacques, 'but what can I do? And you don't have to tell me that my sister and I may find ourselves with four old people on our hands! Because Aunt Berthe could come a cropper all of a sudden! And even Aunt Yvette isn't immune from the hard knocks of life!'

'And neither are you,' Doctor Martel reminded him.

'I won't forget. But all right, that's how it is. Our relatives are the way they are, we'll manage. It'll take as long as it takes. And then, as my father's said to me a thousand times,

25

WITH results which were nothing to be ashamed of, and what was more, with important projects about to be realised, Jacques could have saved himself the expense of an electoral campaign. His sash of office was not in danger. Despite that, he played the game.

First of all out of courtesy towards his fellow citizens – friends or enemies – and also to cock a bit of a snook at Peyrafaure; not too much, just enough to satisfy everyone. For even whilst certain of his victory, the electors would not have understood him leaving a free hand and a clear field to a rival as forceful as Peyrafaure.

The latter conducted his campaign in a frenzy of activity, multiplying meetings, interviews, interminable discussions and other consultations. He lacked neither courage nor audacity, nor that shameless dishonesty not displeasing to certain electors, who regard it as the height of political skill. Peyrafaure did not disappoint them.

Witness the fact that, having announced various sporting developments for the young people, amongst them a tennis court, he now declared that it was all going to cost a fortune, that Jacques had delusions of grandeur, that the community, already crippled with debts, would be ruined for fifty years to come and the taxes would be unimaginably high! Figures in hand, he forecast an intolerable tax increase, as never before seen!

Jacques did not take the trouble to refute this, for his visits to all the homes, even the most far-flung, gave him strength, proved that he had been right to convert the château and that the majority of the electors were delighted at the idea of soon seeing a flock of children on holiday there. Likewise, and he was pleased and surprised by this, people were gratified to know that the village was going to open itself to the outside world, to welcome visitors, to bring in new life thanks to the photo exhibition. Finally, everyone was now anxious to see the auberge opened again.

That was decided; Lacombe's brother-in-law, his wife and six children – four of them were already enrolled at the school – would be moving to the village before the summer. Lacombe also reported, and this was great news, that not only was his brother-in-law all set to open a fixed menu restaurant, but his sister, after studying the market, was contemplating keeping a small grocery store, with bread counter!

But there again, Peyrafaure found an excuse for spiteful gossip, when Lacombe was not there. Without daring to specify the colour of the impending arrivals, he insinuated that one did not know too much about the people one was going to be dealing with ... Because, basically, who could stand guarantee for an individual who had spent part of his army career in the colonial wars and now trebled his monthly pension thanks to child benefit payments?

Peyrafaure would never have made such a suggestion three months earlier, when Lacombe was part of his team within the council. With Martin, Castellac, Delmas and himself, they formed the opposition. But, probably because that turncoat Lacombe wanted his sister and brother-in-law to start on a sound basis with the mayor, he had changed his tune and joined the camp of Jacques, Delpeyroux, Delmond, Coste, Duverger and Brousse; that is, of the majority!

And a majority which was going to be re-elected at the first ballot! An honour which Peyrafaure had no certainty of securing. He was therefore aggressive and vindictive, but not at all dangerous to Jacques and his team.

In any case, Jacques did not particularly resent his excesses. He did not forget that Peyrafaure was among those who had come running when he lay paralysed beside his tractor. That gesture really required him to turn a bit of a deaf ear at the time of an electoral campaign.

Besides, he knew that everything would subside again like a soufflé the day after the second ballot. As soon as the celebration wine toasting the elected members was swallowed, the council would return to its old ways, its monotony, with occasional rows and always Peyrafaure's grand perorations. It was fine like that.

Louise's condition deteriorated drastically two days before the first round of the elections. Although, like Pierre-Edouard, she had got through the winter without any great problem. True, the weather had been mild, the temperature kind. To such an extent that Pierre-Edouard had been able to go out almost every day with Berthe for his little walk in the village; not far, down to the church square; and sometimes even, when he was very bold, as far as Mauricette's, beside the school.

By contrast, Louise no longer went out, no longer moved. Rising early, which is to say soon after Mathilde, who was eager to be the first up to rekindle the fire, she drank the bowl of milk which now represented her main meal of the day. That done, she installed herself in the settle, and the few words she exchanged with Mathilde or Pierre-Edouard, he too an early-riser, grew less frequent, quickly becoming rather disjointed, joining in the conversation after too long a gap.

Thus, without appearing to suffer, she sank into an increasingly impenetrable silence and estrangement, although full of smiles, almost seraphic. She seemed to surface when Berthe sat down at her side to pass the afternoon. She then took some pleasure in her sister's prattling, as she commented on the newspaper, the television programme, the village gossip, and gave news of the family. And it was Berthe too who made sure that she fed herself a little; for she no longer even came to sit at table, but contented herself with nibbling a few morsels of biscuit which she dipped into half a glass of milk sweetened with a spoonful of honey.

When darkness fell, she left her corner by the fire without a sound, informing those around her quietly: 'It's late, I'm going to bed', and disappeared into her room until the following morning.

So on Friday, 11 March, Mathilde was worried not to see her up at her usual time. Apprehensively she entered the bedroom, turned on the light and understood.

Rigid in her bed, half her face deformed by a terrible

grimace, Louise appeared dead. But Mathilde, upset as she was, prevented herself from uttering the slightest exclamation, to avoid any sudden shock to Pierre-Edouard. It was in leaning over her sister-in-law that she discovered she was still alive. Stricken by hemiplegia, the whole of her right side was frozen, inert. But her expression was alive, understanding everything, appealing for help.

Without hesitation, Mathilde continued into the next bedroom, that of Berthe. She always rose much later, having preserved her Parisian habits which often kept her up until midnight. Despite that, she woke as soon as Mathilde pushed open the door. Immediately lucid, understanding that a serious occurrence had caused her sister-in-law to burst in, she called:

'Is it Pierre-Edouard?'

'No, Louise.'

'Is she . . .?'

'No, paralysed.'

'That's all we needed,' said Berthe, rising and slipping on her dressing-gown. 'Have you called Martel?'

'Not yet.'

'Do it right away, tell him it's urgent! Does Pierre-Edouard know?'

'No.'

'I'll take care of that. We don't want anything to happen to him as well.'

Thanks to one of those letters, rather infrequent but very detailed, sent to him by his mother, Dominique learned of his aunt's health trouble and his grandfather's renewed cardiac alert at the same time.

His aunt, fortunately treated in time, seemed stable for the moment. But her paralysis, despite encouraging improvements, made a great deal of work for the household. To such an extent that Félix had come down to Saint-Libéral to give his aunts support for a while.

As for Pierre-Edouard, although exhausted and in defiance of doctor's orders, he demanded to be helped to rise every morning, to dress himself, to shave. Afterwards he installed

368

himself on the settle, swallowed his bowl of milky chicory coffee, and waited until someone came to read the newspaper to him. That took him until the mealtime. He ate it at the fireside, then returned to his bedroom and had a nap.

Afterwards, weather permitting, he asked Félix to accompany him to take some air. Not far, a few steps outside the door, in exceptional circumstances into the garden. Then he came back in, had the television or radio turned on, and waited patiently in this way until it was time for supper. Only after that would he agree to return to his bed.

But all that is very tedious for everyone . . . explained the letter.

The same letter also announced that his father had been overwhelmingly re-elected as the head of the mairie. That the château had been opened with great pomp by all the invited dignitaries; and that, during the coming Easter holidays, the people from the Lierson and Meulen firm were going to meet there for a seminar.

Finally, to conclude, the information that his father was rearing his last batch of pigs. That he had at last found, for 25,000 francs, a very good second-hand tractor, a 55cv which only had 3,500 hours on the clock and could therefore do twice as many again without any problem. With the help of this machine, he was going to resow all his pastures, grub out the old plum and apple trees, set to work again on all sides. After that, cautiously, he would probably begin to turn towards the production of pedigree cattle.

'At last! Some good news!' sighed Dominique, folding up the letter again.

What she had told him at the beginning saddened him greatly. Certainly he had known for a long time that his aunt was failing, but to picture her paralysed touched his heart. And he was also very distressed for his grandfather. And worried to such an extent that he could not help thinking that, perhaps, the latter would not await their return before joining Léon . . .

Actually, his mother's letter had arrived at an awkward moment, and he reacted badly. Already very annoyed about a series of failed experiments – it was not his fault, but that did not improve his temper! – he was also concerned about Béatrice. He found her tired, and would have liked her to rest much more than she did. Instead of which, she had not even stopped work at the maternity hospital. She considered she was better placed than him to know what she ought to do. All he could do was nurse his anger and count the days until their return to France.

'You can see the poor girl hasn't time to look after the garden any more,' remarked Pierre-Edouard, observing the beds where peas, carrots, white onions and garlic were growing.

Everything was flourishing, and well-advanced, but to those who knew about gardening, it was obvious that the crops were in need of attention. Lacking sticks, the peas were beginning to collapse, and weeds were invading the carrots. In addition, the ground prepared to receive the new potatoes was still empty.

'Poor little thing,' sighed Pierre-Edouard, 'we give her too much work. You should look after this garden a bit, just to help Mathilde. I'm sure it must depress her to see it like this.'

'Promise, I'll set to,' agreed Félix, who considered it useless to point out that he had already taken the trouble to hoe between the rows of onions and garlic.

'Ought to put in some chavignounes, they're a good sort of potato.'

'All right. And tomorrow, if it's fine, I'll stake the peas and you'll help me!'

'Oh, help you! Wish I still could! But I'll keep you company,' promised Pierre-Edouard.

'That's really what I meant. Do you want to go back in now?' suggested Félix. 'I wouldn't like you to catch cold.'

He had taken advantage of a ray of sunshine between two showers to accompany Pierre-Edouard, who was keen to see the kitchen garden. Actually they had not been able to go out for several days because Easter week, although not cold, had nevertheless been changeable and damp.

'Cold?' said Pierre-Edouard. 'No, it's fine. Listen to the cuckoos, how they're enjoying themselves, that's a sign of fine weather. Come on, help me get out of here, we're going to walk a bit in the main street.'

'You're not too tired, now?'

'No, no! And then all those nonsensical medicines and injections Martel gives me ought to be some use. Well, I can't complain, when I see your mother . . .'

On discovering, a month earlier, the state his sister had sunk into, Pierre-Edouard had felt his heart could not cope with this new emotion, this too-severe shock. And he suddenly felt as weak as a newborn babe, with somewhere in the top part of his chest a heaviness, a pain which constricted his breathing. Luckily, Doctor Martel was there looking after Louise . . .

'So you're sure, you want to take a turn in the main street? You feel fit for it?' Félix checked.

He considered it pointless and absurd to pretend to the old man that he was allowed to do anything and had never been in such good health. For although it was true his new treatment had alleviated the moments of absentmindedness or apparent delirium which were so disturbing, it did not permit him to remain standing for long, or to walk more than fifty metres without having to stop to gather his strength.

Besides, Pierre-Edouard was completely lucid and aware of his condition; he had no illusions about the little time he had left to live. With him, lies were useless. He had already seen so many, many people die, that he in particular could not be deceived in any way on that matter. Now, all he was hoping for was to see his grandson again. Jacques, knowing how much it would please him, had made him party to Dominique's plans: one day – maybe in twenty years' time, maybe more, but one day – his grandson wanted to come and live at Coste Roche, to work there.

And Pierre-Edouard wanted to hear that for himself, spoken by his grandson, to be certain. And then, God willing, but that was perhaps asking too much of him, and he hardly dared think about it, it seemed so far off, he would have loved to know that his first great-grandson – or daughter – had been born.

After that he would be able to rest at last and wait until his time came. It would come very soon. And nobody could do anything about it. And even the distress and love he read in Mathilde's eyes, when a bout of weakness forced him to swallow several life-preserving pills, would be unable to change anything at all. Even her prayers would be in vain.

But whilst waiting, and as he still had a remnant of strength, he wanted to take advantage of the burgeoning spring and this April afternoon full of such fine lilac blossom.

'Come on, help me,' he repeated, 'we'll walk a bit in the street. Ought to let everyone know that Père Vialhe is still upright!'

They were emerging from the garden when an old Citröen 2CV, its bodywork pitted by rust, braked behind them and then stopped on a level with them.

'Ah! It's you?' said Pierre-Edouard, recognising Father Soliers.

A month earlier, although very busy with all his parishes, Father Soliers had insisted on making a visit to the Vialhes as soon as he had been informed of Louise and Pierre-Edouard's condition.

His arrival had been a great comfort to Mathilde and Yvette; much less so to Berthe, who considered it premature and in very poor taste. It is true that her contact with consecrated places was barely more regular than Pierre-Edouard's. True as well that she was rather too independent a character to conform blindly to rituals which she considered were often questionable, not to say ridiculous. It was therefore rare for her to go to church more than three or four times a year.

Despite that, because she was well-mannered she did not remark to the priest that his visit was open to misinterpretation. Malicious minds might actually see in it, not a simple and friendly polite convention, but the opportunistic action of one who dispensed extreme unction and was suffering from a shortage of the dying.

However, since the only provisions Father Soliers had brought were a bar of milk chocolate and a packet of sponge fingers, and she had clearly seen a contented beam in her sister-in-law's expression, she had kept quiet. And now she behaved very nicely at each fresh visit by the priest.

He made the effort to come almost every week, and Louise always seemed happy to see him again. Always in a hurry, he only stayed a few minutes, time enough to note the progress made by the invalid and congratulate her on it. Then he assured everyone of his prayers, climbed back into his wreck of a 2CV and jolted along to the next invalid, often bedridden in the depths of some other distant parish.

'Well, well, Monsieur Vialhe, you seem to be in fine form!' he said, getting out of his car.

'Fine form? Don't exaggerate, but after all, I'll hang on a bit longer . . .'

'You're right! That's it, try to stay determined like that. Fine, I must go and pay my respects to your sister, I've still lots to do before dark.'

'He does what he can, the poor fellow,' said Pierre-Edouard as soon as the priest had entered the house.

'Yes, and it's good, what he's doing there,' agreed Félix.

'But all the same, it was a different matter in the time of Father Feix or Father Verlhac,' said Pierre-Edouard, advancing with short steps into the main street. 'Yes, when they went to see a sick person it was no trouble to them to spend an hour or two there.'

'They had the time . . .'

'Well, yes. That poor fellow, with all the parishes they've loaded on him, he can't keep up! But all the same, our old ministers were better. They didn't look at their watches. They were almost part of the family; he's just a visitor. That doesn't mean we don't like him, but he's just a visitor . . .'

Although so brief, Christian and Josyane's visit gave a great deal of pleasure to the whole Vialhe family. First, because the couple had come down from Paris to sign the contract for their future holiday home; there was therefore the assurance that they would be coming often. Then, because it was very comforting to hear Josyane's laugh as she responded to her grandmother's worries about her.

As a matter of fact, Mathilde considered that her

373

granddaughter was behaving during her pregnancy with a detachment and casualness which bordered on rashness. So she never stopped warning her and commending the benefits of rest.

'You really should take care, my dear, an accident can happen in a trice! And you, Christian, you're not being sensible! That's a fair old step you're intending to cover, and it's uphill!' she considered it her duty to tell them, when she learned the couple were setting out to walk around the plateau. Truly this late April afternoon, filled with sunshine and perfume, was magnificent, but all the same!

'Now, now, bonne-maman, how dare you say that to me?' teased Josyane. 'To listen to you, anyone would swear you never worked in the fields or stables when you were expecting Maman and my uncles! So our walk, in comparison!'

'It wasn't the same for me! And then . . . It wasn't the same, that's all!' repeated Mathilde.

'That's right, tell me straight out I'm a weakling!'

'No, but I don't think you take enough care of yourself!'

'I love you, bonne-maman! Come on, don't worry, everything's fine, the baby's well settled in, everything's normal. And besides it's not an illness! That's what my gyno is always telling me!'

'You're talking about your doctor, are you? Those people, they trot out nothing but rubbish!'

'That's the first sensible thing you've said for five minutes!' Pierre-Edouard intervened.

He had insisted on sitting on the threshold. Propped up in a cane armchair, his head in the shade thanks to the porch, but his legs in the sun, he was feeling fine.

'Ahah! You see,' teased Josyane, 'even Grandfather thinks I'm right!'

'Naturally, the moment he gets a chance to contradict me!' replied Mathilde with a shrug.

'Don't listen to your grandmother, dear,' said Pierre-Edouard. 'When she gave birth to your mother, it was touch and go whether I could get her out of the cowshed a quarter of an hour beforehand! And if I'd let her, she would have been back there again that same evening!' he finished with a chuckle.

374

He coughed a bit and caught his breath, for even laughing was an effort to him now.

'You mustn't believe a word he says,' Mathilde assured her, bending over him to pull up the cover which had slipped from his shoulders.

'Do you hear her?' Pierre-Edouard called on Josyane and Christian as witnesses. 'Do you hear her?' He clung on to Mathilde's hand, held it between his own. 'You know,' he added, 'she always told me I was so full of mischief and tall stories, I'd end up in hell! Like poor old Léon did!'

'Stop it,' she smiled, 'you're still telling them!'

'And I always replied . . .' He coughed once more, squeezed Mathilde's hand and whispered with a little laugh: 'I replied: There's no chance of that, there's no one in hell. That's why the devil is bored and comes to torment us on earth!'

'And what's more you talk like a heathen!' she cried, without believing a word she said.

He smiled at her, let go of her hand and signalled to Josyane and Christian to come closer.

'And your little one, when's it due?' he asked.

'In June, six or seven weeks.'

'That's still a long time off, a long time . . .' he murmured.

'No it isn't,' Josyane assured him. 'We'll come and show it to you this summer. That way, with Béatrice's, you'll have one for each knee. And Christian will take loads of lovely photos!'

'That's still a long time off, all that,' he repeated. He coughed a little, cleared his throat: 'And what will it be called?'

'David or Marianne,' said Josyane, who had the tact not to remind him that she had given the same answer the previous evening.

'David? David? he murmured. He reflected, his brow furrowed: 'We hid a child during the war, yes, he was called David, him too. And his brother? His brother . . .?'

'Benjamin,' whispered Mathilde.

'That's it. They were nice kids, both of them . . . God knows what became of them . . . Well, that's the way it is . . .'

He shook his head, as if to banish some unpleasant memories, then asked:

'So, it's really true, you've bought Meyjonade's place, at Fonts Perdus?'

'Not Meyjonade's,' Mathilde intervened, 'I've already told you, his daughter married a Mouly. Anyway, you know full well it's Meyjonade's grandson who sold it!'

'It's the same thing,' he said irritably,'to me it's still Meyjonade's.' He fell silent, meditated: 'Before the war, that was a fine farm. The Meyjonades kept six or seven cows, yes, a fine farm . . . And then it's a beautiful spot, Fonts Perdus. Once upon a time, you always flushed at least two covies of red-legs there. And there were hares too. So, now it's yours?'

'Yes,' confirmed Josyane. 'It'll be lovely there. You must come and see us as soon as we've organised it a bit. Since it hasn't been inhabited for a while, there's some work to do . . .'

'And the fields?' he continued.

'You know very well that Valade and Duverger bought them a long time ago!' Mathilde reminded him.

'Ah, that's right,' he murmured, after thinking about it. 'That's true, it was good land . . .'

He pulled the rug around his shoulders, coughed a little and gestured to Mathilde:

'Help me get up, it's too cold now to stay outside.'

'Would you like Christian to help you?' suggested Josyane to her grandmother.

'No, Félix will come, he's in the vegetable garden. You go and take your walk,' she said, and she added quietly: 'It's beautiful and warm, make the most of it.'

If Dominique still had any illusions about his employers at Mondiagri, they were destroyed when he perused the letter he received a week before setting out for France. At first he did not believe what he was reading, then he checked the date and swore volubly:

'Jesus Christ Almighty! They're doing it on purpose! I swear they're doing it on purpose, the bastards!' he called to Béatrice.

She had at last stopped work at the maternity hospital, and was making the most of her free time by resting.

'What's up?' she asked, without moving from the chaise longue.

'That pack of exploiters at Mondiagri are bugging me, that's what's up! Talk about dickheads! They know fine in Paris that I'm taking my leave next week! I told them more than six months ago, the morons!' he shouted, brandishing the letter and pounding out each word heavily with his fist on the table.

'What's up?' she asked again patiently.

'I'm stuck here! That's what's up! And all because those buggers in Paris – because they're real buggers, those people! – are sending me two more idiots! Two hypocrites with the task of arranging a visit to the centre by the Tunisians responsible for food and agriculture! And all just to screw them as fast as possible! Because that's all they're coming for, those vultures!'

'If you'd kept calm, you'd have given me the dates of their visit by now.'

'The fourth and fifth of May! And our leave begins on the twenty-eighth of April! Oh, marvellous! I tell you, they do it on purpose! It's the second time they've played that trick on me! But this time they can go and get stuffed! I'm resigning!'

'There's no question of that,' she said without raising her voice.

'You don't think I'm going to let you leave and have the baby alone, while I'm here trying to convince the poor suckers that there's no salvation for their God-forsaken country besides Mondiagri! Are you out of your mind?'

'Not for one minute. To resign, you have to have the means! You have absolutely no safe place to go to in the immediate future. And just because Ali assures you they'll take you back whenever you like in Algeria, don't think it would be so easy. So no dreaming, if you don't mind? I'll leave on the planned date, and I'll wait for you before going into labour, promise!' she joked.

'No, no, no! That won't do! I'm not letting you leave alone!'

'Bah, there's two of me!' she said, patting her stomach. 'Come on,' she smiled, 'fetch a beer, that'll calm you down. I

377

don't like it when you get worked up like that! And nor does the baby, it responds by pummelling me with its feet! And look, if it's any comfort to you, I'll go earlier and wait for you at Coste-Roche. Over there I'll rest even better than here. But I mean it, seriously!'

'I'm not going to leave you to have the baby alone.'

'Stop going on about it! You know what my gyno said, and I trust her, she's very competent: the baby will be there at the right time, no more and no less! So if you arrive on the sixth, that'll be fine.'

'Hey! Stop it with your infallible dates! That only works in books! Don't forget, as far as this is concerned, you're on the same system as cows. And that I do know about! Just because a cow is pregnant for two hundred and seventy-five days, it doesn't mean the calf arrives at that exact moment! So, stop talking nonsense, if you don't mind!'

'Thanks for the comparison,' she teased. 'Well, I escaped being like a goat, that's something I suppose!'

'One hundred and fifty-five days for a goat! Three months, three weeks and three days for a sow! A hundred and fifty-five days for a ewe! Do you want some more?' He saw that she was laughing and shrugged his shoulders. 'Fine,' he said, suddenly calmed down, 'after all, perhaps you're right. But you must admit these Mondiagri people are real bastards!'

'Why shouldn't they be? It works! The proof is you can't do anything but follow their directives, at least for the moment . . .'

'You did well to add "for the moment"! The time's not far off when they'll realise that Vialhes aren't sheep.'

Although everyone had been told to conceal from Pierre-Edouard that Domique would be at least a week late, he guessed the truth. Probably Yvette, Berthe, Mathilde or Jacques had said one word too many; perhaps someone had gone so far as to mention Béatrice, who was already at Coste-Roche and was staying put there.

As a matter of fact the whole family had been in agreement in telling her that it was pointless to go and visit the old man. One had to face facts, and recognise that it was not her he was waiting for. She had quite understood and was in no way upset.

But this delay played a great deal on the old man's spirits. He went into a rapid and devastating decline. This was all the more poignant since he remained clear-headed. It was just that, instead of calling early to be helped out of bed, he took to dozing there until the end of the morning. At that point, it was obvious he was calling on his reserves to drag himself from his torpor and this paralysing weariness which was crushing him. Then he would call to Félix or Mathilde:

'Have to get me out of here, it's high time,' he would say.

And then he would try to get down from the big wooden bed by himself. Afterwards, when Félix had shaved him, and he felt clean, he had himself brought to the corner by the hearth or, if there was sunshine, to a cane armchair placed in front of the window.

Once there, he waited until evening, punctuating the afternoon with long periods of drowsiness. He asked to be taken to bed as soon as darkness fell, but demanded each evening before lying down:

'Dominique's arriving when?'

'Very soon,' Mathilde would say, not wishing to venture a precise date.

However, on the evening of 6 May, as she leaned over to kiss him on the forehead, she could anticipate his question and announce:

'He'll be there tomorrow, definitely. Do you hear? Tomorrow!'

He sighed, nodded his head and patted her on the arm:

'The devil, he's kept us waiting!' he said at last. But he felt immediately less anxious. And the night was peaceful.

Although shocked to discover Pierre-Edouard's condition, Dominique and Béatrice knew how to put up a good show when they came to visit him on the Saturday evening.

But there were too many people for Pierre-Edouard to feel like talking or even hearing what his grandson had to say to him. So, despite the evident contentment in his beaming expression, he did not say very much. He simply whispered to Dominique, just before going to bed:

'Come tomorrow morning, we must talk.'

'Promise. Well, unless Béatrice decides to go into labour in the meantime!'

'That would be good,' smiled the old man.

He squeezed Dominique's arm and went off towards his bedroom, supported by Félix and Mathilde.

'And now, don't think you have to lie to me!' she said to Dominique and Béatrice, when she returned after putting him to bed. 'I know very well that he's . . .'

'Come on, you can't possibly know,' attempted Dominique.

'Yes, I can,' she sighed as she lowered herself into the settle. She pushed several twigs into the flames, looked at Béatrice: 'So when's it to be?'

'Any day now.'

'The same as for him, then,' she murmured, 'the same as for him . . .'

'How is Aunt Louise?' asked Dominique, to change the subject a little.

Béatrice and he, arriving late, had not wanted to go and disturb her in her bedroom when she was probably already asleep.

'Better day by day,' said Félix.

'She's regained movement in her arm and leg,' clarified Berthe, 'and she's even beginning to try to speak. Oh, not much, but still. In any case, she was never very talkative!'

'But what about you, have you moved down here for good?' Dominique asked Félix.

'No. But I wasn't going to leave your aunt dependent on everyone else and sit around doing nothing. But I'll go back when she's improving.'

Later on, as Dominique and Béatrice were climbing back up to Coste-Roche, Béatrice wanted to know.

'Tell me, don't take it amiss, but just one question: it's the custom with you not to send the sick to hospital?'

'The sick, yes, when there's really nothing else to be done. Old people, no, never. And I think it's very good that way.'

380

'I didn't say it was wrong. I'm finding out, that's all. With you Vialhes, you learn something new every day!'

'So it's really true what your father told me, you'll be coming back to look after the land? That's definite?' insisted Pierre-Edouard.

'Yes. But I can't say when,' explained Dominique.

'That doesn't matter, the main thing is that you come back! And then you'll see, it passes so quickly, time, so quickly . . . So you'll be coming back one day? That's good,' smiled the old man, pulling his rug around him.

Despite uncertain weather, he had still demanded to go and take some air on the threshold. Not for very long, just a few minutes, to be alone with his grandson and hear what he wanted to know. And now he was calm, at peace.

'Tell me, I hope you've still got it?' he asked suddenly.

'What?'

'The napoléon I gave you I don't know how long ago . . .'

'Ah! The twenty-franc coin you gave me for my bac? Of course I've got it! Not on me, but I've got it!'

'Very good. So one day, you must give it to your grandson,' said Pierre-Edouard.

He was seized by a bad fit of coughing which exhausted him. And between gasps continued:

'You tell him you had it from your grandfather, who got it from his . . . For my school certificate . . . You tell him, eh? And then, talk to him a bit about me . . . And about your grandmother . . . Don't forget anything! It's important, to pass on memories, important . . . And now, help me back in. I'm cold. And afterwards, tell your father to come and see me.'

Jacques came down that same evening. As it was still quite light, he hoped to find his father up. But Mathilde informed him that he had already returned to his bed more than an hour earlier.

'Is he asleep?' asked Jacques.

'No, he's asking for you.'

'I couldn't come earlier, what with the animals . . .'

'I know,' she said, 'that's what I told him, he understood. But go and see him now.'

Jacques entered the room and approached the double bed.

'Ah, you're there,' said Pierre-Edouard, opening his eyes. 'Come closer.' He waited until his son was next to him and whispered: 'Go and send for the priest. Yes, yes, I insist on it! That surprises you,' he said, with a ghost of a smile. 'Yes, you're surprised, I can see! But it's not for me . . .'

'I don't understand.'

'Yes, you do!' said Pierre-Edouard with an irritated gesture. 'I've nothing to say to him myself, the poor curé! We've never exchanged more than ten sentences since we've known each other! Not going to start today! But all the same, he must come and see me. You understand, it'll make your mother so happy . . . Call him, straight away.'

'All right, I'll see to it.'

'And mind you tell your mother that it's me who's asking for him, all my own idea. She'll be pleased that I thought of it. Go on . . . Ah, yes, perhaps you ought also tell Guy that . . . Well . . .'

'Don't worry, he phones every evening.'

'Oh, good . . . So he'll know all right to come when it's necessary . . . Now call the priest, it'll make your mother so happy.'

During the following three days, Pierre-Edouard remained in a stable condition. Obstinate to the end, he demanded that they continue to help him get up every morning. Then, slowly, step by step, he moved towards the cane chair which awaited him in front of the fire, where he spent the whole day dozing peacefully. He already seemed detached from the world.

But it was still he who reacted first when the telephone rang in the early hours of 12 May. Day was barely dawning. It looked fine, clear.

'That's it, that's Dominique's baby,' he murmured. He felt about quietly beside him, placed his hand on Mathilde's shoulder as she still slept, exhausted.

'That's Dominique's baby,' he repeated, gently stroking her cheek.

But Félix had already answered it. Awake at last, Mathilde rose, simultaneously worried and happy, and went out of the room to seek news. She returned at once, radiant, almost rejuvenated:

'It really is Béatrice. They took her to Brive in the night. She's just gone into the delivery room. That was Mauricette calling just now, she thought we'd already be up.'

'Help me to get up,' he said.

'Already?'

'Yes.'

She slipped him into his dressing-gown, pulled back the curtains, and supported him so that he could sit up.

'Call Félix,' he said, 'I want to go and take some air . . .'

'You're not to think of it!' she protested.

'Yes I am! It's beautiful, I want to see the sun.'

It took more than five minutes for Félix to help him walk as far as the door. The first rays of the rising sun welcomed them as they finally appeared on the doorstep.

'It's a really fine day,' sighed Pierre-Edouard. 'It'd be so lovely to climb on the peaks, things must be growing again up there . . .'

He screwed up his eyes a little, then leaned heavily on Félix again:

'My armchair,' he said.

He settled into it breathing heavily, pushed away the bowl of milk Mathilde offered, and began to wait, dozing.

He jumped when the telephone rang again towards ten o'clock. Rather confusedly, he made out the smiling, happy faces of Mathilde, Berthe, Yvette and Félix. And through a distant, woolly fog he heard Mathilde.

'He's arrived! He weighs 3.25 kilos! Béatrice is very well!'

Then he woke up properly, even tried to get up.

'Don't move,' said Mathilde, coming to hug him, 'you have a great-grandson. And he's called Pierre! Like you!'

'Pierre?' he murmured as he embraced her. 'Pierre, is that true?'

'Yes!' She said, leaning over him once more to kiss him again. 'Dominique just told me so. He said to tell you that his son is called Pierre, Jacques, Edouard Vialhe!'

'Oh, that's good, that's very good!' the old man smiled as he squeezed her hand.

Two days later, in the morning, when the sun was streaming in through the open window and a pair of cuckoos were calling to each other in the pinewood by the château, Pierre-Edouard announced to Mathilde that he would not be getting up.

Marcillac, 6 mai 1990